Generalization
of Knowledge

Generalization
of Knowledge

Multidisciplinary Perspectives

Marie T. Banich and Donna Caccamise

EDITORS

Psychology Press
Taylor & Francis Group

New York   London

Psychology Press
Taylor & Francis Group
270 Madison Avenue
New York, NY 10016

Psychology Press
Taylor & Francis Group
27 Church Road
Hove, East Sussex BN3 2FA

Printed in the United States of America on acid-free paper
10 9 8 7 6 5 4 3 2 1

International Standard Book Number: 978-1-84872-898-1 (Hardback)

Library of Congress Cataloging-in-Publication Data

Generalization of knowledge : multidisciplinary perspectives / editors, Marie T.
     Banich and Donna Caccamise.
          p. cm.
     Includes bibliographical references and index.
     ISBN 978-1-84872-898-1 (hard back : alk. paper)
     1. Cognitive learning. I. Banich, Marie T., 1957- II. Caccamise, Donna.

LB1590.3.G45 2010
370.15'2--dc22   2009054342

Visit the Taylor & Francis Web site at
http://www.taylorandfrancis.com

and the Psychology Press Web site at
http://www.psypress.com

Contents

SECTION 3 REPRESENTATIONS THAT SUPPORT GENERALIZATION

SECTION 4 EDUCATIONAL AND TRAINING APPROACHES TO GENERALIZATION

SECTION 5 TECHNOLOGICAL APPROACHES TO GENERALIZATION

Preface

Although the notion of generalization fits prominently into cognitive theories of learning, there is surprisingly little in the literature that provides an overview of the issue from a broad multifaceted perspective. Rather, a current literature review finds that the issue is studied using very specific tasks based on very specific assumptions. Yet whether these assumptions carry across studies or across tasks is not an issue that has been considered in detail. Hence the need to try to generalize upon research on the generalization of learning!

This volume evolved from a 3-day symposium in Boulder, Colorado, that was supported by a National Science Foundation Science of Learning Catalyst Center Grant (NSF SBE 0518699). The goal was to take a multidisciplinary perspective on generalization of knowledge from fields associated with cognitive science, including cognitive neuroscience, computer science, education, linguistics, developmental science, and speech, language and hearing sciences, among others. To bring continuity to the conference and to this volume, we asked each speaker to address three important questions:

- How does your field define *generalization*?
- What practices, representations, processes, systems, and so on in your field are thought to support generalization?
- When is generalization detrimental or not needed?

The ultimate goal of the conference was to see if some general principles about generalization could be derived from triangulation across different disciplines and approaches.

The conference, like the volume, was divided into five sections, representing five different perspectives or approaches to generalization. The first section, entitled "Cognitive Neuroscience Approaches to Generalization," with chapters by Huff and LaBar, Williams and Tanaka, and Poldrack, Carr, and Foerde, examines the neural systems that can support generalization of knowledge for both cognitive and emotional processes. The second section, "Developmental Perspectives on Generalization," with chapters from Gerken and Balcomb, Fisher, and Laney and Gomez, examines generalization from the perspective of patterns of learning over development, focusing on the mechanisms that allow young children to learn to generalize and how that interacts with other cognitive processes, most notably language. The third section, "Representations That Support Generalization," with chapters by Griffiths, Huenerfauth, and Levering and Kurtz, considers what aspects of information or their structure allow for generalization. The fourth section, "Educational and Training Approaches to Generalization," with chapters by Graesser, Lin, and D'Mello; Hall, Wieckert, and Wright; and Thompson, considers how educational and training experiences can aid in generalization of knowledge and how generalization can occur across social systems. The final section, "Technological Approaches to Generalization," with chapters by McGrenere, Bunt, Findlater, and Moffatt; Butcher and de la Chica; and Carmien and Fischer, considers the difficult issue of how computerized systems and other modern-day technologies can be created to allow them to generalize, and how they can be organized to help users learn to generalize.

Collectively, these chapters on generalization will allow us to think about this concept in useful ways that inform 21st-century research into theory and application, including tutoring, assistive technology, and endeavors involving collaboration and distributed cognition.

List of Contributors

Frances K. Balcomb
Department of Psychology
University of Arizona
Tucson, AZ

Marie T. Banich
Institute of Cognitive Science and
    Department of Psychology
University of Colorado at Boulder
Boulder, CO

Andrea Bunt
Department of Computer Science
University of British Columbia
Vancouver, BC, Canada

Kirsten R. Butcher
Learning Research and Development
    Center
University of Pittsburgh
Pittsburgh, PA

Donna J. Caccamise
Institute of Cognitive Science
University of Colorado at Boulder
Boulder, CO

Stefan Parry Carmien
Department of Neuroengineering
Fatronik Technological Foundation
San Sebastian, Spain

Valerie Carr
Department of Psychology and
    Interdepartmental Neuroscience
    Program
University of California, Los Angeles
Los Angeles, CA

Sidney D'Mello
FedEx Institute of Technology
University of Memphis
Memphis, TN

Leah Findlater
Department of Computer Science
University of British Columbia
Vancouver, BC, Canada

Gerhard Fischer
Center for Lifelong Learning and
    Design
University of Colorado at Boulder
Boulder, CO

Anna V. Fisher
Department of Psychology
Carnegie Mellon University
Pittsburgh, PA

Karin Foerde
Department of Psychology
University of California, Los Angeles
Los Angeles, CA

LouAnn Gerken
Department of Psychology
University of Arizona
Tucson, AZ

Rebecca L. Gómez
Department of Psychology
University of Arizona
Tucson, AZ

Arthur C. Graesser
Department of Psychology and
    Institute for Intelligent Systems
University of Memphis
Memphis, TN

Tom Griffiths
Department of Psychology
University of California, Berkeley
Berkeley, CA

Rogers Hall
Department of Teaching and Learning
Vanderbilt University
Nashville, TN

Matt Huenerfauth
Department of Computer Science
Queens College, The City University of
    New York
Flushing, NY

Nicole C. Huff
Department of Psychology and
    Neuroscience
Duke University
Durham, NC

Kenneth J. Kurtz
Department of Psychology
Binghamton University, State
    University of New York
Binghamton, NY

Kevin S. LaBar
Center for Cognitive Neuroscience
Duke University
Durham, NC

Jill Lany
Department of Psychology, Waisman
    Center–Infant Learning Lab
University of Wisconsin–Madison
Madison, WI

Kimery Levering
Department of Psychology
Binghamton University, State
    University of New York
Binghamton, NY

David Lin
Department of Computer Science
University of Memphis
Memphis, TN

Joanna McGrenere
Department of Computer Science
University of British Columbia
Vancouver, BC, Canada

Karyn Moffatt
Department of Computer Science
University of British Columbia
Vancouver, BC, Canada

Russell A. Poldrack
Department of Psychology, Brain
    Research Institute, Department
    of Psychiatry and Biobehavioral
    Sciences, and Interdepartmental
    Neuroscience Program
University of California, Los Angeles
Los Angeles, CA

James Tanaka
Department of Psychology
University of Victoria
Victoria, BC, Canada

Cynthia K. Thompson
Department of Communication
    Sciences and Disorders
Northwestern University
Evanston, IL

Kären Wieckert
College of Business Administration
Belmont University
Nashville, TN

Rankin W. McGugin
Department of Psychology
Vanderbilt University
Nashville, TN

Kenneth Wright
Department of Biostatistics
Vanderbilt University
Nashville, TN

Section 1

Cognitive Neuroscience Approaches to Generalization

1

Generalization and Specialization of Conditioned Learning

NICOLE C. HUFF and KEVIN S. LABAR

INTRODUCTION

C lassical conditioning is a fundamental form of learning and memory by which organisms learn to associate which stimuli in the environment lead to reinforcing and punishing outcomes. This form of learning is critical to survival, as it helps organisms identify likely sources of food in the environment and situations and places where a predator is likely to be encountered. Although theoretical accounts of classical conditioning were initially described in terms of reflexive chaining of simple stimulus–response associations, it is now known that many levels of learning occur when organisms evaluate the conditions that lead to biologically salient events (Rescorla, 1988). A century ago, Ivan Pavlov (1927) discovered the basic tenets of classical conditioning through his famous physiologic experiments on salivation of dogs in response to the ringing of bells that predict food delivery. Although Pavlov described a form of conditioned learning for items that an organism wants (known as *appetitive learning*), recent research in neuroscience has focused more on learning the relationships among stimuli that predict delivery of noxious stimuli, resulting in the acquisition of fear responses that occur through conditioning.

Certain aspects of learning that develop through association and conditioning (often called *conditioned learning*) are particularly interesting to consider in the context of understanding mechanisms of generalization. Here we review behavioral and neurobiological evidence that learning of a fear association is initially generalized but with experience becomes specialized. The first section will address evidence for generalization of conditioned learning, and the second section will feature specialization of conditioned learning. We present behavioral and neural data from both human and nonhuman animals throughout the chapter. Although the focus is on fear conditioning (given that most advances have been made in this domain), relevant research using appetitive-conditioning paradigms is introduced where appropriate. We then discuss the behavioral outcome and potential neural dysfunction in anxiety disorders that reflect maladaptive fear generalization. Finally, we highlight recent clinical interventions derived from animal-conditioning models to help patients cope with their overgeneralization of fear.

Historical Perspective

One of the earliest studies of generalization of fear learning in humans was demonstrated in an individual known as Little Albert. In a landmark study conducted by Watson and Raynor (1920), which by today's standards would be deemed unethical, Albert B., a 9-month-old infant, was presented with a variety of furry stimuli, such as a white rat, a rabbit, a dog, a monkey, masks with and without hair, and cotton. The 9-month-old showed no signs of fear to these stimuli. However, he did demonstrate a normal fear response (crying) to the loud sound of a hammer striking a steel bar. At 11 months of age, Albert was again presented with the white rat. This time, when he reached for it, the presentation of the rat was followed by the loud noise of the hammer striking a steel bar. Watson and Raynor repeated this pairing seven times, after which Little Albert cried and crawled away at the sight of the white rat. Interestingly, when observed months later, Albert was also fearful of other objects that looked similar to the white rat, such as a rabbit, a fur coat, and a dog. This observation shows that Little Albert had generalized his conditioned fear response to stimuli that shared similar visual features, and this generalization of the fear response was retained over a relatively long period of time (at least for the life of an infant).

Ivan Pavlov (1927) was the first scientist to formally recognize stimulus generalization and stimulus discrimination in his classic studies of conditioned learning. Pavlov noted that dogs trained to salivate to a bell that predicted the occurrence of food also salivated to a light that happened to be lit around the same time, even though the light was not directly followed by the food reward. This finding exemplifies *cross-modal* (auditory-visual) *generalization* of conditioned learning. However, Pavlov found that with subsequent bell–food pairings (and no light–food pairings), the salivation response became selective to the bell only, which demonstrates *stimulus discrimination*. Thus, following an initial generalization of conditioned responding, the organism learns to discriminate predictive stimuli from nonpredictive ones, which functions to specialize the learning to those predictors most closely associated with the reinforcer. Nonetheless, Pavlov continued to observe *intramodal generalization* following stimulus discrimination—even though salivation was selective to the tone, it still occurred to tones of similar (but not identical) frequencies. In this way, Pavlov discovered multiple layers of generalization and specialization of knowledge within his initial description of this important learning phenomenon. His discoveries show how intricately entwined the concepts of generalization and specialization are to the principles of conditioned learning, and the complexities and malleability of the associations learned during what, at first glance, appears to be a very simple training paradigm.

It is interesting to note that several decades after Pavlov's initial findings on generalization and specialization of conditioning learning, Humphrey (1951) wrote in his seminal book on thinking,

> It is doubtful whether the "generalization" of the conditioned reflex should be considered to be the same process [as other forms of generalization] ... for it seems to depend on the absence of psychological activity ... whereas the process of relating [stimuli] ... is essentially positive [active]. (pp. 266–267)

Humphrey was suggesting that conditioning was a passive, reflexive process that did not require any "thinking" on the part of the organism, and thus generalization of conditioning was unrelated to generalization of other psychological phenomena (such as those described in the present volume). However, as described below, decades of behavioral and neuroscientific work since this time have shown that conditioned learning is psychologically "active" and instantiated in distributed neural networks in the brain that overlap with other forms of learning.

Definitions of Generalization and Specialization

In defining the generalization and specialization of classical conditioning, we consider the theoretical framework described by Holyoak and Nisbett (1988), who postulated two forms of generalization for rule-based learning paradigms, of which conditioning is an example. The first form—*instance-based learning*—occurs when a new rule is applied to predict properties found in observed instances of a known category. As described above, Little Albert learned to avoid all white fuzzy things as a broad form of instance-based learning even though only the white rat should have been feared based on his experience. Within the framework of instance-based learning, *specialization* occurs when a new rule is formed by adding constraints to an existing rule. Presumably later in life, Little Albert learned that the experimental context created by Watson and Raynor was the only situation where loud noises followed the sight of a rat, and thus his fear response became less generalized over time. The second form—*conditioned-simplifying learning*—occurs when qualifying conditions are dropped to make a rule more general. This form of generalization has less relevance to the present discussion because fear responses are initially acquired quite broadly without much attention to the qualifying conditions regarding the eliciting conditions, such as the time or place of occurrence.

As applied to fear learning, instance-based generalization is found during acquisition of novel fears to cues and environments that predict negative reinforcers. Following acquisition of the initial fear association, instance-based generalization is exemplified by the presence of a conditioned fear response to the same cue but in varying contexts or situations, or in response to novel cues and environments that share features with the exemplar. For example, a child who is knocked over by a neighbor's large Saint Bernard may learn to fear not only that particular dog but also all dogs, regardless of whether it is the neighbor's dog or some other dog. In contrast, specialization of fear learning occurs when an organism learns to discriminate which stimuli in the environment control fear behavior. Specialization requires learning when and where fear should be expressed given the predictive relationship between the presence of specific cues and contexts and an aversive outcome. For example, the child may learn to fear only those dogs that are large enough to knock him or her over or only those dogs belonging to the neighbor.

Two examples of specialization of fear learning include stimulus–context discrimination (see Pavlov example, discussed in the "Historical Perspective" section) and *extinction*. During extinction training, a conditioned stimulus that had previously predicted aversive outcomes is no longer paired with a reinforcer. Consequently, the organism learns that the stimulus is no longer threatening, and the fear response subsides. Extinction can be considered a form of specialization of knowledge because a temporal constraint is placed upon the learning that originally took place during acquisition training. Specialization of fear learning has important clinical implications because generalized fear can be distilled down to a more specific, rational, and logical expression. When specialization of fear learning does not occur, fears can become *overgeneralized* to a variety of inappropriate contexts or cues, which is a behavioral hallmark of many anxiety disorders.

ACQUISITION AND GENERALIZATION OF CONDITIONED LEARNING

Behavioral Evidence

A landmark study by Guttman and Kalish (1956) demonstrated that pigeons generalize in a graded manner to stimuli that they have learned can signal their ability to obtain a reward. In this study, pigeons were provided with food rewards when they pecked at an illuminated key light (a yellow-orange color) with a wavelength of 580 nanometers (nm). The birds were subsequently tested with other wavelengths of light without reinforcement in a random order to ascertain the intramodal (i.e., visual) generalization of the conditioned response (in this case, key pecking). Although pigeons responded most strongly to the original wavelength of 580 nm, they also had considerably high response rates to lights of 570 to 590 nm. However, conditioned responding decreased as a function of the distance of the wavelength from the original value. By plotting the response rate across different light wavelengths, a *generalization gradient* is obtained (Figure 1.1) that indicates the extent to which learning the specific stimulus wavelength presented at training generalizes to stimuli sharing visual features. Further work has shown that pigeons can readily differentiate these wavelengths of light in this range, so the generalization gradient was not an artifact of poor color acuity. To our knowledge, this study provided the first systematic investigation that demonstrated a gradient of generalization for a feature used in conditioning. These early findings support the idea that conditioned behavior is characterized by instance-based learning because the pigeons demonstrated a specific response to the reinforced wavelength that also modestly carried over (generalized) to nearby wavelengths.

As derived from an experimental procedure that is now referred to as *classical* (or *Pavlovian*) *conditioning* (Pavlov, 1927), fear conditioning occurs when an environmental cue such as a distinct sound or a visual image (conditioned stimulus,

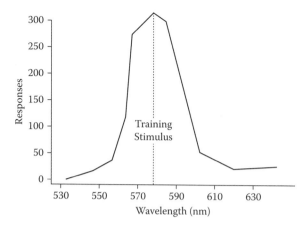

Figure 1.1   Stimulus generalization gradient for pigeons that were trained to peck a colored light of 580 nm wavelength for a food reward and were then tested in the presence of other colors. From Guttman and Kalish (1956), adapted from Domjan (1998, p. 221).

or CS) reliably predicts the presence of an aversive event (unconditioned stimulus, or US). Consequently, a conditioned response develops to the cue that engages defensive biological reactions indicative of a state of fear (such as "freezing" or immobility of the body, increased heart rate and sweat gland activity, higher blood pressure, potentiation of startle reflexes, and stress hormone release). *Cued fear conditioning* occurs when the CS is a discrete sensory cue, such as the sounding of a tone. Fear is then associated with subsequent presentations of the tone CS. *Contextual fear conditioning* occurs when fear responses are elicited by a room (environment) where a noxious US was previously encountered, even in the absence of a discrete sensory CS.

Standard fear-conditioning procedures demonstrate instance-based generalization in several ways. First, early during acquisition training, fear responses tend to generalize to other discrete sensory cues present in the environment (similar to what Pavlov described originally during appetitive conditioning). To illustrate, consider a human fear-conditioning study in which repeated presentations of a picture of a snake (a CS that is predictive of a negative event, or *predictive CS+*) are followed by a shock, whereas presentations of a picture of a spider are not (a CS that is not predictive of a negative event, or *nonpredictive CS–*) (Zorawski, Cook, Kuhn, et al., 2005). During the initial training trials, there is generalization of fear (as indicated by an increase in skin conductance responses) to both the CS+ and CS–, despite the fact that (a) the CS– does not predict reinforcement; and (b) individuals had been habituated to the stimuli, so this response could not reflect an increased skin conductance driven by the novelty of the stimuli (Figure 1.2). That is, the mere introduction of a noxious stimulus will increase fear in a nonspecific way to sensory stimuli present in the environment. However, as training progresses and the predictive relations among the stimuli are apparent, the fear response becomes specified to the CS+ and decreases to the CS–. This aspect of conditioned learning that emerges over time (stimulus discrimination) is discussed

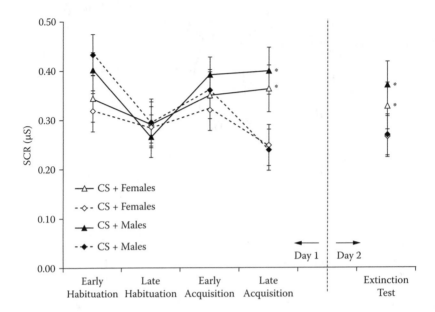

Figure 1.2   Generalization of fear conditioning in early acquisition in males and females. The CS+, a snake image, is followed by a shock, but the CS−, a spider image, is not. The graph displays generalization of the fear response (SCR) to both the CS+ and CS− at early acquisition. Adapted from Zorawski, Cook, Kuhn, and LaBar (2005).

further in the "Stimulus Discrimination" section with respect to mechanisms of specialization of knowledge.

Two other aspects of generalization are readily demonstrated in nonhuman animals. First, conditioned fears will generalize from specific sensory cues to environmental contexts. For example, when a tone is played in a specific testing chamber, rats will initially acquire strong fears to the tone, but they will also display fear to the chamber in the absence of the tone. The magnitude of contextual fear is typically smaller than that to the more predictive tone and sometimes has a more protracted learning rate (e.g., LaBar & LeDoux, 1996).

Second, fears to specific cues generalize across multiple contexts. For example, Huff and Rudy (2004) placed rats in a specific context, a testing chamber where they received several tone (CS) and shock (US) pairings. The following day, the rats were returned to the same context, no shocks or tones were presented, and the rats were observed for their contextual fear responses (in this case, freezing behavior). Consistent with the example above, the rats exhibited fear. Approximately 6 hours later, rats were put into a new context, consisting of a red light and a grated floor distinct from the conditioning and testing chamber, and were presented with the tone to assess their fear behavior to a discrete sensory cue encountered in a novel context. The rats exhibited a fear response again, demonstrating generalization of cued fear from the training context to another one when in the presence of the CS (Figure 1.3). These findings support Holyoak and Nisbett's (1988) framework of instance-based generalization in that fear to a specific CS (tone) is expressed

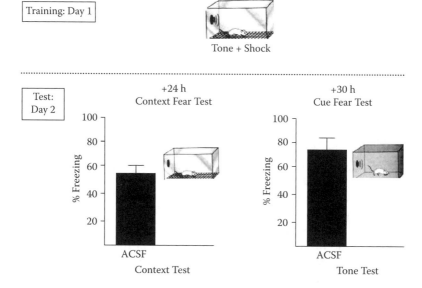

Figure 1.3 A typical fear-conditioning paradigm in rats consists of training to a tone–shock pairing on Day 1. The following day, there is fear testing in the context (no shock), and then 6 hours later to the tone in a novel context. Freezing is the measure of learned fear. Generalization is observed from a cue to the context in the first test and to the same tone in a variant context in the subsequent test. Adapted from Squire and Kandel (1999) and data from Huff & Rudy (2004).

in a novel context that was not part of the initial learning experience. This study also supports Humphrey's (1951) definition, which characterizes *generalization* as a consistent response to a stimulus presented in varying contexts. Thus, fear-conditioning procedures illustrate dynamic engagement of several generalization processes to multiple features of the environment during learning.

Neural Substrates

From extensive research in nonhuman animals, the neurocircuitry, neurotransmitters, and intracellular changes that support fear learning have been delineated. Here we will provide a brief overview of the neural structures necessary for the processing and expression of learned fear and describe neural mechanisms that likely contribute to cue and context generalization.

The amygdala, a structure deep in the brain located in the medial temporal lobe, has emerged as a critical neural region for fear learning. By lesioning this structure, it has been shown that the amygdala mediates the processing of CS–US associations (Fanselow & LeDoux, 1999). In addition, protein synthesis in the amygdala during and immediately following fear conditioning is critical for the consolidation of both cued and contextual fear memories during learning (Huff & Rudy, 2004; Schafe & LeDoux, 2000). Thus, not only is an intact amygdala necessary during the training itself, but also active processing within the amygdala following learning facilitates long-term memory of fear and generalization of cued fear to other contexts.

During fear conditioning, the amygdala receives sensory input directly from the thalamus and also indirectly from the cortex. The thalamus is a subcortical structure in the brain that helps to route and reorganize sensory information as it comes from the sensory receptors (e.g., eyes and ears) on its way to the cortex. These pathways can mediate conditioning to discrete cues, such as tones and shocks (Romanski & LeDoux, 1992). Importantly, the direct thalamo-amygdala pathway is adaptive for an organism in that it provides rapid information about a threat, without the need for information to go to the cortex first. However, in an intact organism this pathway can only process sensory information very crudely. In contrast, the thalamo-cortico-amygdala pathway is an indirect and less rapid connection to the amygdala, but it conveys more complex information about the nature of an environmental cue (LeDoux, 1995). It is thought that the direct route primes the amygdala to receive more detailed sensory and perceptual information about danger. Information about discrete sensory cues from both pathways (originating in the thalamus) converges on neurons in the lateral nucleus of the amygdala (LA) (Li, Stutzman, & LeDoux, 1996).

During fear acquisition, information gets integrated in various ways. The LA integrates sensory information (such as visual and auditory) about the CS and US (Romanski & LeDoux, 1992). The LA relays information to other nuclei in the amygdala, including the basal and central nuclei where additional learning takes place. Outputs from the central nucleus to brainstem and hypothalamic structures then trigger behavioral (freezing or startle) and autonomic (skin conductance, respiration) fear responses (LeDoux, 1995; Maren & Quirk, 2004). Information about context is conveyed to the basal and lateral nuclei of the amygdala from the hippocampus, a neighboring structure in the medial temporal lobe. These connections are particularly important for contextual fear conditioning (see Figure 1.4). The basal and lateral nuclei of the amygdala also send information to regions of the frontal and temporal lobes that are involved in multimodal and associative processing (Kilcross, Robbin, & Everitt, 1997; Maren & Quirk, 2004; Pitkanen, 2000) as well as the striatum, which is involved in motor behaviors that may help initiate reactions to the threatening stimulus (such as fleeing).

Lesion studies provide strong evidence that communication between the amygdala and hippocampus is necessary for normal contextual fear learning. A landmark study (Phillips & LeDoux, 1992) demonstrated that there is partial independence of cue and contextual fear learning. Rats were given lesions to either the amygdala or the hippocampus prior to auditory cued fear conditioning. Rats with amygdala lesions showed no fear conditioning to either the tone or the context. In contrast, rats with hippocampal lesions displayed fear to the auditory cue, but showed significantly less fear to the context. Thus, the amygdala is critical for acquiring fear associations generally, but context conditioning depends additionally on the integrity of the hippocampus. The amygdala also has an important role in strengthening or "modulating" emotional memories that are stored in other brain regions such as the cortex, hippocampus, or striatum so that they remain durable and vivid for long-term recall (McGaugh, 2000).

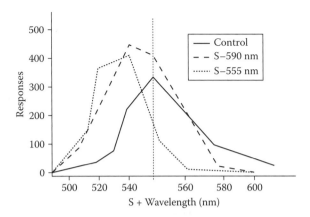

Figure 1.4 Evidence for a generalized peak shift. This study examined the effects of intradimensional discrimination training on stimulus control. Three groups of pigeons were reinforced for pecking at a 550 nm wavelength light (CS+). One group was trained on a CS– of 590 nm. The other group was trained on a CS– of 555 nm. The third group did not receive a CS–. The test for generalization to the above wavelengths demonstrates a peak shift in responding in the two groups that received discrimination training, but not in the control group. The behavioral response pattern depends on both what is reinforced (CS+) and what is not (CS–). From Hanson (1959), adapted from Domjan (1998).

Electrophysiological studies suggest that the amygdala is biased to generalize fear early in acquisition of the association (Rogan, Staubli, & LeDoux, 1997). As reviewed above, one route to the amygdala conveys crude sensory information about the CS while another sends a more complex sensory representation about environmental threats. Specifically, recordings of LA neurons in awake rats show that the most prominent cellular responses occur to the CS within 15 milliseconds of onset. This observation suggests that the thalamo-amygdala pathway, which is a shorter route to the amygdala than via the cortex, initially processes the CS–US association very quickly but in a relatively unspecific manner (Maren, Yap, & Goosens, 2001; Quirk, Armory, & LeDoux, 1997; Quirk, Repa, & LeDoux, 1995). Other brain regions, including the cortex, show changes in neuronal firing in response to the CS as well, but they occur later in time and after more training trials (Maren, 2000; Pascoe & Kapp, 1985; Quirk et al., 1997). These electrophysiological features of fast subcortical pathways may contribute to the initial generalization of fear processing, whereas the slower subcortical pathway may contribute to the later specialization of conditioned fear responses.

Extensive neurochemical investigations in both living and nonliving tissue also implicate the amygdala as playing a causal role in fear conditioning. Long-term potentiation (LTP) is a phenomenon in which a neuronal pathway is stimulated multiple times at a high frequency, resulting in long-lasting responsiveness to subsequent stimuli processed along that pathway. Consistent with recordings of LA neurons during CS and CS–US presentations (Quirk et al., 1995, 1997), LTP has been evoked in the direct thalamo-amygdala pathway and in the indirect thalamo-cortico-amygdala pathway. Importantly, it has been observed that behavioral fear conditioning induces LTP in these pathways as well (McKernan & Shinnick-Gallagher, 1997; Rogan & LeDoux, 1995; Rogan et al., 1997; Tsvetkov, Carlezon, Benes, Kandel, & Bolshakov, 2002). The cellular changes associated with LTP are thought to provide the molecular substrates for long-term memory of fear learning (Lamprecht & LeDoux, 2004).

A recent report investigating the role of LTP in generalization of fear conditioning implicated a neurotransmitter, gamma-aminobutyric acid (GABA), which is involved in neural inhibition, as playing an important role (Shaban et al., 2006). Mice were genetically altered so that they lacked a certain subtype of receptor for this neurotransmitter ($GABA_B$). As discussed above, induction of LTP in the LA is thought to underlie the acquisition of classical fear conditioning in rodents. LA neurons receive input from both the thalamus and the cortex, which are simultaneously active during a sensory experience, such as fear conditioning. This neuronal coactivation is termed *associative LTP*, and is the benchmark for a conditioned association at the neural level. However, when the $GABA_B$ receptor subtype is blocked prior to artificial stimulation at cortical-amygdala projection neurons, nonassociative LTP occurred, suggesting that in an intact organism cortical neurons would fire without a coactivator, such as a CS–US pairing. We suggest that the $GABA_B$ receptor is a mechanism to constrain nonassociative firing of cortical-amygdala neurons, which is important for preventing fear generalization. When $GABA_B$ is not blocked, nonassociative LTP will not occur through a single stimulation train at cortical connections to LA. Moreover, behaviorally, the genetically altered mice exhibited an abnormal fear response in that they showed generalization to an unreinforced control stimulus (CS–) that was not predictive of the US. The findings suggest that this neuronal receptor in the amygdala may be critical for mediating appropriate discrimination and generalization to environmental stimuli.

LTP has also been observed in the amygdala-to-hippocampus pathway (Abe, Niikura, & Misawa, 2003; Akirav & Richter-Levin, 2002), which may be important for mediating the generalization of fear to contexts. For example, we know that the amygdala influences (modulates) hippocampal-dependent memory for context, contextual fear conditioning, and avoidance learning (Huff et al., 2006; Huff & Rudy, 2004; Huff, Wright-Hardesty, Higgins, Matus-Amat, & Rudy, 2005; McGaugh, 2000). Huff and colleagues (2006) demonstrated that inactivation of the amygdala in rats impairs memory for a context, and reduces a protein coded by genes that is generated in the hippocampus during contextual fear conditioning. Taken together, these findings suggest that bidirectional communication between the amygdala and hippocampus is likely to play a role in the generalization of fear to contexts.

Functional neuroimaging and studies of patients with focal brain lesions have shown that the basic neural circuitry for conditioned fear learning is similar in humans to that observed in rats, although the molecular and electrophysiological substrates remain to be determined. Studies of human patients with amygdala damage show that they are impaired in acquiring conditioned fear, as measured by skin conductance responses (Bechara et al., 1995; Hamann, Monarch, & Goldstein, 2002; LaBar, LeDoux, Spencer, et al., 1995; Peper, Karcher, Wohlfarth, Reinshagen, & LeDoux, 2001; Phelps, LaBar, & Anderson, 1998). As predicted by neural recordings in the rodent amygdala (e.g., Quirk et al., 1997), the amygdala is activated during conditioned fear learning in healthy humans. Moreover, individuals who exhibited more amygdala activation exhibited greater responses of the autonomic nervous system that are typically used as indices of conditioning (Furmark, Fischer, Wik, Larsson, & Fredrikson, 1997; Büchel, Morris, Dolan, & Friston, 1998; LaBar, Gatenby, Gore, LeDoux, & Phelps, 1998). Subsequent functional neuroimaging studies of healthy adults during conditioned fear acquisition have revealed activation not just in the amygdala but also in a broader network of associated structures including the thalamus (LaBar & Cabeza, 2006). However, the relative roles of cortical and subcortical routes to fear learning and their contribution to generalization processes remain to be elucidated in humans.

Note that the neuroimaging studies reviewed above do not highlight hippocampal involvement, as they employed cued fear paradigms rather than contextual fear paradigms. Identifying the neural correlates of contextual fear in humans is difficult. Unlike studies in rodents, humans cannot be readily moved from one testing chamber to another while monitoring neural activity in order to observe hippocampal responses to changes in environmental context. Studies employing virtual-reality manipulations of context during neuroimaging are likely to be useful in this regard, although a recent study has confirmed hippocampal involvement during conditioning to threat cues presented in specific visual background contexts (Marschner, Kalisch, Vervliet, Vensteenwegen, & Büchel, 2008). The binding together of information to spatial and temporal contexts is a defining characteristic of declarative (explicit) memory (see chapter 3 by Poldrack, Carr, & Foerde, this volume) in humans, which we know is critically dependent on the hippocampus (Squire, 1992). Thus, probing declarative memory for fear-conditioning episodes can be used as a proxy for determining hippocampal involvement in contextual binding of fear representations in humans. Two studies have shown that amnesic patients with damage restricted to the hippocampus show physiological signs of acquiring conditioned fear responses, such as changes in skin conductance, but they cannot report any declarative knowledge about the conditioning episode (e.g., stating the CS–US contingency) when asked about it shortly afterward (Bechara et al., 1995; LaBar & Phelps, 2005). The opposite patterns of performance between patients with amygdala damage (no ability to acquire cued fear conditioning but an ability to report the contingencies) and those with hippocampal damage (an ability to acquire cued fear conditioning but an inability to report the contingencies) parallel those seen in rodents with regard to contextual versus cued fear memory (Phillips & LeDoux, 1992). Hence, the evidence across species suggests at least partial independence of learning processes and pathways within the fear circuitry.

Taken together, the neurobiological findings suggest that the amygdala is critical for acquiring fear generally, but communication with the hippocampus is important for acquiring contextual representations of fear. It is likely that generalization of fear conditioning across sensory cues (as seen in early acquisition) is facilitated by the operating characteristics of the rapid direct thalamo-amygdala pathway as well as cellular mechanisms of plasticity underlying LTP. Generalization to unconditioned stimuli can also occur when there is not inhibition of appropriate regions of the amygdala (as shown in mice lacking the $GABA_B$ receptor). Thus, one could postulate that an overactive amygdala alters communication with the hippocam-pus and other cortical regions. This situation results in pervasive anxiety and an inability to use flexible processing in order to make stimulus and contextual dis-criminations, which yield inappropriate fear generalization. Cognitive mechanisms that may support these aspects of fear generalization are introduced in the follow-ing section on theoretical mechanisms.

Theoretical Mechanisms

Two theoretical frameworks have been proposed to describe cognitive mecha-nisms that support associative learning, which can be applied to the study of generalization (Rudy & Wagner, 1976). From behavioral and neurobiological evidence, one can argue that there are two independent ways in which memo-ries are stored in the brain, often referred to as *dual representations* (Nadel & Willner, 1980; Nadel, Willner, & Kurtz, 1985; Rudy & O'Reilly, 1999; Rudy, Huff, & Matus-Amat, 2004). One is the *elemental* (or *unitary/featural*) *account*, which suggests that learning occurs to the individual elements (features) of a stimulus or context. Features are each associated independently with a given reinforcer (Wagner & Brandon, 2001; Rescorla & Wagner, 1972). With regard to fear conditioning, such an association would occur via strengthening the amygdala's connections with the hippocampus (which provides contextual infor-mation), or it can occur independently of the hippocampus and be mediated by the amygdala's connections with cortical areas (Rudy et al., 2004). The other view is the *configural* (or *conjunctive*) *account*. The configural account suggests that the combinations of all attributes associated with the fearful event (e.g., visual information, sounds, and/or smells) are stored as whole unique represen-tations that then enter into associations with reinforcers (Pearce, 1994; Rudy & O'Reilly, 1999). Critical to this view is the assumption that from a subset of cues the hippocampus can generate the entire stored memory representation, which is termed *pattern completion* (Marr, 1971; McNaughton & Morris, 1987; O'Reilly & McClelland, 1994). Pattern completion can be viewed as a process that supports generalization of learning.

It is important to note that human declarative memory is postulated to rely on the ability of the hippocampus to pattern complete, for example by recalling a detailed memory (such as a summer's day in your grandmother's kitchen) in response to a specific retrieval cue (such as the smell of apple pie) (Squire, 1992; Tyler & DiScenna, 1986). In contrast, there is a competing function of *pattern separation* (Marr, 1971; O'Reilly & McClelland, 1994) in which events are sepa-rately represented in the brain. Behavioral and more recent neurobiological stud-ies provide evidence in support of these distinct functions of the hippocampus in a variety of tasks in rodents (Guzowski, Knierim, & Moser, 2004; Kiernan & Westbrook, 1993; Rudy & O'Reilly, 2001). Pattern separation provides a way to reduce generalization of similar experiences or stimuli by comparing and then separating the distinct hippocampal representations. Pattern separation may sup-port specialization of fear acquisition and extinction, although this hypothesis has not been explicitly tested.

The elemental and configural accounts as applied to generalization of classical conditioning have been examined in a handful of behavioral studies. Rudy and O'Reilly (1999) demonstrated that preexposure to only the entire conditioning context (but not features of it) facilitated contextual fear conditioning, and that generalization of fear conditioning to other similar contexts is enhanced by prior exposure to the context used to test for generalization. The results were interpreted as indicating pattern completion to the preexposed context during conditioning. These results support the idea that a configural representation plays an important role in establishing a context memory, and that it is mediated by pattern completion processes. In contrast, evidence from contextual fear conditioning in rats (Gonzalez, Quinn, & Fanselow, 2003) and contingency learning in humans (Wheeler, Amundson, & Miller, 2006) shows that subtracting a physical element of the conditioned context or of a compound (i.e., multisensory) CS produces sharper generalization gradients (less generalized and more specialized responses) than adding an element. These findings are in agreement with the elemental view because the representation is not recognized as the same *configuration* when a feature is subtracted. In other words, an elemental representation was stored, which is then still recognized as the same collection of features. Thus, at present there appears to be evidence that both elemental and configural mechanisms contribute to the degree of generalization of conditioned learning. Future behavioral and neurobiological work is needed to further elucidate the conditions (type of conditioning, phase of learning at which manipulation occurs, etc.) under which these processes contribute to various aspects of fear generalization and their instantiation in neural circuits.

SPECIALIZATION OF CONDITIONED LEARNING

Stimulus Discrimination

A landmark behavioral study by Jenkins and Harrison (1960) demonstrated that, during discrimination training, both what is reinforced and what is *not* reinforced determine how specialized learning is when an organism must emit a behavior in response to a cue that leads to a reward (known as *conditioned instrumental learning*) (Jenkins & Harrison). In this study, three groups of pigeons were trained to key peck at an auditory cue. Group 1 was trained with a reinforcing CS+ tone of 1000 Hz and no tone as the unreinforced CS–. Group 2 had a CS+ tone of 1000 Hz and a CS– tone of 950 Hz, and Group 3 had no discrimination training but received a CS+ tone of 1000 Hz only. Upon subsequent testing using multiple tone frequencies, Group 2 showed the steepest generalization gradient, that is, the most specific and least generalized responding. These results show that discrimination training to tones of specific frequencies controls behavior differentially, and that the more precise the CS+/CS– parameters are in terms of sharing a given stimulus feature (such as tone frequency), the more specialized the learning becomes.

Around the same time, another investigation of the factors that control conditioned responding provided evidence for Spence's (1936) earlier theoretical model predicting generalization gradient shifts (Hanson, 1959) (see Figure 1.5).

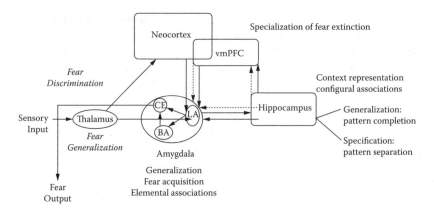

Figure 1.5 Model of fear learning and extinction circuitry. Acquisition of fear recruits projections from the thalamus to the lateral amygdala (LA) directly and indirectly via the cortex. Cortical and hippocampal projections to the amygdala support contextual and declarative fear conditioning. Output from the central nucleus of the amygdala (CE) results in a physical fear response. Following extinction, medial prefrontal (mPFC) neurons exert inhibitory control over LA and CE neurons, resulting in decreased fear responding. Context modulation of extinction could occur through projections of the hippocampus to either the LA or mPFC. Subcortical structures are represented as ovals, and cortical structures are rectangular. Solid line represents acquisition of fear-conditioning pathways. Dotted line represents extinction pathways. Potential sites for generalization and specialization of conditioned fear learning are indicated.

This model states that a stimulus that is reinforced (i.e., CS+) acquires excitatory properties, whereas a stimulus that is not reinforced (i.e., CS−) acquires inhibitory properties. Discriminative responding in the presence of a CS+ and CS− is thought to reflect both the excitation of the CS+ and the inhibition of the CS−. Thus discrimination training is a net value of inhibition and excitation, and not just a positive response value to the rewarded stimuli. Using stimulus discrimination training in which the cue varied within the same dimension, in this case wavelength of light, three groups of pigeons were reinforced with food when they pecked at a key light. The control group did not receive discrimination training, but were always rewarded for pecking to a light CS+ of 550 nm wavelength. Group 2 received presentations of a 550 nm CS + and a 590 nm CS−. The third group was trained with presentations of a 550 nm CS+ and a 555 nm CS−. Subsequently, pigeons were tested with stimuli of varying wavelengths between 500 and 620 nm. The results showed that the maximum responding in the control group was at the 550 nm CS+ wavelength. The control-group responses generalized to stimuli close in range, gradually decreasing to those as a function of wavelength distance from the CS+. Thus, this group demonstrated a gradient that extended from the wavelength on which they had been trained. However, the second group responded most to a stimulus that was not presented during training—they responded maximally to a wavelength of 540 nm. The peak of their generalization gradient shifted away from the original CS+. The third group displayed an even more dramatic response gradient shift: They showed little responding to the CS+ wavelength but instead generated maximum response rates to wavelengths between 530 and 540 nm, to which they were never exposed. This behavioral evidence demonstrates that learning can easily generalize to a variant of the same stimulus type, and that learning is occurring to the nonreinforced stimulus presentations as well as the reinforced stimulus presentations. Moreover, it suggests that specialization of learning is a cumulative response.

Spence (1936) predicted the results of Hanson (1959) and others in his *peak-shift theory*. He postulated that a generalization gradient is actually the net effect of the excitatory generalization gradient (CS+ trials) minus the inhibitory generalization gradient (CS– trials). His formula subtracts the assumed gradient of inhibition centered at the CS– value from the assumed gradient of excitation centered at the CS+ value. This simple formula predicts the experimental evidence later reported in empirical studies. Thus, according to the peak-shift theory, generalization of learning is the net cumulative response to stimuli that have been reinforced *and* that have not been reinforced.

Contextual Control

The question of whether the "background" features of an environment that are not explicitly reinforced can serve to influence conditioned responses has received much attention in many different learning paradigms from behavioral theorists. For example, can the environment (context) in which learning occurs determine the specialization of a conditioned response? In an example of instrumental learning (Thomas, McElvie, & Mah, 1985), pigeons were trained to key peck in response to lights containing lines of different orientations in different contexts, only one of which was positively reinforced. In Context 1, pigeons were trained to peck to a key light with a line orientation of 0 degrees (CS+) and to not peck to a line orientation of 90 degrees (CS–). This relationship was reversed in Context 2 for the same group of birds. Upon subsequent testing for generalization of learning to the CS+ and CS– in Context 1 and Context 2, the birds responded with a generalization gradient that reflected the stimulus training paradigm specific to the training context. Thus, the same exact cue elicited opposite responses in different contexts such that the specific context served as an *occasion setter* to control behavior. There was no difference in response rate between the two contexts, suggesting that each context activated a specific memory of the reinforcement contingency unique to that context. This study provides an example from instrumental conditioning in which the context serves to specify the form of conditioned responding to a given cue, which is also referred to as the *context specificity effect*.

The context specificity effect has also been demonstrated in Pavlovian conditioning paradigms (Hall & Honey, 1990; Honey, Willis, & Hall, 1990). In these studies, rats were conditioned to cue A in Context 1 and to cue B in Context 2. Upon testing, rats displayed more conditioning to cue A when in Context 1 than when it was in Context 2, and likewise more conditioning to cue B when in Context 2 than in Context 1. These findings provide strong support for the idea that the rat has stored a unitary conjunctive memory representation of the cue and the context together (Rudy & O'Reilly, 1999). If it were an elemental association to just the cue, then responding to cue A and cue B would be equivalent regardless of the context in which they were tested. But this was not the case; instead, the memory representation appears to be stored as a conjunction of cue and context together. The experiments described above demonstrate how learning can be *specified*, instead of generalized, to a compound context and cue memory representation.

Fear Extinction and Recovery

Following fear conditioning, presentations of the CS without presentation of a US will yield a decrease in (i.e., extinction of) conditioned fear. Extinction is known to require the learning of a new association, specifically that the CS no longer predicts the aversive US (and is now "safe"). According to the framework of Holyoak and Nisbett (1988), learning when and what *not* to fear is a function of behavioral and neural specialization, as it requires modifying an existing rule ("CS leads to US") to accommodate new constraints. When discrimination between fear and safety cues does not occur, fear may remain when it is no longer warranted and/or fear may generalize over time to inappropriate contexts or stimuli, resulting in a prolonged and dysfunctional state of fear and anxiety.

Extensive studies have shown that animals and humans readily extinguish a fear response when they receive repeated presentations of the CS without the US following fear conditioning (e.g., Bouton, 2004; Davis, 1992; Myers & Davis, 2002; LaBar et al., 1998; Zorawski, Cook, Kuhn, et al., 2005). It has been repeatedly demonstrated that extinction involves new learning and that it is not mere forgetting of the fear association. This is demonstrated by the fact that the fear response may spontaneously reappear with the passing of time. Thus extinction does not cause erasure or forgetting of a fear memory, but instead extinction is a separate learned response (suppression of fear) that competes with the original fear association (e.g., Bouton, 2004). Interestingly, fear that has been extinguished also returns when an organism experiences fear-associated stimuli outside of the context in which the extinction occurred. A large body of systematic studies in rats (and a few recent investigations in humans) demonstrates that after extinction training within the context in which the association was acquired, fear responses can be *renewed* when the organism returns to the acquisition context or in a novel context (Bouton, 2004, 2006; Corcoran & Maren, 2004; Milad, Orr, Pitman, & Rauch, 2005; Vansteenwegen et al., 2005). In other words, the "safety" associations set up during extinction training are bound to the specific context in which extinction took place (Bouton, 2004; Corcoran & Maren, 2001, 2004). In this regard, extinction learning differs from the initial acquisition of fear learning in that the extinction learning that takes place is less generalizable to other contexts, whereas fear to a stimulus can reoccur in a variety of other contexts. In addition, fear that has been extinguished can be *reinstated* when a rat or human experiences a stressor in a novel context and then subsequently encounters the CS in the original fear acquisition context (Bouton & Bolles, 1979; LaBar & Phelps, 2005). The phenomena of fear renewal and fear reinstatement plague cognitive-behavioral treatment of anxiety disorders, because fear responses may be controlled in a clinic setting via exposure therapy (a form of extinction training) but then relapse when the patient encounters feared stimuli and/or stressors in other contexts.

A recent behavioral study in humans examined whether fear relapse can be prevented by conducting extinction with a more general CS than the one associated with fear. The experimental group experienced a modified CS+ and CS– in a novel context but were tested back in the original context to the original CS+ and CS– (ABA design). This group was compared to those participants who were extinguished to the original CS in the conditioning context and then tested for fear relapse in a novel context to the modified CS (AAB design) (Vervliet, Vansteenwegen, & Eelen, 2004). This study demonstrated that there were comparable discrimination and extinction to the modified CS+ and CS– in the context-shift group. However, fear relapse ensued when the participants were tested with the original CSs in the original context. In contrast, if subjects were presented with the original CSs at extinction, they were able to maintain their extinction response to subsequent presentations of a modified CS+ (thus showing intramodal generalization of extinction training) in a novel context. It can be argued that because generalization of extinction training from the new CS to the original CS did not occur, these subjects demonstrated a relapse of fear. These findings suggest that extinction of the conditioned response with a similar but not exact CS does not overcome the relapse of fear when subjects are reexposed to the original CS. Further research is needed to identify extinction-training parameters that yield more generalizable representations of safety and less recovery of fear.

Neural Mechanisms: Stimulus Discrimination

A collection of rodent studies by Weinberger and colleagues demonstrates that the intrinsic response of the neural circuitry can be changed by conditioned learning. For instance, electrophysiological recordings from a single cell in the rat auditory cortex revealed that although it preferred to fire at a specific response frequency of 0.75 kHz (750 times per second), after 30 trials of 2.5 kHz tone–shock pairings, the cell shifted its firing frequency to the CS (2.5 kHz) (Weinberger, 2003). This electrophysiological evidence demonstrates a learning-induced shift of sensory sensitivity in the brain, and a specificity of the response at the single-cell level. Such a specific, learning-induced change in the cell's preferential firing rates to features of a sensory stimulus is referred to as *receptive field plasticity*.

In a separate study (McLin, Miasnikov, & Weinberger, 2002), behavioral generalization of auditory fear conditioning was demonstrated in rats that received tone and neural stimulation pairings, but not in a control group that received unpaired (random) tone and neural stimulation presentations. Presentations of an auditory stimulus (6.0 kHz tone) were paired with electrical stimulation of the nucleus basalis in the basal forebrain. Changes in respiration rate, the behavioral measure of learning, was the greatest at the trained stimulus value (6.0 kHz), and declined in a graded manner the further away the test tones were from this frequency. Importantly, the specificity of responding in receptive fields of sensory regions of the brain and generalization gradients is a general phenomenon that has been observed across a variety of training tasks in rats, such as avoidance in an instrumental-conditioning paradigm (Bakin, South, & Weinberger, 1992) and classical conditioning with either positive or aversive reinforcement (Kisley & Gerstein, 2001). These studies show how the plasticity of the nervous system signals the behavioral salience of specific stimuli acquired through conditioning procedures.

Neural Mechanisms: Extinction and Recovery

Studies in rats have revealed the neural circuitry that maintains extinction behavior, which has implications for understanding brain regions and neurotransmitter systems that may be critical to target for treatment of anxiety disorders (Maren & Quirk, 2004; Ressler et al., 2004; Wood & Bouton, 2006). As introduced above, the amygdala and hippocampus are critical brain regions for cued and contextual fear learning, respectively, and these regions are also important for extinction learning and its context specificity. In addition to these structures, the ventromedial prefrontal cortex (vmPFC) is important for maintaining extinction memory. Specifically, lesions of the vmPFC impair the ability of rats to retain a memory of extinction training, and they require many more training trials to suppress a previously acquired fear response (Morgan & LeDoux, 1993). Electrophysiological studies have revealed a temporal dissociation between responses in neurons of the LA (lateral nucleus) of the amygdala and the vmPFC during the acquisition and extinction of fear, suggesting that they play distinct roles in these processes. With the use of single-unit electrical recordings, Goosens, Hobin, and Maren (2003) demonstrated that firing of neurons in the LA occurs selectively to a CS+ but not a CS− and that this neural signature corresponds with conditioned fear behavior. Whereas LA neurons are active during fear learning, the vmPFC is not significantly more active from baseline at this time. During extinction, however, LA neurons are no longer significantly active and fear behavior is reduced. At the same time, neurons in a region of vmPFC, known in rodents as the *infralimbic region*, increase signaling in response to the extinction context (Milad & Quirk, 2002). Thus, neurons in amygdala and vmPFC have opposing but complementary activation patterns in establishing fear associations. Moreover, they have different roles in maintaining new extinction memories that serve to specialize fear knowledge and control its expression.

As discussed above, extinction is context dependent, meaning that it is expressed only in the context in which it was learned (Bouton, 2006; Corcoran & Maren, 2004). The hippocampus is involved in acquiring context memories, and accordingly the context-dependent nature of extinction depends on the integrity of the hippocampus (Corcoran & Maren, 2001; Corcoran et al., 2004). Following extinction, vmPFC neurons exert inhibitory control over the firing of amygdala neurons, resulting in decreased fear responding, although the exact mechanism is a matter of debate. Context specificity of extinction could occur through projections of hippocampus to either the LA or vmPFC, although currently several models are proposed, and the details of these interactions are not yet established (Maren & Quirk, 2004; Sotres-Bayon, Bush, & LeDoux, 2004).

In humans, the circuitry for fear extinction and its recovery are just beginning to be investigated, but the studies to date implicate similar brain regions as in rodents. Consistent with rodent electrophysiological recordings, during extinction training, the activity in the amygdala was temporally graded such that its activity was strongest during the early portion of extinction training and decreased as the safe nature of the stimulus became well established (LaBar et al., 1998). In a more recent extinction study, Phelps et al. (2004) also reported significant regions of activation in the vmPFC and amygdala, and the magnitude of amygdala activation during extinction predicted the magnitude of conditioned learning expressed physiologically as measured by the skin conductance response. Accordingly, as extinction progressed, both the amygdala and skin conductance response declined. Activity in the subgenual anterior cingulate, a portion of the ventromedial prefrontal cortex in humans, predicted subsequent extinction behavior and was negatively correlated with the amygdala response late in extinction training. This pattern is consistent with electrophysiological evidence in rodents that the vmPFC inhibits fear signaling in the amygdala during extinction. Taken together, the vmPFC seems to provide a critical top-down signal for the specialization of learning that takes place during fear extinction.

In sum, based on the evidence from cross-species conditioned-learning paradigms involving fear acquisition, extinction, and recovery, we propose the following potential model. Crude perceptual tuning along thalamo-amygdala pathways early in acquisition training facilitates generalization of fear from one sensory cue to another. It also allows for generalization from sensory cues to contexts via a pathway between the amygdala and the hippocampus. However, later in acquisition, the specialization of context representations that modulate expression of fear and extinction responses are mediated by top-down influences of the vmPFC, the hippocampus, and other cortical regions onto the amygdala (and, in turn, to the sensory cortex). These tune the neuronal responsiveness to different perceptual representations as well as the conditioned associations to provide stimulus discrimination and flexibility of fear responses, which specializes the learning to specific contexts in both time and space (Figure 1.4).

OVERGENERALIZATION OF FEAR CONDITIONING

Dysregulation of prefrontal-amygdalo-hippocampal circuitry is hypothesized to play a key role in the overgeneralization of fear responses seen in anxiety disorders (e.g., Charney, Deutch, Krystal, Southwick, & Davis, 1993). Individuals with posttraumatic stress disorder (PTSD), for instance, exhibit hyperarousal and often have exaggerated fear responses to sensory stimuli (such as loud noises or claps of thunder) that resemble events related to the source of their trauma (e.g., a round of gunshot fire). In addition, the perseverative and generalized fear response to certain classes of stimuli in specific phobias (e.g., a phobia specific to snakes or a phobia specific to spiders) resembles the case of Little Albert. In both disorders, the stimuli are often confined to contexts that should be considered safe and are temporally remote from any adverse encounter in the past (although some phobias do arise without a clear antecedent event). Such maladaptive fear behaviors can be understood in terms of overgeneralization of conditioned fear principles and a failure of extinction, stimulus discrimination, or contextual control.

Experimental work in populations with PTSD or specific phobias has supported the idea of generalized or exaggerated conditioned fear responding and aberrant function in the relevant brain pathways. For example, fear conditioning to CS–US pairings of colored circles (CS) and electrical shock (US) in PTSD subjects induced exaggerated heart rate, skin conductance, and electromyographic changes during both acquisition and extinction phases of learning relative to controls (Orr et al., 2000). Moreover, only PTSD subjects continued to show skin conductance responses to the CSs during extinction. Phobic individuals also show exaggerated conditioned fear responses to fear-relevant CSs (e.g., snakes or spiders) even when the stimuli are presented subliminally (that is, without individuals being consciously aware of their presentation), and this response also persists longer in extinction (for a review, see Ohman & Mineka, 2001).

These responses appear to be driven by changes in the brain at both the cellular and regional levels. Patients with PTSD have been shown to have a smaller volume of hippocampal tissue, decreased activation of regions of the vmPFC, but enhanced amygdala activation (Bremner, 2006; Charney et al., 1993). One consequence of impairments in this neural circuitry may be an inability to discriminate contextual cues (pattern separation), and therefore PTSD patients may be biased to pattern complete, resulting in contextually generalized fear associations. Research with rats suggests that such changes may be driven by the stressful nature of the fear. Analysis of cellular structure in rats reveals that atrophy of hippocampal neurons but enhanced elaborations of the connective branches of amygdala neuron arborizations are associated with increased stress (McEwen, 2001; Sapolsky, 1996; Vyas, Mitra, Shankaranayana, & Chattarji, 2002).

With regard to implications for therapeutic treatments, recent research on the neurobiological mechanisms of extinction learning in nonhuman animals suggests that targeting neurotransmitter receptors in the amygdala may hold promise. In these studies, an agent targeting N-methyl-D-aspartic acid (NMDA) receptors in the amygdala is given prior to extinction training, and the degree of fear suppression is markedly enhanced and maintained over time relative to rats who receive a placebo injection instead (Walker, Ressler, Lu, & Davis, 2002). A recent clinical research study suggests that extinction learning can also be facilitated and maintained following context-specific exposure therapy in patients with specific phobias by administration of the NMDA receptor partial agonist d-cycloserine (Ressler et al., 2004). In this study, brief d-cycloserine administration in conjunction with virtual reality exposure therapy in a simulated elevator facilitated retention of extinction training and reduced symptoms in acrophobics (i.e., people with a fear of heights) for up to 3 months later. The researchers assessed fear by monitoring skin conductance responses during exposure therapy, and then at follow-up time points with self-reports of anxiety, as well as reports from independent assessors. Although this initial result is promising, it is important to note that a recent report found that administration of d-cycloserine in rats in conjunction with extinction in a secondary context facilitated learning of extinction (fear suppression), but it did not prevent fear relapse when rats were returned to the original conditioning context (Woods & Bouton, 2006). Thus, although researchers have made promising steps toward facilitating extinction learning in phobic populations, evidence also suggests that the potential for context-modulated relapse still exists. Further research into neurobiological mechanisms that control context modulation of fear relapse is necessary for developing better therapeutic interventions.

SUMMARY

In summary, three main concepts should be taken into account when considering the issue of the neural systems supporting generalization within the domain of conditioned learning: (a) Initial fear learning is mediated by an amygdala-dependent implicit memory system whose properties support generalization to novel contexts and to stimuli that share features; (b) specialization of learning with continued training alters tuning of perceptual cortical representations and recruits prefrontal and hippocampal processing for temporal and contextual control over fear expression; and (c) overgeneralization related to hyperactive amygdala responses during fear learning and lack of cortical control during extinction training contribute to emotional memory persistence and inappropriate fear expression, which is exaggerated in anxiety disorders.

From a cognitive perspective, behavioral evidence suggests that both configural representations and pattern completion support fear learning to a context. But decrements in generalization (i.e., specialized responses) may rely on elemental processing that is supported conversely by pattern separation. Intact functioning of the fear neuroanatomy circuitry enables humans to properly access these two distinct but complementary cognitive mechanisms so as to generate appropriate fear responses. In populations with anxiety disorders, these neural systems are compromised, and the ability to discriminate fear cues and to learn and retain safety signals (extinction) is impaired. Additional behavioral and neurobiological research into the mechanisms underlying these phenomena will greatly benefit our understanding of generalization mechanisms and will advance treatment of affective illness.

ACKNOWLEDGMENTS

This work was supported by National Institutes of Health (NIH) Grant No. 2 P01 NS041328 and National Science Foundation (NSF) CAREER award No. 0239614 to Kevin S. LaBar, and by NIH Grant No. F32 MH078471 to Nicole C. Huff.

REFERENCES

Abe, K., Niikura, Y., & Misawa, M. (2003). The induction of long-term potentiation at amygdalo-hippocampal synapses in vivo. *Biological & Pharmaceutical Bulletin, 26,* 1560–1562.

Akirav, I., & Richter-Levin, G. (2002). Mechanisms of amygdala modulation of hippocampal plasticity. *Journal of Neuroscience, 22*, 9912–9921.

Bakin, J. S., South, D. A., & Weinberger, N. M. (1992). Sensitization induced receptive field plasticity in the auditory cortex of the guinea pig during instrumental avoidance conditioning. *Behavioral Neuroscience, 110*, 905–913.

Bechara, A., Tranel, D., Damasio, H., Adolphs, R., Rockland, C., & Damasio A. R. (1995). Double dissociation of conditioning and declarative knowledge relative to the amygdala and hippocampus in humans. *Science, 269*, 1115–1118.

Bouton, M. (2004). Context and behavioral processes in extinction. *Learning & Memory, 11*, 485–494.

Bouton, M. E., & Bolles, R. C. (1979). Role of conditioned contextual stimuli in reinstatement of extinguished fear. *Journal of Experimental Psychology, 5*, 368.

Bouton, M. E., Westbrook. R. R., Corcoran, K. A., & Maren, S. (2006). Contextual and temporal modulation of extinction; behavioral and biological mechanisms. *Biological Psychiatry, 60*, 352–60.

Brandon, S. E., & Wagner, A. R. (2001). A componential theory of Pavlovian conditioning. In R. R. Mowrer & S. B. Klein (Eds.), *Handbook of contemporary learning theories* (pp. 23–64). Mahwah, NJ: Lawrence Erlbaum.

Bremner, J. D. (2006). Stress and brain atrophy. *CNS Neurological Disorders Drug Targets*, 5503–5512.

Büchel, C., Morris, J., Dolan, R., & Friston, K. (1998). Brain systems mediating aversive conditioning: An event-related fMRI study. *Neuron, 20*, 947–957.

Charney, D. S., Deutch, A. Y., Krystal, J. H., Southwick, S. M., & Davis, M. (1993). Psychobiologic mechanisms of posttraumatic stress disorder. *Archives of General Psychiatry, 50*(4), 295–305.

Cohen, Y. E., Theunissen, F., Russ, B. E., & Gill, P. (2007). The acoustic features of rhesus vocalizations and their representation in the ventrolateral prefrontal cortex. *Journal of Neurophysiology, 97*, 1470–1484.

Corcoran. K. A., & Maren, S. (2001). Hippocampal inactivation disrupts contextual retrieval of fear memory after extinction. *Journal of Neuroscience, 21*, 1720–6.

Corcoran, K. A., & Maren, S. (2004). Factors regulating the effects of hippocampal inactivation on renewal of conditional fear after extinction. *Learning & Memory, 11*, 598–603.

Davis, M. (1992). The role of the amygdala in conditioned fear. In J. P. Aggleton (Ed.), *The amygdala: Neurobiological aspects of emotion, memory, and mental dysfunction* (pp. 255–306). New York: Wiley-Liss.

Domjan, M. (1998). *Principles in learning and behavior* (4th ed., pp. 221–238). Belmont Park, CA: Brooks/Cole.

Fanselow, M. S., & LeDoux, J. E. (1999). Why we think plasticity underlying Pavlovian fear conditioning occurs in the basolateral amygdala. *Neuron, 23*, 229–232.

Furmark, T., Fischer, H., Wik, G., Larsson, M., & Fredrikson, M. (1997). The amygdala and individual differences in human fear conditioning. *Neuroreport, 8*, 3957–3960.

Garcia, R., Vouimba, R. M., Baudry, M., & Thompson, R. F. (1999). The amygdala modulates prefrontal cortex activity relative to conditioned fear. *Nature, 402*, 294–296.

Gonzalez, F., Quinn, J. J., & Fanselow, M. S. (2003). Differential effects of adding and removing components of a context on the generalization of conditional freezing. *Journal of Experimental Psychology: Animal Behavior Processes, 29*(1), 78–83.

Goosens, K., Hobin, J., & Maren, S. (2003). Auditory-evoked spike firing in the lateral amygdala and Pavlovian fear conditioning: Mnemonic code or fear bias? *Neuron, 40*, 1013–1022.

Guttman, N., & Kalish, H. I. (1956). Discriminability and stimulus generalization. *Journal of Experimental Psychology, 51*, 79–88.

Guzowski, J., Knierim, J., & Moser, E. (2004). Ensemble dynamics of hippocampal regions CA3 and CA1. *Neuron, 44*, 581–584.

Hamann, S., Monarch, E., & Goldstein, F. (2002). Impaired fear conditioning in Alzheimer's disease. *Neuropsychologia, 40*, 1187–1195.

Hanson, H. M. (1959). Effects of discrimination training on stimulus discrimination. *Journal of Experimental Psychology, 58*, 321–333.

Holyoak, K. J., & Nisbett, R. E. (1988). Induction. In R. J. Sternberg & E. E. Smith (Eds.), *The psychology of human thought* (pp. 50–91). New York: Cambridge University Press.

Honey, R., & Hall, G. (1990). Context-specific conditioning in the conditioned-emotional-response procedure. *Journal of Experimental Psychology: Animal Behavior Processes, 16*, 271–278.

Honey, R., Willis, A., & Hall, G. (1990). Context specificity in pigeon autoshaping. *Learning and Motivation, 21*, 125–136.

Huff, N. C., Frank, M., Wright-Hardesty, K., Sprunger, D., Matus-Amat, P., Higgins, E., et al. (2006). Amygdala regulation of immediate-early-gene expression in the hippocampus induced by contextual fear conditioning. *Journal of Neuroscience, 26*, 1616–1623.

Huff, N. C., & Rudy, J. W. (2004). The amygdala modulates hippocampus-dependent context memory formation and stores cue-shock associations. *Behavioral Neuroscience, 118*(1), 53–62.

Huff, N. C., Wright-Hardesty, K., Higgins, E., Matus-Amat, P., & Rudy, J. W. (2005). Context pre-exposure obscures amygdala modulation of contextual-fear conditioning. *Learning and Memory, 12*, 456–460.

Humphrey, G. (1951). *Thinking: An introduction to its experimental psychology* (pp. 256–257). New York: John Wiley.

Jarrell, T. W., Gentile, C. G., Romanski, L. M., McCabe, P. M., & Schneiderman, N. (1987). Involvement of cortical and thalamic auditory regions in retention of differential bradycardia conditioning to acoustic conditioned stimuli in rabbits. *Brain Research, 412*, 285–294.

Jenkins, H. M., & Harrison, R. H. (1960). Effects of discrimination training on auditory generalization. *Journal of Experimental Psychology, 59*, 246–253.

Kiernan, M. J., & Westbrook, R. F. (1993). Effects of exposure to a to-be-shocked environment upon the rat's freezing response: Evidence for facilitation, latent inhibition, and perceptual learning. *Quarterly Journal of Experimental Psychology: Comparative and Physiological Psychology, 46*(B), 271–288.

Kilcross, S., Robbin, T., & Everitt, B. (1997). Different types of fear-conditioned behaviour mediated by separate nuclei within amygdala. *Nature, 388*, 377–380.

Kisley, M. A., & Gerstein, G. L. (2001). Daily variation and appetitive conditioning-induced plasticity of auditory cortex receptive fields. *European Journal of Neuroscience, 13*, 1993–2003.

LaBar, K. S., & Cabeza, R. (2006). Cognitive neuroscience of emotional memory. *Nature Reviews Neuroscience, 7*, 54–64.

LaBar, K. S., Gatenby, J. C., Gore, J. C., LeDoux, J. E., & Phelps, E. A. (1998). Human amygdala activation during conditioned fear acquisition and extinction: A mixed trial fMRI study. *Neuron, 20*, 937–945.

LaBar, K. S., LeDoux, J. E., Spenser, D. D., & Phelps, E. A. (1995). Impaired fear conditioning following unilateral temporal lobectomy in humans. *Journal of Neuroscinece, 15*, 6846–55.

LaBar, K. S., & LeDoux, J. E. (1996). Partial disruption of fear conditioning in rats with unilateral amygdala damage: Correspondence with unilateral temporal lobectomy in humans. *Behavioral Neuroscience, 110*, 991–997.

LaBar, K. S., & Phelps, E. A. (2005). Reinstatement of conditioned fear in humans is context-dependent and impaired in amnesia. *Behavioral Neuroscience, 119*, 677–686.

Lamprecht, R., & LeDoux, J. E. (2004). Structural plasticity and memory. *Nature Review Neuroscience, 5*, 45–54.

LeDoux, J. E. (1995). Emotion: Clues from the brain. *Annual Review Psychology, 46*, 209–235.

Li, X., Stutzman, G., & LeDoux, J. (1996). Convergent but temporally separated inputs to lateral amygdalal neurons from the auditory thalamus and auditory cortex use different post synaptic receptors: In vivo intracellular and extracellular recordings in fear conditioning pathways. *Learning & Memory, 3*, 229–242.

Maren, S. (2000). Auditory fear conditioning increases CS-elicited spike firing in lateral amygdala neurons even after extensive overtraining. *European Journal of Neuroscience, 12*, 40–47.

Maren, S., & Quirk, G. J. (2004). Neuronal signaling of fear memory. *Nature Reviews Neuroscience, 5*, 844–852.

Maren, S., Yap, S. A., & Goosens, K. A. (2001). The amygdala is essential for the development of neuronal plasticity in the medial geniculate nucleus during auditory fear conditioning in rats. *Journal of Neuroscience, 21*, RC135.

Marr, D. (1971). Simple memory: A theory for archicortex. *Philosophical Transactions of the Royal Society of London B, 262*, 23–81.

Marschner, A., Kalisch, R., Vervliet, B., Vensteenwegen, D., & Büchel, C. (2008). Dissociable role for the hippocampus and amygdala in cued and contextual fear conditioning. *Journal of Neuroscience, 28*(36), 9030–9036.

McEwen, B. S. (2001). Plasticity of the hippocampus: Adaptation to chronic stress and allostatic load. *Annals of the New York Academy of Science, 933*, 265–277.

McGaugh, J. L. (2000). Memory: A century of consolidation. *Science, 287*, 248–251.

McKernan, M. G., & Shinnick-Gallagher, P. (1997). Fear conditioning induces a lasting potentiation of synaptic currents in vitro. *Nature, 390*, 607–611.

McLin, D. E., III, Miasnikov, A. A., & Weinberger, N. M. (2002). Induction of behavioral associative memory by stimulation of the nucleus basalis. *Proceedings of the National Academy of Sciences, 99*, 4002–4007.

McNally, G. V., & Westbrook, F. R. (2006). Predicting danger: The nature, consequences, and neural mechanisms of predictive fear learning. *Learning and Memory, 13*, 245–253.

McNaughton, B. L., & Morris, R. G. M. (1987). Hippocampal synaptic enhancement and information storage within a distributed memory system. *Trends in Neuroscience, 10*, 408–415.

Milad, M. R., Orr, S. P., Pitman, R. K., & Rauch, S. L. (2005). Context modulation of memory for fear extinction in humans. *Psychophysiology, 42*, 456–464.

Milad, M. R., & Quirk, G. J. (2002). Neurons in medial prefrontal cortex signal memory for fear extinction. *Nature, 420*, 70–4.

Mineka, S., Mystkowski, J. L., Hladek, D., & Rodriquez, B. I. (1999). The effects of changing contexts on return of fear following exposure treatment for spider fear. *Journal of Consulting and Clinical Psychology, 67*, 599–604.

Morris, J., Öhman, A., & Dolan, R. (1999). Subcortical pathway to the right amygdala mediating "unseen" fear. *Proceedings of the National Academy of Sciences, 96*, 1680–1685.

Myers, K. M., & Davis, M. (2002). Behavioral and neural analysis of extinction. *Neuron, 36*, 567–584.

Nadel, L., & Willner, J. (1980). Context and conditioning: A place for space. *Physiology and Behavior, 8*, 218–228.

Nadel, L., Willner, J., & Kurz, E. M. (1985). Cognitive maps and environmental context. In P. Balsam & A. Tomie (Eds.), *Context and learning* (pp. 385–406). Hillsdale, NJ: Lawrence Erlbaum.

Ochsner, K. N., & Gross, J. J. (2005). The cognitive control of emotion. *Trends in Cognitive Science, 5,* 242–249.

Ohman, A., & Mineka, S. (2001). Fears, phobias, and preparedness; toward an evolved module of fear and fear learning. *Psychological Review, 108,* 483–522.

Ohman, A., & Soares, J. J. F. (1993). On the automatic nature of phobic fear: Conditioned electrodermal responses to masked fear-relevant stimuli. *Journal of Abnormal Psychology, 102,* 121–132.

O'Reilly, R. C., & McClelland, J. L. (1994). Hippocampal conjunctive encoding, storage, and retrieval: Avoiding a trade off. *Hippocampus, 4,* 661–682.

O'Reilly, R. C., & Rudy, J. W. (2001). Conjunctive representations in learning and memory: Principles of cortical and hippocampal function. *Psychological Review, 108,* 311–345.

Orr, S. P., Metzger, L. J., Lasko, N. B., Macklin, M. L., Peri, T., & Pitman, R. K. (2000). De novo conditioning in trauma-exposed individuals with and without posttraumatic stress disorder. *Journal of Abnormal Psychology, 109*(2), 290–298.

Pascoe, J., & Kapp, B. S. (1985). Electrophysiologial characteristics of amygdaloid dentral nucleus neurons during Pavlovian fear conditioning in the rabbit. *Behavioral Brain Research, 16,* 117.

Pavlov, I. P. (1927). *Conditioned Reflexes: An Investigation of the Physiological Activity of the Cerebral Cortex.* Translated and Edited by G.V. Anrep, London: Oxford University Press.

Pearce, J. M. (1994). Similarity and discrimination: A selective review and a connectionist model. *Psychological Review, 101,* 587–607.

Peper, M., Karcher, S., Wohlfarth, R., Reinshagen, G., & LeDoux, J. E. (2001). Aversive learning in patients with unilateral lesions of the amygdala and hippocampus. *Biological Psychology, 58,* 1–23.

Phelps, E. A., Delgado, M. R., Nearing, K. I., & LeDou, J. E. (2004). Extinction learning in humans: role of the amygdala and vmPFC. *Neuron, 43,* 897–905.

Phelps, E., LaBar, K. S., & Anderson, A. (1998). Specifying the contributions of the human amygdala to emotional memory: A case study. *Neurocase, 4,* 527–540.

Phelps, E. A., & LeDoux, J. E. (2005). Contributions of the amygdala to emotion processing: From animal models to human behavior. *Neuron, 48,* 175–187.

Phillips, R. G., & LeDoux, J. E. (1992). Differential contribution of amygdala and hippocampus to cued and contextual fear conditioning. *Behavioral Neuroscience, 106,* 274–285.

Pitkanen, A. (2000). Connectivity of the rat amygdaloid coplex. In J. P. Aggleton (Ed.), *The amygdala: A functional analysis* (2nd ed.). Oxford: Oxford University Press.

Quirk, G. J., Armony, J. L., & LeDoux, J. E. (1997). Fear conditioning enhances different temporal components of tone-evoked spike trains in auditory cortex and lateral amygdala. *Neuron, 19,* 613–624.

Quirk, G. J., Repa, J. C., & LeDoux, J. E. (1995). Fear conditioning enhances short-latency auditory responses of lateral amygdala neurons: Parallel recordings in the freely behaving rat. *Neuron, 15,* 1029–1039.

Rescorla, R. A. (1988). Pavlovian conditioning: It's not what you think it is. *American Psychologist, 43,* 151–160.

Rescorla, R. A., & Wagner, A. R. (1972). A theory of Pavlovian conditioning: Variations in the effectiveness of reinforcement and nonreinforcement. In A. H. Black & W. F. Prokasy (Eds.), *Classical conditioning: II. Current research and theory* (pp. 64–99). New York: Appleton-Century-Crofts.

Ressler, K. J., Rothbaum, B. O., Tannenbaum, L., Anderson, P., Graap, K., Zimand, E., et al. (2004). Cognitive enhancers as adjuncts to psychotherapy: Use of D-cycloserine in phobic individuals to facilitate extinction of fear. Arch Gen Psychiatry. 61(11), 1136–1144.

Rogan, M.T. & LeDoux, J. E. (1995). LTP is accompanied by commensurate enhancement of auditory-evoked responses in a fear conditioning circuit. Neuron, 15, 127–36.

Rogan, M. T., Staubli, U. V., & LeDoux, J. E. (1997). Fear conditioning induces associative long-term potentiation in the amygdala. Nature, 390, 604–607.

Romanski, L. M., Clugnet, M. C., Bordi, F., & LeDoux, J. E. (1993). Somatosensory and auditory convergence in the lateral nucleus of the amygdala. Behavioral Neuroscience, 104, 444–450.

Romanski, L. M., & LeDoux, J. E. (1992). Equipotentiality of thalamo-amygdala and thalamo-cortico-amygdala circuits in auditory fear conditioning. Journal of Neuroscience, 12(11), 4501–4509.

Rudy, J. W., Huff, N. C., & Matus-Amat, P. (2004). Understanding contextual fear conditioning: Insights from a two-process model. Neuroscience and Biobehavioral Reviews, 28, 675–685.

Rudy, J. W., & O'Reilly, R. C. (1999). Contextual fear conditioning, conjunctive representations, pattern completion, and the hippocampus. Behavioral Neuroscience, 113(5), 867–880.

Rudy, J. W., & O'Reilly, R. C. (2001). Conjunctive representations, the hippocampus, and contextual fear conditioning. Cognitive, Affective, & Behavioral Neuroscience, 1, 66–82.

Rudy, J. W., & Wagner, A. R. (1976). Stimulus selection in associative learning. In W. K. Estes (Ed.), Handbook of learning and cognitive processes: Conditioning and behavior theory (Vol. 2, pp. 269–302). Hillsdale, NJ: Lawrence Erlbaum.

Sapolsky, R. M. (1996). Why stress is bad for your brain. Science, 273, 749–750.

Schafe, G. E., & LeDoux, J. E. (2000). Memory consolidation of auditory Pavlovian fear conditioning requires protein synthesis and protein kinase A in the amygdala. Journal of Neuroscience, 20, RC96.

Shaban, H., Humeau, Y., Herry, C., Cassasus, G., Shigemoto, R., Ciocchi, S., et al. (2006). Generalization of amygdala LTP and conditioned fear in the absence of presynaptic inhibition. Nature Neuroscience, 9(8), 1028–1035.

Shin, L. M., Wright, C. I., Cannistraro, P. A., Wedig, M. M., McMullin, K., Martis, B., et al., (2005). A functional magnetic resonance imaging study of amygdala and medial prefrontal cortex responses to overtly presented fearful faces in posttraumatic stress disorder. Archives of General Psychiatry, 62(3), 273–281.

Sotres-Bayon, F., Bush, D. E. A., & LeDoux, J. E. (2004). Emotional preservation: An update on prefrontal-amygdala interactions in fear extinction. Learning and Memory, 11, 525–535.

Spence, K. W. (1936). The nature of discrimination learning in animals. Psychological Review, 43, 427–449.

Squire, L. R. (1992). Memory and the hippocampus: A synthesis from findings with rats, monkeys and humans. Psychological Review, 99, 195–231.

Squire, L. R., & Kandel, E. R. (1999). Memory: From mind to molecules. New York: Scientific American Library, W. H. Freeman.

Thomas, D. R., McKelvie, A. R., & Mah, W. L. (1985). Context as a conditional cue in operant discrimination reversal learning. Journal of Experimental Psychology: Animal Behavior Processes, 11, 317–330.

Tsvetkov, E., Carlezon, W. A., Benes, F. M., Kandel, E. R., & Bolshakov, V. Y. (2002). Fear conditioning occludes LTP-induced presynaptic enhancement of synaptic transmission in the cortical pathway to the lateral amygdala. Neuron, 34, 289–300.

Tyler, T. J., & DiScenna, P. (1986). The hippocampus memory indexing theory. *Behavioral Neuroscience, 100*, 147–152.

Vansteenwegen, D., Hermans, D., Vervliet, B., Francken, G., Beckers, T., Baeyens, F., et al. (2005). Return of fear in a human differential conditioning paradigm caused by a return to the original acquisition context. *Behaviour Research and Therapy, 43*, 323–336.

Vervliet, B., Vansteenwegen, D., & Eelen, P. (2004). Generalization of extinguished skin conductance responding in human fear conditioning. *Learning & Memory, 11*, 555–558.

Vyas, A., Mitra, R., Shankaranayana, B., & Chattarji, S. (2002). Chronic stress induces contrasting patterns of dendritic remodeling in hippocampal and amygdaloid neurons. *Journal of Neuroscience, 22*, 6810–6818.

Walker, D., Ressler, K., Lu, K., & Davis, M. (2002). Facilitation of conditioned fear extinction by systemic administration or intra-amygdala infusions of D-cycloserine as assessed with fear-potentiated startle in rats. *Journal of Neuroscience, 15*(22), 2343–2351.

Watson, J. B., & Raynor, R. (2000). Conditioned emotional reactions. 1920. *American Psychologist, 55*, 313–7.

Weinberger, N. M. (2003). The nucleus basalis and memory codes: Auditory cortical plasticity and the induction of specific, associative behavioral memory. *Neurobiology of Learning and Memory, 80*, 268–284.

Wheeler, D. S., Amundson, J. C., & Miller, R. R. (2006). Generalization decrement in human contingency learning. *Quarterly Journal of Experimental Psychology, 59*(7), 1212–1223.

Woods, A. M., & Bouton, M. E. (2006). D-cycloserine facilitates extinction but does not eliminate renewal of the conditioned emotional response. *Behavioral Neuroscience, 120*(5), 1159–1162.

Zorawski, M., Cook, C. S., Kuhn, C. A., & LaBar, K.S. (2005). Sex, stress, and fear: individual differences in conditioned learning. *Cognitive Affective and Behavioral Neuroscience, 5*, 191–201.

2

Transfer and Interference in Perceptual Expertise
When Expertise Helps and When It Hurts

RANKIN W. MCGUGIN and JAMES TANAKA

INTRODUCTION

*H*uman learning in the visual domain is best understood as a continuum, characterized by the depth and degree to which a stimulus is encoded, the specific cognitive operations that are engaged, and the distinct neural structures that are recruited. At one end of the continuum, a single presentation of a visual stimulus—so brief as to elude the perceptual awareness of the observer—can nevertheless alter one's subsequent perceptions. For example, studies show that a word stimulus not consciously perceived by the participant can nonetheless facilitate subsequent perceptions of that word (Jacoby & Hayman, 1987). At the other end of the continuum of human learning, changes in perception can result from explicit, purposeful training that occurs over weeks, months, or even a lifetime of practice and experience. For example, farmers learn to differentiate the sex of chickens; musicians learn to distinguish the notes, chords, and instrumental voices in a musical piece; and tennis players learn to anticipate the placement of upcoming shots. In such real-world domains of expertise, the acquisition of information and the refinement of knowledge involve changes in perception, memory, semantics, inference generation, and motor actions (Ericsson, Krampe, & Tesch-Romer, 1993; Palmeri, Wong, & Gauthier, 2004).

It is important to distinguish how perceptual learning and perceptual expertise differ along this continuum of human learning. As shown in Table 2.1, perceptual learning and perceptual expertise can be distinguished in terms of the nature of

TABLE 2.1   Comparing Perceptual Learning and Perceptual Expertise

	Perceptual Learning ↔	**Perceptual Expertise**
Encoding	Brief, incidental	Sustained, intentional
Sensory properties	Low-level features (e.g., orientation and luminance)	High-level objects
Specificity	Hyperspecific	Robust
Neural substrates	Primary visual cortex	Inferior temporal cortex

encoding, the type of stimulus properties encoded, the specificity of learning, and the associated neural substrates. First, perceptual learning and perceptual expertise differ in the nature of information encoded. In perceptual learning paradigms,[1] improved discrimination can be achieved in a single training session and in the absence of attention and awareness, and when the perceptual discrimination is not required by task demands (Seitz, Nanez, Holloway, Koyama, & Watanabe, 2005; Wantanabe, Sasaki, & Nanez, 2001). Real-world perceptual expertise, on the other hand, unfolds over a much longer time course and is typically achieved with years of deliberate practice (Johnson & Mervis, 1997; Tanaka & Taylor, 1991). In laboratory training studies, expert-like performance can be obtained during highly concentrated learning sessions that follow rigorous training protocols (Gauthier & Tarr, 1997a, 1997b; Gauthier, Williams, Tarr, & Tanaka, 1998). Furthermore, whereas research on perceptual learning has focused on the enhanced discrimination of low-level sensory properties such as orientation, surface luminance, or pitch (Ahissar & Hochstein, 1994, 1997, 1998; Fitzgerald & Wright, 2005), studies of perceptual expertise examine more complex, high-level sensory processes involved in the recognition of objects within a specific category (e.g., dogs [Diamond & Carey, 1986], artificial objects called *Greebles* [Gauthier & Tarr, 1997a], or faces). In addition to these differences in the encoding of information, perceptual learning and perceptual expertise also differ in the degree to which they lead to perceptual transfer. Although perceptual learning is hyperspecific to the training stimuli and even their locations in the retinal field (Ahissar & Hochstein, 1993; Shiu & Pashler, 1992; Sigman & Gilbert, 2000), one hallmark of perceptual expertise is its robust ability to generalize to new members of a class (Gauthier et al., 1998).

As predicted from the aforementioned dissociations in encoding and specificity, distinctions between perceptual leaning and expertise also arise at the neural level. For example, perceptual learning studies have shown neural correlates to behavioral improvement in tactile discrimination in the absence of explicit training, attention, or reinforcement in humans (Godde, Stauffenberg, Spengler, & Dinse, 2000; Pleger et al., 2001) and in rats (Godde, Spengler, & Dinse, 1996; Hodzic, Veit, Karim, Erb, & Godde, 2004). In these experiments, behavioral improvement in tactile or grating orientation discrimination (i.e., perceptual learning) was positively correlated with the amount of change in regions of the brain (S1 and S2 in humans) that are the first regions to receive somatosensory information from the peripheral sensory receptors throughout the body. In another study, repeated visual exposure to a specifically oriented grating led to neural changes in visual areas of the brain (i.e., the primary visual cortex, V1; Frenkel et al., 2006). Moreover, repeatedly pairing an auditory tone with stimulation in the ventral tegmental brain area (Bao, Chan, & Merzenich, 2001) or the nucleus basalis of the basal forebrain (Kilgard & Merzenich, 1998), two regions sending widespread projections from early dopaminergic (learning and reinforcement related) neurons to the cortex, leads to increased representation of the tone in early auditory cortical brain regions (i.e., the primary auditory cortex, A1). Although the neural correlates of perceptual learning can be localized to primary sensory areas (S1, V1, and A1), the neural correlates of perceptual *expertise* are typically found in higher order brain areas, such as the inferior temporal cortex, where more complex object processing occurs. Specifically, areas in the middle fusiform gyrus that are routinely activated to faces become similarly responsive to nonface stimuli after extensive training (Gauthier, Curran, Curby, & Collins, 2003).

The focus of this chapter is on the end of the learning continuum that emphasizes perceptual expertise and, largely, expertise in the visual domain in humans. We will first consider the nature of perceptual expertise across a variety of objects and training protocols that optimize this type of expert perceptual learning. Next, we examine the conditions that foster the transfer of perceptual knowledge from one domain to another, as well as the conditions where such transfer fails. Finally, we will discuss perceptual trade-offs related to expertise, whereby perceptual skill in one area of expertise paradoxically hinders performance in another.

BENCHMARKS OF PERCEPTUAL EXPERTISE

What is perceptual expertise? *Expertise* is a generic term that may imply different things to different people. According to our definition, an individual is classified as an "expert" only if he or she satisfies certain behavioral criteria. Generally speaking, experts are expected to have a shared language or classification system. For example, to the average person sitting on the beach, one ocean wave looks just like another. However, to the keen eye of the expert surfer, a wave could be a *bombora*, *cnoid*, *micro-mini*, *honker*, or *slab* depending on its shape, size, and texture. Thus, experts view objects in their domain of expertise at a finer grain of detail than novices. In object recognition, this ability is shown by the level of abstraction at which experts identity familiar objects. Whereas novices identify objects at the basic level (e.g., "dog," "chair," or "car"), experts categorize objects in their domain of expertise at a more specific, subordinate level of abstraction (e.g., "Weimaraner" [dog expert], "Aeron" [chair expert], or "Lexus 400h" [car expert]) (Rosch, Mervis, Gray, Johnson, & Boyes-Braem, 1976). Thus, one hallmark of perceptual expertise is that experts identify objects in their domain of expertise at a more subordinate level of abstraction than novices.

Differences in the perceptual information contained in basic-level and subordinate-level representations may have important consequences on immediate perception and subsequent recognition of a given object. Consider, for example, the basic-level object, *dog*. The representation of this object contains the main parts of a *head*, a *body, four legs*, and a *tail*. Now imagine the subordinate-level description of this animal as a *Weimaraner*. This level of specification requires a modified description of the component parts, such as *medium-sized, oval head*; *compact, brown body*; *long, athletic legs*; and *short, skinny tail*. Whereas the basic-level object representation contains information about the essential parts of an object, the subordinate-level representation provides a more elaborate description of those parts. In visual processing, the broad, coarse-grain descriptions of novices' basic-level judgments rely on data that provide the broad, featural information (i.e., that in low-spatial-frequency channels), whereas the fine-grain descriptions required for experts' subordinate-level categorizations depend on information related to more detailed visual outlines or contours (i.e., that contained in high-spatial-frequency channels) (Collin & McMullen, 2005). Although novices are still capable of analyzing objects at the fine-grain subordinate level, they require relatively more time and effort to do so. That is, it takes longer for a novice to identify an object at the subordinate level of "beagle" or "robin" than it does for them to categorize the same object at the basic level of "dog" or "bird" (Johnson & Mervis, 1997; Tanaka & Taylor, 1991). In contrast, experts are just as fast to categorize objects of expertise at the subordinate level as they are to categorize those objects at the basic level.

Importantly, the subordinate-level descriptions of experts are not stored as separate bits of detailed information, but rather are combined into a unitary, holistic representation. In fact, relative to novices, experts are *less* capable of attending to a single part or feature of an object for which they are an expert (Gauthier et al., 2003). This so-called holistic nature of expert performance suggests that with high levels of learning, distinct components gradually become processed as a single perceptual entity (Ahissar & Hochstein, 2004; Goldstone, 1998). Experts trained in Morse code, for example, decipher the dots and dashes of the message as whole units rather than single bits of information (Ahissar & Hochstein, 2004).

Although we may not all be Morse code aficionados, most everyone qualifies as a "face expert," where faces are arguably the most ubiquitous form of holistic processing. In face perception, people are sensitive to even the slightest changes to a face stimulus. For instance, a subtle modification of a single facial feature (e.g., changing the shape of the mouth) or its spatial configuration (e.g., increasing the distance between the nose and mouth) can impact the perception of other facial features and even alter the perceived holistic identity of the entire face (McGugin & Gauthier, in press; Tanaka & Farah, 1993; Tanaka & Sengco, 1997; Young, Hellawell, & Hay, 1987; but see Wenger & Ingvalson, 2002, for an explanation of holistic effects based on cognitive-decisional as opposed to perceptual processes). Similarly, experts form holistic representations of objects in their domain of expertise. Car experts, for example, can notice slight variations in the relative positions of the grill, front windshield, and side mirrors that change the perception of the whole car, whereas a novice is unaware of such configural changes (Gauthier & Tarr, 1997a).

Importantly, these behavioral markers of perceptual expertise—namely, subordinate-level recognition and holistic processing—have observable neural correlates. It has been well established by functional magnetic resonance imaging (fMRI) that pictures of faces selectively activate inferotemporal regions of the brain and, specifically, an area in the fusiform gyrus referred to as the *fusiform face area* (FFA; Kanwisher, McDermott, & Chun, 1997; Puce, Allison, Gore, & McCarthy, 1995; Sergent, Ohta, & MacDonald, 1992). Rather than being specific or exclusive to faces, however, this neural structure may reflect a more generic, expert recognition module that is activated by faces for most people and by objects of expertise for experts (Tarr & Gauthier, 2000). In support of this view, a similar pattern of activity in the FFA was found in response to faces in control participants, to car stimuli in car experts, and to bird stimuli in bird experts (Gauthier, Skudlarski, Gore, & Anderson, 2000). Similarly, individuals laboratory trained in expert recognition and discrimination of novel objects (i.e., Greebles) showed an increase in FFA activity in response to pictures of those novel objects (Gauthier, Tarr, Anderson, Skudlarksi, & Gore, 1999). See Figure 2.1.

In addition to functional neuroimaging, methods of recording the electrical activity of the brain, such as through event-related potentials (ERPs), have been employed to explore the neural correlates of perceptual expertise. Whereas whole-brain fMRI analyses portray the spatial layout of the neural circuitry involved in a

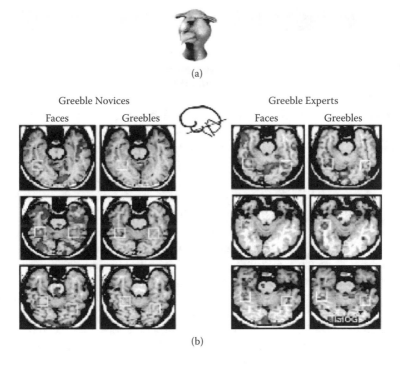

Figure 2.1   Perceptual expertise training with novel objects. (a) An example "Greeble" used for training. (b) Functional neuroimaging group data for Greeble novices (*n* = 3) and Greeble experts (*n* = 3) in a passive-viewing task of faces and Greebles. Passive viewing of objects was used as a statistical baseline condition for brain activation maps. The results show that activation in face-selective regions can increase with expertise for novel objects. White squares indicate the middle fusiform gyri. Arrows indicate the lateral occipital foci. Adapted from Gauthier, Behrmann, and Tarr (1999).

process, ERPs can provide more detailed information regarding the precise timing of neural events associated with expertise. ERP studies have shown that when experts view objects of their expertise, electrodes placed over posterior regions of the brain detect enhanced activity in a particular waveform that occurs 170 ms after the onset of the object (i.e., called "the N170"; Busey & Vanderkolk, 2005; Rossion, Gauthier, Goffaux, Tarr, & Crommelinck, 2002; Tanaka & Curran, 2001). An ERP component that shows similar timing and a similar distribution of activity across different electrodes has been observed when participants view images of faces (Bentin, Allison, Puce, Perez, & McCarthy, 1996). Moreover, the N170 to both faces and objects of expertise is delayed by inversion, suggesting that this manipulation disrupts holistic perception of expert stimuli (Rossion et al., 2002). The enhanced N170 component has thus been interpreted as a general indicator of real-world expertise found in bird, dog (Tanaka & Curran), car (Gauthier et al., 2003), and fingerprint (Busey & Vanderkolk) experts. However, more recent work from training studies has suggested that a second component—the N250—might be more sensitive to the subordinate-level processing associated with the acquisition of expertise (Scott, Tanaka, Sheinberg, & Curran, 2006; Tanaka, Curran, Porterfield, & Collins, 2006; Tanaka & Pierce, 2009).

In summary, results from the cognitive neuroscience studies suggest that face recognition and expert object recognition share common neural substrates and neurophysiological processes, and these structures and processes are amendable to the effects of perceptual experience and training. With a general understanding of the behavioral and neural fundamentals of expertise, we can address the nature of perceptual expertise in unique contexts and training conditions. Focusing on visual perception, we will see when and how expertise *helps* subsequent object processing, and when and how it *hurts* concurrent object processing.

TRANSFER AND GENERALIZATION IN PERCEPTUAL EXPERTISE

In perceptual expertise, transfer involves the generalization of expert recognition from a familiar, learned context to an unfamiliar, novel context. The extent of perceptual transfer in expertise can be viewed as a continuum of weak, intermediate, and strong forms. See Table 2.2. A *weak* form of perceptual transfer occurs when an expert can recognize an object of expertise across changes in viewpoint and viewing conditions. For example, a cattle farmer can identify a specific cow when viewed from different perspectives or lighting conditions. In face recognition, highly familiar faces are less influenced by viewpoint than less familiar faces (Hill, Schyns, & Akamatsu, 1997). Hence, unlike novices who are poor at generalizing recognition learned in one orientation to a new orientation (Edelman & Bülthoff, 1992; Rock & DiVita, 1987; Tarr & Pinker, 1989), experts are less influenced by the effects of changing viewpoints.

Whereas weak transfer involves the mapping of divergent object viewpoints to a common underlying object representation, *intermediate* transfer stresses the process by which different object exemplars are grouped into the same subordinate-level

TABLE 2.2   Summary of Transfer and Interference in Perceptual Expertise

Effect	Description	Example	References
Transfer			
Weak transfer	Expert recognition transfers across novel viewpoints of expert objects.	Training on one object viewpoint transfers to recognition of novel viewpoints.	Edelman and Bülthoff (1992), Gauthier and Tarr (1997b), Hill et al. (1997), Poggio and Edelman (1990), Riesenhuber and Poggio (2000), Rock and DiVita (1987), Ullman (1998), and Weisberg et al. (2007)
Intermediate transfer	Expert recognition transfers to novel exemplars of expert objects.	Training on one set of images of an owl species (e.g., barred owl) transfers to the recognition of novel images of that same owl species (e.g., barred owl).	Scott et al. (2006), Tanaka et al. (2005), and Weisberg et al. (2007)
Strong transfer	Expert learning transfers to new categories within a domain of expertise.	Training on a variety of species of owls (e.g., screech, snowy, and barred) transfers to the learning of new species of owls (e.g., great gray).	Gauthier and Tarr (1997a), Gauthier et al. (1998), Scott et al. (2006), Tanaka et al. (2005), and Yue et al. (2006)
Nontransfer	Previous perceptual expertise neither facilitates nor interferes with expert recognition or learning in other domains.	Training on recognition of owl species does not transfer to or inhibit the recognition of wading bird species, and vice versa.	Gauthier and Tarr (1997a), Gauthier et al. (1998), Mondloch, Maurer, and Ahola (2006), Myles-Worsley et al. (1988), Pascalis et al. (2002), Rhodes et al. (1989), Scott et al. (2006), Tanaka and Droucker (submitted), and Tanaka et al. (2005)
Interference	Expertise in one domain interferes with performance in another expert domain.	Car expertise impeded search for a target face when displayed among car distractors.	Curby and Gauthier (2001), Gauthier et al. (2003), McKeeff et al. (submitted), Rossion et al. (2004, 2007), and Williams et al. (in preparation)

category. Intermediate transfer in normal object recognition occurs at the basic level (e.g., office chairs, easy chairs, and kitchen chairs belong to the same category of *chair*), whereas intermediate transfer of *expertise* demands that objects are categorized at a more specific, subordinate level. The expert birder, for example, is able to classify different instances of Pacific loons whether seen in their winter or spring plumage, or as juveniles or adults. Here, expert categorization is not bound to a specific image or exemplar, but is sufficiently robust that it generalizes across exemplars, even if these exemplars vary considerably in their visual appearance. A study by Tanaka, Curran, and Sheinberg (2005) demonstrated the properties of intermediate transfer where participants learned to classify owls at the subordinate, species (e.g., "barred owl," or "screech owl"), or basic level (e.g., "owl"). When shown novel pictures of the learned species of owls that were not encountered during training, participants in the subordinate-level training condition showed superior discrimination of these stimuli. Thus, subordinate-level training with one set of images of an owl species transferred to the recognition of novel images of the learned owl species (Tanaka et al., 2005; see also Scott et al., 2006).

In contrast to intermediate transfer, which involves the activation of previously learned subordinate-level representations, *strong* transfer requires the generation of new subordinate-level categories. For example, a bird watcher who specializes in North American songbirds should be able to transfer this perceptual knowledge when learning unfamiliar species of songbirds from South America. Evidence for strong transfer was found in a recent study where individuals were trained to expert levels of subordinate-level discrimination of novel objects called "blobs" (Yue, Tjan, & Biederman, 2006). After training, blob experts demonstrated significantly superior performance relative to untrained, novice participants when both groups were tested on a *novel* blob configuration. Similarly, participants trained with a set of artificial objects (Greebles) were faster and more accurate than untrained novices in learning new sets of Greebles (Gauthier et al., 1998). In another study, participants who were trained to discriminate spotted and barred owls were able to transfer their skills to the discrimination of great gray owls, for which they received no training (Tanaka et al., 2005). Blobs, Greebles, and owls all represent object categories whose group members share similar features arranged in a common spatial configuration and, as a result, must be individuated on the basis of quantitative differences in featural and configural information. Presumably, it is the heightened sensitivity to subtle differences in featural and configural information that allows experts to acquire new subordinate-level categories more quickly than novices.

Strong transfer can also occur in the case of learning to recognize faces from other races (Tanaka & Droucker, submitted). A classic finding in the face recognition literature is that people are better at recognizing faces from their own race relative to other-race faces (Bothwell, Brigham, & Malpass, 1989; Meissner & Brigham, 2001). To test perceptual transfer in other-race face recognition, Caucasian participants were trained to discriminate Hispanic and African American faces at either the subordinate level of the individual (e.g., Joe, Bob, or Fred) or the basic level of race (e.g., Hispanic or African American; Tanaka & Droucker). The number of training trials was equivalent in the subordinate and basic training conditions, ensuring that the amount of absolute perceptual exposure was held constant. Whereas subordinate-level training facilitated the recognition of new within-race faces, basic-level training did not improve the recognition of novel faces from the categorized race. For example, participants trained to *individuate* African American faces and *categorize* Hispanic faces were better at recognizing novel African American faces, but not novel Hispanic faces. These findings suggest that it is the level at which experts discriminate objects in their domain, and not the extent of mere exposure, that is critical for the transfer of perceptual expertise. Collectively, these training experiments (Gauthier, Anderson, Tarr, Skudlarski, & Gore, 1997; Tanaka et al., 2005; Tanaka & Droucker; Yue et al., 2006) show that subordinate-level classification facilitates the formation of new category representations. This is the "rich get richer" nature of perceptual expertise, whereby previous perceptual knowledge begets the acquisition of new perceptual knowledge.

In this section, we have characterized the transfer of perceptual expertise as a gradient or continuum. In its simplest form, weak transfer requires recognition of the expert object across changes in viewpoint. Intermediate transfer, although encompassing viewpoint invariance, is more demanding and extends subordinate-level recognition to all exemplars in the category. Whereas weak and intermediate transfer entail the activation of a previously acquired subordinate-level representation, strong transfer emphasizes the ability to generate new subordinate-level representations. Thus, experts not only are distinguished from novices in their ability to quickly and accurately recognize objects in their domain of expertise at the subordinate level, but also have the perceptual advantage when acquiring *new* subordinate-level representations.

LIMITS TO TRANSFER

In the studies presented above, we have explored examples of transfer where expertise obtained in one experimental condition generalized to recognition in another. In these same studies, however, there were also conditions where no transfer was observed. For example, subordinate-level training of Greebles did not transfer to Greeble families with different part structures, owl expertise did not transfer to the recognition of wading birds (and vice versa), and subordinate-level training of Hispanic faces did not improve recognition of African American faces (and vice versa). In these circumstances, perceptual expertise in one domain neither facilitated nor impaired perception of objects from other stimulus domains.

The absence of transfer is informative for understanding the processes *not* influenced by expertise training. For example, it appears that expert training did not improve the general visual attention abilities or perceptual strategies of the participants. Otherwise, those abilities and strategies could have been applied broadly to the other stimulus domains to lead to more generically improved recognition. Nor were participants acquiring metastrategies that facilitated their ability to "learn how to learn." In Gauthier et al. (1998), for example, the amount of transfer exhibited by Greeble experts depended on structural similarity between the Greebles in the training set and Greebles in the transfer set.

Moreover, transfer effects in expertise are not likely to transcend basic-level categories or knowledge domains: for example, being a dog expert does not automatically make one a car expert (Gauthier & Tarr, 1997a; Gauthier et al., 1998). Indeed, even the most robust example of naturally occurring perceptual expertise has its limitations. It has been shown, for example, that adult humans' expertise in face recognition does not always extend to faces in noncanonical orientations (Farah, Wilson, Drain, & Tanaka, 1995; Gauthier & Tarr, 1997a), faces of other species (Mondloch, Maurer, & Ahola, 2006; Pascalis, de Haan, & Nelson, 2002), or faces of other races (Rhodes, Tan, Brake, & Taylor, 1989; Tanaka & Droucker, submitted). Similarly, radiologists' expertise with reading X-rays is restricted to clinically relevant abnormalities (Myles-Worsley, Johnston, & Simons, 1988).

Although expert perception fails to transfer between structurally dissimilar categories, such as between owls and wading birds, it is important to note that *structural dissimilarity* and *structural similarity* are relative terms. Compared to owls and wading birds, for example, the faces of African American and Hispanic individuals are highly similar, sharing the same basic shape, features, and spatial configuration. Yet, the absence of transfer between African American faces and Hispanic faces suggests that similarity, per se, is not determined by the structural geometry of the stimulus categories, but rather by the demands of the identification task at hand (Schyns, 1998).

NEUROIMAGING AND NEUROPHYSIOLOGICAL EVIDENCE OF TRANSFER

Functional neuroimaging (fMRI) and event-related potentials (ERPs) have been employed to better understand the mechanisms through which perceptual expertise "helps" subsequent learning and perception. These studies investigate the patterns of neural activity associated with weak, intermediate, and/or strong forms of perceptual transfer, as well as the brain activity corresponding to contexts of limited transfer. For example, in a recent fMRI study, Weisberg, van Turennout, and Martin (2007) examined the neural circuitry for object recognition while participants visually matched pictures of novel objects (Figure 2.2a) before and after training. Behavioral data acquired during fMRI scans revealed both weak and intermediate forms of transfer: "Experts" were significantly faster than "novices" in posttraining matching tasks of trained exemplars from different orientations (weak transfer) and never-before-seen but visually similar exemplars (intermediate transfer). The brain data showed an interesting pattern of increased neural activity in certain anterior cortical regions (e.g., anterior regions of the left middle temporal gyrus, left intraparietal sulcus, and left premotor cortex) that were specific to the trained exemplars, accompanied by decreases in activity in the ventral temporal cortex (i.e., fusiform gyrus) (see Figure 2.2b). Only the posterior temporal pattern of neural responses generalized across trained and novel object sets. This asymmetry—namely, perceptual specificity in anterior brain regions and perceptual transfer in posterior brain regions—is interpreted as evidence that anterior areas represent more complex object representations compared to posterior regions (Weisberg et al., 2007). Regarding the generalized learning effects in ventral brain regions, the authors suggest that the visual similarity between trained and not-trained novel objects allowed participants to automatically ascribe similar functional properties and/or visual processing resources to the members of the new object category.

In an ERP test of perceptual transfer, Scott et al. (2006) explored the neural markers for behavioral evidence of intermediate and strong forms of transfer. Behaviorally, perceptual discrimination transferred to new instances and new

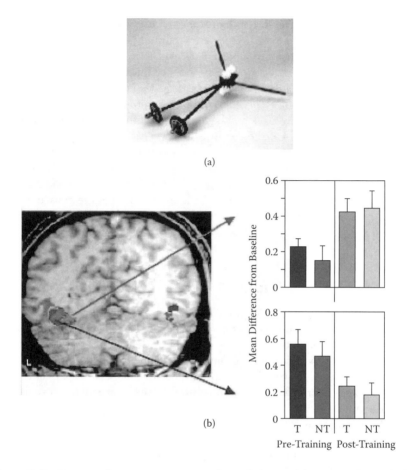

Figure 2.2   Perceptual expertise training with novel objects. (a) An example novel object created from construction toys. (b) Functional neuroimaging group data ($n = 12$) showing learning-induced changes in the ventral temporal cortex. A coronal section with areas activated in the fusiform gyrus. Medial areas in red were more active after training than before, whereas lateral areas in blue were more active before training than after. Learning transferred from the trained objects (T) to the not-trained objects (NT), as shown by an equal magnitude of activation for the two stimulus domains in the medial and lateral fusiform gyrus. Adapted from Weisberg, van Turennout, and Martin (2007).

species for birds initially learned at the subordinate, species level but not for birds learned at the basic, family level. Neurally, the authors recorded an expertise-associated ERP component that occurred about 250 ms after stimulus presentation (i.e., the N250) and was localized to recordings over the occipitotemporal area of both the left and right hemispheres. Following subordinate-level training, the N250 brain potential was observed in response to new exemplars of both learned and unlearned avian species. An earlier component, the N170, showed an enhanced response amplitude when participants received training at either the subordinate- or basic-level categorization, suggesting that this ERP component reflects a more generic perceptual *exposure* (rather than *expertise*) to objects learned at any level of discrimination. Perceptual expertise is more accurately reflected in the N250 component, which reveals transfer of subordinate-level activation to novel exemplars of related subordinate-level categories (intermediate transfer) and to new exemplars of related but untrained subordinate-level categories (strong transfer). Critically, an enhanced N250 was not observed to birds that were learned at the basic level. Similarly, N250 effects have recently been reported after training participants to recognize other-race faces at the subordinate level of the individual (e.g., Joe or Bob). Critically, the N250 component was not observed when the other-race faces were categorized at the basic level of race (e.g., African American or Hispanic) (Tanaka & Pierce, 2009). Distinctions between the nature of N170 and N250 can also be traced to separate neural regions—the medial occipital regions and lateral temporal regions, respectively—supporting suggestions for unique processes for basic- and subordinate-level or novice- and expert-level discriminations (Scott et al., 2006).

INTERFERENCE IN PERCEPTUAL EXPERTISE

In the previous sections, we examined behavioral and neurological mechanisms through which perceptual expertise can "help" new learning via different forms (i.e., weak, intermediate, or strong) of positive transfer. We also explored certain contexts in which expertise can exert null effects on learning. Now we will investigate the opposite side of the coin, conditions where expertise can actually "hurt" learning through interference and competition. In these latter cases, expertise in one domain interferes with perception in other expert domains. Interference occurs when an individual must discriminate targets from among visually or semantically similar stimuli. Theories of perceptual interference assume that certain processing mechanisms are inherently capacity limited and that, all else being equal, these mechanisms can be recruited by different stimuli and/or tasks. Perceptual interference reflects competition for shared and overlapping, yet limited, processing resources (see Kastner, De Weerd, Desimone, & Ungerleider, 1998; Kastner et al., 2001; Kastner & Ungerleider, 2000; Reynolds, Chelazzi, & Desimone, 1999).

Some of the earliest behavioral evidence of interference in perceiving objects of expertise comes from the *composite* effect (Figure 2.3). In one version of the composite task, individuals were consistently slower to name the identity of one half (either the top or the bottom) of a face formed as a composite of two separate individuals when the two halves are perfectly aligned (i.e., forming a new face), compared to when the two halves are slightly offset (i.e., drawing attention to the separate or independent identities of the halves; Young et al., 1987). The composite effect indicates the obligatory processing or automatic perceptual integration of all parts of an object and, as such, is often viewed as a behavioral marker of holistic processing (Gauthier et al., 2003; Gauthier & Curby, 2005). Holistic processing, as discussed in the "Benchmarks of Perceptual Expertise" section, is an important signature of perceptual expertise. It is understandable, then, that the composite effect is not observed with inverted stimuli or with nonface common objects, and yet is robustly observed with human faces and nonface objects for which an

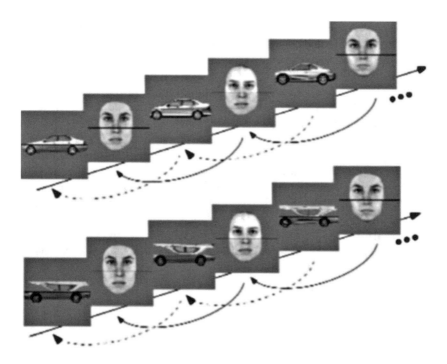

Figure 2.3 Experimental design displaying the composite effect. Participants were told to attend only to the bottom half of all objects and, for each one, to determine whether the bottom part of the present image matched the bottom part of the last image from the same category. Normal faces were intermixed with either normal cars (top row) or cars with an inverted top half (bottom row), which acted as a control condition. Adapted from Gauthier, Curran, Curby, and Collins (2003).

observer has substantial expertise (Gauthier et al., 2003; McKone & Kanwisher, 2005; Young et al.).

Gauthier et al. (2003) investigated interference in expert perception (e.g., holistic processing) via the composite effect. In their study, car experts and car novices were asked to make same-different judgments based on the bottoms of alternating composite face and car images. This was a short-term memory task requiring that the car part be held in memory while participants made a judgment on a face part, or vice versa. The alternating presentation of stimuli allowed the authors to measure whether perceptual interference between processes recruited by faces and cars differed between car experts and novices. Results showed that faces were processed less holistically by car experts, who simultaneously represented cars in a holistic manner, compared to car novices who did not process the two halves of the cars as an integrated whole. These findings reflect competition for holistic processing resources or, more broadly, functional overlap between face and car processing in car experts (Gauthier et al., 2003).

In another study, car experts were tested in a rapid serial visual presentation (RSVP) paradigm in which items were shown for approximately 1/10th of a second in quick succession. In this study, the RSVP stream contained alternating faces and

cars shown at fixation and was used to explore the temporal constraints of perceptual interference (McKeeff, Tong, & Gauthier, submitted). Supporting the predictions that car expertise would lead to more interference, car experts relative to car
novices were slower to identify a previously studied face amongst task-irrelevant
car distractors. In addition to the show of interference in the temporal domain,
evidence of interference has also been shown in the spatial domain using a visual
search paradigm in which car experts were asked to detect a face target presented
amongst car distractors (see Figure 2.4) (McGugin, McKeeff, Tong, & Gauthier,
in preparation). In this task, participants were instructed to study two faces, then
to detect which of the two studied faces appeared in a cluttered search array. The
search array could contain two, four, or eight distractor images from a nontarget
category. This paradigm showed that task-irrelevant distractors from a category
of expertise compete with face detection when all stimuli are simultaneously distributed in space and observers are free to control their eye movements. In accordance with earlier work (Curby & Gauthier, 2001; Gauthier et al., 2003; McKeeff
et al., submitted), car expertise impeded the search for a target face among car
distractors.

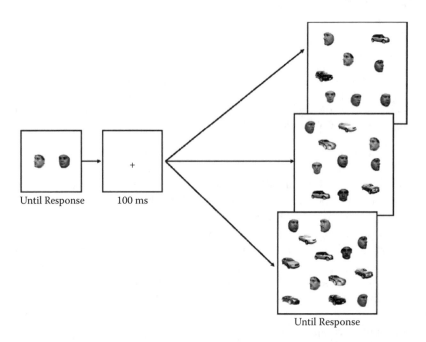

Until Response   100 ms

Until Response

Figure 2.4   Visual search paradigm. Trials began with the presentation of two faces
followed by a fixation cross. With the onset of the cluttered display screen, participants
searched for one of the two studied targets, responding as quickly and accurately as possible. The search display always contained only one studied image, along with five images
from the same category as the studied images and two, four, or eight nontarget distractors.
Adapted from Williams, McKeeff, Tong, and Gauthier (in preparation).

NEUROPHYSIOLOGICAL EVIDENCE OF INTERFERENCE IN EXPERTISE

Neurophysiology has provided important clues as to the neural correlates of behavioral measures of competitive interactions in perceptual expertise. Before diving into the relevant research, it is helpful to consider the underlying neural mechanisms of interference in expertise through a framework of repetition–suppression or adaptation. *Neural adaptation* refers to the brain's ability to make on-line recalibrations of sensory information in accordance with the variable input received from the visual world (Kovacs et al., 2006). Specifically, repetition of particular stimuli or stimulus attributes can result in a weakening of neuronal firing, the hemodynamic fMRI response, and ERP signals originating in areas of the brain responsible for coding the stimuli or stimulus attributes that are repeated. These data suggest that the repeated presentation of the feature(s) requires the same processing resources or same parts of neural tissue and hence becomes attenuated with multiple exposures (Grill-Spector, 2006; Winston, Henson, Fine-Goulden, & Dolan, 2004). For example, prolonged exposure to a face relative to a nonface stimulus (which acts as a control) leads to the suppression of face-related but not non-face-related neural signals (Kovacs et al.).

Importantly, stimuli need not be perceptually identical for habituation effects to be demonstrated. Henson et al. (2000) produced a habituation response in the fusiform gyrus when participants are repeatedly exposed to faces containing contour (i.e., high-spatial-frequency) information. Critically, the habituation response was maintained when participants viewed the same faces containing only global (low-spatial-frequency) information. These findings indicate that high-level adaptation effects can be elicited by visually distinct stimuli if they share a common object category (e.g., distinguishing one face from another) (Gauthier, Curby, Skudlarski, & Epstein, 2005).

Examining interference effects in individuals who are experts with a particular type of visual information supports this conclusion. Like neural adaptation, perceptual interference can occur in cases of either visually (i.e., two identical cups) or functionally (i.e., a tea cup and a coffee mug) overlapping representations. In accordance with the notion that expertise in a given visual domain requires the same common neural-processing mechanisms as expertise in a different visual domain, many ERP studies of expertise have found competition between the physiological responses to faces and nonface objects for which an individual has expertise (Gauthier et al., 2003; Rossion, Collins, Goffaux, & Curran, 2007; Rossion, Kung, & Tarr, 2004). For example, Gauthier et al. (2003) explored situations of concurrent processing of faces and cars in car experts. They recorded ERPs while participants performed the alternating face–car composite visual working memory task described earlier. First, based on their experience, car novices showed a higher amplitude N170 in response to faces, whereas car experts showed a larger N170 amplitude in response to cars. Moreover, the authors predicted that if expertise with cars engages early face-responsive ERP components, then the N170 evoked by faces should be attenuated by the coincidence of a competing object for which the observer has expertise. Indeed, faces presented in the context of cars evoked

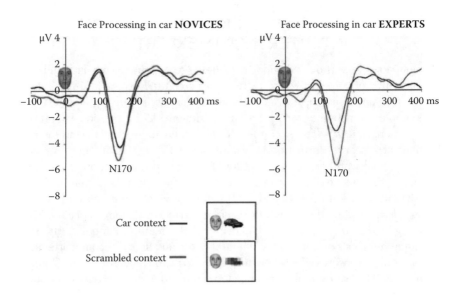

Figure 2.5   Event-related potential (ERP) responses to faces in car experts and novices. Note the reduced signal of the N170 in response to faces in car experts when a car is presented (car context) relative to when a scrambled car is presented (scrambled context). From Rossion, Collins, Goffaux, and Curran (2007).

a reduced N170 in car experts but not car novices (Gauthier et al., 2003). See Figure 2.5.

The neural basis of interference effects observed in individuals with a high level of expertise in identifying a particular visual class of objects has also been demonstrated in training studies using novel objects learned in the laboratory. In fact, two studies of similar experimental design found similar results for laboratory-trained Greeble expertise and naturally occurring car expertise. ERP potentials originating from occipitotemporal regions were recorded in response to a laterally presented face while participants fixated on a concurrently presented Greeble (Rossion et al., 2004) or car (Rossion et al., 2007). Rossion et al. (2004) found that after 8 to 10 hours of Greeble training, Greeble "experts" relative to "novices" produced an N170 response to the distractor face that was reduced by 20% when in the presence of a Greeble. Similarly, Rossion et al. (2007) observed a decrease in the amplitude of the evoked potential elicited by face stimuli when real-world car experts had to concurrently fixate a car (Figure 2.5). Consistent with claims of Gauthier et al. (2003), faces and visual objects with which an individual has expertise compete for early visual-processing mechanisms in occipitotemporal cortex.

The simultaneous presentation procedure used in these studies by Rossion and colleagues (2004, 2007) contrasts with a sequential presentation of information used by Gauthier et al. (2003). Simultaneous presentation provides a measure of competition between perceptual processes and/or representations without introducing effects associated with different phases of visual short-term memory (i.e., encoding, retention, and response). As a test of this difference, Rossion et al. (2007) presented faces and cars to car experts either simultaneously or separated by a brief interval (i.e., 200 ms). Their results revealed a significant recovery from sensory suppression with sequential, temporally spaced presentations. These findings suggest that interference effects become attenuated when presentations of expert objects are sufficiently separated in time even if the object representations rely on similar neural loci (Rossion et al., 2007).

The studies reviewed above show that experts perceiving objects of expertise (e.g., car experts processing cars or Greeble experts processing Greebles) rely on visual mechanisms in the occipitotemporal cortex that compete with those engaged by face processing. Thus, concurrent visual processing of faces and objects of expertise leads to perceptual interference and mutual suppression. Under such circumstances, how does expertise "hurt" perception? Interference findings are typically attributed to one of two possible underlying neurophysiological mechanisms. According to one explanation, interference occurs between classes of objects for which one is an expert because the perception of faces and objects recruits proximal, though independent, neural networks that operate in an overlapping time frame but are mutually inhibitory (Gauthier et al., 2003). In other words, although neural resources engaged by faces and objects of expertise proceed in parallel, sensory suppression between faces and expert objects occurs from mutually suppressive signals relayed from one representative population of neurons to another via local lateral inhibitory connections (Rossion et al., 2007). A second interpretation of such interference effects proposes that the neural substrates supporting processing are not independent but rather overlap at the cellular level (Gauthier et al., 2003; Jacques & Rossion, 2004; Rossion et al., 2007). Hence, cells in the occipitotemporal cortex responding preferentially to face stimuli may respond similarly to nonface objects with which one is expert. Whether best ascribed to overlap at the cellular level or local competition between independent, nearby ensembles of neurons, perceptual interference between the early visual processing of faces and objects of expertise indicates that similar perceptual mechanisms are recruited for both types of expert recognition (Rossion et al., 2004, 2007).

CONCLUSION

So, what can we conclude? Is perceptual expertise good or bad? Does it help or hurt other forms of sensory perception? The answer, simply put, is "It depends." Multiple factors related to stimulus structure, context of learning, and task demands determine the outcome—whether expertise in one domain fosters the transfer of perceptual knowledge to another domain, hinders performance in other domains, or exerts minimal or null influence on learning. From this interaction between conditions of learning and testing, we observe not only instances where perceptual expertise "helps" in the case of perceptual generalization and transfer, but also cases where expertise "hurts" as shown by interference effects. Table 2.2 summarizes the terms of these conditions. As shown, the weakest form of perceptual transfer occurs when expert knowledge facilitates perception across novel viewing conditions and viewing perspectives. An intermediate form is observed when expert recognition transfers to unfamiliar exemplars within an expert's domain. The third and strongest form of perceptual transfer involves the facilitated construction of new subordinate-level categories based on prior expert learning. Importantly, if perceptual transfer fails, perceptual interference does not necessarily result. Rather, certain training and testing contexts interact to yield situations where perceptual expertise neither facilitates nor impairs expert recognition or learning in other domains. Finally, perceptual trade-offs are observed when limited processing resources are simultaneously recruited, such that expertise in one domain interferes with performance in another expert domain. Thus, whether an expert surfer, a skilled cattle farmer, or an ordinary person viewing a crowd of faces, we are all likely to experience situation-dependent episodes of both facilitated learning and inhibited perception. Insights into when and how perceptual expertise helps and hurts perception will provide us a better understanding of how experience shapes the way we see and recognize objects in the world.

NOTE

1. Experimental paradigms that have been employed to induce perceptual learning effects include (a) coactivation studies in the somatosensory cortex whereby improvements in tactile performance and cortical reorganization are achieved through passive unattended stimulation (e.g., Godde et al., 1996, 2000; Pleger et al., 2001), (b) coactivation studies in visual cortices in which repeated passive exposure to a particular orientation of bars can lead to persistent enhancement of neural responses to that orientation (e.g., Frenkel et al., 2006), (c) contextual cuing paradigms in which a repeated configuration of distractors in a visual search display can drive learned associations between context and targets (e.g., Chun, 2000; Chun & Jiang, 1998; Sireteanu & Rettenbach, 2000), and (d) subliminal designs showing that participants can learn as a result of mere exposure to a subliminal stimulus (i.e., a stimulus they didn't actually perceive) (Seitz, Nanez, et al., 2005; Seitz & Watanabe, 2003, 2005; Seitz, Yamagishi, et al., 2005; Watanabe et al., 2001).

REFERENCES

Ahissar, M., and Hochstein, S. (1993). Attentional control of early perceptual learning. *Proceedings of the National Academy of Sciences, 90*, 5718–5722.

Ahissar, M., and Hochstein, S. (1994). Plasticity in auditory cortical circuitry. *Current Opinion in Neurobiology, 4*, 580–587.

Ahissar, M., and Hochstein, S. (1997). Task difficulty and the specificity of perceptual learning. *Nature, 387*, 401–406.

Ahissar, M., and Hochstein, S. (1998). Perceptual learning. In V. Walsh & J. Kulikowski (Eds.), *Perceptual constancies: Why things look as they do* (pp. 455–498). Cambridge: Cambridge University Press.

Ahissar, M., & Hochstein, S. (2004). The reverse hierarchy theory of visual perceptual learning. *Trends in Cognitive Sciences, 8*, 457–464.

Bao, S., Chan, V. T., & Merzenich, M. M. (2001). Cortical remodeling induced by activity of ventral tegmental dopamine neurons. *Nature, 412*, 79–83.

Bentin, S., Allison, T., Puce, A., Perez, E., & McCarthy, G. (1996). Electrophysiological studies of face perception in humans. *Journal of Cognitive Neuroscience, 8*, 551–565.

Bothwell, R. K., Brigham, J. C., & Malpass, R. S. (1989). Cross-racial identification. *Personality and Social Psychology Bulletin, 15,* 19–25.

Busey, T. A., & Vanderkolk, J. R. (2005). Behavioral and electrophysiological evidence for configural processing in fingerprint experts. *Vision Research, 45,* 431–448.

Chun, M. M. (2000). Contextual cueing of visual attention. *Trends in Cognitive Science, 4,* 170–178.

Chun, M. M., & Jiang, Y. (1998). Contextual cueing: Implicit learning and memory of visual context guides spatial attention. *Cognitive Psychology, 36,* 28–71.

Collin, C. A., & McMullen, P. A. (2005). Subordinate-level categorization relies on high spatial frequencies to a greater degree than basic-level categorization. *Perception & Psychophysics, 67,* 354–364.

Diamond, R., & Carey, S. (1986). Why faces are and are not special: An effect of expertise. *Journal of Experimental Psychology: General, 115,* 107–117.

Edelman, S., & Bülthoff, H. H. (1992). Orientation dependence in the recognition of familiar and novel views of three-dimensional objects. *Vision Research, 32,* 2385–2400.

Ericsson, K. A., Krampe, R. T., & Tesch-Romer, C. (1993). The role of deliberate practice in the acquisition of expert performance. *Psychological Review, 100*(3), 363–406.

Farah, M. J., Wilson, K. D., Drain, H. M., & Tanaka, J. R. (1995). The inverted face inversion effect in prosopagnosia: Evidence for mandatory, face-specific perceptual mechanisms. *Vision Research, 35,* 2089–2093.

Fitzgerald, M. B., & Wright, B. A. (2005). A perceptual learning investigation of the pitch elicited by amplitude-modulated noise. *The Journal of the Acoustical Society of America, 118,* 3794–3803.

Frenkel, M. Y., Sawtell, N. B., Diogo, A. C., Yoon, B., Neve, R. L., & Bear, M. F. (2006). Instructive effect of visual experience in mouse visual cortex. *Neuron, 51,* 339–349.

Gauthier, I., Anderson, A. W., Tarr, M. J., Skudlarski, P., & Gore, J. C. (1997). Levels of categorization in visual object studied with functional MRI. *Current Biology, 7,* 645–651.

Gauthier, I., Behrmann, M., & Tarr, M. J. (1999). Can face recognition really be dissociated from object recognition? *Journal of Cognitive Neuroscience, 11,* 349–370.

Gauthier, I., & Curby, K. M. (2005). A perceptual traffic jam on highway N170: Interference between face and car expertise. *Current Directions in Psychological Science, 14,* 30–33.

Gauthier, I., Curby, K. M., Skudlarski, P., & Epstein, R. A. (2005). Individual differences in FFA activity suggest independent processing at different spatial scales. *Cognitive, Affective & Behavioral Neuroscience, 5,* 222–234.

Gauthier, I., Curran, T., Curby, K. M., & Collins, D. (2003). Perceptual interference supports a non-modular account of face perception. *Nature Neuroscience, 6,* 428–432.

Gauthier, I., Skudlarski, P., Gore, J. C., & Anderson, A. W. (2000). Does visual subordinate-level categorisation engage the functionally defined fusiform face area? *Cognitive Neuropsychology, 17,* 143–163.

Gauthier, I., & Tarr, M. J. (1997a). Becoming a "Greeble" expert: Exploring mechanisms for face recognition. *Vision Research, 37,* 1673–1681.

Gauthier, I., & Tarr, M. J. (1997b). Orientation priming of novel shapes in the context of viewpoint-dependent recognition. *Perception, 26,* 51–73.

Gauthier, I., Tarr, M. J., Anderson, A. W., Skudlarski, P., & Gore, J. C. (1999). Activation of the middle fusiform "face area" increases with expertise in recognizing novel objects. *Nature Neuroscience, 2,* 568–573.

Gauthier, I., Williams, P., Tarr, M. J., & Tanaka, J. (1998). Training "Greeble" experts: A framework for studying expert object recognition processes. *Vision Research, 38,* 2401–2428.

Godde, B., Spengler, F., & Dinse, H. R. (1996). Associative pairing of tactile stimulation induces somatosensory cortical reorganization in rats and humans. *NeuroReport, 8,* 281–285.

Godde, B., Stauffenberg, B., Spengler, F., & Dinse, H. R. (2000). Tactile coactivation-induced changes in spatial discrimination performance. *Journal of Neuroscience, 20,* 1597–1604.

Goldstone, R. L. (1998). Perceptual learning. *Annual Review of Psychology, 49,* 585–612.

Grill-Spector, K. (2006). Selectivity of adaptation in single units: Implications for fMRI experiments. *Neuron, 49,* 170–171.

Hill, H., Schyns, P. G., & Akamatsu, S. (1997). Information and viewpoint dependence in face recognition. *Cognition, 62*(2), 201–222.

Hodzic, A., Veit, R., Karim, A. A., Erb, M., & Godde, B. (2004). Improvement and decline in tactile discrimination behavior after cortical plasticity induced by passive tactile coactivation. *Journal of Neuroscience, 24,* 442–446.

Jacoby, L. L., & Hayman, C. A. G. (1987). Specific visual transfer in word identification. *Journal of Experimental Psychology: Learning, Memory, and Cognition, 13,* 456–463.

Jacques, C., & Rossion, B. (2004). Concurrent processing reveals competition between visual representations of faces. *NeuroReport, 15,* 2417–2421.

Johnson, K. E., & Mervis, C. B. (1997). Effects of varying levels of expertise on the basic level of categorization. *Journal of Experimental Psychology: General, 126,* 248–277.

Kanwisher, N., McDermott, J., & Chun, M. M. (1997). The fusiform face area: A module in human extrastriate cortex specialized for face perception. *Journal of Neuroscience, 17,* 4302–4311.

Kastner, S., De Weerd, P., Desimone, R., & Ungerleider, L. G. (1998). Mechanisms of directed attention in the human extrastriate cortex as revealed by functional MRI. *Science, 282,* 108–111.

Kastner, S., De Weerd, P., Pinsk, M. A., Elizondo, M. I., Desimone, R., & Ungerleider, L. G. (2001). Modulation of sensory suppression: Implications for receptive field sizes in the human visual cortex. *Journal of Neurophysiology, 86,* 1398–1411.

Kastner, S., & Ungerleider, L. G. (2000). Mechanisms of visual attention in the human cortex. *Annual Review of Neuroscience, 23,* 315–341.

Kilgard, M. P., & Merzenich, M. M. (1998). Cortical map reorganization enabled by nucleus basalis activity. *Science, 13,* 1714–1718.

Kovacs, G., Zimmer, M., Banko, E., Harza, I., Antal, A., & Vidnyanszky, Z. (2006). Electrophysiological correlates of visual adaptation to faces and body parts in humans. *Cerebral Cortex, 16,* 742–753.

McGugin, R. W., & Gauthier, I. (in press). Perceptual expertise with objects predicts another hallmark of face perception. *Journal of Vision.*

McGugin, R. W., McKeeff, T. J., Tong, F., & Gauthier, I. (In preparation). Expertise effects in a visual search paradigm.

McKeeff, T. J., Tong, F., & Gauthier, I. (Submitted). Expertise reduces the functional cerebral distance between face and object perception.

McKone, E., & Kanwisher, N. (2005). Does the human brain process objects of expertise like faces? A review of the evidence. In S. Dehaene, J. R. Duhamel, M. Hause, & G. Rizzolatti (Eds.), *From monkey brain to human brain.* Cambridge, MA: MIT Press.

Meissner, C. A., & Brigham, J. C. (2001). Thirty years of investigating the own-race bias in memory for faces: A meta-analytic review. *Psychology, Public Policy, and Law, 7,* 3–35.

Mondloch, C. J., Maurer, D., & Ahola, S. (2006). Becoming a face expert. *Psychological Science, 17,* 930–934.

Myles-Worsley, M., Johnston, W. A., & Simons, M. A. (1988). The influence of expertise on X-ray image processing. *Journal of Experimental Psychology: Learning, Memory and Cognition, 14*, 553–557.

Palmeri, T. J., Wong, A. C-N., & Gauthier, I. (2004). Computational approaches to the development of perceptual expertise. *Trends in Cognitive Science, 8*, 378–386.

Pascalis, O., de Haan, M., & Nelson, C. A. (2002). Is face processing species-specific during the first year of life? *Science, 296*, 1321–1323.

Pleger, B., Dinse, H. R., Ragert, P., Schwenkreis, P., Malin, J. P., & Tegenthoff, M. (2001). Shifts in cortical representations predict human discrimination improvement. *Proceedings of the National Academy of Sciences, 98*, 12255–12260.

Poggio, T., & Edelman, S. (1990). A network that learns to recognize three-dimensional objects. *Nature, 343*, 263–266.

Puce, A., Allison, T., Gore, J. C., & McCarthy, G. (1995). Face-sensitive regions in human extrastriate cortex studied by functional MRI. *Journal of Neurophysiology, 74*, 1192–1199.

Reynolds, J. H., Chelazzi, L., & Desimone, R. (1999). Competitive mechanisms subserve attention in macaque areas V2 and V4. *Journal of Neuroscience, 19*, 1736–1753.

Rhodes, G., Tan, S., Brake, S., & Taylor, K. (1989). Expertise and configural coding in face recognition. *British Journal of Psychology, 80*, 313–331.

Riesenhuber, M., & Poggio, T. (2000). Models of object recognition. *Nature Neuroscience, 3*, 1199–1204.

Rock, I., & DiVita, J. (1987). A case of viewer-centered object perception. *Cognitive Psychology, 19*, 280–293.

Rosch, E., Mervis, C., Gray, W., Johnson, D., & Boyes-Braem, P. (1976). Basic objects in natural categories. *Cognitive Psychology, 8*, 382–439.

Rossion, B., Collins, D., Goffaux, V., & Curran, T. (2007). Long-term expertise with artificial objects increases visual competition with early face categorization processes. *Journal of Cognitive Neuroscience, 19*, 543–555.

Rossion, B., Gauthier, I., Goffaux, V., Tarr, M. J., & Crommelinck, M. (2002). Expertise training with novel objects leads to left lateralized face-like electrophysiological responses. *Psychological Science, 13*, 250–257.

Rossion, B., Kung, C. C., & Tarr, M. J. (2004). Visual expertise with nonface objects leads to competition with the early perceptual processing of faces in the human occipitotemporal cortex. *Proceedings of the National Academy of Sciences, 101*, 14521–14526.

Schyns, P. G. (1998). Diagnostic recognition: Task constraints, object information, and their interactions. *Cognition, 67*, 147–179.

Scott, L. S., Tanaka, J. W., Sheinberg, D. L., & Curran, T. (2006). A reevaluation of the electrophysiological correlates of expert object processing. *Journal of Cognitive Neuroscience, 189*, 1453–1465.

Seitz, A. R., Nanez, J. E., Holloway, S. R., Koyama, S., & Watanabe, T. (2005). Seeing what is not there shows the costs of perceptual learning. *Proceedings of the National Academy of Sciences, 102*, 9080–9085.

Seitz, A. R., & Watanabe, T. (2003). Is subliminal learning really passive? *Nature, 422*, 36.

Seitz, A. R., & Watanabe, T. (2005). A unified model for perceptual learning. *Trends in Cognitive Science, 9*, 329–334.

Seitz, A. R., Yamagishi, N., Werner, B., Goda, N., Kawato, M., & Watanabe, T. (2005). Task specific disruption of perceptual learning. *Proceedings of the National Academy of Science, 102*, 14895–14900.

Sergent, J., Ohta, S., & MacDonald, B. (1992). Functional neuroanatomy of face and object processing. *Brain, 115*, 15–36.

Shiu, L. P., & Pashler, H. (1992). Improvement in line orientation discrimination is retinally local but dependent on cognitive set. *Perception & Psychophysics, 52*, 582–588.

Sigman, M., & Gilbert, C. D. (2000). Learning to find a shape. *Nature Neuroscience, 3,* 264–269.

Sireteanu, R., & Rettenbach, R. (2000). Perceptual learning in visual search generalizes over tasks, locations and eyes. *Vision Research, 40,* 2925–2949.

Tanaka, J. W., & Curran, T. (2001). A neural basis for expert object recognition. *Psychological Science, 12,* 43–47.

Tanaka, J. W., Curran, T., Porterfield, A. L., & Collins, D. (2006). Activation of pre-existing and acquired face representations: The N250 ERP as an index of face familiarity. *Journal of Cognitive Neuroscience, 18,* 1488–1497.

Tanaka, J. W., Curran, T., & Sheinberg, D. L. (2005). The training and transfer or real-world perceptual expertise. *Psychological Science, 16,* 145–151.

Tanaka, J. W., & Droucker, D. (Submitted). Reversing the other race effect in adults: A test of the perceptual expertise hypothesis.

Tanaka, J. W., & Farah, M. J. (1993). Parts and wholes in face recognition. *Quarterly Journal of Experimental Psychology, 46A,* 225–245.

Tanaka, J. W., & Pierce, L. J. (2009). The neural plasticity of other-race face training. *Cognitive, Affective, & Behavioral Neuroscience, 9,* 122–131.

Tanaka, J. W., & Sengco, J. A. (1997). Features and their configuration in face recognition. *Memory and Cognition, 25,* 583–592.

Tanaka, J. W., & Taylor, M. (1991). Object categories and expertise: Is the basic level in the eye of the beholder? *Cognitive Psychology, 23,* 457–482.

Tarr, M. J., & Gauthier, I. (2000). FFA: A flexible fusiform area for subordinate-level visual processing automatized by expertise. *Nature Neuroscience, 3,* 764–769.

Tarr, M. J., & Pinker, S. (1989). Mental rotation and orientation dependence in shape recognition. *Cognitive Psychology, 21,* 233–282.

Ullman, S. (Ed.). (1998). *Three-dimensional object recogniton based on the combination of views.* Cambridge, MA: MIT Press.

Watanabe, T., Sasaki, Y., & Nanez, J. (2001). Perception learning without perception. *Nature, 413,* 844–848.

Weisberg, J., van Turennout, M., & Martin, A. (2007). A neural system for learning about object function. *Cerebral Cortex, 17,* 513–521.

Wenger, M. J., & Ingvalson, E. M. (2002). A decisional component of holistic encoding. *Journal of Experimental Psychology–Learning Memory and Cognition, 28*(5), 872–892.

Winston, J. S., Henson, R. N. A., Fine-Goulden, M. R., & Dolan, R. J. (2004). fMRI-adaptation reveals dissociable neural representations of identity and expression in face perception. *Journal of Neurophysiology, 92,* 1830–1839.

Xu, Y. (2005). Revisiting the role of the fusiform and occipital face areas in visual expertise. *Cerebral Cortex, 15,* 1234–1242.

Young, A. W., Hellawell, D. J., & Hay, D. C. (1987). Configural information in face perception. *Perception, 16,* 747–759.

Yue, X., Tjan, B. S., & Biederman, I. (2006). What makes faces special? *Vision Research, 46,* 3802–3811.

3

Flexibility and Generalization in Memory Systems

RUSSELL A. POLDRACK, VALERIE CARR, and KARIN FOERDE

T he concept of qualitatively different memory systems underlying human behavior has a long history (Schacter, 1987; Squire, 1987). One impetus to these ideas has been our common subjective experience: Although we can easily recollect past experiences in a conscious manner, many learned behaviors seem to occur "automatically" whenever the right set of circumstances occurs, without any need to consciously remember past instances of the same behavior. Such a distinction between "memories" and "habits" has received substantial support from neuroscience and neuropsychology since the 1960s. Studies of patients with memory disorders due to brain damage have demonstrated that these different forms of memory can be dissociated from one another, such that damage to particular brain regions can impair one form of memory while leaving the other intact.

These studies of amnesic patients, as well as converging evidence from animal models, have led to consensus on a broad distinction between memory systems that are functionally and neuroanatomically distinct. *Declarative memory* is thought to support conscious recollection of past events as well as learning of new facts, and relies upon the hippocampus and surrounding cortical structures of the medial temporal lobe (Cohen & Eichenbaum, 1993; Squire, 1992). *Nondeclarative memory* is a blanket term used for all other forms of memory that do not rely upon the medial temporal lobe; of particular interest to the present discussion is a form of nondeclarative memory known as *habit memory*, which involves the development of stimulus–response associations with practice over time. The development of habits appears to rely particularly upon the basal ganglia (Mishkin, Malamut, & Bachevalier, 1984; Packard & Knowlton, 2002).

Given that parsimony argues against the unnecessary postulation of multiple memory systems, the multiple systems approach is burdened to explain why it is that multiple systems would have evolved instead of a single integrated system. Sherry and Schacter (1987) presented an evolutionary argument for the existence of multiple memory systems that focused on the concept of *functional incompatibility*, in which a function served by one system is incompatible with some other necessary function. They proposed that the human procedural learning system is specialized to gradually learn about invariant features in the environment, whereas the declarative memory system is specialized to remember the varying features of specific experiences. As an example, the procedural learning system would remember how to drive the car, whereas the declarative memory system would remember where the car is parked today. Failure of the procedural system to discard the details of unique experiences would prevent it from taking advantage of the regularities that exist across experiences (e.g., an inability to drive on a new street after learning on a specific street), whereas failure of the declarative system to retain these same details would render it unable to remember specific episodes due to massive interference from overlapping representations. Thus, the functional incompatibility between these systems reflects the fact that they must retain different types of information that are necessarily incompatible.

The goal of the present chapter is to outline how the computational architectures of the neural systems that underlie declarative and procedural memory might give rise to the processing of specific and invariant features of experiences, respectively. The procedural learning system, involving cortico-basal ganglia (in addition to other cortical and subcortical systems), detects invariant features due to the highly convergent nature of its connectivity, which results in a great deal of dimensionality reduction. That is, only the central tendency of numerous inputs is retained and a record of the specific inputs discarded. The declarative memory system, on the other hand, uses processes that transform very similar inputs into highly distinctive, nonoverlapping memory traces (a process known as *pattern separation*), as well as operations that support retrieval of these specific, detailed experiences based on partial cues (*pattern completion*). The divergent computational architectures that support these different processes provide a basis for understanding how generalization differs between different forms of learning and memory.

THE NEURAL ARCHITECTURE OF DECLARATIVE MEMORY

Since the observation of severe memory deficits following bilateral excision of the medial temporal lobe (MTL) in patient H.M. (Scoville & Milner, 1957), it has been clear that this region is essential for the formation of new declarative memories. Further work over the ensuing decades has provided substantial evidence regarding the mnemonic functions subserved by the many substructures of the MTL, and animal models and computational approaches have provided further insight into the functions supported by these structures. The outline of MTL function provided here is necessarily brief and incomplete; for more detailed discussions, see Squire, Stark, and Clark (2004).

We will focus on those aspects of MTL structure and function that are most relevant to its generalization abilities. First we will outline the anatomical makeup and connectivity of the MTL. We will then discuss how this unique architecture contributes to three processes thought to underlie our ability to form declarative memories: associative plasticity, pattern separation, and pattern completion. Prior to introducing these topics, however, we will begin by presenting a fictional memory that will serve as a helpful guide during each of the following sections: Imagine that you and a friend decide to head to the countryside for the 4th of July, and you take a nice long drive down a tree-lined road with the windows rolled down and your favorite song playing. Several weeks later a coworker inquires as to how you spent the holiday weekend, and you respond by recounting the episode described above, such that you were able to recall each of the individual elements of the episode from the cue of "July 4th."

Connectivity

The MTL can be divided into several subregions that include the hippocampal formation and the cortices that surround it: the perirhinal, parahippocampal, and entorhinal cortices. The hippocampal formation is itself composed of additional subregions, including cornu ammonis (CA) fields 1 and 3, the dentate gyrus, and the subiculum (see Figure 3.1). The perirhinal and parahippocampal cortices serve as the main input regions within the MTL, and receive information from most all other areas of the brain. This includes input from regions that process sensory information, as well as input from regions that allow for higher level processing (e.g., language and spatial processing). The connections between these neocortical regions and the cortices of the MTL are reciprocal, meaning that the MTL not only receives highly convergent, concurrent inputs regarding nearly every aspect of cortical function, but also has the ability to influence these neocortical regions. Upon receiving such convergent input, the parahippocampal and perirhinal cortices pass this information to the entorhinal cortex, which in turn conveys the information to the hippocampus proper. Given that the hippocampus is seated atop this hierarchy of inputs, it is thought to be ideally situated to bind together the multiple elements of an experience (e.g., friend, trees, and song) into a unified memory representation (e.g., what I did for the 4th of July) (Cohen & Eichenbaum, 1993).

In addition to the gross anatomy of the MTL, knowledge of specific regional connectivity between the entorhinal cortex and the hippocampus, as well as within the hippocampus itself, aids our understanding of how the MTL supports declarative memory (see Figure 3.1). During encoding of new memories, a major route of information flow is along perforant path projections from the entorhinal cortex to the dentate gyrus, and from there to area CA3, area CA1, and back again to the entorhinal cortex. A notable anatomical feature of the dentate gyrus is that it consists of approximately tenfold more neurons than the entorhinal cortex, meaning that information fans out as it projects from the cortex to this larger pool of neurons (Gluck & Myers, 2001). This fanning out means that relatively few neurons in

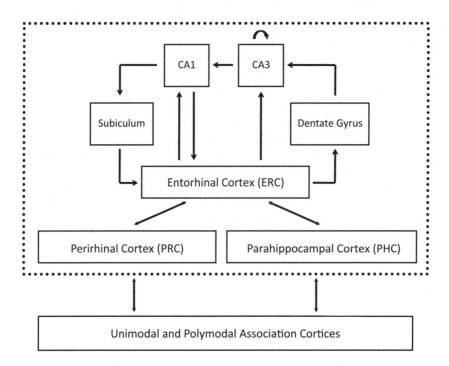

Figure 3.1   A schematic of the structure and connections of the medial temporal lobe. Dashed box denotes MTL structures.

the dentate gyrus are active for a given element of an episode (e.g., the type of tree you saw on your drive). As we shall see in the following section on pattern separation, this sparseness contributes to the formation of memory traces that will not overlap with preexisting, similar memory traces.

From the dentate gyrus these sparse representations are then passed to area CA3, which has the unique anatomical property that it receives a large number of inputs from recurrent connections among CA3 neurons themselves. During encoding, CA3 receives information from the dentate gyrus that represents different aspects of a given episode (e.g., friend, trees, and song), activating multiple CA3 neurons. Connections between these coactive neurons are strengthened via associative plasticity—described in detail below—forming a conjunctive representation of the individual elements of the episode (e.g., a unified memory regarding what I did for the 4th of July).

This conjunctive representation is then passed to area CA1, which has its own set of unique anatomical properties. First, CA1 receives input not only from CA3 but also directly from the entorhinal cortex; thus, this area receives both information already processed by the dentate gyrus (sparse) and CA3 (conjunctive), and unprocessed information directly from the entorhinal cortex. This coactivation creates a key link between the processed and unprocessed representations, allowing CA1 to serve as a "translator" between these two types of information. Second, CA1 both receives information from and feeds back information to the entorhinal cortex; for this reason, the CA1 representation of a given memory is considered to be "invertible." Together, these two features are thought to facilitate later memory retrieval attempts (Rolls & Kesner, 2006), as discussed in further detail under the "Pattern Completion" section.

Associative Plasticity

The structure of neurons is similar to that of a tree with many branches. One neuron can communicate with thousands of other neurons via individual connections, known as *synapses*, at different positions on the branch-like structure. When synaptically connected neurons in the hippocampus fire together within a relatively short time window, the strength of the connection between those neurons increases, such that the cell providing input can more easily excite the cell to which it sends information. This change in strength is known as *long-term potentiation* (or LTP), and although it is by no means limited to the hippocampus, it has been studied extensively in this structure (see Malenka & Nicoll, 1999, for a discussion of the cellular and molecular bases of LTP). In particular, LTP has been shown to be necessary for learning on a range of hippocampus-dependent memory tasks in rodents (e.g., Martin & Morris, 2002).

Because LTP is specific to a given synapse (i.e., connection), it provides the basis for the hippocampus to bind together sets of specific inputs that are concurrently active. Returning to our July 4th example, LTP would serve to bind together individual elements of the episode into a unified memory of the holiday by strengthening connections between neurons representing the date, the friend with whom you were driving, the location of your drive, the song being played, and so on. Furthermore, strengthening of these specific connections allows for later retrieval of the entire memory, based on only a partial cue (e.g., a coworker mentioning the date of July 4th, which then triggers your memory for elements associated with this date). That is, because connections between neurons representing, for example, the date and the song were previously strengthened, activation of one input can now more easily excite other associated inputs, such that all elements of the original memory are recalled.

Pattern Separation

Whereas the procedural memory system is thought to be specialized for slowly developing representations of the general structure of the environment, the hippocampus is thought to specialize in memorizing details of specific events. Learning about specifics at a rapid rate and storing all the constituent information, however, will eventually cause new information to interfere with similar, previously stored patterns. In order to avoid such catastrophic interference, the architecture and physiology of the hippocampal system allow for the formation of distinct, separable memory representations. As outlined below, current computational models of the MTL provide insight into how subregional connectivity contributes to this pattern separation process. These models differ in several regards, but here we attempt to focus on commonalities across models. (For a more in-depth discussion of such models, see, e.g., Gluck & Myers, 2001; Norman & O'Reilly, 2003; Rolls & Kesner, 2006).

Area CA3 of the hippocampus is generally regarded as the storage site of pattern-separated representations. How, then, do convergent, overlapping representations from the entorhinal cortex become separated en route to CA3? First, inputs from the entorhinal cortex to the dentate gyrus are thought to be modifiable via processes of associative plasticity, as described above. Second, information fans out as it leaves the entorhinal cortex and enters the dentate gyrus, such that relatively few neurons are active for a given element of an episode. To give an oversimplified example using our 4th of July scenario, imagine that the entorhinal cortex is composed of five neurons, and that activity in four out of five of these neurons represents the date, the friend, the type of trees, and the song, respectively. Next imagine that these four neurons project to a pool of 50 neurons in the dentate gyrus. Now, rather than four out of five neurons representing a given episode, four out of 50 neurons represent that episode. Thus, information regarding this particular 4th of July experience is represented by only a fraction of the total number of neurons in the dentate gyrus (i.e., sparse representation). In this way, the newly formed memory representation is less likely to overlap with similar memories from past 4th of July experiences, allowing for the formation of unique, independent memory traces. In the entorhinal cortex, on the other hand, information from the current 4th of July is indeed likely to overlap with information from past 4th of July holidays, given that fewer neurons are available to represent the elements of a given episode.

Third, sparse representation in the dentate gyrus is coupled with low levels of neuronal firing activity between this region and CA3, resulting in sparse connectivity between the dentate gyrus and CA3. The net result is that overlapping patterns of activity in the entorhinal cortex are separated by both the dentate gyrus and connections between the dentate gyrus and CA3, creating distinct patterns of activity and thus avoiding interference between memories (Rolls & Kesner, 2006). Resulting pattern-separated representations are then stored in CA3 by changes in plasticity among the recurrent collaterals of CA3; such plasticity changes serve to bind together multiple elements of the input pattern into a unified representation of an episode.

In addition to the manner in which the dentate gyrus and CA3 process entorhinal patterns of activity during encoding, another representation of entorhinal activity is simultaneously formed in CA1. The entorhinal cortex projects directly to CA1, and thus this incoming information is not preprocessed by the dentate gyrus and CA3. As a result, this representation is thought to be less sparse than that stored in CA3, and is also unique in that it is invertible—that is, information both spreads from the entorhinal cortex to CA1 and spreads back from CA1 to the entorhinal cortex. Thus, as we encode new memories, a representation of entorhinal input is formed in CA1, and due to back projections from CA1, an association is formed in the entorhinal cortex with the CA1 representation. Importantly, during encoding, a link between the processed (sparse) CA3 representation and relatively overlapping (unprocessed) CA1 representation is formed along projections from CA3 to CA1. Thus, the processed CA3 representation is linked to the unprocessed

CA1 representation, which is in turn linked to the entorhinal representation due to back projections from CA1 to the entorhinal cortex. As we shall see in the next section, the formation of these links facilitates subsequent retrieval processes by serving as a translator between sparse and overlapping representations.

Pattern Completion

As mentioned in previous sections, the MTL receives overlapping representations from the cortex, but in order to form distinct memories and avoid interference between similar episodes in life (e.g., how you spent this year's 4th of July vs. last year or the year before), the hippocampus separates them as described above. However, once such patterns are separated and stored, there exists a difference between the overlapping entorhinal representations and the sparser CA3 representations. Consequently, when information regarding a particular cue (e.g., the date *4th of July*) is sent from the entorhinal cortex to the hippocampus during a retrieval attempt, you have an incoming pattern that is quite different than the stored pattern, presenting a potential problem for memory retrieval (O'Reilly & McClelland, 1994). In order to solve this problem, it is thought that CA1 serves to translate between the complete, sparse representation in CA3 and the overlapping representation in the entorhinal cortex.

Specifically, during retrieval the entorhinal cortex presents a portion of a previously studied pattern (e.g., mention of the date *4th of July*) to the hippocampus. It is thought that previous strengthening of synapses between the entorhinal cortex and the hippocampus, as well as strengthened connections within recurrent collaterals of CA3 (connections between, e.g., the date and the friend with whom you were driving) allow for reactivation of the entire unified CA3 representation—a process known as *pattern completion*. This completed representation then spreads along the previously established link between the sparse CA3 representation and the unprocessed CA1 representation. Due to the invertible nature of the CA1 representation, activity in CA1 spreads back to the associated representation in the entorhinal cortex. In this way, a comparison between the input cue ("What did you do for the 4th of July?") and the completed memory ("I went to the countryside with my friend so-and-so, where we saw beautiful trees and listened to our favorite song with the windows rolled down") can be successfully matched within the entorhinal cortex (Hasselmo, Wyble, & Wallenstein, 1996; Norman & O'Reilly, 2003; O'Reilly & McClelland, 1994; Rolls & Kesner, 2006).

Summary

The medial temporal lobe serves as a memory system that allows for the formation and retrieval of distinct, detailed memories from our everyday life experiences. The MTL receives information from all areas of the cortex regarding, for example, what happened, where something happened, and when it happened. As we experience a given episode, the unique anatomy and physiology of the hippocampus allow for (a) encoding of each of the elements in a distinct fashion such that they do not overlap with previously experienced elements, and (b) unification of each of these elements into a single, cohesive memory that can then be recalled in entirety based only on presentation of one of the elements. These processes are thought to rely upon pattern separation processes at encoding, coupled with the formation of conjunctive representations via associative plasticity. During retrieval, the ability to recall an entire memory based on a cue is referred to as *pattern completion*, which relies upon previously strengthened connections between individual elements of an episode as well as connections or links formed between different regions of the MTL.

THE NEURAL ARCHITECTURE OF PROCEDURAL MEMORY

The neural systems involved in nondeclarative memory are substantially more heterogeneous than those involved in declarative memory, which is perhaps not surprising given that this class of memory phenomena is defined by exclusion as "anything that does not require the medial temporal lobe." However, it is clear that a wide range of nondeclarative memory phenomena relies upon circuits involving the cerebral cortex and basal ganglia, particularly those phenomena usually referred to as *procedural memory*, which involve the gradual acquisition of skills and behavioral tendencies culminating in "habits." We will focus on this class of phenomena, but we note that there are clearly structures other than the basal ganglia that support nondeclarative memory phenomena, for example the amygdala (see chapter 1 by Huff and LaBar), the cerebellum (Doyon, Penhune, & Ungerleider, 2003; Sanes, Dimitrov, & Hallett, 1990), and various forms of cortical plasticity (Karni et al., 1995; Wagner, Koutstaal, Maril, Schacter, & Buckner, 2000).

There is substantial evidence that the basal ganglia are necessary for acquisition of a broad range of skills and habits. Patients with disorders of the basal ganglia, such as Huntington's and Parkinson's diseases, are impaired at acquiring new motor skills, such as keeping a stylus steady on a target on a rotating platform (Gabrieli, Stebbins, Singh, Willingham, & Goetz, 1997; Heindel, Salmon, Shults, Wallicke, & Butters, 1989), perceptual skills involving reading mirror-reversed text (Martone, Butters, Payne, Becker, & Sax, 1984), and cognitive skills, such as solving complex multimove puzzles where discs must be transferred between pegs to create specific patterns (Saint-Cyr, Taylor, & Lang, 1988); for a review, see Packard and Knowlton (2002). Neuroimaging studies have provided converging evidence for the involvement of basal ganglia in skill acquisition in normal individuals, again across a wide range of skills (for a review, see Poldrack & Willingham, 2006).

The neurobiology of cortico-basal ganglia systems bears an interesting surface resemblance to that of the hippocampal system, in that the striatum (the primary input structure of the basal ganglia, comprising the caudate nucleus, putamen, and nucleus accumbens) receives inputs from nearly every higher order cortical region, and sends connections back to the same regions. However, on closer inspection the computational architecture of cortico–basal ganglia circuits diverges in important ways from the architecture of cortico-hippocampal circuits. We will focus on several aspects of cortico–basal ganglia circuits that appear to be particularly important with regard to generalization: parallel loops, convergent connectivity, and outcome-dependent changes in structure and function.

Parallel Loops

The architecture of the circuits involving the cortex and basal ganglia have been characterized in terms of a set of "loops" that connect the cortex to the basal ganglia, which then output to the thalamus and then return to the same region of the cortex (Alexander & Crutcher, 1990; Alexander, DeLong, & Strick, 1986; and see Figure 3.2). The cortex sends excitatory inputs to the striatum, which sends inhibitory inputs to the pallidum, which inhibits the thalamus, which sends excitatory connections back to the cortex. The net effect of exciting striatal neurons is to further excite the cortex, via the double-inhibitory circuit of the striatum and pallidum. As a result, desired actions can be selected more efficiently.

This same loop pattern is seen throughout the basal ganglia, but each loop courses through a specific subregion of the basal ganglia, a specific subregion of the cortex, and a specific subregion of the thalamus, so that these loops essentially are functionally segregated and work in parallel. Just as there is clustering of neurons dedicated to the hand in the motor region of the neocortex, there is some degree of clustering of neurons dedicated to the hand in the striatum. Although these circuits have traditionally been thought of as strongly segregated (Alexander et al., 1986), more recent work has provided evidence for a substantial degree of interaction between circuits (Bar-Gad, Morris, & Bergman, 2003). The important point here is that, even if the loops are somewhat interactive, information processing across diverse domains (e.g., vision and affective processes) remains largely segregated. Note that whereas the input structures of the MTL are characterized by extensive inter- and intraconnectivity, the input structures (the striatum) of the basal ganglia are less widely interconnected and tend to be connected only

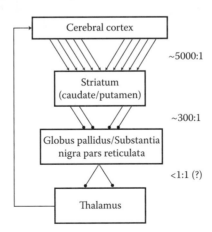

Figure 3.2 A schematic of the structure and connections of cortical-striatal-pallidal-thalamic loops.

very locally. As such, there simply is no architecture to support the association of arbitrary coactivated inputs in the way it is described for the MTL above. Changes in connection strength between neurons are necessarily limited by the physical connections of synapses, and therefore the basal ganglia loops' anatomical semi-segregation limits the inputs amongst which plasticity may occur.

Convergent Connectivity

The anatomy of connections in the basal ganglia can be viewed as a funnel, with a substantial convergence of neurons at each level to the next level (Bar-Gad et al., 2003; Zheng & Wilson, 2002; and see Figure 3.2). Each neuron in the striatum of the basal ganglia receives inputs from roughly ~5,000 cortical neurons, and it is estimated that it requires concurrent excitation from hundreds of cortical neurons to cause the firing of a striatal neuron (Wilson, 1995). At the next level, each neuron in the globus pallidus receives input from ~300 striatal neurons. It appears that the globus pallidus is a bottleneck, at which point concurrent activation of thousands of cortical neurons converges upon globus pallidus neurons. Although not well quantified, it is possible that connectivity from the globus pallidus to the thalamus is slightly divergent, but essentially a high level of dimensionality reduction has occurred by the time information reaches the thalamus and influences the outputs back to the cortex. Unlike the MTL, there is no representation that would support recapitulation of the original input. The idea is that received inputs are reduced to a more focused signal that allows actions to be selected efficiently. As will be discussed below, a special form of plasticity in the basal ganglia allows gradual shaping of the most appropriate actions based on experience.

Outcome-Dependent Plasticity

An important aspect of the functioning of the striatum is that it receives input from neurons in the substantia nigra pars compacta and ventral tegmental area in the midbrain that use dopamine (DA) as a neurotransmitter. Although the function of the dopaminergic system is complex and remains under active investigation, one important role of this input is to provide information as to whether or not expected outcomes have occurred (Schultz, 2006; Schultz, Dayan, & Montague, 1997). Dopamine neuron firing increases when an unexpected reward occurs, whereas it decreases when an expected reward does not materialize. Once it has been learned that a stimulus predicts rewards, DA neuron firing also increases when that stimulus occurs (Hollerman & Schultz, 1998). Indeed, this DA signal functions much like a learning–teaching signal postulated in influential models of reinforcement learning.

The DA error signal appears to play an important role in changes that can occur in the connections between the cortex and the striatum. Coincident firing of connected cortical and striatal neurons leads to strengthening of the connections between those cells, but only in the presence of DA, whereas coincident firing in the absence of DA may lead to decreased synaptic strength (Reynolds, Hyland, & Wickens, 2001; Wickens & Kotter, 1995). This is referred to as the "three-factor" model of cortico-striatal plasticity (Reynolds & Wickens, 2002), whereby the development of cortical plasticity requires presynaptic activity, postsynaptic depolarization, and the presence of DA at the synapse. Hence, dopamine, which is present as a result of a rewarding outcome, can be considered to play a critical role in strengthening selective cortical inputs to the striatum allowing these to more effectively drive the striatum in the future, which in turn makes selection of particular actions more efficient. The gradual shaping of this response ensures that, more likely than not, the action is appropriate. The implication for models of generalization is that this holds true only when the context remains the same. Whereas the ability to retrieve slightly different representations allows responding to slightly different circumstances, in the case of the basal ganglia the currently favored action will be produced across a range of different inputs. In a novel context, the lack of invertibility will not allow determination of which previous experiences best apply in the current situation.

For example, a specific response may be learned to a certain visual pattern if the response is followed with a positive outcome. However, simply performing the response does not recapitulate the visual pattern. This type of pattern completion, as performed by the MTL, does not occur. Interestingly, different types of pattern completion, such as linking multiple motor responses into a single response, may occur. For example, you may learn to play a sequence of notes on the piano. Playing the first note in the sequence may easily lead to completion of the sequence. Notably, playing a note from the middle of the sequence is less likely to lead to completion of the pattern. In this sense, completion of a pattern from partial input is markedly less flexible than what is possible for the MTL. It is this lack of flexibility that makes what has been learned less amenable to use in novel contexts. One must start at the same point every time, or none of the information is available.

It should be noted that the striatum is not unique in receiving dopaminergic inputs that modulate neural plasticity. In fact, the hippocampus also receives inputs from the dopamine system that modulate LTP in that region (Jay, 2003; Lisman & Grace, 2005). In addition, the hippocampus seems to play an important role in activating dopamine discharge to novel stimuli (Lisman & Grace). Thus, in each case the presence of dopamine is likely to increase retention: in the case of the striatum for particular action selections in response to specific stimuli and in the case of the hippocampus for particular combinations of features that make up an episode.

Summary

Although the basal ganglia seem at face value to be organized similarly to the medial temporal lobe with regard to their connectivity, cortico-striatal circuits have architectural features that clearly distinguish them from the MTL. In particular, whereas the MTL creates highly sparse representations that aim to retain the maximal amount of distinctive detail regarding the cortical input patterns, information processing from cortex through the basal ganglia results in a high degree of dimensionality reduction, due to the substantial degree of anatomical "funneling" at each stage. Second, whereas the MTL exhibits a high degree of convergence of information across different cortical systems, information from different cortical regions remains relatively segregated within cortico-striatal loops. Finally, neural plasticity in cortico-striatal systems appears to be heavily modulated by dopamine signals that provide direct feedback regarding the relative utility of actions.

FLEXIBILITY AND GENERALIZATION

Before undertaking a discussion of how generalization differs between procedural and declarative memory systems, it is important to be clear about what is meant by *generalization* in this context, because the meaning of this concept appears to differ substantially across theoretical domains. In this present context, *generalization* is defined as the ability to access the relevant knowledge in contexts outside of the one in which it was originally acquired.

This definition is similar to the concept of *flexibility* that has been used in the memory systems literature. Cohen and Eichenbaum (1993; see also Cohen, Poldrack, & Eichenbaum, 1997) have argued that one of the primary factors that distinguishes declarative from procedural memory is the degree to which the knowledge can be accessed outside of the situation in which it was acquired. Declarative memories are thought to be flexible, in the sense that they can be retrieved based on partial information and, importantly, *any* part of the information. This argument may be somewhat surprising to students of the psychology of memory. The principles of encoding specificity and transfer-appropriate processing have focused attention on the benefits of overlap between the specific context in which encoding and retrieval occur and on the processes engaged during encoding and retrieval of memories. For example, you may learn a set of animal names by reading words or looking at pictures. Then, if you are asked to recognize whether an item is one of the studied animals, you will do better if asked about a picture if you studied pictures and better with words if you studied words. Such phenomena seem to imply a degree of inflexibility for declarative memory.

Without downplaying the importance of encoding–retrieval interactions on declarative memory, it is worth pointing out that these effects are relatively weak; rarely do such context shifts make one amnesic for previous experience in the sense that none of the encoded information is remembered. Being probed for memory of studied animal pictures with words still leads to recall of animal pictures. Other examples are the well-known studies of context effects by Godden and Baddeley (1975) and Eich, Weingartner, Stillman, and Gillin (1975). Although contextual factors, such as studying words underwater and being tested on land, did have significant effects on declarative memory performance, by no means did the subjects become amnesic for their previous experience. This suggests that the principles describing the importance of overlap between encoding and retrieval, although relevant, clearly do not preclude substantial flexibility in these types of memories. Further, the frequency of spontaneous retrieval of past events provides even stronger evidence for the flexibility of declarative memory; if retrieval of a long-lost memory from elementary school required returning to elementary school, where that memory was encoded, retrieval would be all but impossible, whereas in actuality spontaneous retrieval of such memories seems to happen regularly.

The concept of procedural memory has long been understood in terms of direct modifications of the processes involved in task performance (Cohen, 1984; Hirsh, 1974). For example, one modifies one's memory of how to play the piano by actually playing the piano. With practice, the systems that support piano playing are modified. In such a system, it is clear how generalization would be limited to performance of tasks that engage the same processes. In this way, procedural memory exemplifies the concept of transfer-appropriate processing much more strongly than declarative memory: If the same processors are not engaged, then there is no potential for the memory to be expressed, and if the context is different, expression is also severely compromised. For example, if you are given a piano where the keys have been scrambled, it might be impossible to recreate a learned song. It will not be a question of reproducing a little less than with a normal piano, but of reproducing nothing at all.

EVIDENCE FROM NEUROPSYCHOLOGY

Evidence regarding the relative specificity of declarative and nondeclarative memory comes from the study of patients with memory disorders. A number of studies have examined whether amnesic patients can be taught new abilities, such as the use of computer systems, for the purposes of cognitive rehabilitation and vocational training (Glisky, 1995). For example, Glisky, Schachter, and Tulving (1986) examined new learning of computer facts and skills in individuals with damage to the hippocampus and other medial temporal lobe structures. As discussed above, medial temporal lobe structures are thought to support the binding together of different information from different cortical regions. The amnesics were taught specific facts about computers using a method of vanishing cues, in which the same question is presented (and can be answered) with fewer cues as training progresses. Over a number of lessons, four patients were taught to program a computer to perform various actions, as well as learn various system commands. The amnesics showed remarkable retention of the information; by the end of the third session, they were able to perform complex operations on the computer. However, upon closer examination it became clear that the knowledge acquired by the patients differed in character from that acquired by healthy participants. Whereas the healthy participants could easily answer questions about their new knowledge, the amnesics were impaired on questions where the wording was even slightly changed from that of training. In addition, they failed on a transfer task in which they were required to synthesize their knowledge in a way not experienced during training. Glisky et al. concluded that the knowledge acquired by the amnesics was "hyperspecific: it is relatively inflexible, rigidly organized, and only narrowly accessible" (p. 325). Because the MTL system, which supports declarative memory, is damaged in these individuals, any learning must occur via other systems. As such, these results are consistent with the notion that whereas declarative memory supports the generalization of knowledge beyond the initial context of acquisition, nondeclarative memory mechanisms are substantially less flexible.

EVIDENCE FROM NEUROIMAGING

The foregoing analysis suggests that the degree to which knowledge can be generalized outside of the initial context should depend upon which neural system is involved in learning. With healthy humans, it is not possible to directly manipulate which system is involved, as it is in animals via lesions or pharmacological interventions. However, it is possible to use behavioral manipulations to modulate the relative involvement of these systems, and to use neuroimaging to measure the engagement of each system in relation to learning.

Such an approach was used to investigate the involvement of brain systems while participants performed a probabilistic classification task (PCT). On the PCT, participants classify stimuli, consisting of one to three cue cards, into two categories. In total, there are four possible cues, and the 14 stimuli are combinations of those cues. After classifying a stimulus, participants receive feedback indicating what the correct answer is. However, the feedback is probabilistic such that for each cue, a category is shown to be correct on some proportion of trials, and the other category shown as correct the rest of the time. The multiple cue combinations and probabilistic feedback make simple memorization of cue–outcome relations difficult and inaccurate unless sampled across multiple presentations. Previous studies have shown that patients with declarative memory problems (e.g., as a result of medial temporal lobe damage) are able to learn this task (Knowlton, Squire, & Gluck, 1994; Reber, Knowlton, & Squire, 1996), though sometimes these patients may be impaired relative to healthy participants (Hopkins, Myers, Shohamy, Grossman, & Gluck, 2004). Patients with basal ganglia disorders, however, are badly impaired at learning on this task (Knowlton, Mangels, & Squire, 1996; Knowlton, Squire, Paulsen, Swerdlow, & Swenson, 1996; Shohamy et al., 2004), highlighting the critical role of the basal ganglia in learning in the task. Neuroimaging has shown that learning in this task is associated with activation in the basal ganglia and dopamine system (Aron et al., 2004; Poldrack et al., 2001; Poldrack, Prabakharan, Seger, & Gabrieli, 1999), and has suggested that the basal ganglia and MTL systems may be in competition with one another to drive behavior (Poldrack & Packard, 2003; Poldrack & Rodriguez, 2004).

In a recent study, Foerde, Knowlton, and Poldrack (2006) examined whether it was possible to manipulate the relative roles of the basal ganglia and MTL in PCT learning. Participants learned two PCTs, one under single-task conditions and one while performing a concurrent tone-counting task, which required tracking the number of high-pitched tones in a stream of high and low tones. Generally, dual-task conditions, such as counting tones in addition to doing another task, are found to harm declarative memory, whereas procedural learning is characterized as being insensitive to such manipulations. Each PCT had the same underlying structure, but the cues were in different colors, such that the participant clearly learned two separate tasks. After learning each task, a probe task was given where the cues learned under both single- and dual-task conditions were presented interleaved and under single-task conditions. Participants classified these items without receiving feedback, such that no further learning was occurring and the items learned under different conditions could be compared, demonstrating that performance was not statistically different after learning under different conditions.

Additionally, once outside the scanner participants were given tests of their declarative knowledge. For example, they were asked which item they would be most likely to see if they knew a certain category was the outcome (as opposed to selecting a category in response to the item, as during training). One would expect that such tests would tap the functioning of the medial temporal lobe systems because patients with MTL damage are impaired on these measures relative to healthy participants (Reber et al., 1996). On these measures, learning under single- versus dual-task conditions did have an effect. Participants were significantly worse at selecting items learned under dual-task conditions, and their results were in fact no better than chance. These results suggest that although learning under dual-task conditions allows one to perform well in the context of the task one was trained on, this ability does not generalize to situations where knowledge about cue–outcome associations has to be applied differently. It was hypothesized that the source of this difference in ability to generalize was due to the memory systems supporting performance in each case, and this was tested using functional magnetic resonance imaging (fMRI).

The fMRI results showed that when classifying items learned under single-task conditions, activity in the MTL was correlated with accuracy on that task, whereas classification accuracy on the task learned under dual-task conditions was correlated with activity in the basal ganglia. Furthermore, the level of declarative knowledge about the single-task PCT was correlated with MTL activity, whereas there was no such relationship for the dual-task PCT. This result ties the ability to generalize (or flexibly use) knowledge selectively to the MTL. As outlined previously, the architectures of the MTL and basal ganglia make these memory systems differently suited to support generalization. When you learn something in such a way that it depends on your MTL, you will be able to access the knowledge flexibly and generalize it to a different context. In contrast, being asked to do the same when the knowledge depends on the basal ganglia is not successful.

CONCLUSIONS

A substantial body of work has demonstrated that human learning and memory can be best explained via the concept of multiple memory systems. We have outlined here how differences in the neural architectures that support these different forms of memory result in differences in generalization between those memory systems. This approach shows how cognitive neuroscience can provide more than simply mapping cognitive functions onto brain areas; by relating the computational architecture of neural systems to the functional properties of behavior, this approach allows fundamental insights about the nature of neural function to help explain the ways in which memory works.

REFERENCES

Alexander, G. E., & Crutcher, M. D. (1990). Functional architecture of basal ganglia circuits: Neural substrates of parallel processing. *Trends in Neuroscience, 13*(7), 266–271.

Alexander, G. E., DeLong, M. R., & Strick, P. L. (1986). Parallel organization of functionally segregated circuits linking basal ganglia and cortex. *Annual Review of Neuroscience, 9*, 357–381.

Aron, A. R., Shohamy, D., Clark, J., Myers, C., Gluck, M. A., & Poldrack, R. A. (2004). Human midbrain sensitivity to cognitive feedback and uncertainty during classification learning. *Journal of Neurophysiology, 92*(2), 1144–1152.

Bar-Gad, I., Morris, G., & Bergman, H. (2003). Information processing, dimensionality reduction and reinforcement learning in the basal ganglia. *Progress in Neurobiology, 71*(6), 439–473.

Cohen, N. J. (1984). Preserved learning capacity in amnesia: Evidence for multiple memory systems. In L. R. Squire & N. Butters (Eds.), *Neuropsychology of memory* (pp. 83–103). New York: Guilford.

Cohen, N. J., & Eichenbaum, H. E. (1993). *Memory, amnesia, and the hippocampal system.* Cambridge, MA: MIT Press.

Cohen, N. J., Poldrack, R. A., & Eichenbaum, H. (1997). Memory for items and memory for relations in the procedural/declarative memory framework. *Memory, 5*(1–2), 131–178.

Doyon, J., Penhune, V., & Ungerleider, L. G. (2003). Distinct contribution of the cortico-striatal and cortico-cerebellar systems to motor skill learning. *Neuropsychologia, 41*(3), 252–262.

Eich, E., Weingartner, H., Stillman, R. C., & Gillin, J. C. (1975). State dependent accessibility of retrieval cues in the retention of a categorized list. *Journal of Verbal Learning and Verbal Behavior, 14*, 408–417.

Foerde, K., Knowlton, B. J., & Poldrack, R. A. (2006). Modulation of competing memory systems by distraction. *Proceedings of the National Academy of Science USA, 103*(31), 11778–11783.

Gabrieli, J. D., Stebbins, G. T., Singh, J., Willingham, D. B., & Goetz, C. G. (1997). Intact mirror-tracing and impaired rotary-pursuit skill learning in patients with Huntington's disease: Evidence for dissociable memory systems in skill learning. *Neuropsychology, 11*(2), 272–281.

Glisky, E. L. (1995). Computers in memory rehabilitation. In A. D. Baddeley, B. A. Wilson, & F. Watts (Eds.), *Handbook of memory disorders* (pp. 557–576). Chichester, UK: John Wiley.

Glisky, E. L., Schacter, D. L., & Tulving, E. (1986). Computer learning by memory-impaired patients: Acquisition and retention of complex knowledge. *Neuropsychologia, 24*(3), 313–328.

Gluck, M. A., & Myers, C. E. (2001). *Gateway to memory: An introduction to neural network modeling of the hippocampus and learning.* Cambridge, MA: MIT Press.

Godden, D., & Baddeley, A. D. (1975). Context-dependent memory in two natural environments: On land and under water. *British Journal of Psychology, 66*, 325–331.

Hasselmo, M. E., Wyble, B. P., & Wallenstein, G. V. (1996). Encoding and retrieval of episodic memories: Role of cholinergic and GABAergic modulation in the hippocampus. *Hippocampus, 6*(6), 693–708.

Heindel, W. C., Salmon, D. P., Shults, C. W., Wallicke, P. A., & Butters, N. (1989). Neuropsychological evidence for multiple implicit memory systems: A comparison of Alzheimer's, Huntington's; and Parkinson's disease patients. *Journal of Neuroscience, 9*, 582–587.

Hirsh, R. (1974). The hippocampus and contextual retrieval from memory: A theory. *Behavioral Biology, 12,* 421–444.

Hollerman, J. R., & Schultz, W. (1998). Dopamine neurons report an error in the temporal prediction of reward during learning. *Nature Neuroscience, 1*(4), 304–309.

Hopkins, R. O., Myers, C. E., Shohamy, D., Grossman, S., & Gluck, M. (2004). Impaired probabilistic category learning in hypoxic subjects with hippocampal damage. *Neuropsychologia, 42*(4), 524–535.

Jay, T. M. (2003). Dopamine: A potential substrate for synaptic plasticity and memory mechanisms. *Progress in Neurobiology, 69*(6), 375–390.

Karni, A., Meyer, G., Jezzard, P., Adams, M. M., Turner, R., & Ungerleider, L. G. (1995). Functional MRI evidence for adult motor cortex plasticity during motor skill learning. *Nature, 377*(6545), 155–158.

Knowlton, B., Squire, L. R., & Gluck, M. A. (1994). Probabilistic classification in amnesia. *Learning & Memory, 1,* 106–120.

Knowlton, B. J., Mangels, J. A., & Squire, L. R. (1996). A neostriatal habit learning system in humans. *Science, 273,* 1399–1402.

Knowlton, B. J., Squire, L. R., Paulsen, J. S., Swerdlow, N. R., & Swenson, M. (1996). Dissociations within nondeclarative memory in Huntington's disease. *Neuropsychology, 10*(4), 538–548.

Lisman, J. E., & Grace, A. A. (2005). The hippocampal-VTA loop: Controlling the entry of information into long-term memory. *Neuron, 46*(5), 703–713.

Malenka, R. C., & Nicoll, R. A. (1999). Long-term potentiation: A decade of progress? *Science, 285*(5435), 1870–1874.

Martin, S. J., & Morris, R. G. (2002). New life in an old idea: The synaptic plasticity and memory hypothesis revisited. *Hippocampus, 12*(5), 609–636.

Martone, M., Butters, N., Payne, M., Becker, J. T., & Sax, D. (1984). Dissociations between skill learning and verbal recognition in amnesia and dementia. *Archives of Neurology, 41*(9), 965–970.

Mishkin, M., Malamut, B., & Bachevalier, J. (1984). Memory and habits: Some implications for the analysis of learning and retention. In L. R. Squire & N. Butters (Eds.), *Neuropsychology of memory* (pp. 287–296). New York: Guilford.

Norman, K. A., & O'Reilly, R. C. (2003). Modeling hippocampal and neocortical contributions to recognition memory: A complementary-learning-systems approach. *Psychological Review, 110*(4), 611–646.

O'Reilly, R. C., & McClelland, J. L. (1994). Hippocampal conjunctive encoding, storage, and recall: Avoiding a trade-off. *Hippocampus, 4*(6), 661–682.

Packard, M. G., & Knowlton, B. J. (2002). Learning and memory functions of the basal ganglia. *Annual Review of Neuroscience, 25,* 563–593.

Poldrack, R. A., Clark, J., Paré-Blagoev, J., Shohamy, D., Creso Moyano, J., Myers, C., et al. (2001). Interactive memory systems in the human brain. *Nature, 414,* 546–550.

Poldrack, R. A., & Packard, M. G. (2003). Competition among multiple memory systems: Converging evidence from animal and human brain studies. *Neuropsychologia, 41*(3), 245–251.

Poldrack, R. A., Prabakharan, V., Seger, C., & Gabrieli, J. D. E. (1999). Striatal activation during cognitive skill learning. *Neuropsychology, 13,* 564–574.

Poldrack, R. A., & Rodriguez, P. (2004). How do memory systems interact? Evidence from human classification learning. *Neurobiology of Learning and Memory, 82*(3), 324–332.

Poldrack, R. A., & Willingham, D. B. (2006). Functional neuroimaging of skill learning. In R. Cabeza & A. Kingstone (Eds.), *Handbook of functional neuroimaging of cognition* (2nd ed., pp. 113–148). Cambridge, MA: MIT Press.

Reber, P. J., Knowlton, B. J., & Squire, L. R. (1996). Dissociable properties of memory systems: Differences in the flexibility of declarative and nondeclarative knowledge. *Behavioral Neuroscience*, *110*(5), 861–871.

Reynolds, J. N., Hyland, B. I., & Wickens, J. R. (2001). A cellular mechanism of reward-related learning. *Nature*, *413*(6851), 67–70.

Reynolds, J. N., & Wickens, J. R. (2002). Dopamine-dependent plasticity of corticostriatal synapses. *Neural Networks*, *15*(4–6), 507–521.

Rolls, E. T., & Kesner, R. P. (2006). A computational theory of hippocampal function, and empirical tests of the theory. *Progress in Neurobiology*, *79*(1), 1–48.

Saint-Cyr, J. A., Taylor, A. E., & Lang, A. E. (1988). Procedural learning and neostriatal dysfunction in man. *Brain*, *111*, 941–959.

Sanes, J. N., Dimitrov, B., & Hallett, M. (1990). Motor learning in patients with cerebellar dysfunction. *Brain*, *113*(Pt. 1), 103–120.

Schacter, D. L. (1987). Implicit memory: History and current status. *Journal of Experimental Psychology Learning, Memory, and Cognition*, *13*(3), 501–518.

Schultz, W. (2006). Behavioral theories and the neurophysiology of reward. *Annual Review of Psychology*, 57, 87–115.

Schultz, W., Dayan, P., & Montague, P. R. (1997). A neural substrate of prediction and reward. *Science*, *275*(5306), 1593–1599.

Scoville, W. B., & Milner, B. (1957). Loss of recent memory after bilateral hippocampal lesions. *Journal of Neurological and Neurosurgical Psychiatry*, *20*, 11–21.

Sherry, D. F., & Schacter, D. L. (1987). The evolution of multiple memory systems. *Psychological Review*, *94*(4), 439–454.

Shohamy, D., Myers, C. E., Grossman, S., Sage, J., Gluck, M. A., & Poldrack, R. A. (2004). Cortico-striatal contributions to feedback-based learning: Converging data from neuroimaging and neuropsychology. *Brain*, *127*(Pt. 4), 851–859.

Squire, L. R. (1987). *Memory and brain*. New York: Oxford University Press.

Squire, L. R. (1992). Memory and the hippocampus: A synthesis from findings with rats, monkeys, and humans. *Psychological Review*, *99*(2), 195–231.

Squire, L. R., Stark, C. E., & Clark, R. E. (2004). The medial temporal lobe. *Annual Review of Neuroscience*, *27*, 279–306.

Wagner, A. D., Koutstaal, W., Maril, A., Schacter, D. L., & Buckner, R. L. (2000). Task-specific repetition priming in left inferior prefrontal cortex. *Cerebral Cortex*, *10*(12), 1176–1184.

Wickens, J. R., & Kotter, R. (1995). Cellular models of reinforcement. In J. C. Houk, J. L. Davis, & D. G. Beiser (Eds.), *Models of information processing in the basal ganglia* (pp. 187–214). Cambridge, MA: MIT Press.

Wilson, C. J. (1995). The contribution of cortical neurons to the firing pattern of striatal spiny neurons. In J. C. Houk, J. L. Davis, and D. G. Beiser (Eds.), *Models of information processing in the basal ganglia* (pp. 29–50). Cambridge, MA: MIT Press.

Zheng, T., & Wilson, C. J. (2002). Corticostriatal combinatorics: The implications of corticostriatal axonal arborizations. *Journal of Neurophysiology*, *87*(2), 1007–1017.

Section 2

Developmental Perspectives on Generalization

4

Three Observations About Infant Generalization and Their Implications for Generalization Mechanisms

LOUANN GERKEN and FRANCES K. BALCOMB

O ver 3 decades of research on human infants has shown us that they enter the world with an impressive set of sensory abilities (e.g., Eimas, Siqueland, Jusczyk, & Vigorito, 1971; Jusczyk, 1997; Kellman & Arterberry, 2006). Further, the most recent decade has made clear that infants are also equipped with a set of cognitive abilities that allows them to parlay their initial sensory experiences into the beginnings of adult systems, such as language and spatial reasoning (e.g., Gerken, 2005; Oakes, Ross-Sheehy, & Luck, 2006). Through a series of snapshots of infant abilities at different ages, infant researchers are beginning to map out the trajectory of development in different cognitive domains. They are also beginning to hypothesize what sort of learning mechanism(s) might be needed to connect the known points of the developmental path. Of particular interest are mechanisms that might be involved in learners' ability to generalize from a limited set of experiences. Generalization allows learners to behave appropriately when they encounter new input that shares relevant properties with prior experiences, and, importantly, to discriminate new input that shares relevant properties with prior experiences from otherwise similar input that does not share those relevant properties. For example, generalizing from instances of the concept *dog* implies that the learner both behaves appropriately toward the new instances of dog (e.g., refers to them with the word *dog*) and behaves differently toward similar nondogs (e.g., does not refer to horses with the word *dog*).

In this chapter, we make three observations about the generalization mechanism that hold over a number of studies of infant learning. They concern (a) learning rate, (b) learning as loss of ability, and (c) monitoring learning. Our presentation focuses mainly on infant learning of language-like systems; however, examples are taken from other domains to better illustrate various points. Let us briefly fore-shadow the subsequent discussion: Learning rate—and, in particular, the amount of input that is required for generalizations—supports some generalization mechanisms while casting doubt on others. Different computational models require different amounts of input for generalization, and insofar as the models are like or unlike human infants, we can use the models to make inferences about human learning mechanisms. By *developmental loss of generalization*, we mean that some kinds of information in the input that allow generalization in younger infants no longer appear to be a basis of generalization for older infants. Such findings suggest that the generalization mechanism changes over development and that any characterization of that mechanism must take into account these changes. Finally, infants and young children show some evidence of monitoring their learning, turning their attention to input sets that allow the greatest degree of generalization. These observations tell us that, whatever the generalization mechanism, it is not sponge-like, but more self-guided in character. Using these three observations, which are presented in the next three sections, we use the final section to present a rough sketch of a generalization mechanism, as well as highlight the kinds of information that are still needed to make the sketch more refined.

LEARNING RATE

Infants are very rapid learners as measured both by the short amount of time it takes them to encode and generalize from new input and by the amount of input required. In this section, we focus on the number of different examples of a generalization that is needed for learning, as well as on the number of repetitions of each example that is needed. Imagine, for example, that a parent and child are looking at a book with pictures of animals. The parent points to a picture of a terrier and says, "That's a dog." A little later, the parent points to a picture of an Irish wolfhound and says, "That's a dog." For a child at some ages, encountering these two different dogs might be enough to grasp the concept *dog* and generalize it to other members of the species, while differentiating it from similar but different species like wolves and coyotes. However, for a younger child, the book exercise might need to be repeated over several days in order for the child to encode and remember each dog picture and its label. Only after multiple encounters with terriers, Irish wolfhounds, and (as another example) German shepherds is the child able to make the *dog* generalization. In keeping with the concept learning and psycholinguistics literatures, we will refer to the different examples from a particular generalization as *types*. In this case, terriers, Irish wolfhounds, and German shepherds are each different types from the category *dog*. The different encounters with each dog type are often called *tokens*. However, for readers who are not familiar with the type–token distinction, we will refer to multiple occurrences of a type as *versions* of that type.

The reason that the number of types and versions of the type are important in understanding the generalization mechanism is that different theoretical approaches to generalization differ in their implicit or explicit predictions about the amount of input needed. Deductive approaches such as parameter setting (Chomsky, 1981) suggest that, in the limit, a single datum (a single version of a single input type) is sufficient for a learner to rule out an incorrect grammatical rule. Associative approaches tend to be at the other extreme, with generalization requiring many input types (Altmann & Dienes, 1999; Elman, 1999; McClelland & Plaut, 1999; Seidenberg & Elman, 1999a, 1999b; Shastri & Chang, 1999). Bayesian hypothesis selection models tend to fall somewhere in between in terms of the number of input types required (Tenenbaum & Griffiths, 2001; Xu & Tenenbaum, 2007). Although these different approaches to generalization differ in their predictions about the number of input types required, none of them, to our knowledge, directly address the question of how many versions of each input type might be required. Therefore, by studying the number of types and versions of each type required for generalization, we can distinguish among existing approaches and encourage promising approaches to consider the role of multiple versions of each type.

Beginning with the number of input types that are required to generalize a concept or category, several studies have begun to suggest that this number is quite small. Gerken (2006) demonstrated that 9-month-olds familiarized with 17 repetitions (versions) of each of four different types from an AAB or ABA pattern of syllables (*leledi, wiwije, jijili, dedewe,* or *ledile, wijewi, jiliwi, dewede*) were able at test to discriminate AAB versus ABA patterns instantiated in new syllables (*popoga, kokoba* vs. *pogapo, kobako*), indicating that infants had generalized over the four familiarization types.[1] Subsequent research suggests that infants are able to make linguistic generalizations over just three input types. Gerken and Bollt (2008) found that infants exposed to 3- and 5-syllable words that exhibited patterns of stressed and unstressed syllables based on one of two artificial languages were able to generalize the principle "stress syllables ending in a consonant" (heavy syllables) after hearing only three different syllables ending in a consonant (types) in the input. For example, infants in Language 1 were familiarized with words like those in 1a through e (see list), which contained the heavy syllables BOM, KEER, and SHUL. During test, they were able to discriminate new words like those in 1f, which contained the heavy syllable TON from very similar words that did not embody the same generalization (capitals indicate stressed syllables; see further discussion of this set of studies in the next section). Importantly, no words in the familiarization language were stressed on the second and fourth syllables, suggesting that infants were generalizing based on the principle "stress syllables ending in a consonant" and not based on having memorized particular stress patterns (e.g., stressing the first and third syllables).

1a. BOM do re
1b. DO re KEER
1c. DO re SHUL mi fa
1d. DO re mi FA so
1e. BOM bom do RE mi
1f. do TON re MI fa

The importance of three input types is further supported by work in a visual learning domain. Needham and colleagues (Needham, Dueker, & Lockhead, 2005) exposed 4-month-olds to between one and three exemplars (types) of a visual category and then tested them on new items that were either consistent or inconsistent with the category. They found that infants did not generalize based on one or two exemplars of the category, but they did generalize from three exemplars.

We know somewhat less about the number of versions of each type required for learning than we know about the number of types. For example, in the study described above, infants were able to generalize over AAB versus ABA syllable string patterns with four input types distributed over less than 17 repetitions (versions) of each type (Gerken, 2006). That is, 4 × 17 = 68 total 3-syllable words were the input. In the study on which Gerken (2006) was based, 7-month-olds generalized after hearing three repetitions (versions) each of 16 AAB or ABA types (48 total input stimuli) created by crossing the four A syllables *le*, *wi*, *ji*, and *de* with the four B syllables *di*, *je*, *li*, and *we* (Marcus, Vijayan, Rao, & Vishton, 1999). Recent research from our laboratory attempted to push the lower limit on the number of versions of each type by familiarizing 9-month-olds with just a single instance of each of the four word types used by Gerken (2006; *leledi*, *wiwije*, *jijili*, and *dedewe*; four input stimuli total). Infants showed no evidence of learning under this condition, although the same four types did result in generalization when multiple (10 to 20) type repetitions of each type composed the familiarization stimuli (Gerken, 2006; Gerken & Tenenbaum, 2008).

One reason for the importance of understanding the relation of types and versions of each type required for infant generalization concerns the independence of types and versions in learning by infants and by computational models. If types and versions contribute independently to generalization, we might construe the generalization mechanism as one in which multiple versions of each type allow a particular example (type) to be sufficiently encoded in memory. It may be that younger learners or learners new to a domain need more versions of each type in order to generalize. Once each type is encoded in memory, all learners may need only a handful of different types (e.g., three) in order to make a particular generalization. Recall the example of dog concept generalization presented at the beginning of this section, in which younger learners may need to see the same three dogs over several sessions before the information about each dog and its label are encoded in memory. If this example reflects what really happens in generalization, the generalization mechanism might entail separate sorts of computations for encoding the input and for making generalizations over that input. To our knowledge, such a separation is not part of any existing learning models. However, it would be relatively easy to make it part of a Bayesian model (Tenenbaum & Griffiths, 2001). In contrast, there is no differentiation of types and versions of each type in many associative learning models (e.g., Xu & Tenenbaum, 2007). Of course, in the real world, outside of infant experiments and computational models, knowing what counts as two types or two versions of a single type is half of the battle. For example, are two acoustic events different versions of the word *pig*, or are they two different words (types; e.g., *pig* and *big*)? It is very likely that the speed of infant learning we see for a particular generalization in our studies relies on the infant having already sorted out what counts as types versus versions of a type in the relevant domain before they entered the laboratory. We discuss in the next section one approach that infants might use to determine whether two inputs are two different types versus versions of one type.

Whatever the relation between types and versions of a type turns out to be, it is clear that most associative models of generalization have used more input examples (multiple types and/or multiple versions of each type) than are required by infants (Altmann & Dienes, 1999; Elman, 1999; McClelland & Plaut, 1999; Seidenberg & Elman, 1999a, 1999b; Shastri & Chang, 1999). In contrast, hypothesis-testing models generalize from a number of input types in the same range as infants. For example, Kuehne, Gentner, and Forbus (2000) devised a model of learning the AAB versus ABA structure discussed above in which learners looked for analogies between possible abstract descriptions of familiarization and test data in order to determine what the two had in common. The model learned with the same number of types and type repetitions as the infants studied by Marcus and colleagues (1999). Similarly, a Bayesian hypothesis-testing model proposed by Regier and Gahl (2004) converged on the appropriate generalization from a small set of possibilities with five exemplars of the input. In hypothesis-testing models, learners attempt to recover from the input the state of affairs in the world that could have generated such input. In the case of language data, this state of affairs is often called a *grammar*. Such models entail redescribing the raw input data in more abstract terms (e.g., a rule). This more abstract description of the data is then compared with new input (Kuehne et al., 2000; Perfors, Tenenbaum, & Regier, 2006; Regier & Gahl). In contrast, associative approaches that encode patterns of relations among different aspects of the input, without a more abstract redescription, are sufficient for generalization (e.g., Rumelhart & McClelland, 1987). Associative models have the advantage that they do not need to say where the more abstract descriptions come from (a distinct disadvantage of hypothesis-testing approaches). However, if associative models cannot account for data on learning rate as well as hypothesis-testing models, this conceptual advantage is neutralized to some extent.

LEARNING AS LOSS OF ABILITY

You might recall from the introduction that generalization and discrimination can be viewed as two sides of a coin. Generalization entails both treating items that share relevant similarities as the same, and treating items that share no similarities or irrelevant similarities as different. A classic finding in the infant language development literature is that younger infants are able to discriminate pairs of speech sounds that older infants are not (e.g., Polka & Werker, 1994; Werker, Gilbert, Humphrey, & Tees, 1981). Data from a number of studies on perception of vowels and consonants suggest that infants are born with the ability to discriminate most speech contrasts, and through exposure to their native language(s), they lose the ability to discriminate those contrasts that are not phonemic (i.e., that don't differentiate words) in their language. It is important to note that infants lose their ability to perceive nonnative contrasts, particularly vowel contrasts, at ages when they are unlikely to know any or many words of their language. Therefore, it seems likely that they are determining which sounds are being used contrastively and which ones are not based on the statistical distribution of sounds in their input, and not on word meaning (Maye, Werker, & Gerken, 2002).

A common misconstrual of the data showing loss of perception of nonnative contrasts is that infants lose the ability to perceive speech sounds that they do not hear in their input. The inadequacy of this explanation can be illustrated with the following example: The /l/ produced in the phrase *zip lip* is made more forward in the mouth than the /l/ in *back lip*. These two productions of /l/ are "allophones" of the English phoneme /l/; that is, they are differences in pronunciation that depend on the other sounds with which they are combined, but that make no difference to meaning. (Returning to the terminology that we have been using, the two l's are different versions of a single type.) However, in the language Mid-Waghi, which is spoken in New Guinea, these two productions of /l/ are different phonemes, such that two otherwise identical-sounding words produced with the two different versions of /l/ would have different meanings. (They are two different types.) Presumably (although the study has not been done), American infants would discriminate the two versions of /l/ early in life (around 6 months), but they would generalize both sounds to the same phonemic category and hence lose the discrimination later (around 10 months). This example illustrates the point that infants lose the ability to discriminate speech sounds that are not used phonemically in their language, even though they may hear the same sounds as allophonic variants in their native language. We construe the focus on phonemically important acoustic distinctions as one in which the learner attempts to determine the source of acoustic variation that accounts for the most data. In terms of the current example, we assume that English-exposed infants hear words like *lip* produced in a variety of contexts (after /p/, after /k/, in isolation, etc.). Therefore, they will hear variation in the way that the /l/ is produced, but the distribution of acoustic variants will likely be unimodal. That is, there will be an acoustic variant of /l/ that is produced most often and some less frequent, acoustically similar variants. In contrast, the distribution of acoustic variants of /l/ for a Mid-Waghi speaker will likely be bimodal. That is, there will be two frequent acoustic variants, one for each of the two phonemes. If learners can detect the form of acoustic distributions and, crucially, use this distribution to infer the state of affairs in the world that gave rise to the particular distribution they encounter, they can make a guess as to whether acoustic variations arise from two underlying sources, categories, or types (bimodal distribution) or whether acoustic variation is continuous and not reflecting underlying categories but rather versions of a single category or type (unimodal distribution). Importantly, they might come to ignore acoustic distinctions that exhibit a unimodal distribution.

Maye et al. (2002) tested this hypothesis by presenting 6- and 8-month-old infants with either unimodal or bimodal distributions of an 8-step continuum of speech sounds along a particular acoustic dimension that is not used in English. Infants exposed to a unimodal continuum were unable to discriminate the endpoints at test, whereas infants exposed to a bimodal continuum were. These results suggest that the distribution of speech sounds in infants' input can provide a cue to whether a set of acoustic variants are produced as allophones of a single phoneme (unimodal distribution) or as two distinct phonemes (bimodal distribution). The fact that infants' behavior is affected by the shape of an input distribution suggests that they are sensitive to such information (see Gerken, 2005, for a review of the kinds of input statistics found to affect infant learning).

The loss of ability to perceive acoustic differences that do not account for much variance in the input is often discussed as a narrowing of attention (Werker & Tees, 1984). Recently, the same kind of narrowing of attention that appears to describe infants' learning of the phonemic structure of their native language has also been found in a quite different linguistic domain—detecting principles for assigning stress to syllables in multisyllabic words. In many languages, word stress does not occur in fixed positions (e.g., the first syllable or last syllable); rather, stress is assigned to each word based on a set of interacting stress principles, such as "Stress alternating syllables," or "Stress syllables ending in a consonant." Gerken (2004; Gerken & Bollt, 2008) found that 9-month-olds exposed to 3- and 5-syllable words exhibiting the stress assignment principles for one of two artificial languages were able to generalize to new words that obeyed the same principles. For example, infants exposed to words like those in 1a through e (see list), as part of their familiarization language, listened longer to words like 1f than very similar words that did not fit the generalizations in the language. Recall from the previous section that no words in the familiarization language were stressed on the second and fourth syllables, suggesting that infants were generalizing based on the principles and not based on having memorized particular stress patterns (e.g., "Stress first and third syllables").

The 9-month-olds' ability to generalize the principle "Stress syllables ending in a consonant" stands in contrast to their ability to learn a similar principle: "Stress syllables beginning with /t/" (Gerken & Bollt, 2008). The latter principle is not found in human languages, whereas the former is. Interestingly, however, 7-month-olds were able to generalize the "Stress syllables beginning with /t/" principle. An examination of the statistics of English word stress demonstrates that, although English has no absolute rule that syllables ending in a consonant should be stressed, more stressed than unstressed syllables end in a consonant, providing some reason for English learners to consider syllable ending as a basis for generalizing about stress. In contrast, English provides no statistical evidence that more stressed than unstressed syllables begin with /t/. We hypothesize that, whereas 7-month-olds are open to a range of generalizations about word stress, 9-month-olds have narrowed their focus to those bases of generalization that have some statistical support in their input language.

Data from studies employing the same word stress stimuli with English-speaking adults suggest that learners narrow their bases of generalization even further as they are exposed to the statistics of English (Gerken & Bollt, 2008; Guest, Dell, & Cole, 2000). In these studies, adults were unable to generalize the principle "Stress syllables ending in a consonant" when exposed to the same input that allowed this generalization in 9-month-olds. We hypothesize that the apparent loss of abilities to learn new stress principles is due to the fact that adult English speakers have discovered a more statistically reliable cue to word stress—word location. Because 87% of English words begin in a stressed syllable (Cutler & Carter, 1987), there is little need for English speakers to rely on principles such as "Stress syllables ending in a consonant" for assigning stress to words. The notion that English-speaking adults expect stress to occur in a fixed syllable location is supported by the fact that they were able to discriminate new test items consistent with their familiarization language from similar items if the familiarization and test items shared a stress pattern (e.g., stress on the second and fifth syllables). That is, adults are able to learn a new language system, but only if the system uses the same kinds of generalizations (e.g., which syllable locations are stressed) used in their own language. The adult data provide another example that becoming proficient in a cognitive domain entails narrowing one's attention to certain statistically reliable dimensions of the input and ignoring others.

A third example of learning entailing the loss of abilities comes from studies in which infants come to use a particular type of information in one cognitive domain and not another. Marcus and colleagues (Marcus, Fernandes, & Johnson, 2007) recently reported that 7.5-month-olds could generalize an AAB versus ABB pattern for spoken syllables but not musical tones. Dawson and Gerken (2009) replicated the null result with 7.5-month-olds familiarized with chord sequences, but found that 4-month-olds were able to generalize from AAB or ABA chord sequences to new sequences exhibiting the same pattern. This study demonstrates that tuning of attention not only occurs within a cognitive domain, such as language, but also allows different cognitive domains to be treated as distinct from each other. On this view, music and language are treated similarly early in development, but diverge over development. Dawson and Gerken argued that what defines a domain (e.g., language or music) is the statistics within that domain. If the variance in two kinds of input data can be explained by referring to the same kinds of statistical regularities (e.g., identity relations among adjacent or near-adjacent elements), then the two kinds of input are treated as a single domain. However, if two sets of input data exhibit different kinds of statistical regularities, the two sets are treated as belonging to different domains.

Returning to the specific example, the loss of ability to generalize to new musical sequences exhibiting AAB or ABA patterns may be due to the fact that dependency relations between adjacent and nearby items are crucial for processing language, whereas they are not relevant in music. Just as English-exposed infants hear different acoustic versions of /l/, infants hear music in which AAB and ABA patterns are present. For example, the first measure of "Brahms' Lullaby" (BL) follows an AAB pattern, whereas the first measure of "This Old Man" (TOM) follows an ABA pattern. However, in many melodies that infants and children hear, there is no identity relation among adjacent or near-adjacent notes. For example, in "Hot Cross Buns" (HCB), the notes in the first measure are different from each other, following an ABC pattern. In the face of an apparently uninformative statistical distribution of relations among individual notes, most melodies that infants and children hear share more predictive properties on other dimensions. For example, the first and last notes of the first measure of BL, TOM, and HCB are two steps apart. In BL and TOM, the last note in the measure is the fifth note of the key (e.g., the last note is G when the key is C). In HCB, the last note is the first note of the key (C in the key of C). Ending a measure on 1 or 5 is typical of many folk and popular songs. Therefore, the relation between musical key and the final note of a measure accounts for more variance in music than relations among individual notes.

A variety of computational models attempt to capture the attentional filtering that can be observed in laboratory studies with adults (e.g., Crawford, Huttenlocher, & Hedges, 2006; Kruschke, 2003, 2006).[2] In these studies, participants are exposed to input that can be characterized on several dimensions. Models of participants' performance assign greater weight to those dimensions that are better predictors of outcomes or future events. Although these models typically examine change in the weights that different dimensions of the stimuli are given over the course of a single study, they appear to be applicable to developmental change over months. Applying these models to the music example, learners would eventually come to use the greater statistical reliability of "ends on 1 or 5" to narrow their attention to tonal relations at the expense of discerning note identity relations.

MONITORING LEARNING

Learners in the real world are confronted with multiple sources of information and therefore multiple simultaneous potential generalizations. Although many models of learning depend on reinforcement, infants often accomplish rapid and sophisticated learning, both in the real world and in complex experimental tasks, with no explicit goal, and little to no feedback guiding specific learning trajectories. Furthermore, most learning problems presented to human infants and computer models alike are restricted, such that little extraneous information is given. However, learners in the real world are surrounded by extraneous information for each learning domain. For example, an infant playing with two adults could attempt to make generalizations about language the adults are using, about the toys they are playing with, or about the nature of adult–adult versus adult–child social interactions, just to name a few. Perhaps learners just select at random some pieces of input to attend to and attend until they have made some generalization. However, not all generalizations are likely to be within the cognitive grasp of learners at all developmental stages, and some potential generalizations may turn out to be dead ends for learners at any developmental stage. Given how rapidly infants and children learn, the apparent lack of external feedback, and the complexity of learning problems, especially outside of the laboratory, it seems that learners must have some way of deciding which aspects of their environment offer the most promising generalizations and which should be avoided.

One possible source of information available to learners that is discussed in animal learning literature is that internal reinforcement is provided by a reduction of uncertainty. In other words, infants operate with the goal of making the environment more predictable, and reinforcement comes from latching upon the information sources that allow the most successful generalizations about the environment. Thus, infants show increased attention to and reliance on aspects of their input that account for large parts of the variance (e.g., attending to phonemic differences that are meaningful, such as /l/ and /r/ for English speakers) and reduced attention to distinctions that, while they exist, account for little variance (e.g., not attending to phonemic differences such as /l/ and /r/ that are not meaningful to Japanese speakers). Given how rapidly infants learn, even in complex environments, we can infer that they are able to access implicit knowledge about their rate of uncertainty reduction and use that knowledge to select to which source(s) of information to attend. The findings on learning as loss of ability and/or attention are consistent with this inference.

It is important to emphasize that what appears to be reinforcing is reduction of uncertainty, not low uncertainty in itself. If given the choice between a well-known learning domain, in which the parameters of generalization are already established, and a new one, a goal of low uncertainty would seem always to drive the learner to the well-known (albeit already learned) space. However, this description does not seem accurate. Rather, adults are able to consciously assess their knowledge state as well as their likely learning rate (rate of uncertainty reduction). For example, a patient with a newly diagnosed medical condition from a general physician may seek opinions from other sources, including another general physician and some basic reading material, each of which gives similar but slightly different opinions. After consulting with a number of information sources, the patient may begin to generalize across consistent input and discriminate individual nonsignificant variations that are not relevant to the question. At this point, having sought enough information to gain an understanding of the issue, the patient may choose to seek opinions from a specialist in that area or more professionally oriented reading material, seeking more specialized information to build on the knowledge base. Thus, when faced with understanding a new information type, a person will assess their level of understanding as compared to the level of information offered by various sources and choose a source that will result in optimal learning, or an optimal decrease in their lack of knowledge (or uncertainty), which changes dynamically throughout the learning process.

To posit that metacognition is a viable mechanism contributing to generalization in infancy, we need evidence for metacognition at young ages. Until recently a compendium of evidence suggested that metacognitive abilities did not emerge until early school years. However, recent work in our lab using methods employed with nonhuman primates suggests that evidence for implicit metacognition can be found at earlier ages.

In traditional tasks that address children's ability to monitor their learning and memory, most research has been directed at school-aged children. This research reveals a strong developmental trend in what are typically called *metacognitive abilities*, such that older children's assessments of what they know are more accurate than relatively younger children's throughout childhood (Lockl & Schneider, 2002). For example, in a feeling-of-knowing study, kindergarten, first-grade, and third-grade children were presented with line drawings and asked to name them. If a child failed to correctly name an item, the child was asked if she or he would recognize the correct label if she or he heard it. Subsequently, children were presented with an array of nine pictures and one verbal label, and asked to point to the matching picture. Third-grade children were significantly better at predicting which picture–label matches they would be able to recognize than first-grade children, who in turn outperformed kindergarten children (Wellman, 1977).

However, evidence for implicit memory monitoring comes from comparative research. Recent research with rhesus monkeys has indicated that they are able to manifest at least rudimentary metacognition skills. In one such study, Smith and colleagues (Smith, Shields, Washburn, & Allendoerfer, 1998) presented a serial list to adult humans and monkeys and gave them a choice of responding to the task or choosing an "uncertain" response. Humans and monkeys were more likely to choose the uncertain response for items in the middle of the list (more difficult) than items in the beginning and end of the list, indicating memory-monitoring abilities.

Further evidence for nonverbal memory monitoring comes from research with young children in our lab. In these experiments children aged 3.5 years demonstrated memory-monitoring skills by responding on a nonverbal task originally developed for nonhuman animals, in which they had to access their knowledge states. Children watched a movie with 15 animal–object matching pairs. It was assumed that by the end of the movie, they would remember some pairs and would have forgotten others (thus having "known" and "unknown" item matches). At test, for each trial children saw one item of a pair and got to choose whether they wanted to try to find its mate, or to skip that trial. Subsequently their memory was tested for all trials to assess accuracy. If children can monitor their memory, they should choose to find the match for the trials they remember, and skip the ones they have forgotten, resulting in higher accuracy on accepted than skipped trials. This was the observed pattern of performance, suggesting that young children are able to alter behavioral responses based on implicit memory monitoring, at least during recall. A second finding from this research was that children who demonstrated better memory-monitoring performance also demonstrated better overall recognition memory performance than children who either over- or underestimated their memory, suggesting that metacognition is linked to the process on which it acts, such that performance in one domain is inherently linked to performance in the other. Our finding on individual differences in memory monitoring is consistent with problematicity theory (Prins, Veenman, & Elshout, 2006), in which metacognition and intellectual ability are interlinked components, interacting to influence learning and problem solving depending on task demands. Learners assess both their skills and the difficulty of a task to determine the best strategy for responding, resulting in different strategies for novices and experts across varying levels of difficulty.

If children can use metacognition to acquire knowledge, perhaps they can similarly use it to generalize knowledge as well. In fact, an assumption underlying commonly used methods in infant learning and generalization paradigms is that infants' differential preference for what is novel versus what is familiar in commonly used methods is due to their seeking an optimal level of new and old information to promote learning (Hunter & Ames, 1988). A standard way of interpreting direction of preference effects in infant research is that it reflects a tacit understanding by the infant of degree of learning, such that infants will show a novelty preference at test if they have mastered the information in training, and a familiarity preference if they have not. That is, infants will attend to a novel input type if they have learned and generalized the information to novel stimuli items, but will show a familiarity preference if they have not mastered the information, and hence their generalization does not account for the variance in the training input.

Indeed, there is evidence that level of experience can predict familiarity or novelty preferences in infants. For example, in one study, 8- and 12-month-old infants were introduced to a complex array of toys, and allowed to play freely with them. One group was allowed to play with the toys until they were habituated and compared to the second group, who were familiarized with but not habituated to the toys. At test, infants were given both the familiar array and a novel array of toys to choose from. Infants who had habituated showed a significantly greater preference for novel toys than infants who had been familiarized but not habituated, suggesting that infants differentially sought out novel toys only after attaining sufficient experience with the familiar (Hunter, Ames, & Koopman, 1983). This study suggests that infants have some control over how they are learning, using their level of competence to guide their behavioral responding to manipulate learning opportunities. In fact, direction of preference from familiarity to novelty can be reversed by increasing exposure to stimuli based on the assumption that increased exposure time will result in higher competency with training (Thiessen, Hill, & Saffran, 2005).

Currently, the question of whether 17-month-old infants demonstrate differential behavioral responding based on self-assessed level of competence is under investigation in our lab. As described above, an assumption in standard infant research paradigms is that infant looking behavior reflects some understanding on the infant's part of his or her own level of competence with a given behavior. For example, in habituation paradigms, it is assumed that infants will attend to novel information until they have reached a level of tacit understanding of that material, at which point they will habituate, or look away. Following this assumption, infants who habituate to a new stimulus should show a greater level of behavioral competence with information in that stimulus than infants who have not yet habituated and are, in theory, still learning the material. In an experiment currently under investigation in our lab, 17-month-old infants are presented with a spatial learning task in a standard habituation paradigm. Infants watch a movie that shows the locations of three balls hidden in an array of six boxes, and subsequently are presented with the box and encouraged to retrieve the balls from the hidden locations. Infants are split into two groups: those who watch the movie until they habituate (no longer attend to the movie), and those whose viewing is interrupted before they have habituated. If, indeed, habituation is an infant's way of indicating a level of mastery with the presented material, those infants who habituate should show a greater level of competence at finding the balls in the array than those infants whose viewing times are interrupted. Results from this study may reveal that long before children can reliably report on their knowledge states, they are able to access information about their level of learning, and use it to guide how they respond on a learning task. Importantly, if we can find evidence that learners choose the domains over which they attempt to generalize based on an internally generated signal of uncertainty reduction, models in which learning depends on reinforcement may need to be revised to allow for internally generated reinforcement.

SUMMARY AND CONCLUSION

In this chapter, we discuss three properties of infant generalization that have been observed across learning domains. The properties are that infants generalize from a small number of input types if there are multiple versions of these types, that generalization is characterized by losses of ability as well as gains, and that infants are able to implicitly monitor their own knowledge states and use this ability to select generalization domains. If these observations hold up to further investigation, our models of learning and generalization need to be modified in several ways. First, insofar as models that engage in some form of hypothesis testing demonstrate learning rates more on par with those of infant learners, these models are to be preferred over models that more passively accumulate input statistics but do not redescribe these statistics at a higher level of abstraction. Second, more dynamic models are needed, such that the units of analysis and the statistics applied to these units change over development based on previous successes and failures of generalization. Third, the growing body of data suggesting that learners are able to monitor their own generalization in a domain suggests that generalization models that employ some sort of internally generated reinforcement may capture important properties of real-world learning. We hope that our tying together these three heretofore distinct lines of research will spark discussion in the fields of human development and machine learning, and perhaps lead to new behavioral studies as well as new generalization models.

ACKNOWLEDGMENT

The writing of this chapter and many of the studies to which we refer were supported by NICHD grant #HD042170.

NOTES

1. Unless otherwise noted, all of the infant studies presented here employ the headturn preference procedure (Kemler Nelson et al., 1995), in which infants are familiarized with an auditory stimulus for approximately 2 minutes and subsequently presented with new stimuli that are either consistent or inconsistent with the familiarization stimulus. Significant listening times to consistent versus inconsistent test items are taken to indicate learning and generalization during familiarization.
2. Guenther and Gjaja (1996) have modeled the types of data found by Maye et al. (2002). However, their model is one of neural tuning, suggesting that the ability to access nonphonemic contrasts is lost. Findings that adults can use nonphonemic contrasts in speech segmentation would appear to contradict such a model (e.g., Gaskell & Marslen-Wilson, 1996). What is needed is a model that narrows the focus to dimensions of the input that account for variance *in particular contexts*.

REFERENCES

Altmann, G., & Dienes, A. (1999). Rule learning by 7-month-olds and neural networks. *Science, 284*, 875.

Balcomb, F. K., & Gerken, L. A. (2008). Three-year old children can access their own memory to guide responses on a visual matching task. *Developmental Science,11*, 750–760.

Chomsky, N. (1981). *Lectures on government and binding*. Dordrecht: Foris.

Crawford, L. E., Huttenlocher, J., & Hedges, L. V. (2006). Within-category feature correlations and Bayesian adjustment strategies. *Psychonomic Bulletin & Review, 13*, 245–250.

Cutler, A., & Carter, D. (1987). The predominance of strong initial syllables in the English vocabulary. *Computer Speech and Language, 2*, 133–142.

Dawson, D., & Gerken, L. A. (2009). Learning to learn differently: The emergence of domain-sensitive generalization in the second six months of life. *Cognition, 111*, 378–382.

Eimas, P., Siqueland, E., Jusczyk, P. W., & Vigorrito, K. (1971). Speech perception in infants. *Science, 171*, 303–306.

Elman, J. (1999). Generalization, rules, and neural networks: A simulation of Marcus et al. (1999). Unpublished manuscript, University of California, San Diego.

Gaskell, M., & Marslen-Wilson, W. (1996). Phonological variation and inference in lexical access. *Journal of Experimental Psychology: Human Perception and Performance, 22*, 144–158.

Gerken, L. A. (2004). Nine-month-olds extract structural principles required for natural language. *Cognition, 93*, B89–B96.

Gerken, L. A. (2005). What develops in language development? In R. Kail (Ed.), *Advances in child development and behavior* (Vol. 33, pp. 153–192). San Diego, CA: Elsevier.

Gerken, L. A. (2006). Decisions, decisions: Infant language learning when multiple generalizations are possible. *Cognition, 98*, B67–B74.

Gerken, L. A., & Bollt, A. (2008). Three exemplars allow at least some linguistic generalizations: Implications for generalization mechanisms and constraints. *Language Learning and Development, 4*(3), 228–248.

Gerken, L. A., & Tenenbaum, J. B. (2008). Can infant generalization be characterized as model selection? Unpublished manuscript.

Guenther, F. H., & Gjaja, M. N. (1996). The perceptual magnet effect as an emergent property of neural map formation. *Journal of the Acoustical Society of America, 100*, 1111–1121.

Guest, D. J., Dell, G. S., & Cole, J. S. (2000). Violable constraints in language production: Testing the transitivity assumption of optimal theory. *Journal of Memory & Language, 42*(2), 272–299.

Hunter, M., & Ames, E. (1988). A multifactor model of infant preferences for novel and familiar stimuli. *Advances in Infancy Research, 5*, 69–95.

Hunter, M., Ames, E., & Koopman, R. (1983). Effects of stimulus complexity and familiarization time on infant preferences for novel and familiar stimuli. *Developmental Psychology, 19*(3), 338–352.

Jusczyk, P. W. (1997). *The discovery of spoken language*. Cambridge, MA: MIT Press.

Kellman, P. J., & Arterberry, M. E. (2006). Infant visual perception. In D. Kuhn, R. S. Siegler, W. Damon, & R. M. Lerner (Eds.), *Handbook of child psychology: Vol 2. Cognition, perception, and language* (6th ed., pp. 109–160). Hoboken, NJ: John Wiley.

Kemler Nelson, D., Jusczyk, P. W., Mandel, D. R., Myers, J., Turk, A. E., & Gerken, L. A. (1995). The headturn preference procedure for testing auditory perception. *Infant Behavior and Development*, *18*, 111–116.

Kruschke, J. (2003). Attentional learning. *Current Directions in Psychological Science*, *12*, 171–175.

Kruschke, J. (2006). Locally Bayesian learning with applications to retrospective revaluation and highlighting. *Psychological Review*, *113*, 677–699.

Kuehne, S. E., Gentner, D., & Forbus, K. D. (2000). Modeling infant learning via symbolic structural alignment. In *Proceedings of the 22nd annual conference of the Cognitive Science Society*. Mahwah, NJ: Lawrence Erlbaum.

Lockl, K., & Schneider, W. (2002). Developmental trends in children's feeling-of-knowing judgments. *International Journal of Behavioral Development*, *26*(4), 327–333.

Marcus, G. F., Fernandes, K., & Johnson, S. P. (2007). Infant rule learning facilitated by speech. *Psychological Science*, *18*(5), 387–391.

Marcus, G. F., Vijayan, S., Rao, S. B., & Vishton, P. M. (1999). Rule learning by 7-month-old infants. *Science*, *283*, 77–80.

Maye, J., Werker, J. F., & Gerken, L. A. (2002). Infant sensitivity to distributional information can affect phonetic discrimination. *Cognition*, *82*(3), B101–B111.

McClelland, J. L., & Plaut, D. C. (1999). Does generalization in infant learning implicate abstract algebraic rules? *Trends in Cognitive Sciences*, *3*, 166–168.

Needham, A., Dueker, G., & Lockhead, G. (2005). Infants' formation and use of categories to segregate objects. *Cognition*, *94*, 215–240.

Oakes, L. M., Ross-Sheehy, S., & Luck, S. J. (2006). Rapid development of feature binding in visual short-term memory. *Psychological Science*, *17*(9), 781–787.

Perfors, A., Tenenbaum, J. B., & Regier, T. (2006, July 30–August 1). Poverty of the stimulus? A rational approach. Paper presented at the 28th annual conference of the Cognitive Science Society, Vancouver, British Columbia.

Polka, L., & Werker, J. F. (1994). Developmental changes in perception of nonnative vowel contrasts. *Journal of Experimental Psychology: Human Perception and Performance*, *20*, 421–435.

Prins, F. J., Veenman, M. V. J., & Elshout, J. J. (2006). The impact of intellectual ability and metacognition on learning. *Learning and Instruction*, *16*(4), 374–387.

Regier, T., & Gahl, S. (2004). Learning the unlearnable: The role of missing evidence. *Cognition*, *93*, 147–155.

Rumelhart, D., & McClelland, J. (1987). Learning the past tenses of English verbs: Implicit rules or parallel distributed processing? In B. MacWhinney (Ed.), *Mechanisms of language acquisition* (pp. 195–248). Mahwah, NJ: Lawrence Erlbaum.

Seidenberg, M. S., & Elman, J. (1999a). Do infants learn grammar with algebra or statistics? *Science*, *284*, 435–436.

Seidenberg, M. S., & Elman, J. (1999b). Networks are not hidden rules. *Trends in Cognitive Sciences*, *3*, 288–289.

Shastri, L., & Chang, S. (1999). *A spatiotemporal connectionist model of algebraic rule-learning* (No. TR-99-011). Berkeley: University of California.

Smith, J. D., Shields, W. E., Washburn, D., & Allendoerfer, K. (1998). Memory monitoring by animals and humans. *Journal of Experimental Psychology*, *127*(3), 227–250.

Tenenbaum, J. B., & Griffiths, T. L. (2001). Generalization, similarity, and Bayesian inference. *Behavioral and Brain Sciences*, *24*, 629–640.

Thiessen, E., Hill, E., & Saffran, J. (2005). Infant-directed speech facilitates word segmentation. *Infancy*, *7*(1), 53–71.

Wellman, H. (1977). Tip of the tongue and feeling of knowing experiences: A developmental study of memory monitoring. *Child Development*, *48*(1), 13–21.

Werker, J. F., Gilbert, J. H. V., Humphrey, K., & Tees, R. C. (1981). Developmental aspects of cross-language speech perception. *Child Development*, *52*, 349–355.

Werker, J. F., & Tees, R. C. (1984). Cross-language speech perception: Evidence for perceptual reorganization during the first year of life. *Infant Behavior and Development*, *7*, 49–63.

Xu, F., & Tenenbaum, J. B. (2007). Word learning as Bayesian inference. *Psychological Review*, *114*, 245–272.

5

Mechanisms of Induction Early in Development

ANNA V. FISHER

*T*he ability to generalize knowledge from the known to the unknown is crucially important: As Steven Sloman (1993) succinctly put it, "[O]ur knowledge that leopards can be dangerous leads us to keep a safe distance from jaguars" (p. 321). It has been amply demonstrated that even infants and very young children are capable of simple inductive generalizations (Baldwin, Markman, & Melartin, 1993; Gelman & Markman, 1986; Rakison, 2003; Sloutsky & Fisher, 2004a; Sloutsky, Lo, & Fisher, 2001; Welder & Graham, 2001), although the mechanisms underlying induction early in development remain hotly debated. Consider the example above: One might rely on several sources of information to keep a safe distance from jaguars after having learned that leopards are dangerous. First, both leopards and jaguars belong to the same animal family referred to as *big cats*. Second, both leopards and jaguars are found in similar habitats, namely, the rainforest (in Africa and South America, respectively). Third, both leopards and jaguars are predators. Fourth, leopards and jaguars look similar to each other. Are these sources of information equally important, or are some more important than others? Does the role of different sources of information (i.e., conceptual knowledge versus appearance similarity) change with development? These questions remain contested, and several theoretical accounts have been proposed to explain the mechanisms of induction in children and adults.

Rips (1975) was one of the first researchers to undertake a systematic investigation of inductive generalization using familiar categories. In his study, Rips presented participants with fictitious scenarios; for example, participants could have been told that scientists discovered that all robins on a distant island have a new contagious disease. Participants were then asked to estimate what proportion of other bird species on this island (e.g., sparrows, geese, and ostriches) would also have the disease. Rips identified two factors that influenced people's inductive inferences: (a) the similarity of the given category to the target category, and (b) the typicality of the given category. Specifically, the more similar the given category to the target category, the more willing people are to generalize the property in question; for example, if participants are told that all *geese* have the new disease, then participants will be more likely to generalize this property to *ducks* than to *sparrows*, because ducks are more similar to geese than sparrows are to geese. Similarly, the likelihood of generalization to the target category increases with the increase in the typicality of the given category (with regard to its superordinate category); for example, if participants are told that all *robins* have the disease, people are more likely to assume that other bird species also have the disease than if they are told that all *ostriches* have the disease, because people consider robins to be more typical birds than ostriches (at least in the continental United States).

These findings have been interpreted as evidence of similarity-based as well as category-based induction in adults. In particular, category knowledge is not required to estimate how similar items are to each other. For example, one does not need to know that geese and ducks belong to the category *birds* in order to perform similarity judgment. Furthermore, to estimate the similarity of geese to ducks, one does not need to know what other species also belong to the category *birds* (e.g., robins, eagles, and owls); this information is irrelevant in the estimation of similarity. However, this information is relevant if one needs to estimate how typical a given item is (i.e., how representative it is of the category to which it belongs; Rips, 1975), because typicality can be established only with regard to the whole category.

Osherson and colleagues (Osherson, Smith, Wilkie, Lopez, & Shafir, 1990) further developed and formalized Rips' (1975) account of induction in their similarity–coverage model, in which *coverage* refers to reliance on the knowledge of categories and taxonomies. Osherson et al. obtained evidence for the 11 phenomena predicted by the model, some of which rely only on the *similarity* component, whereas others require a *category coverage* component. However, the view that adults both possess the knowledge about taxonomies and rely on this knowledge to perform induction has been challenged by Steven Sloman. In several of his studies, Sloman (1993, 1998) presented adults with arguments similar to the ones below:

(1)
   Birds have an ulnar artery.

   Robins have an ulnar artery.

(2)
   Birds have an ulnar artery.

   Penguins have an ulnar artery.

Both of these arguments should be equally strong from the normative perspective, because both robins and penguins are members of the category *birds*; thus, conclusion categories in both arguments occupy the same level in the animal taxonomy. Therefore, if adults rely on their taxonomic knowledge to perform induction (i.e., the category coverage component), they should judge these arguments as equally strong. However, Sloman predicted that because robins share more features with other birds than penguins (and therefore are more similar to other birds than penguins), adults might judge the first argument to be stronger than the second argument. Over 90% of participants presented with these and other similar arguments considered the first argument stronger than the second, supporting Sloman's prediction. These findings provided support to Sloman's (1993) model of feature-based induction, according to which strength of inductive arguments increases with increased overlap between features of the premise and conclusion categories.

In contrast to the above-mentioned models arguing that adults rely on similarity at least to some extent during induction, Bayesian models of induction are often explicitly formulated as similarity-free models (Heit, 1998; Sanjana & Tenenbaum, 2002). For example, Kemp and Tenenbaum's (2009) model relies on the idea that induction is based on background knowledge captured by a structure that represents relationships among categories comprising this structure. In the case of natural-kind categories (e.g., animals, plants, and rocks), background knowledge is often represented in the form of a tree-structured taxonomy. Within this approach, similarity effects observed in induction are an artifact of the proximity of categories in a taxonomy—the closer two categories are in a taxonomy, the more they will have in common. Overall, models of mature induction range from similarity-only models (Sloman, 1993) to knowledge-only models (Heit; Kemp & Tenenbaum).

THEORETICAL ACCOUNTS OF EARLY INDUCTION

Similar to the study of mature induction, the study of induction early in development has not been without controversy, and several theoretical accounts have been proposed to account for the mechanisms of early induction. According to one position, often referred to as a *naïve theory approach*, even early in development induction is driven by children's knowledge about language and the world. When

> trying to determine whether to draw an inference from object A to object B, a child would not simply calculate the similarity between the two objects. Rather the child would determine whether A and B belong to members of the same natural kind category that encompasses both A and B. (Gelman & Coley, 1991, p. 185)

Knowledge that allows even very young children to perform induction in this manner comes in the form of conceptual assumptions, three of which are especially important for induction.

The *category assumption* is the belief that all natural-kind entities are members of more general categories and that members of the same category share many unobserved properties (such as DNA, internal organs, etc.). The *linguistic assumption* is the belief that linguistic labels (unless they are proper names) denote categories rather than individuals. When performing induction, children as well as adults rely on these assumptions to conclude that entities sharing a label belong to the same kind, and therefore share many unobservable properties. The *label centrality assumption* is a belief that various sources of information form a conceptual hierarchy, with some properties being more important, or *central*, than others for determining category membership and generalizing properties of natural-kind objects; for example, it is argued that object labels are more central to the category membership of objects than their appearances (Gelman & Coley, 1991; Jaswal, 2004; Keil, Smith, Simons, & Levin, 1998). In other words, it is assumed that even early in development, (a) induction is category based, and (b) labels are proxies of category membership and are central for induction, and as such their contribution to induction is greater than that of peripheral properties, such as appearances.

According to the alternative approach, early in development induction is an automatic generalization process based on the overall similarity of compared entities. As Sloutsky and colleagues have suggested (Sloutsky, 2003; Sloutsky & Fisher, 2004a; Sloutsky, Lo, & Fisher, 2001), early in development linguistic labels are attributes of objects, and the similarity of compared entities is thus computed over both appearance and labeling attributes. These intuitions were implemented in a recently proposed similarity-based model of early generalization. According to the *similarity-induction-naming-categorization model* (SINC), early in development induction is a function of the overall perceptual similarity computed over weighted visual and auditory attributes (Sloutsky & Fisher, 2004a). The theory underlying SINC assumes that due to auditory dominance, auditory information (including linguistic labels) often has greater attentional weights than visual information early in development. Support for this assumption comes from the finding that auditory input, including labels, often overshadows (or attenuates the processing of) corresponding visual input early in development (Napolitano & Sloutsky, 2004; Robinson & Sloutsky, 2004, 2007; Sloutsky & Napolitano, 2003; Sloutsky & Robinson, 2008). Although auditory overshadowing decreases with age, these effects are pronounced and reliable in 3- to 5-year-old children (Robinson & Sloutsky, 2004a). As a result of attenuated visual processing in the presence of auditory information, young children perceive entities that share the same auditory label as looking more similar than the same entities presented without a label (Sloutsky & Fisher, 2004; Sloutsky & Lo, 1999). In other words, according to SINC, early in development common labels are features directly contributing to perceived similarity rather than markers denoting common category membership. Within this approach, conceptual knowledge (such as beliefs that individual items belong to categories and that labels indicate category membership) is viewed as a potential outcome of development and learning, rather than a prerequisite for it.

Overall, the SINC model can be characterized as a similarity-only model, whereas the naïve theory approach can be characterized as mostly knowledge based. Note that proponents of the naïve theory approach agree that children can rely on perceptual similarity information; however, they argue that children do so only when other, more central sources of information (e.g., category labels) are not available. Hence, this approach is characterized here as mostly knowledge based rather than knowledge only.

Although both theoretical approaches to induction have generated empirical support, similar findings often have been taken as evidence supporting both approaches. Consider, for instance, a typical induction task known as the *triad task*, in which 4-year-old children are presented with a *target* item and several *test* items (i.e., Test A and Test B), and asked whether the target item is more likely to share a biological property with Test A or Test B. For example, children may be shown a picture of a brown starfish (the target), a brown pinecone (Test A), and a red starfish (Test B). Children are then told that the pinecone has little seeds inside and the red starfish (referred to as *"a starfish"*) has little eggs inside. Participants' task is to decide whether the target starfish (referred by the same label as Test B, *"a starfish"*) has little eggs inside or little seeds inside. For the test item depicted in Figure 5.1, 4-year-old children are likely to generalize that Test B rather than Test A shares the property with the target (Gelman & Markman, 1986; Sloutsky & Fisher, 2004a).

Proponents of alternative approaches to early induction propose markedly different explanations to account for this pattern of responses. According to the similarity-based approach, early in development common labels contribute to the overall perceived similarity of presented entities. Therefore, when both Test A and Test B share appearance features with the target (as in Figure 5.1), common labels increase the perceived similarity of Test B to the target, thus promoting generalization from Test B to the target (Sloutsky & Fisher, 2004a; Sloutsky & Lo, 1999). According to the naïve theory approach, "[C]hildren assume that a label provides direct access to an object's kind, and that an object's kind determines what nonobvious properties it is likely to have" (Jaswal, 2004, p. 1872). Therefore, we need to rely on paradigms other than the triad task to distinguish between the naïve theory and similarity-based approaches to induction. In the remaining sections, I will review evidence from two tasks designed to elucidate the mechanisms of early induction. I will specifically focus on (a) studies utilizing recognition memory tasks, and (b) studies manipulating attention allocated to labels and appearances.

Test A: **Pinecone**   Test B: **Starfish**

Target: **Starfish**

Figure 5.1   Example of a triad used originally in Gelman and Markman (1986) and in Sloutsky and Fisher (2004a) a replication of the original study.

MECHANISMS OF INDUCTION: EVIDENCE FROM MEMORY INTRUSIONS

The idea behind this line of research is that memory traces formed in the course of an induction task can elucidate the mechanisms of induction. The inspiration for this idea came from the line of research on true and false recognition in adults. In particular, it has been demonstrated that deep semantic processing increased the level of correct recognition of presented words compared to shallow processing. For example, Craik and Tulving (1975) presented participants with a list of words to study and asked them to answer one of the following three types of questions about each word: (a) whether the word is in capital letters (visual-processing condition), (b) whether the word rhymes with another word (phonemic-processing condition), or (c) whether the word can be used in a particular sentence (semantic-processing condition). The results indicated that participants could recognize more words on a subsequently administered memory test if they were engaged in semantic but not visual or phonemic processing. However, semantic processing results not only in higher rates of correct recognition but also in higher levels of false recognition of nonpresented items that are semantically related to the presented items (often referred to as *critical lures*) (e.g., Rhodes & Anastasi, 2000; Thapar & McDermott, 2001). At the same time, engaging participants in perceptual processing results in high rates of true recognition (often referred to as *hits*) and low false recognition (often referred to as *false alarms*) (Brainerd, Reyna, & Forrest, 2002; Marks, 1991). Therefore, if memory accuracy is measured as a difference between true and false recognition, then semantic processing leads to overall low recognition accuracy, whereas perceptual processing leads to overall high recognition accuracy in adults.

Research findings briefly described above suggest that a memory test administered after an induction task may reveal differential encoding of information during induction: Category-based induction should be based on semantic processing and thus lead to low discrimination of studied items from critical lures during a memory test (compared to a no-induction baseline condition). However, similarity-based induction should be based on shallow perceptual processing and thus lead to accurate discrimination of studied items from critical lures. To test these predictions, Sloutsky and Fisher developed an induction-then-recognition (hereafter, ITR) paradigm (Fisher & Sloutsky, 2004, 2005a; Sloutsky & Fisher 2004a, 2004b). The ITR paradigm consists of a recognition phase preceded by a study phase, which may include several conditions. In the *induction* condition, participants are first presented with a picture of an animal (i.e., a *cat*), and informed that the animal has "beta-cells inside its body." Participants are then presented with 30 pictures of animals (i.e., *cats, bears,* and *birds*), one picture at a time, and asked whether each presented animal also has beta-cells inside. After responding, participants are provided with "yes/no" feedback indicating that only *cats* (but not *bears* or *birds*) had beta-cells inside their bodies. In the *baseline* condition, participants are presented with pictures of animals identical to those presented in the induction condition, and instructed to remember these pictures as accurately as possible. Following the study phase, participants are presented with a recognition memory test, with half of the recognition pictures being old (i.e., *old cats* and *bears*) and half being new (i.e., novel *cats*, which served as critical lures, and *squirrels*, which served as catch items). Participants are asked to determine whether each picture presented during the recognition phase is "old" (i.e., exactly the same as the one presented during the study phase) or "new."

According to the naïve theory approach, mechanisms of induction are similar in children and adults: When presented with items that belong to familiar categories, similar to adults young children are assumed to perform induction relying on their knowledge of category membership. At the same time, the similarity-based approach argues that category-based induction is an outcome of learning and development, and unlike adults young children engage in similarity-based induction. Because, unlike adults, young children were expected to perform similarity-based induction, this reasoning led to a nontrivial prediction that after performing induction, young children may exhibit better performance than adults. In particular, it was predicted that adults should experience a postinduction decrease in recognition accuracy compared to the baseline condition, whereas young children should remain accurate in both the induction and baseline conditions.

These predictions have received empirical support, and Figure 5.2 presents a summary of results across three published reports that used the ITR paradigm (Fisher & Sloutsky, 2004, 2005a; Sloutsky & Fisher, 2004a, 2004b). Recognition accuracy in these studies was measured using memory sensitivity A-prime scores. A-prime is a nonparametric analogue of the signal detection d-prime statistic (Snodgrass & Corwin, 1988); an A-prime score of .5 indicates that participants do not discriminate old items from critical lures, and as discrimination accuracy increases, A-prime scores approach 1. As can be seen in Figure 5.2, after performing inductive generalizations with members of familiar animal categories, adults' memory accuracy attenuated markedly compared to the no-induction baseline (A-prime scores of .58 and .78 in the induction and baseline conditions, respectively), and these effects of induction were robust across a wide range of animal categories (Fisher & Sloutsky, 2004). At the same time, young children were accurate in both the baseline and induction conditions (A-prime scores of .74 and .68,

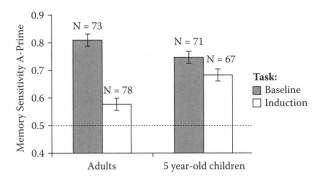

Figure 5.2 A-prime scores in 5-year-old children and adults aggregated across all published studies using the ITR paradigm. Error bars represent the standard errors of the mean. The dashed line represents the point of no sensitivity.

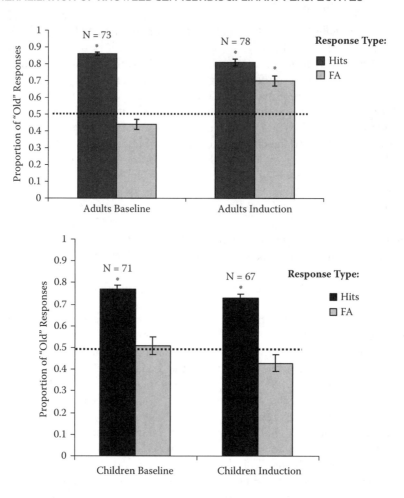

Figure 5.3 Proportions of hits and false alarms (FA) in adults (panel A) and children (panel B) aggregated across all published reports. Error bars represent the standard errors of the mean. Dashed line = chance level. ° = above chance, $p < .05$.

respectively). Further analyses of hits and false alarms, presented in Figure 5.3, indicated that postinduction decrease in recognition accuracy observed in adults stemmed from the pattern of high hits and high false alarms (.81 and .70, respectively), a "signature" pattern of deep semantic processing (Rhodes & Anastasi, 2000; Thapar & McDermott, 2001). A "signature" pattern of perceptual processing was found in the baseline condition in adults (the rate of hits and false alarms was .86 and .44, respectively) and in both induction and baseline conditions in 5-year-olds (the rate of hits and false alarms was .73 and .45 in the induction condition and .77 and .51 in the baseline condition).

These findings suggest that both children and adults amply encode item-specific information about presented entities in the baseline condition. However, when a recognition test is preceded by an induction task, adults are likely to encode predominantly category-level information, whereas children encode predominantly item-specific information. Therefore, when presented with members of familiar categories, children, unlike adults, do not spontaneously perform induction based on their knowledge of category membership, relying on item-level rather than category-level processing.

It could be argued that 5-year-olds exhibit no decrease in recognition accuracy after performing induction because they fail to perform induction accurately (i.e., to accurately infer during the study phase that the property of beta-cells should be attributed only to cats). However, evidence suggests that this was not the case: Even though adults' induction accuracy (89% correct) is somewhat higher than that of 5-year-olds (79% correct), young children's rate of correct induction was well above chance level (50%). Furthermore, the correlation between induction accuracy and A-prime scores was negligible, with correlation coefficients never surpassing ±0.1, suggesting that recognition accuracy after performing induction was not associated with less accurate induction performance.

Additional evidence supporting the argument that similarity-based generalization is a developmental default comes from a study in which participants were tested in the ITR paradigm while their eye movements were tracked. When adult participants were presented with pairs of pictures used in the ITR paradigm and asked to decide whether these pairs depicted identical animals (similarity judgment condition) or animals belonging to the same category (categorization condition), eye-tracking data indicated that category judgments elicited significantly fewer fixations than similarity judgments (2.6 and 5.2 fixations per item, respectively). Therefore, encoding item-specific information during induction should lead to attenuated visual fixations compared to the baseline, whereas encoding of item-specific information should not.

This prediction was supported when children and adults were tested in the induction and baseline conditions of the ITR paradigms while their eye movements were tracked (Fisher & Sloutsky, 2005b): As shown in Figure 5.4, when adult participants were tested in the baseline condition, they averaged 11.4 fixations per item during the study phase, and the number of fixations decreased dramatically in the induction condition, in which participants averaged 5.4 fixations per item. Children, on the other hand, exhibited no decrease in the number of visual fixations in the induction condition compared to the baseline (8.8 and 7.6 fixations, respectively). These findings indicate that attention to visual input was attenuated in the induction condition in adults but not in 5-year-olds.

These findings were further corroborated by an analysis of the two critical regions of the stimuli, the face region and the body region. First, young children sustained their attention to both face and body regions of the presented stimuli for equal amounts of time in the baseline and induction conditions; however, adults exhibited more protracted looking in the baseline condition than in the induction condition. More importantly, children and adults exhibited different patterns of fixations across the regions of interest. Figure 5.5 presents visual fixations on the face and the body regions in the induction condition adjusted to fixations in the baseline condition. Negative scores indicate a decrease in looking compared to the

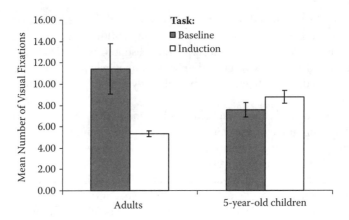

Figure 5.4   Mean number of visual fixations in children and adults in the induction and baseline conditions. Error bars represent standard errors of the mean.

baseline condition, whereas positive scores indicate an increase in looking. As can be seen in Figure 5.5a, adults exhibited a marked drop in looking in the induction compared to the baseline condition across both regions of interest. In contrast, young children increased looking to the face region in the induction condition compared to baseline (Figure 5.5b). Overall, eye-tracking data obtained in the ITR paradigm mirror recognition accuracy data, suggesting differential encoding patterns in 5-year-olds and adults during induction.

Follow-up studies (Fisher & Sloutsky, 2005a) indicated that transition from similarity-based to spontaneous category-based induction is gradual, such that 7-year-olds exhibit no postinduction decrease in recognition accuracy similar to 5-year-olds, whereas 11-year-olds exhibit some decrease, but the magnitude of this decrease is less than that of adults (Figure 5.6). However, these findings leave open a possibility that younger children encoded both category-level and item-specific information during induction, and encoding differences described above stemmed from younger children exhibiting greater interest in pictures than older children and adults. This possibility was addressed in a series of training studies, in which children were trained to perform "adult-like" category-based induction. In the course of training, children were presented with picture cards of familiar animals that belonged to categories other than the ones used in the induction-then-recognition paradigm (i.e., *bunnies*, *lions*, and *dogs*). Training consisted of six categorization trials (in which children were asked to group together animals of the same kind) and six induction trials (in which children were taught a novel property about one of the animals and asked which other animals would also have this property). The training was aimed at teaching children the following principles: (a) Animals that look similar belong to the same kind, (b) animals that belong to the same kind share many properties, and (c) animals that share the same name belong to the same kind and share many properties. Notice that according to the knowledge-based approach, the last two principles come in the form of conceptual assumptions that young children already possess even without training. Also, notice that

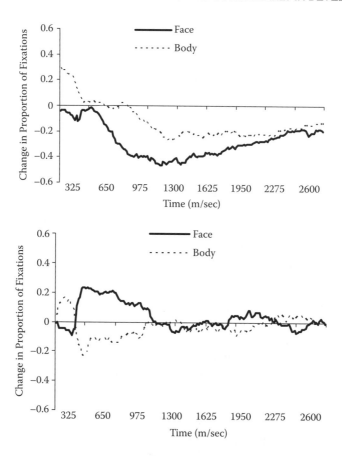

Figure 5.5 Visual fixations on the face and body regions of the target category in the induction condition compared to the baseline in adults (panel A) and children (panel B).

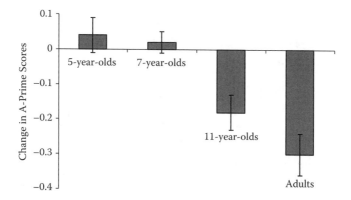

Figure 5.6 Change in the A-prime scores in the induction compared to the baseline conditions across different age groups. Error bars represent standard errors of the mean.

training did not deemphasize the importance of perceptual information, because children were repeatedly told that "animals that look alike are the same kind of animal that have the same name and similar stuff inside." Therefore, if in the previous experiments children were encoding category-level information in addition to item-specific information, this training should not have any effect on children's postinduction recognition accuracy. If, however, training taught children to perform category-based generalizations, then we should observe decreased postinduction recognition accuracy, and this prediction received empirical support: After being trained to perform category-based induction, recognition accuracy of both 5- and 7-year-olds decreased to the level of adults (Fisher & Sloutsky, 2005a). At the same time, training did not attenuate children's accuracy in the baseline condition—even after training, 5- and 7-year-olds exhibited high recognition accuracy. Therefore, observed postinduction decrease in recognition memory accuracy is attributable to specific effects of training to perform category-based induction rather than to general factors, such as fatigue. These findings suggest that both 5- and 7-year-olds could be successfully trained to perform category-based induction. However, a follow-up study indicated that only 7-year-olds can successfully retain the effects of training over a delay: When training in category-based induction and testing in the ITR paradigm were separated by a 2-week delay, the recognition memory of 5-year-olds returned to the high pretraining levels, whereas the accuracy of 7-year-olds did not (Figure 5.7).

Findings discussed above indicate that spontaneous category-based induction is likely a product of learning and development rather than a developmental default. It is possible that children learn through observation and interaction with the world that similar objects are likely to share many properties. It is also possible that children learn at school that things can be classified into categories and that category names are good predictors of category membership (with some rare exceptions, such as *seahorse* or *guinea pig*), with older children being more likely to retain this knowledge for longer periods of time than younger children. Therefore, based on the observation and interaction with objects in the real world, schooling,

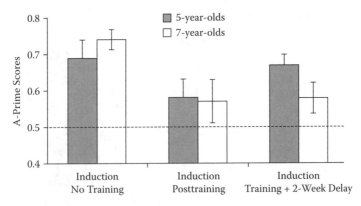

Figure 5.7   Pre- and posttraining A-prime scores in the induction condition in 5- and 7-year-old children.

and the development of general cognitive abilities, people may gradually develop conceptual beliefs and assumptions, such as the *label* and *category* assumptions.

MECHANISMS OF INDUCTION: EVIDENCE FROM FLEXIBLE ADJUSTMENT OF ATTENTION ALLOCATED TO LABELING AND APPEARANCE ATTRIBUTES

As discussed above, both the naïve theory approach and SINC recognize the importance of labels for induction early in development; however, they posit vastly different mechanisms by which labels influence induction. According to the former position, the importance of labels stems from top-down conceptual influences (such as the *label centrality assumption*), whereas according to the latter position it stems from a low-level attentional mechanism rooted in auditory overshadowing.

One way of distinguishing between the two hypotheses is to examine the flexibility of reliance on different sources of information, such as labels and appearances. If reliance on labels and appearances stems from the automatic allocation of attention to these sources of information, then changing the amount of attention directed to these attributes should affect children's willingness to rely on labels and appearances in a subsequent induction task. Conversely, if children believe that labels are more theoretically central than appearances, then such a change should be difficult if not impossible, because beliefs are notoriously resistant to change. In particular, when people hold strong beliefs, children as well as adults tend to disregard evidence inconsistent with their beliefs (Hamilton & Rose, 1980; Johnston & Jacobs, 2003; Lord, Ross, & Lepper, 1979; Meehan & Janik, 1990). Although the former theoretical position predicts a high degree of flexibility in relying on both labeling and appearance attributes, the latter position predicts that the status of conceptually central attributes (i.e., labels) and conceptually peripheral attributes (i.e., appearances) should be relatively fixed.

There is ample evidence suggesting that attention allocated to perceptual attributes can be flexibly changed in both animals and humans by manipulating their predictive values: When a particular cue is consistently predictive, attention allocated to this cue increases, whereas when a cue is consistently nonpredictive, attention allocated to this cue decreases (see Hall, 1991, for a review). It is therefore reasonable to expect that manipulating predictive values of labels and appearances should change reliance on these attributes in the course of induction. To test this hypothesis, Fisher and Sloutsky (2006) presented 5-year-old children with a task in which attention allocated to labels and appearances was manipulated through associative training. In particular, children were not explicitly instructed to increase attention to either attribute; instead, changes in the allocation of attention to labels and appearances were achieved through feedback.

Children were presented with a game in which a witch had captured many animals and kept them in a cage, and children could help free these animals by correctly answering the experimenter's questions. The questions asked during training were biological induction questions presented in the context of a triad task (see Figure 5.8a for an example of a training triad). For example, children could

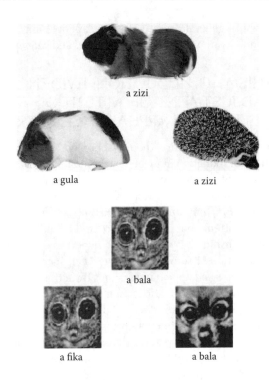

Figure 5.8   Example of a training triad (top) and a testing triad (bottom).

be told that the target item had "thick blood inside" and asked to predict whether Test Item A (that looked like the target) or Test Item B (that shared its name with the target) also had "thick blood inside." Children were provided with corrective feedback depending on the experimental condition. In the *label training condition*, children were provided with positive feedback for making label-based choices and with negative feedback for making appearance-based choices. In the *appearance training condition*, children were provided with positive feedback for making appearance-based choices and with negative feedback for making label-based choices. In the *baseline training condition*, children were presented with an unrelated task (i.e., they were asked to predict whether the target liked to play with Test A or Test B) and provided with positive feedback on 75% of the trials regardless of their responses: 75% of correct responses during training was the learning criterion used in the label and appearance training conditions, so therefore we provided participants in the baseline condition with positive feedback on 75% of the trials to ensure that participants in this condition received experience comparable to that of participants in the label and appearance training conditions, without affecting their allocation of attention to labeling and appearance attributes. Positive feedback was given in the form of short cartoons depicting an animal being freed from the cage. Negative feedback consisted of a still picture of the witch in front of the caged animals.

After training, children were presented with a testing task that, similar to a training task, consisted of biological induction questions presented in the context of a triad task (see Figure 5.8b for an example of a testing triad). If children rely on labels in the course of induction because they realize that labels convey category membership information and are therefore theoretically central properties of objects, then associative training should not change reliance on labels in the course of induction. In this case, there should be no change in induction performance in the appearance and label training conditions compared to the baseline. However, if reliance on labels and appearances during induction stems from automatic allocation of attention to these predictors, then changing the amount of attention allocated to labels and appearances should affect reliance on these predictors in a subsequent task. Fisher and Sloutsky's (2006) results point to the latter outcome. As Figure 5.9 illustrates, participants in the label training condition were more likely to rely on labels during a subsequent induction task compared to participants in the baseline condition (88% vs. 56% of label-based responses), whereas participants in the appearance training condition were more likely to rely on appearances compared to the baseline (32% vs. 56% of label-based responses). These findings suggest that the amount of attention allocated to labeling and appearance attributes can change flexibly in the course of associative training: When either attribute became consistently nonpredictive in the course of the training task, reliance on this attribute decreased markedly during testing.

Similar flexibility effects have also been demonstrated by Sloutsky and Spino (2004), who used different materials and a different procedure. In their task, 4-year-old children were presented with testing sets depicting fictitious animals, such that each test set consisted of a target and three test items, and each test item shared one feature with the target: appearance, label, or biological inheritance information (i.e., participants could be told that the target animal "gave birth" to

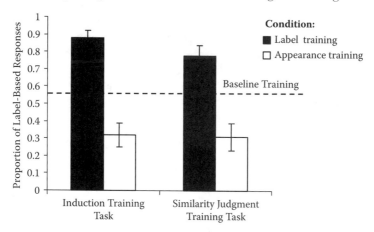

Figure 5.9   Proportion of label-based responses in the label and appearance training conditions in 5-year-old children. Dashed line represents the proportion of label-based responses in the baseline training condition. Error bars represent standard errors of the mean.

the test animal). Children were trained to rely on only one of these three features during induction using feedback-based associative training, and effects of this training were sustained for up to 3 months.

However, it is possible that the effects discussed above stemmed from spontaneous rule discovery rather than associative training. In particular, it is possible that participants discovered the "rule of the game" during training and then applied the rule during testing. There are two different types of rules that participants could discover during training. First, participants could discover a general rule of the following form: "In this game I need to choose animals with the same name/appearances." Participants could also discover a more specific rule, such as the following "In this game animals with the same name/appearances have similar stuff inside." If children discovered either of these rules, then effects of training described above stemmed from deliberate (i.e., strategic) focusing of attention on the predictive attributes rather than from nondeliberate (i.e., automatic) adjustment in attention allocated to labels and appearances. There is evidence suggesting that 3- to 5-year-old children often have difficulty with deliberate control of attention (Dempster, 1992; Hommel, Li, & Li, 2004; Napolitano & Sloutsky, 2004; Trick & Enns, 1998); however, the possibility that effects of training were driven by rule discovery was tested in two follow-up experiments.

Effects of nondeliberate adjustment in attention allocation can be differentiated from discovering a task-specific rule and deliberately focusing attention on predictive attributes when participants are presented with a different task during training and testing phases: If a rule is discovered during training in one task, there is no reason to expect that this rule should be applied to a *different* task presented in the course of testing. However, if training effects stem from nondeliberate adjustments in the allocation of attention to labels and appearances, for a specific set of tasks training effects may be evident even when different tasks are used in the course of training and testing. In particular, it has been suggested that for young children (a) labels are attributes of objects, contributing to a perceived similarity of presented entities; and (b) generalization is a function of perceptual similarity computed over weighted appearance and labeling attributes (Sloutsky & Fisher, 2004a). Therefore, if inductive generalization is a function of the overall similarity (with both labels and appearances contributing to similarity), then adjustment in the amount of attention allocated to labels and appearances in the course of similarity judgment should affect performance on a subsequent induction task.

To test the possibility that participants discovered a task-specific version of the rule, Fisher and Sloutsky (2006) changed the nature of the training task: Induction training (used in Experiment 1) was substituted with similarity judgment training. In the course of the similarity judgment task, children were asked whether the target looks more like Test A or Test B, and provided with feedback that rewarded label-based choices in the label training condition and appearance-based choices in the appearance training condition. If, during similarity judgment training, children discover a rule of the form "The ones that have the same name are similar" (in the label training condition) or "The ones that look alike are similar" (in the appearance training condition), then this rule should not be applied during the testing phase, which uses a *different* task (i.e., an inductive generalization instead of a similarity judgment task). In this case, there should be no effects of similarity judgment training on children's induction performance. However, if training effects described above stemmed not from discovering a task-specific rule and deliberately focusing on the predictive attributes, but from nondeliberate adjustment in the amount of attention allocated to labels and appearances, then similarity judgment training should affect performance on an induction task. The latter prediction was supported: As shown in Figure 5.9, participants who were trained to rely on labels in a similarity judgment task were more likely to rely on labels on a subsequent induction task compared to the baseline (78% vs. 56% of label-based responses), whereas participants who were trained to rely on appearances in a similarity judgment task were more likely to rely on appearances on a subsequent induction task compared to the baseline (31% vs. 56% of label-based responses). These findings suggest that it is unlikely that effects of induction training described above stemmed from discovering a task-specific version of the rule. At the same time, these findings provide additional support for the idea that early inductive generalization is a function of perceived similarity automatically computed over labeling and appearance attributes.

However, the possibility remains that training effects discussed above could also stem from discovering a general (rather than a task-specific) version of the rule, such as the following: "In this game, choose the one with the same name." To test this possibility, in the next experiment we substituted associative (i.e., feedback-based) training with an explicit explanation of the rule. If effects of training described above stemmed from children first discovering a general version of the rule during training and then applying the rule during testing, then children should have no difficulty following the rule when it is explained to them. Prior to testing, participants were told that either names or appearances were "not important in this game" (in the *ignore labels* and *ignore appearances* conditions, respectively), and asked to answer the experimenter's questions based only on the other available attribute (i.e., appearances in the ignore labels condition and labels in the ignore appearances condition). Participants were then introduced to a stuffed animal named Zizi and told that Zizi is going to play the game after they are done. Participants were asked to help Zizi play the game well by explaining to him the rule of the game. All children were successfully able to do so, thus demonstrating understanding of the rule. In the course of testing, participants were reminded of the rule at the onset of *each* induction trial. At the conclusion of testing, participants were asked to remind Zizi what the rule of the game was, and all children were successfully able to do this as well.

Performance in the ignore labels and ignore appearances conditions was compared to performance in three baseline conditions: the *no instructions baseline condition* (in which participants were given no special instructions to attend to or ignore either attribute), *no labels baseline condition* (in which no labels were presented during induction so that children could respond only on the basis of appearance information), and *no appearances condition* (in which no appearance information was presented during induction so that children could respond only on the basis of label information; this manipulation was achieved by presenting participants with three pictures of identical trees and telling them that the animals were hiding behind the trees). If effects of training in the previous study stemmed from rule discovery and deliberate focusing on predictive attributes, then participants should be successful in following the rule presented by the experimenter at the onset of *each* trial. In this case, the level of performance in the ignore labels and ignore appearances conditions should be (a) different from the no instructions baseline and (b) comparable to the level of performance in the no labels condition and no appearances condition, respectively. However, an opposite pattern of performance was observed: As shown in Figure 5.10, instructing children to ignore labeling or appearance attributes at the onset of each trial did not change their performance compared to the no instructions baseline, whereas children had no difficulty relying on the labeling and appearance attributes alone when no conflicting information was presented. These findings render it unlikely that effects of training presented in Figure 5.8 stemmed from discovering a general version of the rule rather than from nondeliberate adjustment in attention allocated to labeling and appearance attributes in the course of associative training.

Results presented above indicate that reliance on labeling and appearance attributes in the course of induction is flexible: When either attribute became consistently nonpredictive in the course of training, reliance on this attribute decreased markedly during testing. At the same time, such flexibility in 5-year-old children could be achieved only through associative training but not through deliberate instructions. Overall, these results challenge the position that effects of labels on induction stem from young children's belief in their conceptual importance: It is not clear how this hypothesis can account for the fact that associative training, but not explicit instructions, resulted in flexible shifts of attention away from predictors that are claimed to be theoretically central (i.e., linguistic labels) to those that are claimed to be theoretically peripheral (i.e., appearances). At the same time, these findings support the notion that reliance on labels and appearances in the course of

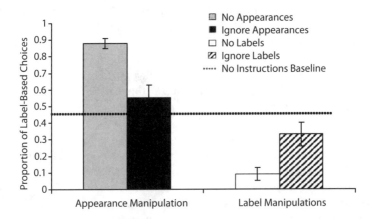

Figure 5.10 Proportion of label-based responses in an inductive generalization task in 5-year-old children under *no instructions* and *explicit instructions* conditions.

induction stems from automatic allocation of attention to predictive attributes and not from theoretical beliefs about the centrality of certain attributes over others.

ALIGNING THEORETICAL ASSUMPTIONS WITH A BROADER BODY OF KNOWLEDGE

Evidence about the mechanisms of induction early in development obtained from the studies on memory intrusions and flexible adjustment in attention allocated to various object attributes provides support to the view that early generalization relies predominantly on the low-level mechanisms of perception, attention, and memory. At the same time, this evidence challenged the view that these low-level mechanisms are insufficient and conceptual assumptions are necessary to account for induction early in development. However, theories can and should be evaluated not only on the basis of whether they can generate supporting evidence but also on the basis of the consistency of their underlying assumptions with a broader body of knowledge.

According to the naïve theory approach, sophisticated behaviors exhibited early in development are based on representational constraints, limiting the dimensions of the environment that learners attend to (Gelman, 2003; Gelman & Medin, 1993; Keil et al., 1998; Woodward, 2000). In particular, it has been argued that children's categories are constructed "on the basis of children's beliefs and assumptions about the world and the way language works" (Jaswal, 2004). According to the alternative approach, early generalization is based on the process of automatic computation of the overall similarity of presented entities (Sloutsky, 2003; Sloutsky & Fisher, 2004a, 2004b, 2005). Proponents of this approach have argued that early learning is constrained by the regularities in the input and information processing rather than representational constraints. In particular, when a certain cue is highly predictive in a certain context, attention allocated to this cue within this context automatically increases, whereas attention to cues that have low predictive power in the same context automatically decreases (Fisher & Sloutsky, 2006; Sloutsky & Fisher, 2008).

In other words, both approaches assume some sort of attentional selectivity allowing children to allocate attention to properties relevant to the task at hand and ignore irrelevant information. However, assumed mechanisms of this selectivity are radically different. On the one hand, it is argued that this early selectivity is automatic and "relatively inaccessible to deliberate and strategic controls" (Smith, Jones, & Landau, 1996, p. 144; see also Samuelson & Smith, 2000; Sloutsky, 2003; Sloutsky & Fisher, 2005). On the other hand, it has been suggested that even early in development, generalization could be a reasoning process relying on "conscious and deliberate weighting and ignoring of different aspects of the situation" (Gelman & Medin, 1993, p. 164; see also Keil, 1991). However, although both of these theoretical approaches are internally consistent, it is important to consider the consistency of their underlying assumptions with the general processing constraints early in development.

The ability to reason in a conscious and deliberate manner and to ignore information irrelevant to the task at hand requires a rather high degree of executive control, "the ability to orchestrate thought and action in accordance with internal goals" (Miller & Cohen, 2001). There is evidence that rudimentary elements of executive control are present by the end of the first year of life; however, it is not until later in development that children can voluntarily engage and disengage their attention (Ruff & Rothbart, 1996). The following then becomes a crucial question: Is voluntary selective attention sufficiently developed to support conceptually driven learning in infancy and early childhood? In other words, do young learners have sufficient control to inhibit attention to perceptually salient but conceptually irrelevant cues, allocate their attention to conceptually relevant cues, and switch attention among cues (because different cues can be relevant for different tasks)?

Research suggests that even newborns are not indifferent to what they attend to, preferring to look at some visual stimuli over others (Fantz, 1963). However, this selectivity can be characterized as stimulus driven or automatic, rather than person driven or voluntary: Early selectivity is driven by the properties of the stimulus, such as its brightness, intensity, and novelty (Ruff & Rothbart, 1996), rather than by infants' intentions. Transition from stimulus-driven to person-driven selectivity takes place during the preschool years (Rueda, Posner, & Rothbart, 2005; Ruff & Rothbart, 1996), with immaturity of executive control being documented in a variety of different tasks (Akshoomoff, 2002; Napolitano & Sloutsky, 2004; Robinson & Sloutsky, 2004; Zelazo, Frye, & Rapus, 1996; for discussion, see Fisher, 2007). Difficulties in performing tasks requiring voluntary control of attention have been attributed to the immaturity of the prefrontal cortex (PFC) (Bunge, Dudukovic, Thomason, Vaidya, & Gabrieli, 2002; Miller & Cohen, 2001). In particular, there is neuroimaging and postmortem evidence indicating that the PFC follows a delayed maturation course compared to other brain areas (Bunge et al.; Casey, Giedd, & Thomas, 2000; Durston et al., 2002). Furthermore, prefrontal lesions in adults and nonhuman primates lead to impaired performance on the tasks requiring executive control (Miller & Cohen). Overall, currently there is no evidence to support the possibility suggested by Gelman and Medin (1993) that attention to various attributes during induction early in development could be based on deliberate allocation of attention.

CONCLUSIONS

Adult models of induction discussed at the beginning of the chapter are likely poor approximations of induction early in development for two main reasons. First, adult models assume reliance on the knowledge of categories in the course of induction. For instance, even Sloman's (1993) feature-based model of induction relies on the computation of similarity relations between *categories* of items rather than *individual* entities. However, findings emerging from the induction-then-recognition paradigm indicate that 4- to 7-year-old children are unlikely to encode category membership of presented entities in the course of induction (even when these entities belong to familiar categories). Second, adult models of induction involve a reasoning component, and reasoning is a process that likely requires deliberate control of attention. However, research on development of executive attention suggests that young children's ability to focus and shift attention deliberately may not be developed enough to support reasoning. As discussed above, both of these criticisms apply to the naïve theory approach as well as models of mature induction. SINC, on the other hand, does not presuppose knowledge of categories and reliance on this knowledge during induction, and well-developed executive attention early in development. Therefore, SINC and theory underlying SINC can successfully account for children's performance on traditional induction tasks, as well as predict new phenomena, such as flexibility in relying on labeling and appearance attributes and effects of induction on recognition memory. These findings add to the body of literature suggesting that associative mechanisms play an important role in the learning of human infants and adults as well as many other species (Hall, 1991; Smith, 2000), whereas deliberate reasoning appears to be not only uniquely human but also a relatively late developmental achievement. Therefore, although there exist separate plausible accounts of early and mature induction that would be consistent with all available data, this remains a realm of future reseach.

REFERENCES

Akshoomoff, N. (2002). Selective attention and active engagement. *Developmental Neuropsychology, 22,* 625–642.

Baldwin, D. A., Markman, E. M., & Melartin, R. L. (1993). Infants' ability to draw inferences about nonobvious object properties: Evidence from exploratory play. *Child Development, 64,* 711–728.

Brainerd, C. J., Reyna, V. F., & Forrest, T. J. (2002). Are young children susceptible to the false-memory illusion? *Child Development, 73,* 1363–1377.

Bunge, S. A., Dudukovic, N. M., Thomason, M. E., Vaidya, C. J., & Gabrieli, D. E. (2002). Immature frontal lobe contributions to cognitive control in children: Evidence from fMRI. *Neuron, 33,* 1–20.

Casey, B. J., Giedd, J. N., & Thomas, K. M. (2000). Structural and functional brain development and its relation to cognitive development. *Biological Psychology, 54,* 241–257.

Craik, F. I., & Tulving, E. (1975). Depth of processing and the retention of words in episodic memory. *Journal of Experimental Psychology: General, 104,* 268–294.

Dempster, F. N. (1992). The rise and fall of the inhibitory mechanism: Toward a unified theory of cognitive development and aging. *Developmental Review, 12,* 45–75.

Durston, S., Thomas, K. M., Yang, Y., Uluğ, A. M., Zimmerman, R. D., & Casey, B. J. (2002). A neural basis for the development of inhibitory control. *Developmental Science, 5,* 9–16.

Fantz, R. L. (1963). Pattern vision in newborn infants. *Science, 140,* 296–297.

Fisher, A. V. (2007). Are developmental theories of learning paying attention to attention? *Cognition, Brain, and Behavior, 11,* 635–646.

Fisher, A. V., & Sloutsky, V. M. (2004). Categorization and memory: Representation of category information increases memory intrusions. In *Proceedings of the XXVI annual conference of the Cognitive Science Society.* Mahwah, NJ: Erlbaum.

Fisher, A. V., & Sloutsky, V. M. (2005a). When induction meets memory: Evidence for gradual transition from similarity-based to category-based induction. *Child Development, 76,* 583–597.

Fisher, A. V., & Sloutsky, V. M. (2005b). Effects of category labels on early induction. Paper presented at the 4th biannual conference of the Cognitive Development Society.

Fisher, A. F., & Sloutsky, V. M. (2006). Flexible attention to labels and appearances in early induction. In R. Sun & N. Miyake (Eds.), *Proceedings of the 28th annual conference of the Cognitive Science Society*. Mahwah, NJ: Erlbaum.

Gelman, S. A. (2003). *The essential child: Origins of essentialism in everyday thought*. Oxford: Oxford University Press.

Gelman, S. A., & Coley, J. (1991). Language and categorization: The acquisition of natural kind terms. In S. A. Gelman & J. P. Byrnes (Eds.), *Perspectives on language and thought: Interrelations in development* (pp. 146–196). New York: Cambridge University Press.

Gelman, S. A., & Markman, E. (1986). Categories and induction in young children. *Cognition, 23*, 183–209.

Gelman, S. A., & Medin, D. L. (1993). What's so essential about essentialism? A different perspective on the interaction of perception, language, and concrete knowledge. *Cognitive Development, 8*, 164.

Hall, G. (1991). *Perceptual and associative learning*. New York: Oxford University Press.

Hamilton, D. L., & Rose, T. L. (1980). Illusory correlation and the maintenance of stereotypic beliefs. *Personality and Social Psychology, 39*, 832–845.

Heit, E. (1998). A Bayesian analysis of some forms of inductive reasoning. In M. Oaksford & N. Chater (Eds.), *Rational models of cognition* (pp. 248–274). Oxford: Oxford University Press.

Hommel, B., Li, K. Z. H., & Li, S.-C. (2004). Visual search across the life span. *Developmental Psychology, 40*, 545–558.

Jaswal, V. K. (2004). Don't believe everything you hear: Preschoolers' sensitivity to speaker intent in category induction. *Child Development, 3*, 279–300.

Johnston, K. E., & Jacobs, J. E. (2003). Children's illusory correlations: The role of attentional bias in group impression formation. *Journal of Cognition and Development, 4*, 129–160.

Keil, F. C. (1991). Intuitive belief systems and informal reasoning in cognitive development. In J. F. Voss, D. N. Perkins, and Segal (Eds.), *Informal Reasoning and Education*, 247–263, Earlbaum.

Keil, F. C., Smith, W. C., Simons, D. J., & Levin, D. T. (1998). Two dogmas of conceptual empiricism: Implications for hybrid models of the structure of knowledge. *Cognition, 65*, 103–135.

Kemp, C., & Tenenbaum, J. B. (2009). Structured statistical models of inductive reasoning. *Psychological Review, 116*(1), 20–58.

Lord, C. G., Ross, L., & Lepper, M. R. (1979). Biased assimilation and attitude polarization: The effects of prior theories on subsequently considered evidence. *Journal of Personality and Social Psychology, 37*, 2098–2109.

Marks, W. (1991). Effects of encoding the perceptual features of pictures on memory. *Journal of Experimental Psychology: Learning, Memory, and Cognition, 17*, 566–577.

McClelland, J. L., & Rogers, T. T. (2003). The parallel distributed processing approach to semantic cognition. *Nature Reviews Neuroscience, 4*, 1–5.

Meehan, A. M., & Janik, L. M. (1980). Illusory correlation and the maintenance of sex role stereotypes in children. *Sex Roles, 22*, 83–95.

Miller, E. K., & Cohen, J. D. (2001). An integrative theory of prefrontal cortex function. *Annual Review of Neuroscience, 24*, 167–202.

Napolitano, A. C., & Sloutsky, V. M. (2004). Is a picture worth a thousand words? Part II: The flexible nature of modality dominance in young children. *Child Development, 75*, 1850–1870.

Osherson, D. N., Smith, E. E., Wilkie, O., Lopez, A., & Shafir, E. (1990). Category-based induction. *Psychological Review*, 97, 185–200.

Rakison, D. H. (2003). Parts, motion, and the development of the animate–inanimate distinction in infancy. In D. H. Rakison & L. M. Oakes (Eds.), *Early category and concept development: Making sense of the blooming, buzzing confusion* (pp. 159–192). New York: Oxford University Press.

Rhodes, M. G., & Anastasi, J. S. (2000). The effects of a levels-of-processing manipulation on false recall. *Psychonomic Bulletin & Review*, 7, 158–162.

Rips, L. J. (1975). Inductive judgments about natural categories. *Journal of Verbal Learning and Verbal Behavior*, 14, 665–681.

Rips, L. J., Shoben, E. J., & Smith, E. E. (1973). Semantic distance and the verification of semantic relations. *Journal of Verbal Learning and Verbal Behavior*, 12, 1–20.

Robinson, C. W., & Sloutsky, V. M. (2004). Auditory dominance and its change in the course of development. *Child Development*, 75, 1387–1401.

Robinson, C. W., & Sloutsky, V. M. (2007). Visual processing speed: Effects of auditory input on visual processing. *Developmental Science*, 10, 734–740.

Rueda, R. M., Posner, M. I., & Rothbart, M. K. (2005). The development of executive attention: Contributions to the emergence of self-regulation. *Developmental Neuropsychology*, 28, 573–594.

Ruff, H. A., & Rothbart, M. K. (1996). *Attention in early development*. New York: Oxford University Press.

Samuelson, L., & Smith, L. B. (2000). Grounding development in cognitive process. *Child Development*, 71(1), 98–106.

Sanjana, N., & Tenenbaum, J. B. (2002). Bayesian models of inductive generalization. In S. Becker, S. Thrun, & K. Obermayer (Eds.), *Advances in neural information processing systems* (pp. 51–58). Cambridge, MA: MIT Press.

Sloman, S. A. (1993). Feature-based induction. *Cognitive Psychology*, 25, 231–280.

Sloman, S. A. (1998). Categorical inference is not a tree: The myth of inheritance hierarchies. *Cognitive Psychology*, 35, 1–33.

Sloutsky, V. M. (2003). The role of similarity in the development of categorization. *Trends in Cognitive Sciences*, 7, 246–251.

Sloutsky, V. M., & Fisher, A. V. (2004a). Induction and categorization in young children: A similarity-based model. *Journal of Experimental Psychology: General*, 133, 166–188.

Sloutsky, V. M., & Fisher, A. V. (2004b). When development and learning decrease memory: Evidence against category-based induction in children. *Psychological Science*, 15, 553–558

Sloutsky, V. M., & Fisher, A. V. (2005). Similarity, induction, naming, and categorization (SINC): Generalization or inductive reasoning? Response to Heit and Hayes. *Journal of Experimental Psychology: General*, 134, 606–611

Sloutsky, V. M., & Fisher, A. V. (2008). Attentional learning and flexible induction: How mundane mechanisms give rise to smart behaviors. *Child Development*, 79, 639–651.

Sloutsky, V. M., & Lo, Y.-F. (1999). How much does a shared name make things similar? Part 1. Linguistic labels and the development of similarity judgment. *Developmental Psychology*, 35, 1478–1492.

Sloutsky, V. M., Lo, Y.-F., & Fisher, A. V. (2001). How much does a shared name make things similar: Linguistic labels and the development of inductive inference. *Child Development*, 72, 1695–1709.

Sloutsky, V. M., & Napolitano, A. (2003). Is a picture worth a thousand words? Preference for auditory modality in young children. *Child Development*, 74, 822–833.

Sloutsky, V. M., & Robinson, C. W. (2008). The role of words and sounds in infants' visual processing: From overshadowing to attentional tuning. *Cognitive Science*, 32(2), 342–365.

Sloutsky, V. M., & Spino, M. A. (2004). Naïve theory and transfer of learning: When less is more and more is less. *Psychonomic Bulletin & Review, 11*, 536–541.

Smith, L. B. (2000). Avoiding associations when it's behaviorism you really hate. In R. Michnick Golinkoff, K. Hirsh-Pasek, L. Bloom, L. B. Smith, A. L. Woodward, N. Akhtar, et al. (Eds.), *Becoming a word learner: A debate on lexical acquisition*. New York: Oxford University Press.

Smith, L. B., Jones, S. S., & Landau, B. (1996). Naming in young children: A dumb attentional mechanism. *Cognition, 60*, 143–171.

Snodgrass, J. G., & Corwin, J. (1988). Pragmatics of measuring recognition memory: Applications to dementia and amnesia. *Journal of Experimental Psychology: General, 117*, 34–50.

Thapar, A., & McDermott, K. B. (2001). False recall and false recognition induced by presentation of associated words: Effects of retention interval and level of processing. *Memory & Cognition, 29*, 424–432.

Trick, L. M., & Enns, J. T. (1998). Life-span changes in attention: The visual search task. *Cognitive Development, 13*(3), 369–386.

Welder, A. N., & Graham, S. A. (2001). The influences of shape similarity and shared labels on infants' inductive inferences about nonobvious object properties. *Child Development, 72*, 1653–1673.

Woodward, A. L. (2000). Constraining the problem space in early word learning. In *Becoming a word learner: A debate on lexical acquisition*. London: Oxford University Press.

Zelazo, P. D., Frye, D., & Rapus, T. (1996). An age-related dissociation between knowing rules and using them. *Cognitive Development, 11*, 37–63.

6

Prior Experience Shapes Abstraction and Generalization in Language Acquisition

JILL LANY and REBECCA L. GÓMEZ

G eneralization, or the ability to extend what one has learned beyond instances or exemplars already encountered, is central to human behavior. To give just a few examples, we easily recognize new instances of dogs, apples, and cars, and we recognize the labels for those objects even when they are pronounced in an unfamiliar voice or accent. The study of generalization thus sheds light on fundamental learning processes across diverse domains, such as perception, categorization, and language acquisition.

One important question addressed by studies of generalization is how abstractions are formed, or how common structure is distilled from a set of specific instances. As a result of this process, new exemplars can be appropriately recognized as instances of a learned pattern or category, and learning is thereby generalized. In this chapter we use the term *generalization* to mean the extension of knowledge to new instances or situations (the process itself), and *abstraction* to refer to the learning, or representational changes, supporting the ability to generalize. Numerous studies have focused on the factors contributing to successful generalization, or what information learners use to form and extend abstractions. On one view, learners use perceptual information, or how objects look, feel, and sound, to form categories such as *dog* and recognize new instances of such categories. On another view, these categories are formed on the basis of conceptual information, such as what it *means* to be a dog, or what a dog *is*, rather than on perceptual features (for a discussion of this issue, see Mandler, 2000a, 2000b; and replies by Carey, 2000; Gibson, 2000; Nelson, 2000; Quinn & Eimas, 2000; and Reznik, 2000; as well as Goldstone & Barsalou, 1998).

In the domain of language acquisition, there are similar questions about what kinds of information infants use to form syntactic categories, such as *noun* and *verb*. For example, words from different syntactic categories have different semantics (e.g., nouns often, but not always, refer to objects, people, or animals, whereas verbs generally refer to actions or events). Words from different syntactic categories also have different distributional properties, or tend to be used in different sentence contexts (e.g., nouns often follow determiners such as *a* and *the*, whereas verbs are more likely to occur after pronouns such as *he* or *she*). Furthermore, words from different syntactic categories have different phonological properties, with nouns tending to have more syllables than verbs, and verbs more often having consonant cluster onsets and reduced vowels (Christiansen & Monaghan, 2006; Farmer, Christiansen, & Monaghan, 2006; Kelly, 1992; Monaghan, Chater, & Christiansen, 2005). Some have argued that grouping words into syntactic categories primarily relies on semantic information (Pinker, 1984), whereas others argue that infants begin to form such categories by attending to words' distributional and phonological properties (e.g., Christiansen & Monaghan; Gerken, Wilson, & Lewis, 2005; Gómez & Lakusta, 2004; Maratsos & Chalkley, 1980; Mintz, 2003; Mintz, Newport, & Bever, 2002; Monaghan et al.).

A second focus of research on generalization is the extent to which learners' sensitivity to a pattern is abstract, or separable from the specific characteristics of learned instances. This is an important question because it sheds light on how far learning can be extended beyond familiar instances. Learners' ability to generalize is a particularly contentious issue in the domain of language acquisition because language use requires substantial abstraction beyond the specific sentences a learner has already encountered, and the extent to which these grammatical patterns are learned versus innately given is a matter of long-standing controversy. Understanding the degree to which we can learn and generalize grammatical patterns is thus critical to accounts of language acquisition. In studies that assess how abstract learning is, participants are typically trained on strings of spoken syllables conforming to a pattern, and then tested on strings in which each syllable was replaced by a tone or, to test the extent of transfer even further, an arbitrary graphic symbol (Altmann, Dienes, & Goode, 1995).

Thus far, we have discussed two aspects of generalization. The first concerns what kinds of input learners require to form a particular abstraction, such as whether semantic versus distributional and phonological cues are used to form syntactic categories. The second concerns the nature of the abstraction itself, or what has actually been learned or generalized about a pattern, as in the case of studies of transfer. Although these questions are central to understanding generalization and abstraction, a focus on these two aspects alone can lead to a static view of generalization, in which learners encounter a set of items and abstract commonalities among them. The abstraction that results might be used to recognize novel exemplars and even to infer something about them, but it is inert, neither changing nor interacting with subsequent learning of new patterns or structures. In the real world, and particularly during early development, learning is unlikely to end with the formation of an isolated abstraction. Instead, learners encounter new examples that may change the nature of a previously formed abstraction and the generalizations they are able to make. Thus, a comprehensive understanding of generalization entails the study of how abstractions are shaped by ongoing learning, either by being adapted in response to new information or by supporting the learning of new and more complex patterns.

Gerken (2005) took this into account when she investigated how infants' generalizations are shaped and later modified by subsequent learning. She first tested how the nature of learners' input affects their generalizations by exposing 9-month-old infants to a subset of strings generated by an artificial language. Critically, the particular set of strings that infants heard was chosen to highlight different aspects of the language structure. For example, one group of infants heard four words in which the first two syllables (referred to as A *syllables*) were identical, but the third (referred to as a B *syllable*) was different from the first two (e.g., *leledi*). Across the input words, all of the A and B syllables were different (i.e., the words were *leledi, wiwije, jijili,* and *dedewe*), and thus these strings conformed to an AAB pattern. A second group of infants also heard strings in which the first two syllables were the same, but the final syllable was always *di* (i.e., *leledi, wiwidi, jijidi,* and *dededi*). These words are consistent with an AAB pattern, in that the first two syllables of the word are identical and the last syllable is different. But because all words ended in *di*, infants could also learn an AA*di* pattern, or "All words end in *di*." Infants appeared to learn the abstraction that most closely fit their input, generalizing to AAB words containing novel syllables in the first case, and forming a narrower AA*di* abstraction in the latter case, generalizing to novel words only if they ended in the syllable *di*.

This first experiment addresses the question of how input properties contribute to generalization, or what kind of input is necessary to form a particular abstraction. More recently, Gerken (in press) has investigated how these generalizations are influenced by ongoing learning. They found that infants exposed to an AA*di* language enlarge their generalization if given exposure to instances that support the broader AAB generalization. In other words, even when trained predominantly on AA*di* words, if the last few familiarization words start with the AA pattern but end with a syllable other than *di*, these infants generalize to new AAB words in which the B syllable is not *di*. This demonstrates an impressive flexibility in generalization, and suggests that infants can rapidly change their generalizations to fit their experience.

In addition to adapting abstractions to accommodate new information, learners may also use one abstraction to form a new one. One example of this is the ability to "scaffold" sensitivity to complex or higher order structure on sensitivity to simpler structure. In the domain of word learning, Smith and colleagues (Colunga & Smith, 2003, 2005; Jones & Smith, 2002; Smith, Jones, Landau, Gershkoff-Stowe, & Samuelson, 2002) suggested that children initially learn word meanings through repeated associations between objects and labels, but once a critical mass of labels has been acquired, they detect higher order regularities that characterize those associations. For example, object labels such as *cup, ball,* and *phone* refer to a set of objects that have a common shape. Children may initially learn the association between the label *ball* and things that are round, and the association between *cup* and things that are cup shaped. A higher order abstraction that object labels tend to pick out groups of things with similar shapes (i.e., "X's are X shaped") might then emerge from these specific associations. Such a generalization allows children to extend object labels on the basis of objects' shape as opposed to other features, such as their color or texture. As a result, upon hearing the label *crayon* referring to a red crayon, they can use it to refer to new crayon-shaped objects regardless of their color. Thus, novice word learners slowly acquire specific label–object associations through repeated experience, but then higher order associations emerge that facilitate the rapid formation of new label–object associations, and the appropriate extension of those labels according to object shape.

These examples suggest that *generalization* is multifaceted and dynamic, encompassing the formation of an abstraction, the ability to recognize a new item as an instance of a pattern or abstraction, and the influence of such knowledge on the learning of new patterns. Although all three of these dimensions are critical aspects of learning, the role of prior learning in generalization is poorly understood because of the difficulty inherent in accurately measuring and quantifying prior experience. To illustrate with a simple example, the amount of experience a particular child has had with dogs—live dogs, toy dogs, pictures of dogs, or even the word *dog*—will differ depending on whether the child has a pet dog, reads books about dogs, sees dogs on television, and the like. Moreover, prior experience can impact many levels of sensitivity (e.g., sensory processing, stimulus familiarity, and the strength of associations between stimuli), and there is a great deal of potential for interaction between these experiences and maturational or developmental changes.

Despite the difficulty of identifying the relevant sources of prior experience, studying prior learning can provide insights into the learning mechanisms underlying sensitivity to different kinds of structure. A common approach to assessing the nature of learning mechanisms is to test what kinds of patterns learners successfully acquire, and where learning breaks down. This approach is quite valuable, yet it is also important to consider that what naïve learners can learn is often quite different than what can be acquired by more experienced learners. This is true in the field of language acquisition, where researchers have sought to establish limits on human learning mechanisms in order to better specify how language is acquired. To the extent that the ability to learn a pattern or structure is difficult to demonstrate within the context of an isolated learning experience, it is important to recognize that such learning may be bootstrapped from the learning of simpler structure. Theories taking prior experience into account may postulate very different kinds of learning mechanisms than those that do not, or may focus on a different aspect of the learning problem. For example, on one account, children's ability to rapidly acquire and appropriately extend object labels arises from innately given biases. Object kinds are one kind of relationship between items that children might use when extending labels (e.g., extending a label to an object of the same kind or category, such as extending *ball* to new balls and other round objects). However, another possibility would be extending labels on the basis of thematic relationships, or to objects that are closely associated, (e.g., extending the label *ball* to bats, because bats are used to hit balls). The fact that children are able to appropriately extend labels to novel objects within a category (i.e., to new instances of a ball, but not to thematically related objects like bats) is taken as evidence that they are innately constrained to privilege taxonomic relationships, or relationships between object kinds, in labeling tasks (Markman, 1990; Markman & Hutchison, 1984). By this view, learning focuses on the child's ability to extend these innate biases, but does not question how these biases come to exist. Because labels could, in theory, be extended on the basis of any number of properties, it is indeed difficult to explain how infants appropriately extend them based on taxonomic relationships and not thematic ones without considering the effect of learning many label–object type associations in which a particular label is applied to objects of the same shape, as per the work of Smith and colleagues (Colunga & Smith, 2003, 2005; Jones & Smith, 2002; Smith et al., 2002). Thus, considering the role that prior experience plays in acquisition may fundamentally change our theories of learning, as well as provide a basis for new theories.

In this chapter, we focus on the dynamic nature of learning and generalization in the acquisition of syntax-like structure in language. At the level of syntax, or word combinations, learners' sensitivity to grammatical patterns must generalize beyond familiar combinations of words (i.e., "The dog is barking" is a grammatical construction, but "Is dog the barking" is not) to how words of different categories can be combined (i.e., that determiners like *a* and *the* predict nouns such as *dog* and *cat*, whereas auxiliaries like *is* and *was* predict verbs like *barking* or *running*).

The challenge of learning these patterns may be lessened if some of these abstractions can be built upon lower-level sensitivity to language structure. As previously mentioned, the abstract principles governing *word learning* (i.e., the tendency to generalize labels on the basis of common shape) may arise from learning about individual label–object associations (Colunga & Smith, 2003, 2005; Jones & Smith, 2002; Smith et al., 2002). Here we focus on how prior learning might bootstrap sensitivity to complex *syntactic patterns*, and specifically how prior learning impacts the acquisition of nonadjacent dependencies in language, which are predictive relationships that do not occur in immediate sequence. These experiments focus on how nonadjacent relationships are learned. However, by focusing on how such learning builds upon prior experience, we can provide a unique window into learning and generalization more broadly.

ADJACENT AND NONADJACENT RELATIONSHIPS IN LANGUAGE

Adjacent relationships are those pertaining to elements that are in immediate sequence in time or space, whereas *nonadjacent relationships* pertain to elements that are separated by other elements. For example, the presence of a determiner such as *a* or *the* predicts the occurrence of a noun such as *dog* or *cat*. The noun might be adjacent to the determiner, as in "The dog ran away," but can also be nonadjacent, as in "The Smiths' dog ran away." Similarly, in the sentence "John is running in the race" the auxiliary *is* predicts the presence of *-ing*, as both are necessary to signal that the verb *run* is in the progressive tense; however, these elements are separated by the verb root itself. Interestingly, nonadjacent relationships can be more difficult for learners to acquire than adjacent ones (Gómez, 2002; Newport & Aslin, 2004).

Given the importance of nonadjacent relationships in language structure, it is critical to investigate how learners acquire them. One possibility is suggested by the nature of the language we use with infants: speech to infants and children tends to consist of shorter, simpler utterances than speech to adults (Newport, Gleitman, & Gleitman, 1977; Pine, 1994), and thus they may encounter adjacent dependencies between words and word categories before nonadjacent ones. It is thus possible that experience with adjacent relationships facilitates or generalizes to learning nonadjacent ones. We recently tested this hypothesis with adult learners by exposing them to a language with nonadjacent dependencies after exposure to either a language containing similar adjacent relationships, or a matched language lacking such relationships (Lany, Gómez, & Gerken, 2007). We first describe the structure of the artificial languages incorporating adjacent and nonadjacent structures, and then describe our experimental methodology.

LEARNING AN *AX BY* PATTERN

Our artificial language, containing adjacent relationships that consisted of the word categories denoted by *a*, *b*, *X*, and *Y*, was similar to artificial languages used by Braine (1987), Frigo and MacDonald (1998), Gerken et al. (2005), and Gómez and LaKusta (2004). This artificial language incorporated restrictions on how words from these categories were combined into strings, such that *a* elements were paired with *X* elements and *b* elements with *Y* elements, but not vice versa. Figure 6.1 presents a schematic of the *aX bY* pattern. Note that the *aX bY* pattern is similar to the co-occurrence relationship between determiners and nouns in English—determiners predict nouns (*the dog* is a grammatical sequence), whereas auxiliaries predict verbs (*is barking* is grammatical) but not nouns (*is dog* is an ungrammatical sequence). Thus, testing how learners acquire the *aX bY* structure sheds light on learning mechanisms relevant to natural language acquisition.

Studies investigating how *aX bY* patterns are acquired suggest that learners readily detect the positional regularities present in the language, such as whether a particular word always occurs in an initial or final position within a string (*a*'s and *b*'s occur in the string–initial position, whereas *X*'s and *Y*'s always occur in the

	X_1	X_2	X_3	X_4	X_5	X_6
a_1	a_1X_1	a_1X_2	a_1X_3	a_1X_4	a_1X_5	a_1X_6
a_2	a_2X_1	a_2X_2	a_2X_3	withheld	a_2X_5	a_2X_6

	Y_1	Y_2	Y_3	Y_4	Y_5	Y_6
b_1	b_1Y_1	b_1Y_2	b_1Y_3	withheld	b_1Y_5	b_1Y_6
b_2	b_2Y_1	b_2Y_2	b_2Y_3	b_1Y_4	b_2Y_5	b_2Y_6

Figure 6.1   A typical *aX bY* pattern. Learners are exposed to a subset of the grammatical pairings of markers and content words. Learners are tested to see if they will respond correctly to both heard and unheard (or withheld) pairings. Reprinted from *Cognitive Science*, 31, J. Lany, R. L. Gómez, and L. A. Gerken, "The role of prior experience in language acquisition," © 2007, with permission from the Cognitive Science Society.

final position; Smith, 1969). Learners also readily track co-occurrence information pertaining to individual words. For example, they are sensitive to the fact that a_1 is followed by X_1 and X_2 but not by Y_1 or Y_2 (Braine, 1987). This kind of co-occurrence information is also referred to as *distributional information*, or the likelihood that an element is preceded or followed by some other element.

The fact that X elements occur in similar distributional contexts (they occur with both a_1 and a_2), and those contexts are distinct from the contexts in which Y elements occur, is a cue that could be used to group X's and Y's into separate categories (Maratsos & Chalkley, 1980). Learners sensitive to the co-occurrence patterns of a, b, X, and Y categories (as opposed to individual elements) *should* generalize to novel aX and bY combinations. In other words, upon hearing the string a_1X_4, learners sensitive to the $aX bY$ structure should generalize to an a_2X_4 while rejecting b_1X_4 and b_2X_4 (see Figure 6.1). However, it seems that learning the co-occurrence relationships between word categories is heavily dependent on the presence of correlated cues to category membership (Braine, 1987; Frigo & MacDonald, 1998; Gerken et al., 2005; Gómez & Lakusta, 2004). For example, if X's share a common phonological property (e.g., the number of syllables they contain, or common morphology such as a distinctive ending) in addition to having similar distributional characteristics, learners successfully learn and generalize the category relationships. The overlap between distributional cues and phonological features is sometimes referred to as a *correlated cue*, as the two types of cues to category membership are totally or partially coupled to (or redundant with) one another. In this case, correlations between distributional and phonological cues seem to facilitate learning by highlighting the fact that a and b elements predict different word categories, such that learners notice the $aX bY$ dependencies because a's and b's more obviously predict different kinds of words. Importantly, in natural languages, words from different syntactic categories are distinguished by both distributional (Cartwright & Brent, 1997; Mintz, 2003; Mintz et al., 2002; Monaghan et al., 2005; Redington, Chater, & Finch, 1998) and phonological cues (Christiansen & Monaghan, 2006; Farmer et al., 2006; Kelly, 1992; Monaghan et al.).

GENERALIZING TO AN *ACX BCY* PATTERN

Previous studies (Braine, 1987; Frigo & MacDonald, 1998; Gerken et al., 2005; Gómez & LaKusta, 2004; Wilson, 2002) focused on how the $aX bY$ pattern is abstracted, and the degree to which it is dependent on the presence of correlated cues between words' distributional and perceptual features. We extended these findings by asking how exposure to an artificial language containing co-occurrence restrictions affects subsequent acquisition of a related artificial language. Given that languages contain both adjacent and nonadjacent co-occurrence restrictions on word categories, we asked whether learners who had acquired adjacent relationships would be able to generalize to nonadjacent ones, which are generally quite difficult for learners to acquire.

To test this, we first trained and tested adult learners on an $aX bY$ language, and then trained and tested them on an $acX bcY$ language that contained completely novel vocabulary. Like the *aX bY* language, the *acX bcY* language required learning about co-occurrence restrictions on word categories. However, it differed in that the *aX* and *bY* relationships were separated by a *c* element. We compared this group to a control group exposed to an "uncued" *aX bY* language, which contained the same vocabulary as the *aX bY* language, but lacked correlated cues marking *X*'s and *Y*'s (*a*'s and *b*'s could occur with both *X*'s and *Y*'s). Both groups were then transferred to the *acX bcY* language. In previous research (Braine, 1987; Frigo & MacDonald, 1998; Smith, 1969), learners exposed to languages lacking correlated cues typically fail to learn the category-level co-occurrence relationships. We therefore predicted that learners given prior experience with the *aX bY* language would learn the nonadjacent relationships in the *acX bcY* language better than the control learners who lacked such prior experience. Critically, the two groups' prior experience was matched in terms of all other aspects of the language (e.g., vocabulary and positional information). Exposure to category-level dependencies was the only difference, thus providing a stringent comparison.

THE ARTIFICIAL LANGUAGE MATERIALS

The aX bY Language (The Experimental Group)

We constructed two versions of an *aX bY* language, each with its own vocabulary (see Table 6.1). In both versions the *a* and *b* elements were monosyllabic, whereas the *X* and *Y* elements were bisyllabic, and were distinguished from each other by the presence of a distinctive ending. For example, in Version A, all *X*'s ended in the syllable *oo*, and all *Y*'s ended in the syllable *ee*, and in Version B the *X*'s ended in the syllable *it* and *Y*'s ended in the syllable *ul*.

TABLE 6.1   *aX bY* Language Materials

Version A				Version B			
a_1 X_{1-6}	a_2 X_{1-6}	b_1 Y_{1-6}	b_2 Y_{1-6}	a_1 X_{1-6}	a_2 X_{1-6}	b_1 Y_{1-6}	b_2 Y_{1-6}
alt juhnoo	pel juhnoo	erd nusee	vot nusee	ush keerit	dak keerit	ong bivul	rud bivul
alt wifoo	pel wifoo	erd lemee	vot lemee	ush lepit	dak lepit	ong choopul	rud choopul
alt tamoo	pel tamoo	erd sufee	vot sufee	ush feegit	dak feegit	ong habbul	rud habbul
alt feenoo	pel feenoo	erd vaymee	vot vaymee	ush soolit	dak soolit	ong jerul	rud jerul
alt zinoo	pel zinoo	erd raffee	vot raffee	ush yohvit	dak yohvit	ong pogul	rud pogul
alt deechoo	pel deechoo	erd durpee	vot durpee	ush zamit	dak zamit	ong vummul	rud vummul

Source: Adapted from *Cognitive Science, 31*, J. Lany, R. L. Gómez, and L. A. Gerken, "The role of prior experience in language acquisition," © 2007, with permission from the Cognitive Science Society.

Note: Learners were exposed to a subset of the 24 possible strings from either Version A or B, and then tested on familiar and withheld grammatical strings, and on nongrammatical strings.

The Uncued aX bY Language (The Control Group)

We created two versions (A and B) of an uncued language by recombining elements from the $aX\,bY$ languages (see Table 6.2). In the $aX\,bY$ language, a elements were paired with X_{1-6}, and b elements were paired with Y_{1-6}. Because all X's and Y's were marked with a phonological feature indicating their category membership, this language contained correlated cues to category membership. In the uncued language, however, a elements were paired with X_{1-3} and Y_{4-6}, whereas b elements were paired with Y_{1-3} and X_{4-6}. The uncued language thus contained distributional cues to word categories (a's and b's predicted nonoverlapping sets of X's and Y's) while lacking correlated cues to category membership (a's and b's did not each predict a set of words with a common ending). However, the uncued language was perfectly matched to the $aX\,bY$ language in its vocabulary, positional regularities (a's and b's occurred string-initially, and X's and Y's occurred string-finally), and prosody. Thus, the only difference between the uncued and $aX\,bY$ languages was the presence of correlated cues indicating co-occurrence restrictions between a's and X's, and between b's and Y's in the $aX\,bY$ language.

The acX bcY Language

The $acX\,bcY$ language was created from the $aX\,bY$ language by inserting a c element between the a and X elements, and between the b and Y elements. There were two versions (A and B) of the $acX\,bcY$ language, each with distinct vocabulary (see Table 6.3).

Immediately following exposure to each of the languages, participants were tested using a grammaticality–judgment task. They listened to a set of strings, one at a time, and were instructed to make a "yes or no" judgment as to whether the string followed the pattern present in the training language. They heard four kinds of test strings. There were two kinds of grammatical strings—strings that had been presented during their training set (grammatical-heard strings, or GH),

TABLE 6.2   Uncued aX bY Language Materials

Version A				Version B			
$aX_{1-3},\,aY_{4-6}$		$bX_{4-6},\,bY_{1-3}$		$aX_{1-3},\,aY_{4-6}$		$bX_{4-6},\,bY_{1-3}$	
a_1	a_2	b_1	b_2	a_1	a_2	b_1	b_2
alt juhnoo	pel juhnoo	erd nusee	vot nusee	ush keerit	dak keerit	ong feegit	rud feegit
alt wifoo	pel wifoo	erd lemee	vot lemee	ush lepit	dak lepit	ong soolit	rud soolit
alt feenoo	pel feenoo	erd durpee	vot durpee	ush zamit	dak zamit	ong yohvit	rud yohvit
alt sufee	pel sufee	erd tamoo	vot tamoo	ush bivul	dak bivul	ong habbul	rud habbul
alt vaymee	pel vaymee	erd zinoo	vot zinoo	ush choopul	dak choopul	ong jerul	rud jerul
alt rafee	pel rafee	erd deechoo	vot deechoo	ush pogul	dak pogul	ong vummul	rud vummul

Source: Adapted from *Cognitive Science*, 31, J. Lany, R. L. Gómez, and L. A. Gerken, "The role of prior experience in language acquisition," © 2007, with permission from the Cognitive Science Society.

Note: Learners were exposed to a subset of the 24 possible strings from either Version A or B, and then tested on familiar and withheld grammatical strings, and on nongrammatical strings.

TABLE 6.3   *acX bcY* Language Materials

Version A					Version B				
a	**b**	**c**	**X**	**Y**	**a**	**b**	**c**	**X**	**Y**
alt	erd	hes	juhnoo	nusee	ush	ong	tash	keerit	bivul
pel	vot	kaf	wifoo	lemee	dak	rud	fis	lepit	choopul
		sij	tamoo	sufee			nep	feegit	habbul
			feenoo	vaymee				soolit	jerul
			zinoo	raffee				yohvit	pogul
			deechoo	durpee				zamit	vummul

Source: Adapted from *Cognitive Science, 31,* J. Lany, R. L. Gómez, and L. A. Gerken, "The role of prior experience in language acquisition," © 2007, with permission from the Cognitive Science Society.

Note: These elements were combined into strings of the form *acX* and *bcY.* Learners were exposed to a subset of the 72 possible strings from either Version A or B, and were then tested on familiar and withheld grammatical strings, and on nongrammatical strings.

and grammatical strings that had been withheld during familiarization (grammatical-unheard strings, or GUH). There were also two kinds of nongrammatical strings: NGH strings, which were "matched" to GH strings in that they consisted of the same X and Y elements paired with an ungrammatical a or b element. Thus, if a_1X_1, or "alt feenoo," was a GH test string, then b_1X_1, or "erd feenoo," was an NGH test string. The NGUH test strings were nongrammatical strings matched to grammatical-unheard (GUH) strings, such that if a_2X_2, or "pel wifoo," was a GUH test string, then b_2X_2, or "vot wifoo," was an NGUH test string. Test strings were divided into two blocks, with the instructions repeated in between.

The GH, GUH, NGH, and NGUH test strings from the *acX bcY* language were chosen in the same manner. In the *acX bcY* familiarization strings, all c elements were preceded equally often by a and b elements, and were followed by X elements as often as by Y elements. As a result, adjacent relationships (i.e., the $ac, bc, cX,$ and cY transitions) could not be used to discriminate between grammatical and nongrammatical strings at test. Thus, only learners focusing on nonadjacent relationships could discriminate grammatical from nongrammatical test strings. Training on this task took place over 2 consecutive days. On the first day, participants in both groups were familiarized with their respective training language followed by a test. The experimental group was exposed to Version A or B of the *aX bY* language, whereas the control was exposed to Version A or B of the uncued language. On the second day, participants in both groups were trained and tested on an *acX bcY* language, such that if they had been exposed to a Version A language on day 1, they were exposed to Version B of the *acX bcY* language on day 2, and vice versa. Thus, the language that participants learned on day 2 was instantiated in new vocabulary.

We first report performance on the *acX bcY* language. Table 6.4 displays the mean endorsement rates to the four kinds of test strings separately for the control (the uncued *aX bY* language group) and experimental groups (the *aX bY* language group). Significantly, higher endorsement rates to GH strings than to UGH strings could represent both memory for familiar combinations and the *a_X b_Y* pattern,

TABLE 6.4   Adults' Mean Endorsement Rates With Standard Error of the Mean in Parentheses

	Block 1				Block 2			
	GH	GUH	NGH	NGUH	GH	GUH	NGH	NGUH
Day 1								
Control (Uncued)	.78	.68	.68	.64	.67	.61	.65	.57
	(.044)	(.038)	(.048)	(.050)	(.040)	(.043)	(.039)	(.045)
Experimental (aX bY)	.86	.76	.64	.51	.78	.62	.58	.53
	(.031)	(.044)	(.057)	(.064)	(.035)	(.046)	(.052)	(.049)
Day 2								
Control (acX bcY)	.64	.56	.63	.60	.63	.62	.62	.55
	(.030)	(.042)	(.038)	(.036)	(.042)	(.036)	(.037)	(.043)
Experimental (acX bcY)	.73	.68	.57	.53	.62	.60	.53	.53
	(.031)	(.043)	(.048)	(.046)	(.044)	(.035)	(.045)	(.046)

Source: Reprinted from *Cognitive Science*, *31*, J. Lany, R. L. Gómez, and L. A. Gerken, "The role of prior experience in language acquisition," © 2007, with permission from the Cognitive Science Society.

Note: *GH* refers to grammatical-heard test strings, and *NGH* to their matched nongrammatical counterparts. Similarly, *GUH* refers to grammatical-unheard test strings, and *NGH* to their nongrammatical counterparts.

whereas greater endorsement of GUH than UGUH strings represents generalization to novel strings, and thus indicates sensitivity to the *a_X b_Y* pattern.

As predicted, we found that learners in the experimental group were better able to learn the nonadjacent dependencies than controls. The experimental group's advantage held primarily in the first test block, with sensitivity to the nonadjacent relationships declining over the course of testing. This decline may be due to the fact that participants are exposed to both grammatical and ungrammatical strings at test, and exposure to these ungrammatical instances may weaken sensitivity to the grammatical nonadjacent relationships. Participants in the experimental group discriminated GH and GUH strings from ungrammatical ones in the first test block, but the control group showed no such discrimination.

Our hypothesis is that the experimental group's enhanced sensitivity to the nonadjacent relationships in the *acX bcY* language results from their prior experience with the adjacent co-occurrence restrictions on similar categories in the *aX bY* language. This hypothesis is in line with the control versus experimental groups' performance during the initial learning phase of the experiment (see Table 6.4). The control group's recognition of familiar strings was marginal, and they showed no ability to generalize to unheard strings. We can therefore conclude that the control group was not sensitive to the co-occurrence restrictions of their language, and even their ability to recognize familiar stings was weak.

In contrast, the experimental group's performance on the *aX bY* language suggests that they successfully acquired the language's co-occurrence restrictions (see Table 6.4). Their sensitivity to GH strings was robust across the two blocks of testing, and they were also able to discriminate GUH strings from nongrammatical ones in the first test block. This sensitivity to the *aX bY* pattern, which was absent in learners exposed to the uncued language, is likely to have promoted the experimental group's sensitivity to the nonadjacent relationships in the $acX\,bcY$ language.

These findings suggest that sensitivity to adjacent relationships between word categories in the $aX\,bY$ language bootstraps learning of the more difficult nonadjacent relationships in the $acX\,bcY$ language. Additionally, because the $aX\,bY$ and uncued languages were equivalent in their vocabulary, prosodic characteristics, and positional regularities of a, b, X, and Y elements, the findings rule out the possibility that exposure to these surface properties, rather than the $aX\,bY$ structure itself, accounts for the experimental group's ability to learn the $acX\,bcY$ language.

WHAT ABOUT INFANTS?

As previously mentioned, the fact that speech addressed to infants and toddlers tends to consist of shorter, simpler utterances than speech addressed to adults (Newport et al., 1977; Pine, 1994) suggests that infants may be exposed to simple constructions before more complex ones. For example, they are likely to hear sentences like "It's a ducky," in which the predictive relationship between determiners and nouns holds between adjacent elements, before sentences like "It's a yellow ducky," in which these elements are separated by an adjective. Thus, it is plausible that infants' experience with adjacent dependencies in simple constructions plays a role in their ability to learn nonadjacent dependencies in their native language. However, for this to be so, infants would have to generalize from adjacent to nonadjacent dependencies despite the fact that the surface features of the strings containing such relationships can be quite dissimilar. The adult learners in our studies were able do so, but there is considerable debate over the extent to which infants can achieve such generalization in early language acquisition (see Tomasello, 2000; versus Fisher, 2002; and Gertner, Fisher, & Eisengart, 2006 for an interesting debate of this issue), and thus the extent to which infants benefit from prior experience in language acquisition is unclear. We thus asked whether infants' experience with adjacent dependencies between word categories bootstraps sensitivity to nonadjacent ones in an artificial language–learning task despite differences in the surface features of the strings containing adjacent versus nonadjacent dependencies.

We also probed the factors influencing the developmental trajectory of sensitivity to nonadjacent dependencies. Although infants demonstrate robust sensitivity to adjacent relationships by 8 months of age, several studies suggest that the ability to learn nonadjacent dependencies emerges somewhere between 15 and 18 months (Gómez & Maye, 2005; Santelmann & Jusczyk, 1998). Although maturation and concomitant increases in processing capacity surely contribute to older infants' ability to learn nonadjacent relationships, prior experience may also play a critical role. Although older infants have increased processing and memory capacity (Bauer, 2007), they also have more language experience. In particular, they have accumulated more experience with simpler constructions in which dependent elements are adjacent. This experience could enhance their sensitivity to nonadjacent relationships between such elements, perhaps by attuning them to these predictive relationships. Because Gómez and Maye found that the ability to track nonadjacent relationships does not emerge until 15 months of age, even under the most conducive circumstances, we tested whether 12-month-old infants could learn them if given relevant prior experience.

As a first step, we tested whether infants' experience with adjacent relationships enables them to recognize nonadjacent relationships containing the same items. To do so, infants would have to generalize from two- to three-element strings with a novel prosodic contour, and containing both a novel word separating familiar *aX* and *bY* elements, and novel adjacent relationships involving that word. Infants in the experimental group were familiarized to an artificial language containing adjacent dependencies, and then were habituated to strings in which those dependencies were nonadjacent. Control infants were familiarized to a language lacking predictive adjacent dependencies, but matched to the consistent language in vocabulary and prosody, and were then habituated to strings containing nonadjacent dependencies, just like the experimental group. The logic of the habituation phase was that infants sensitive to the nonadjacent relationships should dishabituate to strings containing violations of those dependencies in the subsequent test phase. If prior exposure to adjacent dependencies is critical to detecting nonadjacent ones, experimental but not control infants should dishabituate to such violations.

Familiarization

The *aX bY* Language   Infants in the experimental group were familiarized to *aX bY* strings while playing quietly with a parent and an experimenter (see Table 6.5). The language was similar to the *aX bY* language used with adults, the major exception being that syllable number was used to distinguish *X* elements from *Y* elements (*X*'s were monosyllabic, and *Y*'s were disyllabic).

The Uncued *aX bY* Language   Infants in the control group were familiarized with an uncued *aX bY* language similar to the uncued language used in the adult experiment (see Table 6.5). Each phrase of the language contained an *a, b, X,* and *Y* element; however, *a*'s occurred with all six *X*'s and *Y*'s, as did the *b* elements. The uncued language provided equivalent exposure to individual vocabulary elements as the *aX bY* language, and had the same intonational patterns and positional regularities as the *aX bY* language. Critically, however, it did not conform to an *aX bY* generalization.

The Habituation Test

The *acX bcY* Language   After familiarization to either the *aX bY* language or the uncued *aX bY* language, infants were exposed to strings containing nonadjacent relationships. These strings were created by inserting a novel *c* element, *hes*, in the center of *aX* and *bY* phrases (see Table 6.5). This allowed us to test whether familiarization to adjacent relationships facilitates detection of these relationships when they are subsequently presented nonadjacently. Although 12-month-olds typically fail to detect nonadjacent relationships, we hypothesized that infants familiarized

TABLE 6.5   Materials Testing 12-month-olds' Ability to Generalize to Familiar Combinations

Familiarization Materials

a	b	X	Y
ong	alt	coomo	deech
erd	ush	fengle	ghope
		kicey	jic
		loga	skige
		paylig	vabe
		wazil	tam

Habituation Materials

a_1X	a_2X	b_1Y	b_2Y
ong hes coomo	erd hes coomo	alt hes deech	ush hes deech
ong hes fengle	erd hes fengle	alt hes ghope	ush hes ghope
ong hes kicey	erd hes kicey	alt hes jic	ush hes jic
ong hes loga	erd hes loga	alt hes skige	ush hes skige
ong hes paylig	erd hes paylig	alt hes vabe	ush hes vabe
ong hes wazil	erd hes wazil	alt hes tam	ush hes tam

Test Materials (With Violations of the aX and bY Relationships)

a_1Y	a_2Y	b_1X	b_2X
ong hes deech	erd hes deech	alt hes coomo	ush hes coomo
ong hes ghope	erd hes ghope	alt hes fengle	ush hes fengle
ong hes jic	erd hes jic	alt hes kicey	ush hes kicey
ong hes skige	erd hes skige	alt hes loga	ush hes loga
ong hes vabe	erd hes vabe	alt hes paylig	ush hes paylig
ong hes tam	erd hes tam	alt hes wazil	ush hes wazil

Note: The familiarization elements were combined to form *aX*, *bY*, *aY*, and *bX* strings. Experimental infants were exposed only to *aX* and *bY* strings, whereas control infants were exposed to *aX*, *bY*, *aY*, and *bX* strings. The two groups were exposed to the same set of habituation and test strings.

to the *aX bY* language (the experimental group) should detect the nonadjacent relationships between these categories, given their exposure to these co-occurrence restrictions. In contrast, infants exposed to the uncued *aX bY* language (control infants) lacked experience with co-occurrence restrictions between word categories and should therefore fail to detect the nonadjacent relationships.

We tested sensitivity to the nonadjacent relationships using a habituation paradigm. Habituation is a procedure commonly used to test infant learning, and relies on infants' tendency to show increased attention to a novel stimulus relative to a stimulus with which they have just been extensively familiarized. During habituation and test trials, infants were seated on their parent's lap facing a screen. At the start of each trial, an animated cartoon of a baby jumping up and down (an "attention getter") was projected onto the screen. Once infants looked at the attention getter, the image changed to a colorful bull's-eye, and habituation strings began to play from a speaker. The strings continued to play until infants looked away from the screen for more than 2 consecutive seconds. At that point, a new trial began. Thus, infants controlled how long they listened to the strings by looking toward and away from the pictures. In these experiments, the habituation procedure entailed exposing infants to the *acX bcY* strings until they showed a 50% decrement in attention to them. Once they had habituated to those strings, they were presented with two test trials, which were identical to habituation trials except that infants heard strings containing nongrammatical nonadjacent relationships (see Table 6.5). Infants tracking the nonadjacent relationship in the habituation strings should notice that the relationships in the test strings contain violations of those relationships, and should therefore listen to them longer than to the last two habituation strings.

As a baseline, we used the listening time to the final two habituation trials that were given prior to the test trials. Indeed, the experimental group listened significantly longer to the test trials than to the final two habituation trials, although there was no difference in the control group's mean listening to these trials (see Figure 6.2). This suggests that only the experimental group, who had prior experience with adjacent *aX* and *bY* combinations, noticed the nonadjacent relationships in the habituation strings. A comparison of the two groups' increase in listening time to the test strings was marginally significant, suggesting that the experimental group's sensitivity to the nonadjacent dependencies was greater than that of the control group's. The two groups did not differ in the amount of their exposure to nonadjacent dependencies during habituation, and thus differences in exposure cannot account for the experimental group's advantage.

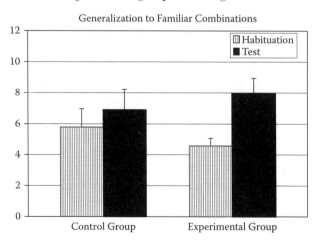

Figure 6.2   12-month-olds' mean listening times to the final two habituation trials and the two test trials. A significant increase in looking to the two test trials over the final two habituation trials suggests that infants noticed the nonadjacent relationships in the habituation strings, and the violation of these relationships in the test strings. Experimental but not control infants showed such an increase.

These findings suggest that 12-month-old infants can detect nonadjacent relationships if they first have experience with adjacent relationships between those elements. We recently extended these findings to ask whether 12-month-olds can generalize from adjacent relationships between word categories to unfamiliar nonadjacent combinations (Lany & Gómez, 2008). We addressed this question by familiarizing infants to an $aX\ bY$ language with particular aX and bY strings withheld. They will then be habituated to strings containing nonadjacent relationships between the withheld aX and bY combinations, and tested with strings containing violations of the nonadjacent relationships. These infants, but not control infants, recognized *new* instances of that pattern when they occurred nonadjacently.

CONCLUSIONS

These data shed light on how potentially difficult natural language structures might be acquired. Despite the fact that dependencies between syntactic categories can be nonadjacent, naïve learners in our experiments had difficulty acquiring them. Importantly, if given prior experience with similar adjacent dependencies, both infant and adult learners were able to generalize to nonadjacent ones. This suggests that the complex abstractions involved in language can be built on experience with simpler structure.

Our findings also speak to learners' ability to generalize or transfer across instances with dissimilar surface structure, a central topic in the domain of language acquisition. Recent empirical studies of infant learning indicate that infants can form generalizations relevant to natural language syntax. For example, Gómez and Lakusta (2004) demonstrated that 12-month-old infants can learn and generalize co-occurrence relationships between word categories. Specifically, infants exposed to an $aX\ bY$ language similar to that used in our infant experiment can discriminate between grammatical and ungrammatical strings containing novel X and Y elements if they are marked by distinctive features (i.e., X's are bisyllabic and Y's are monosyllabic). Moreover, using a similar paradigm, Gerken et al. (2005) found that if a majority of X's and Y's were marked by distinctive features, 17-month-old infants can learn the predictive relationships between a's and b's and those distinctive features. Moreover, they found that infants generalized to novel strings even if the X's and Y's in those strings were not marked by distinctive features. In other words, if infants heard a_1X_4 but not a_2X_4, they were able to distinguish a_2X_4 from b_1X_4 and b_2X_4 (see Figure 6.1) even if X_4 lacked the distinctive feature marking X's. The current findings extend previous work on generalization by showing that infants can generalize from adjacent to nonadjacent co-occurrence relationships based on their prior learning, and can even do so across strings with substantial differences in their surface characteristics (i.e., the familiarization and habituation strings differed in length and prosodic contour, contained a novel c word, and contained novel transitions between words). Our findings with adult learners provide evidence for even further generalization, as prior experience with adjacent relationships facilitated learning nonadjacent relationships in a language with completely novel vocabulary. Thus, these experiments add to the evidence that learners can form generalizations relevant to natural language structure, and also suggest that prior experience facilitates this process.

Additionally, these findings highlight the complex and dynamic nature of generalization in learning. Although generalization entails the ability to recognize a new item as a member of a learned category or pattern, it also frequently involves the influence of prior learning on acquiring novel structure, such as the adaptation of an abstraction in the face of new information (as in the case of Gerken and Tenenbaum's [in preparation] study of infants learning an AAB pattern), as well as the influence of such knowledge on learning new patterns (as in the case of Smith and colleagues' studies of children learning about the relationship between labels and the perceptual features of different objects; Colunga & Smith, 2003, 2005; Jones & Smith, 2002; Smith et al., 2002). These aspects of generalization may complement one another, and in fact, it can be difficult to draw a firm distinction between them. For example, it may be difficult to clearly distinguish between a case where a higher order generalization arises from lower order associations, and a case where encountering new examples enlarges a generalization. For example, in our experiment testing adults' transfer from an $aX\,bY$ language to an $acX\,bcY$ language, it may be that experience with the $aX\,bY$ language results in sensitivity to the specific predictive relationships between words in the initial position and the endings on adjacent words. Upon exposure to another language containing similar predictive relationships between words and the endings on nonadjacent words, learners may form a *higher order* abstraction that words belong to categories marked by salient features, and there are restrictions on how these word categories can be combined. Another possibility is that exposure to the $aX\,bY$ language results in sensitivity to the fact that word categories in sentence-initial position predict the category of adjacent words, and that exposure to the $acX\,bcY$ language encourages the *broader* generalization that there are co-occurrence restrictions on word categories, be they adjacent or nonadjacent. On either explanation, however, learners' sensitivity to this complex nonadjacent structure rests upon their prior learning of adjacent relationships.

In this chapter we have discussed evidence from our own studies as well as others' examining how learning and generalization build upon prior experience in the domain of language acquisition. These principles apply across many other domains, such as processing of visual patterns (Needham, Dueker, & Lockhead, 2005; Quinn & Bhatt, 2005; Quinn & Schyns, 2003), and suggest that considering how learning and generalization are shaped and supported by prior experience provides a unique window into the acquisition of complex and abstract patterns.

ACKNOWLEDGMENTS

The research reported in this chapter was supported by the National Institute of Child Health and Human Development (HD42170–07). The authors thank the infants and families who participated in this research; Linsey Curtis, Crystal Garcia, Tara Grover, and Katherine Chapman for assistance with data collection; and Jessica Payne for helpful comments on earlier drafts.

REFERENCES

Altmann, G. T. M., Dienes, Z., & Goode, A. (1995). Modality independence of implicitly learned grammatical knowledge. *Journal of Experimental Psychology: Learning, Memory, and Cognition, 21*, 899–912.

Bauer, P. J. (2007). *Remembering the times of our lives: Memory in infancy and beyond.* Mahwah, NJ: Laurence Erlbaum Associates.

Braine, M. D. S. (1987). What is learned in acquiring word classes: A step toward an acquisition theory. In B. MacWhinney (Ed.), *Mechanisms of language acquisition.* Hillsdale, NJ: Erlbaum.

Carey, S. (2000). The origins of concepts. *Journal of Cognition and Development, 1*, 37–41.

Cartwright, T. A., & Brent, M. R. (1997). Syntactic categorization in early language acquisition: Formalizing the role of distributional analysis. *Cognition, 63*, 121–170.

Christiansen, M. H., & Monaghan, P. (2006). Discovering verbs through multiple-cue integration. In K. Hirsh-Pasek & R. M. Golinkoff (Eds.), *Action meets word: How children learn verbs.* Oxford: Oxford University Press.

Colunga, E., & Smith, L. B. (2003). The emergence of abstract ideas: Evidence from networks and babies. *Philosophical Transactions of the Royal Society, 358*, 1205–1214.

Colunga, E., & Smith, L. B. (2005). From the lexicon to expectations about kinds: A role for associative learning. *Psychological Review, 112*, 347–382.

Farmer, T. A., Christiansen, M. H., & Monaghan, P. (2006). Phonological typicality influences on-line sentence comprehension. *Proceedings of the National Academy of Sciences, 103*, 12203–12208.

Fisher, C. (2002). The role of abstract syntactic knowledge in language acquisition: A reply to Tomasello (2000). *Cognition, 82*, 259–278.

Frigo L., & MacDonald, J. (1998). Properties of phonological markers that affect the acquisition of gender-like subclasses. *Journal of Memory and Language, 39*, 448–457.

Gerken, L. A. (2005). Decisions, decisions: Infant language learning when multiple generalizations are possible. *Cognition, 98*, B67–B64.

Gerken, L. A. (in press). Infants use rational decision criteria for choosing among models of their input. *Cognition.*

Gerken, L. A., Wilson, R., & Lewis, W. (2005). Seventeen-month-olds can use distributional cues to form syntactic categories. *Journal of Child Language, 32*, 249–268.

Gertner, Y., Fisher, C., & Eisengart, J. (2006). Learning words and rules: Abstract knowledge of word order in early sentence comprehension. *Psychological Science, 17*, 684–691.

Gibson, E. J. (2000). Commentary on perceptual and conceptual processes in infancy. *Journal of Cognition and Development, 1*, 43–48.

Goldstone, R. L., & Barsalou, L. W. (1998). Reuniting perception and conception. *Cognition, 65*, 231–262.

Gómez, R. L. (2002). Variability and detection of invariant structure. *Psychological Science, 13*, 431–436.

Gómez, R. L., & Lakusta, L. (2004). A first step in form-based category abstraction in 12-month-old infants, *Developmental Science, 7*, 567–580.

Gómez, R. L., & Maye, J. (2005). The developmental trajectory of nonadjacent dependency learning. *Infancy, 7*, 183–206.

Jones, S. S., & Smith, L. B. (2002). How children know the relevant properties for generalizing object names. *Developmental Science, 5*, 219–232.

Kelly, M. H. (1992). Using sound to solve syntactic problems: The role of phonology in grammatical category assignments. *Psychological Review, 99*, 349–364.

Lany, J., & Gómez, R. L. (2008). Twelve-month-old infants benefit from prior experience in statistical learning. *Psychological Science, 19*, 1247–1252.

Lany, J., Gómez, R. L., & Gerken, L. A. (2007). The role of prior experience in language acquisition. *Cognitive Science, 31*, 481–507.

Mandler, J. M. (2000a). Perceptual and conceptual processes in infancy. *Journal of Cognition and Development, 1*, 3–36.

Mandler, J. M. (2000b). Reply to commentaries on perceptual and conceptual processes in infancy. *Journal of Cognition and Development, 1*, 67–79.

Maratsos, M., & Chalkley, M. A. (1980). The internal language of children's syntax: The ontogenesis and representation of syntactic categories. In K. Nelson (Ed.), *Children's language* (Vol. 2). New York: Gardner Press.

Markman, E. M. (1990). Constraints children place on word meanings. *Cognitive Science, 14*, 57–77.

Markman, E. M., & Hutchison, J. E. (1984). Children's sensitivity to constraints on word meaning: Taxonomic vs. thematic relations. *Cognitive Psychology, 16*, 1–27.

Mintz, T. H. (2003). Frequent frames as a cue for grammatical categories in child directed speech. *Cognition, 90*, 91–117.

Mintz, T. H., Newport, E. L., & Bever, T. G. (2002). The distributional structure of grammatical categories in speech to young children. *Cognitive Science, 26*, 393–424.

Monaghan, P., Chater, N., & Christiansen, M. H. (2005). The differential role of phonological and distributional cues in grammatical categorization. *Cognition, 96*, 143–182.

Needham, A., Dueker, G. L., & Lockhead, G. (2005). Infants' formation and use of categories to segregate objects. *Cognition, 94*, 215–240.

Nelson, K. (2000). Global and functional: Mandler's perceptual and conceptual processes in infancy. *Journal of Cognition and Development, 1*, 49–54.

Newport, E. L., & Aslin, R. N. (2004). Learning at a distance I: Statistical learning of non-adjacent dependencies. *Cognitive Psychology, 48*, 127–162.

Newport, E. L., Gleitman, H., & Gleitman, L. R. (1977). Mother, I'd rather do it myself: Some effects and non-effects of maternal speech style. In C. Snow & C. Ferguson (Eds.), *Talking to children: Language input and acquisition* (pp. 109–149). Cambridge: Cambridge University Press.

Pine, J. M. (1994). The language of primary caregivers. In C. Gallaway & C. J. Richards (Eds.), *Input and interaction in language acquisition* (pp. 38–55). Cambridge: Cambridge University Press.

Pinker, S. (1984). *Language learnability and language development*. Cambridge, MA: Harvard University Press.

Quinn, P. C., & Bhatt, R. S. (2005). Learning perceptual organization in infancy. *Psychological Science, 16*, 511–515.

Quinn, P. C., & Eimas, P. D. (2000). The emergence of category representations during infancy: Are separate and conceptual processes required? *Journal of Cognition and Development, 1*, 55–61.

Quinn, P. C., & Schyns, P. G. (2003). What goes up may come down: Perceptual process and knowledge access in the organization of complex visual patterns by young infants. *Cognitive Science, 27*, 23–935.

Redington, M., Chater, N., & Finch, S. (1998). Distributional information: A powerful cue for acquiring syntactic categories. *Cognitive Science, 22*, 435–469.

Reznik, S. J. (2000). Interpreting infant conceptual categorization. *Journal of Cognition and Development, 1*, 63–66.

Santelmann, L. M., & Jusczyk, P. W. (1998). Sensitivity to discontinuous dependencies in language learners: Evidence for limitations in processing space. *Cognition, 69*, 105–134.

Smith, K. H. (1969). Learning co-occurrence restrictions: Rule learning or rote learning? *Journal of Verbal Behavior, 8*, 319–321.

Smith, L. B., Jones, S. S., Landau, B., Gershkoff-Stowe, L., & Samuelson, L. (2002). Object name learning provides on-the-job training for attention. *Psychological Science, 13,* 13–19.

Tomasello, M. (2000). Do young children have adult syntactic competence? *Cognition, 74,* 209–253.

Section 3

Representations That Support Generalization

7

Bayesian Models as Tools for Exploring Inductive Biases

THOMAS L. GRIFFITHS

G eneralization—reasoning from the properties of observed entities to those of entities as yet unobserved—is at the heart of many aspects of human cognition. As several of the chapters in this book indicate, generalization plays a key role in language learning, where learners need to make judgments about the linguistic properties of utterances (such as their meaning or grammaticality) using their previous experience with a language. It also underlies our ability to form and use categories, allowing us to identify which objects are likely to belong to a category based on a few examples, and is central to learning about causal relationships, where we predict how one event will influence another by drawing on past instances of those events. Language learning, categorization, and causal induction are three of the most widely studied topics in cognitive science, and allow us to communicate about, organize, and intervene on our environment. They are also three examples of problems for which human performance exceeds that of automated systems, setting the standard to which artificial intelligence and machine learning research aspires. This raises a natural question: What makes people so good at generalization?

The ubiquity and importance of generalization in cognitive science derive in part from its close relationship to inductive inference. The definition of *generalization* given above emphasizes its relationship to the classic problem of induction (e.g., Hume, 1739/1978), in which one forms predictions about future events based on examples from the past, such as anticipating that the sun will rise tomorrow because of the many days on which the sun has risen in the past. We can also think of generalization in terms of extracting a general rule from these events that can be used to make further predictions. For instance, Figure 7.1 shows a collection of (x,y) pairs produced by a simple function $y = f(x)$ together with additive noise. The dotted line shows a new value of x, for which the value of y is unknown.

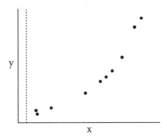

Figure 7.1   A schematic example of a generalization problem. The solid black points indicate a set of (x,y) pairs—the data supplied to the learner. The task is predict the value of y for a new value of x. The set of possible y values for a particular value of x is indicated by the dotted line. This prediction can be made by inferring the function relating x and y.

Predicting the value of y for this new x based on the other (x,y) pairs is a problem of generalization. In forming a prediction, you might take into account the different forms that the function $f(x)$ relating x and y might take on. Identifying the underlying function is an inductive problem. This simple example clearly has parallels in human causal learning, where people might want to understand the nature of the relationship between a cause and an effect, and there is an extensive literature exploring how people learn functions of this kind (for a review, see Busemeyer, Byun, DeLosh, & McDaniels, 1997).

The connection between generalization and induction means that the question of how to produce good generalizations becomes the question of what makes a good inductive learner. One reason why inductive problems such as language learning, categorization, and causal induction are particularly interesting from the perspective of cognitive science is that the hypotheses under consideration are not directly determined by the observed data. In order to choose among the many hypotheses that might provide equally good accounts of the data, the learner has to inject some subjective preferences for those hypotheses. This observation, which has a long history in cognitive science (e.g., Helmholtz, 1866/1962; Kant, 1781/1964), has two consequences. First, the way that people solve inductive problems can be uniquely revealing about the structure of the mind, as the conclusions people reach are a function of both data and their internal dispositions, which I will refer to as *inductive biases*. Second, these biases make the difference between a good inductive learner and a bad one, so understanding the consequences of having different inductive biases will provide an answer to the question of what makes a good inductive learner.

In this chapter, I explore the question of what makes a good inductive learner, emphasizing the role of inductive biases and the potential of Bayesian models of cognition as tools for revealing those biases. As a first step in this exploration, I consider the possibility that what makes a good inductive learner is simply being able to entertain a richer set of hypotheses as to the structure contained in observed data. An example suffices to illustrate that this is not the whole story: Richer hypothesis spaces can come with serious disadvantages. This motivates the discussion of a simple but deep result in mathematical statistics—the bias–variance trade-off—which provides a way to understand the relevance of inductive biases to human learning. I then argue that probabilistic models in which inductive inference is performed using Bayes' rule provide a way to formalize these biases, and summarize two methods of using Bayesian models to determine human inductive biases: making models with different biases and testing them against human data, and using the predictions of Bayesian models to design experiments that are explicitly intended to reveal inductive biases.

INDUCTIVE INFERENCE AND THE RICHNESS OF THE HYPOTHESIS SPACE

At an abstract computational level (Anderson, 1990; Marr, 1982), we can formalize inductive problems as follows. The goal of the learner is to generalize accurately from observed data. Denoting the data d, the learner seeks to identify the hypothesis h that will result in the greatest generalization accuracy. The hypothesis h will be selected from a set of hypotheses H, which I will refer to as the *hypothesis space*. A learning algorithm is a procedure for using the data d to select a hypothesis h from a hypothesis space H. To make these ideas more concrete, in the simple function learning problem from Figure 7.1, the data d are the (x,y) pairs, a hypothesis h is a function relating x and y, and a simple learning algorithm is selecting the function that most closely matches the points in d from the set of functions in the hypothesis space H. Using this formal framework, the question of what makes a good inductive learner reduces to asking what makes a good learning algorithm.

Theories of cognitive development and the history of formal models of learning in cognitive science both suggest a simple answer to this question: that better learning algorithms are characterized by richer hypothesis spaces. Jean Piaget's influential account of cognitive development suggested that as children develop, they become capable of entertaining more sophisticated hypotheses about the structure of their environment (e.g., Inhelder & Piaget, 1958). This change in representational capacity is viewed as the major force allowing children to acquire the knowledge associated with the adult state, a claim that has drawn criticism on logical grounds (e.g., Fodor, 1980). A similar trend appears in the history of models of human learning based on artificial neural networks. Initially, there was enthusiasm for simple two-layer neural networks such as Rosenblatt's (1958) perceptron, which automatically learned a set of weights that described how much a given input in the first layer should be linearly influencing a given output in the second layer. However, Minsky and Papert (1969) pointed out that these models were severely limited in the input–output mappings that they could learn. Specifically, perceptrons were able to learn only distinctions between sets of inputs that were linearly separable. This problem could be addressed by using multilayer perceptrons in which the outputs of one layer underwent a nonlinear transformation and became the inputs of the next, and Rumelhart, Hinton, and Williams (1986) introduced the back-propagation algorithm for training multilayer networks. The basic procedure for selecting a hypothesis was based on the same criteria as those used in the perceptron: choosing the weights of connections between layers in the model that allowed the model to most closely match the training data. The innovation was the expansion of the hypothesis space to make it possible to overcome the constraint of linear separability.

The idea that richer hypothesis spaces are the key to better inductive inference provides an attractively simple answer to the question of what makes a good inductive learner. However, it is straightforward to demonstrate that richer hypothesis spaces are not sufficient to guarantee good inductive inferences, and can actually prove detrimental. Consider three possible learning algorithms for solving the function learning problem depicted in Figure 7.1. As mentioned above, here the data are the (x,y) pairs and the hypotheses are functions relating x and y, producing predictions $h(x)$. The first learning algorithm selects the linear function $h(x) = q_0 + q_1x$ that minimizes the squared error between the prediction of the function at x and the true value of y, $(h(x) - y)^2$. The second and third learning algorithms use the same procedure to select a quadratic function $h(x) = q_0 + q_1x + q_2x_2$, and an 8th-degree polynomial

$$h(x) = q_0 + \sum_{k=1}^{8} q_k x^k$$

respectively. Because the criterion for selecting a function is the same in each case—minimizing the squared error—all that differs is the hypothesis space H from which the function is selected. We can describe these hypothesis spaces as sets of functions, or equivalently as sets of numbers corresponding to the parameters of the functions. For example, we can think of the function $y = 1 + 2x$ as a line in x,y space, or as the parameter vector $(2,1)$. Representing functions in this way, the hypothesis space of the first learning algorithm is $H_1 = (q_0,q_1) \in R^2$, where R is the set of real numbers. The hypothesis space of the second learning algorithm is $H_2 = (q_0,q_1,q_2) \in R^3$, and is strictly richer than H_1, because any linear function can be produced by setting $q_2 = 0$ (i.e., the functions contained in H_1 form a strict subset of H_2, with functions like $y = 1 + 2x + x^2$ being contained in H_2 but not H_1). Likewise, $H_3 = (q_0,...,q_8) \in R^9$, and is strictly richer than H_2.

The consequences of using these three learning algorithms are shown in Figure 7.2.[1] For these data, the linear hypothesis space H_1 produces a function that does not correspond particularly closely to the data; the quadratic hypothesis space H_2 produces lower error, in that the function falls closer to the points; and the set of 8th-degree polynomials H_3 results in very little error on any of the points. So, richer hypothesis spaces produce functions that match the data more closely, as should be expected because these spaces provide more options from which to select. However, this does not guarantee that algorithms using richer hypothesis spaces will always do a better job of generalization. Looking at the three functions in Figure 7.2, which would you select to make your prediction of y for the new value of x? In fact, these data were generated from a quadratic function, very similar to that found using H_2. Consequently, in this case, the algorithm using H_2. would generalize better than that using H_3. The more powerful learning algorithm,

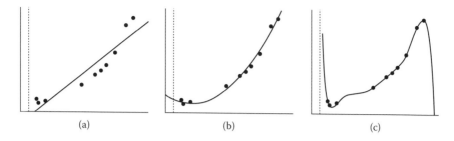

Figure 7.2   Consequences of selecting function minimizing squared error to observed data, using hypothesis spaces of (a) linear functions, (b) quadratic functions, and (c) 8th-degree polynomials.

the one with the richer hypothesis space, would perform worse. So, why is a richer hypothesis space not sufficient for improved generalization?

THE BIAS–VARIANCE TRADE-OFF

A simple explanation for why richer hypothesis spaces can be problematic is that having more options makes it possible to fit noise in the data. The points shown in Figure 7.1 were generated by adding random noise to the true underlying function. As a consequence, a learning algorithm can "overfit" the data, capturing the noise as well as the systematic variation produced by the underlying function. This makes the algorithm extremely sensitive to the specific points that are observed, and leads to a great deal of variability in its predictions. However, the example considered above also illustrates that richer hypothesis spaces can be beneficial: The learning algorithm considering only linear functions performed poorly, because the true function (in this case, a quadratic) was outside its hypothesis space. So, richer hypothesis spaces seem to aid generalization in some cases, and hinder it in others.

We can begin to understand how the assumptions made by different learning algorithms affect generalization by formally analyzing the factors contributing to generalization performance. In this section, I will briefly summarize an elegant result from the statistics literature, showing that generalization error decomposes into two parts—the bias of a learning algorithm, and its variance (Geman, Bienenstock, & Doursat, 1992). Although I will focus on the case of learning functions, this kind of analysis can be performed for simple inductive problems of many kinds, including categorization problems (Domingos, 2000; Friedman, 1997; James & Hastie, 1997; Tibshirani, 1996), and the general spirit of the results is recapitulated in many other formal analyses of learning (Kearns & Vazirani, 1994; Vapnik, 1995). The presentation here follows that of other discussions of the bias–variance trade-off in the machine-learning literature (Bishop, 2006; Hastie, Tibshirani, & Friedman, 2001), and goes into a fair amount of mathematical detail. The less mathematically inclined reader can skip ahead to the paragraph just past the last equation, where there is a more qualitative summary of this reasoning.

In the function learning example, our data are produced by selecting a set of x values from a distribution $p(x)$, and then generating corresponding y values from a distribution $p(y|x)$ that is Gaussian with mean $f(x)$ and standard deviation σ. This defines a joint distribution $p(x,y)$ on (x,y) pairs. A learning algorithm returns a hypothesis h, which we will take to be a function $y = h(x)$, for data d consisting of n points drawn from this distribution. The generalization error, GE, associated with such a function will be the average of the error associated with a particular (x,y) pair over the distribution $p(x,y)$, or

$$GE = \iint (y - h(x))^2 p(x, y) dx dy = E_{p(x,y)} \left[(y - h(x))^2 \right] \tag{7.1}$$

where $E_{p(x)}[f(x)] f(x)$ is the expectation of $f(x)$ over the distribution $p(x)$. With some algebra, we can simplify this to

$$GE = E_{p(x,y)}[(y - f(x) + f(x) - h(x))^2] \tag{7.2}$$

$$= E_{p(x,y)}[(y - f(x))^2] + E_{p(x,y)}[(f(x) - h(x))^2] \tag{7.3}$$

$$= \sigma^2 + E_{p(x)}[(f(x) - h(x))^2] \tag{7.4}$$

where the second line uses the linearity of expectation and the fact that $E_{p(x,y)}[(y - f(x))(f(x) - h(x))]$ is zero, and the third line uses the definition of $p(y|x)$ and the observation that y does not appear in $f(x)$–$h(x)$ (see Geman et al., 1992, for details).

The basic conclusion suggested by Equation 7.4 is that generalization error can be attributed to a combination of intrinsic error due to the noise in y, represented by σ^2, and systematic error resulting from the difference between the true function $f(x)$ and the function selected by the learning algorithm $h(x)$. A good hypothesis—one that produces low generalization error—will thus be one that makes $(f(x) - h(x))^2$ small for arbitrary x. However, we need to take into account the fact that the hypothesis $h(x)$ chosen by the learning algorithm depends on the data d. To do this, we need to compute the expected generalization error of a learning algorithm, EGE, over data d. This is simply

$$EGE = E_{p(d)}[GE] \tag{7.5}$$

where $p(d)$ is the probability distribution that results from drawing n points from $p(x,y)$, and GE is given in Equation 7.1. A good learning algorithm—one that produces low expected generalization error—will thus be one for which the expectation of its error, $(f(x) - h(x))^2$, over possible data sets d is small. We can express this as

$$E_{p(d)}[(f(x) - h(x))^2] = (f(x) - E_{p(d)}[h(x)])^2 + E_{p(d)}[h(x) - E_{p(d)}[h(x)])^2] \tag{7.6}$$

where the derivation is similar to that used in Equations 7.2 through 7.4, adding and subtracting $E_{p(d)}[h(x)]$ in the same way we added and subtracted $f(x)$ in Equation 7.2.

Equation 7.6 might seem relatively arcane at first glance, but it actually has a simple and intuitive interpretation. The first term on the right-hand side reflects differences between the true function $f(x)$ and the predictions made by the learning algorithm when averaged over all data sets. This is a measure of the *bias* of the learning algorithm—its overall capacity to capture the right form of the function. Formally, the bias at a point x is defined to be

$$\text{bias} = f(x) - E_{p(d)}[h(x)] \tag{7.7}$$

The second term on the right-hand side expresses the degree to which the hypothesis selected by the learning algorithm changes as a function of d. This is the *variance* of the learning algorithm, by analogy to the variance of a probability distribution, being the expected squared difference between the predictions and their average. Formally, the variance at a point x is

$$\text{variance} = E_{p(d)}[(h(x) - E_{p(d)}[(h(x)])^2] \tag{7.8}$$

Thus, we can rewrite Equation 7.6 as

$$E_{p(d)}[(f(x) - h(x))^2] = \text{bias}^2 + \text{variance} \tag{7.9}$$

making it clear that the performance of the learning algorithm can be described in terms of just these two factors. It follows from Equations 7.4 and 7.5 that the expected generalization error is just σ^2 plus the expectation of the sum of the squared bias and the variance with respect to $p(x)$.

The decomposition of the expected generalization error into bias and variance provides a simple framework for understanding the properties of different learning algorithms. I will illustrate the contributions of these factors by returning to the three learning algorithms introduced above, which differ only in the hypothesis spaces that they use. These learning algorithms are simple enough that we can directly compute their bias and variance, if we make some assumptions about the distribution $p(x,y)$ from which (x,y) pairs are being generated. For the purpose of illustration, assume that the true function $f(x)$ is the quadratic function used above, that the probability of a given value of x is equal over the entire range of possible x values shown in the graphs in Figures 7.1 and 7.2, and that the noise level σ^2 (i.e., the amount that observed values of y vary around the true function) is fixed. I then generated 100 samples of 10 data points ($n = 10$) from this distribution, and applied the three learning algorithms (i.e., minimizing error for linear, quadratic, and 8th-degree polynomials) to these data, producing 100 instances of $h(x)$ for each algorithm. These 100 hypotheses are thus samples from the distribution of the hypotheses produced by the learning algorithms when applied to data generated in this way (i.e., samples from $p(d)$). The resulting 100 samples are shown in Figure 7.3 (the light gray lines), together with a function produced by averaging these predictions (the black line), and the true function $f(x)$ (the dashed black line).

Figure 7.3 provides an intuitive illustration of the meaning of bias and variance, and how they contribute to generalization error. The bias of a learning algorithm is

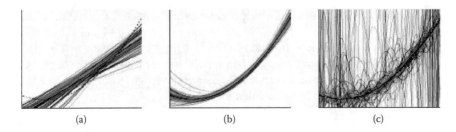

(a)   (b)   (c)

Figure 7.3   Bias and variance. Each panel shows the results of applying a learning algorithm to 100 randomly generated sets of 10 points. The gray lines are the model predictions,
the black line is the average of these predictions, and the dotted line is the true function
$f(x)$ from which the data were generated. (a) A hypothesis space of linear functions results
in a high bias, with the average function differing significantly from the true function, and
a moderate amount of variance around that average function. (b) A hypothesis space of
quadratic functions results in both low bias and low variance. (c) A hypothesis space of 8th-
degree polynomials results in low bias, with the average function being close to the truth,
but an enormous amount of variance, with predictions depending strongly on the specifics
of the data.

the difference between its average predictions (shown in black) and the true function (the dotted line). Its variance is the amount of variation (i.e., the spread) that
it shows around that average. The hypothesis space of linear functions results in a
high bias, with the average function differing significantly from the true function,
but reasonably low variance, as illustrated by the fact that learned functions (the
gray lines) do not deviate much from the average function. In contrast, the hypothesis space of 8th-degree polynomials results in low bias, with the average function
being close to the true function, but incredibly high variance, with very different
predictions being produced by different samples of d. The hypothesis space of quadratic functions has both low bias and low variance, producing an average function
close to the true function and exhibiting little variation across samples.

The decomposition of expected generalization error into bias and variance provides us with a way to understand how richer hypothesis spaces can sometimes
help generalization, and sometimes hurt it. Richer hypothesis spaces help because
they reduce bias. Going from linear functions to quadratic functions adds enough
flexibility so that it becomes possible to actually match the true function. Richer
hypothesis spaces hurt because they increase variance. Going from quadratic functions to 8th-degree polynomials adds so much flexibility that it becomes possible
to overfit the data, producing highly variable predictions. This transition from one
source of error to another is the *bias–variance trade-off*, and much of the work in
designing learning algorithms is about trying to hit the sweet spot between bias
and variance for a given problem.

Before considering the implications of this analysis for understanding human
inductive inference, it is worth noting two subtle points about how bias and variance depend on different factors involved in learning. The first is that this formal
notion of bias is relative. From Equation 7.7, it should be clear that the bias is the
result of the relationship between the learning algorithm and the true function,

$f(x)$. If the true function were linear, then the algorithm using the linear hypothesis space would have a low bias. If the true function were cubic, then the algorithm using the quadratic hypothesis space would have a high bias. The dependence of the bias on the true function is somewhat counterintuitive, so I use the term *inductive biases* to describe the dispositions that guide learners in solving inductive problems, reflecting the extent to which they favor one kind of hypothesis over another. These inductive biases will be the same regardless of the true function. For example, the learning algorithm using the linear hypothesis space will always produce a linear function, and we can describe its inductive biases in these terms.

The second subtlety of the bias–variance trade-off is that variance is strongly affected by the amount of data provided to the learning algorithm. Figure 7.4 shows the results of repeating the procedure used to construct Figure 7.3, but with $n = 100$ rather than $n = 10$. Now, whether the hypothesis space is quadratic functions or 8th-degree polynomials has little effect on the variance of the learning algorithm: The data are sufficient to strongly determine a solution either way. The sweet spot between bias and variance thus changes as the amount of data increases, with richer hypothesis spaces being less problematic when data are plentiful.

IMPLICATIONS FOR HUMAN INDUCTIVE INFERENCE

The bias–variance trade-off suggests that the answer to the question of what makes a good inductive learner is going to depend on the kind of problems that the learner will face. If the learner will be provided with only small amounts of data, then variance is a real concern and the only way to guarantee accurate generalization is by having inductive biases that match the problem at hand (i.e., that make the bias, in the formal sense, small). If the learner will be provided with large amounts of data, and needs to be able to solve a variety of problems, then variance is a less significant issue and bias is dominant: The learner needs to be flexible enough to accommodate the different solutions that could be needed for different problems.

Interestingly, these two perspectives map loosely onto the two extreme positions found in discussion of human inductive biases in cognitive science: that the relevant biases are strong and specific to particular learning domains (such as

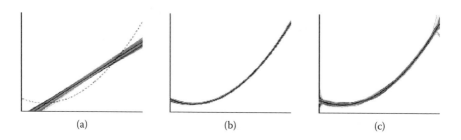

(a)   (b)   (c)

Figure 7.4   Adding more data reduces variance for all three learning algorithms. The predictions shown here are from 100 sets of 100 randomly generated points. (a) The linear hypothesis space still results in a high bias, but hypothesis spaces of (b) quadratic functions and (c) 8th-degree polynomials now result in more similar predictions.

acquiring language; e.g., Chomsky, 1965), or that the biases are weak and are the result of learning mechanisms that are called *domain general* because they can be used to acquire what seem to be a variety of different kinds of representations from different kinds of input data (e.g., connectionist models; Elman et al., 1996; Rogers & McClelland, 2004; Rumelhart & McClelland, 1986). Arguments supporting the idea that people have strong biases emphasize limitations in the amount or the quality of data provided to learners, setting up the problem as one in which reducing variance is dominant (e.g., you might want to draw different conclusions from a few sentences in a novel language than from a few steps in a dance routine). *Domain specificity* is a natural corollary of this view, because different domains will provide different targets for learning, and require different inductive biases. Arguments supporting the idea that people have weak biases focus on the possibility of a single learning algorithm that can be applied across many domains—something that requires flexibility in their use (e.g., one algorithm that can be used to learn both languages and the sequences of motor movements that comprise a dance). An example of a hypothesis space of this kind is the large space of nonlinear functions that can be produced by multilayer neural networks. These approaches downplay the issue of the amount of data available to learners. For example, algorithms such as back-propagation that seek to minimize error on some training data treat the amount of data and the number of iterations of learning equivalently, meaning that a small but representative sample will result in the same predictions as a larger sample in which the same points appear many times.

More generally, the bias–variance trade-off makes it clear that understanding human inductive inference means understanding human inductive biases. The key to good generalization is having inductive biases that provide a good compromise between bias and variance across a range of problems. By identifying the biases that guide human inductive inference, we can examine whether either of these two extreme views is correct. We can also explore the continuum of positions between these two extremes. However, in order to do so we need a good way to systematically and transparently characterize the inductive biases of a learner.

BAYESIAN INFERENCE AND INDUCTIVE BIASES

Bayesian inference is a formalism that makes the inductive biases of learners particularly clear. It also provides a rational account of how learners should go about revising their beliefs in light of evidence (e.g., Robert, 1994). In this section, I will summarize the basic ideas behind this approach and illustrate them using the example of learning functions. My emphasis here will be on a Bayesian analysis of inductive inference in broad terms. A Bayesian analysis of generalization in the stricter sense of reasoning from observed properties of a set of objects to the unobserved properties of another object is given in Tenenbaum and Griffiths (2001), building on that of Shepard (1987).

The basic assumption behind Bayesian inference is that learners are willing to express their degrees of belief in different hypotheses using probabilities. Several formal arguments can be made in support of this assumption (Cox, 1961; Jaynes, 2003), and once it is accepted the process of revising beliefs becomes straightforward, being a matter of applying *Bayes' rule*. Assume that a learner has a *prior* probability distribution, $p(h)$, specifying the probability assigned to the truth of each hypothesis h in a set of hypotheses H before seeing d. Bayes' rule states that the probability that should be given to each hypothesis after seeing d—known as the *posterior probability*, $p(h|d)$—is

$$p(h \mid d) = \frac{p(d \mid h)p(h)}{\displaystyle\sum_{h \in H} p(d \mid h)p(h)} \qquad (7.10)$$

where $p(d|h)$—the *likelihood*—indicates how probable d is under hypothesis h. The sum in the denominator simply guarantees that this process produces a probability distribution, ensuring that the resulting probabilities sum to one.

Bayes' rule provides an elegant way to characterize the inductive biases of learners, through the prior distribution over hypotheses $p(h)$. Interpreted probabilistically, priors indicate the kind of world a learner expects to encounter, guiding his or her conclusions when provided with data. The prior probability associated with each hypothesis reflects the probability with which a learner expects that hypothesis to be the solution to an inductive problem. Intuitively, Bayes' rule just tells us how to combine the inductive biases expressed in the prior with the information provided by the data, which is characterized by the likelihood $p(d|h)$. Any inductive inference has to trade off these two sources of constraints on hypotheses, and the mathematical form of Bayes' rule sets the terms of this trade-off, with both sources playing a direct role in determining the posterior probability of a hypothesis.

To provide a simple example, consider the problem of predicting the weather. In this case, we will consider just two hypotheses: sun or rain. A person living on the east coast of the United States—say, in Boston or Providence—might predict that, all other things being equal, there is a 50% chance of rain on a given day. Thus, the prior probability of rain would be $p(\text{rain}) = 0.5$. This prior probability could differ across people, especially if they live elsewhere. For example, a person living on the west coast—say, in Berkeley or San Francisco—might set $p(\text{rain}) = 0.1$. Upon seeing an ominous gray cloud in the sky, it would become necessary to revise one's beliefs. This observation constitutes our data, and is fairly diagnostic of rain, with $p(\text{cloud}|\text{rain}) = 0.8$ and $p(\text{cloud}|\text{sun}) = 0.3$. Applying Bayes' rule, our east-coast person would compute $p(\text{rain}|\text{cloud})$ to be approximately 0.73 and look for an umbrella, whereas our west-coast person would obtain $p(\text{rain}|\text{cloud})$ of approximately 0.23 and be confident walking home. It should be clear that the prior probability that people are assigning to rain has a significant effect on their conclusions, and reflects a bias appropriate to their environment—if they switched places, the west-coast person would constantly get wet and the east-coast person would often carry a superfluous umbrella.[2]

We can easily translate the function learning problem that I have been using as a running example into a problem of Bayesian inference. Once again, the treatment here will be relatively technical, and the less mathematically inclined reader can safely skip ahead to the next section provided the idea that priors can express inductive biases is clear. In the case of function learning, the assumption that y is generated from a Gaussian distribution with mean $h(x)$ and standard deviation s gives us our likelihood function $p(d|h)$, and means that the likelihood is maximized by minimizing the sum of the squared errors $(y - h(x))^2$. If we define our priors to be uniform over all functions in our hypothesis space, giving constant prior probability to every function in the set, then the hypothesis with maximum posterior probability is simply the hypothesis in that set with highest likelihood. Selecting the hypothesis with maximum posterior probability would thus be equivalent to the learning algorithm that chooses the function in the hypothesis space that minimizes the sum of the squared errors.

Using this simple method of setting a prior—choosing a hypothesis space and assigning probabilities uniformly within that space—and selecting the hypothesis with highest posterior probability produce exactly the same results for the linear, quadratic, and 8th-degree polynomial hypothesis spaces as in our example in Figure 7.2. However, it helps to explain why we saw those results. The prior expresses the expectations of a learner, and a learner who assigns equal prior probability to every 8th-degree polynomial believes that it lives in a world where it is likely to encounter extremely complex functions. Although the function shown in Figure 7.2c seems like a wild conjecture to us, it is just as plausible a priori as any other 8th-degree polynomial to the learner. The issue is that its beliefs are poorly calibrated to the quadratic world in which it lives.

More generally, priors can be used not just to limit the set of hypotheses but also to constrain their plausibility. In our function learning example, we can use 8th-degree polynomials as our hypothesis space, providing us with the potential to produce complex functions, but define a prior that favors simpler functions. This can be done by giving higher prior probability to those functions for which the parameters of the polynomial, q_k, are small (when all q_k are zero, the function is just a flat line at zero, and increasing q_k increases the extent to which the function differs from this). One approach is to take a Gaussian prior for each q_k, with a mean of 0 and a standard deviation of ab^k. For $b < 1$, the variance decreases geometrically with k, meaning that the coefficients of higher powers of x are increasingly likely to be small. Figure 7.5 shows samples from this prior for three different values of b, illustrating how the prior probability of different kinds of functions is affected by this parameter. Figure 7.6 shows the consequences of choosing the hypothesis with maximum posterior probability using the Gaussian likelihood introduced above together with these three priors.[3] As with constraining the hypothesis space directly, the resulting predictions vary in how well they correspond to the true function. However, one significant difference is that a learner using any of these three priors could ultimately learn any 8th-degree polynomial, if there are enough data that suggest that this complexity is warranted, rather than being stuck within a limited hypothesis space. Assigning graded degrees of plausibility across a large hypothesis space is an effective way to define models that are sufficiently constrained that they can generalize well from small amounts of data, yet sufficiently flexible that they can learn complex functions from large amounts of data. Variants on this approach are widely used in machine learning (Bishop, 2006; Hastie et al., 2001).

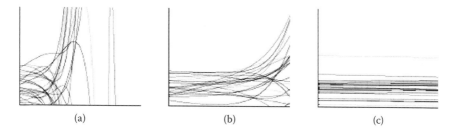

Figure 7.5 Samples of functions from different priors on the hypothesis space of 8th-degree polynomials. All priors were defined by assuming that the parameter q_k, being the coefficient of x^k, followed a Gaussian distribution with mean zero and standard deviation ab^k. Varying b varies the extent to which coefficients are expected to be small as k increases. The scale is the same as that used in the other figures exploring this example. (a) $b = 0.3$ results in a prior in which functions can have relatively high curvature. (b) $b = 0.1$ penalizes higher powers of x more strongly, resulting in less curved functions. (c) $b = 0.01$ favors functions that have no curvature and little slope, giving extremely small values to all q_k except q_0.

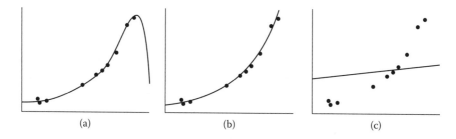

Figure 7.6 Consequences of using different priors in making predictions. The final predictions are a compromise between the prior and the likelihood. The priors are those used to generate the functions that appear in the corresponding panels in the previous figure. (a) With a prior that favors functions with high curvature ($b = 0.3$), a highly curved function is selected. (b) A prior favoring functions that have a little curvature ($b = 0.1$) does well in reproducing the true function, having inductive biases appropriate for the problem at hand. (c) A prior favoring functions with no curvature and little slope does poorly, although the predictions it makes based on the data are notably different from the functions sampled from the prior, having a nonnegligible slope. With more data, this prior would eventually be overwhelmed, allowing the learner to make more accurate predictions.

Finally, it is important to note that the prior distribution assumed by a learner should not be interpreted simply as reflecting innate constraints on learning. The prior simply collects together all of the factors affecting how plausible a learner finds a particular hypothesis. There are many such factors other than innate constraints that could affect this, such as data from other domains that are independent of the data observed in this domain but might provide a source of hypotheses, or information-processing constraints, such as limitations on working memory. It should also be clear that many learning algorithms, including those used with multilayer neural networks, can be interpreted as having a prior over some hypothesis space. That prior might just be relatively weak, like the uniform priors over hypothesis spaces of functions discussed in this section. For example, when viewed from this perspective, the learning algorithms typically used with multilayer neural networks can be interpreted as defining a uniform prior over the hypothesis space of functions that can be expressed through their weights (Mackay, 1995; Neal, 1992).

REVEALING INDUCTIVE BIASES

Bayesian models provide a way to express a variety of inductive biases, through the prior distribution over hypotheses that they assume. These models make predictions about which hypotheses people should select as a consequence of observing different kinds of data. This suggests at least two ways to explore the inductive biases of human learners: comparing human judgments to Bayesian models that assume different priors, and using the assumptions behind Bayesian models to design experiments that are explicitly intended to reveal the priors of the participants. I will outline these two approaches, providing examples of cases in which they have been successful.

Testing Assumed Biases

The simplest approach to using Bayesian models to reveal human inductive biases is to construct a set of models that assume different priors, and examine which of these models best characterizes human performance on a task. This approach is consistent with a long tradition of computational modeling in cognitive science, in which parameterized models are fit to human data and compared in order to evaluate claims about the processes behind behavior. For example, a variety of models have been proposed to explain how people perform learning tasks in which people have to learn a function that relates one variable (x) to another (y), like that used in our example (Busemeyer et al., 1997; DeLosh, Busemeyer, & McDaniel, 1997; Kalish, Lewandowsky, & Kruschke, 2004). Although not expressed in Bayesian terms, these models differ in the inductive biases that they ascribe to learners, and tests of these models explore what kinds of biases seem to give a better account of human judgments.

Several studies have explicitly used Bayesian models in this way. Anderson (1990; Anderson & Milson, 1989) introduced a probabilistic model of memory, in which retrieval was viewed as a process of inferring whether an item in memory was likely to be needed based on a cue. This model required a prior distribution over items in memory, indicating the probability assigned to a given item being needed at a particular time. This "need probability" was originally estimated using a model based on the circulation patterns of books in a library, but Anderson and Schooler (1991) subsequently estimated distributions from three environmental sources: headlines in the *New York Times*, a corpus of child-directed speech, and people who sent e-mail to Anderson. In each case, they computed the probabilities of items being needed at a given time as a function of the times at which they were encountered in the past. These distributions could then be used to make predictions about basic effects seen in standard list memory tasks, such as retention curves, the effects of practice, and the spacing of exposures, just by computing the need probability for each item based on the times at which it was studied. The success of this approach provides a particularly elegant explanation for these phenomena, grounding them in a prior obtained directly from the environment. Similar methods are commonly used in perception research, showing that human judgments can be accounted for by an ideal observer (i.e., an observer using Bayesian inference to try to reconstruct the structure that produced a given sensory stimulus) using knowledge of the probabilities with which different structures exist in the environment (e.g., Geisler, Perry, Super, & Gallogly, 2001).

Other analyses have more directly compared the consequences of using different priors. For example, Wason (1966) found that people often make what seem to be errors when asked what information they would need to test a simple rule about the relationship between two properties of a set of objects. These judgments were errors when the task was viewed from the perspective of deductive logic, but Oaksford and Chater (1994) showed that they could be explained as the result of a rational Bayesian inference provided the properties involved are rare—that is, true for only a small subset of objects. McKenzie and Mikkelsen (2000) made a similar point in the context of covariation assessment, where people evaluate the extent to which two properties seem to be related based on the frequencies with which they co-occur. McKenzie and Mikkelson (2000) argued that long-standing results concerning the relative weight assigned to different kinds of evidence could be explained as the result of a belief that predicates are rare. A number of subsequent studies have tested these explanations, examining the consequence of manipulating the rarity of predicates for people's judgments in these tasks, finding support for this Bayesian analysis (McKenzie & Mikkelsen, 2007; Oaksford & Chater, 2001; Oaksford, Chater, & Grainger, 1999; Oaksford, Chater, Grainger, & Larkin, 1997).

If the goal is to identify people's priors, then inferences from small amounts of data have the potential to be most informative, as they will be most strongly influenced by priors because the probability of the data will be similar under a range of hypotheses. To return to our example of predicting the weather, the conclusions drawn from observing a single dark cloud are more likely to be affected by whether one lives on the east coast or the west coast, whereas a sky filled with dark clouds is so much more probable under the hypothesis of rain than under the alternative that prior probabilities have little effect on the conclusion. Griffiths and Tenenbaum (2006) studied inferences from small samples to show that people have remarkably accurate knowledge of the distributions associated with different aspects of daily life, and use this knowledge in the way prescribed by Bayes' rule (see Figure 7.7). For example, the probability distributions for human life expectancy (in years) and the amount of money made by a movie (in millions of dollars) are quite different, being similar to a Gaussian distribution in the first case and a much more skewed power–law distribution in the second (see Figure 7.7). In the experiment, people were asked to make a prediction based on a single piece of data. For example, if you were assessing the prospects of a 60-year-old man, how much longer would you expect him to live? If you heard that a movie had made $40 million so far at the box office, how much would you expect it to make in

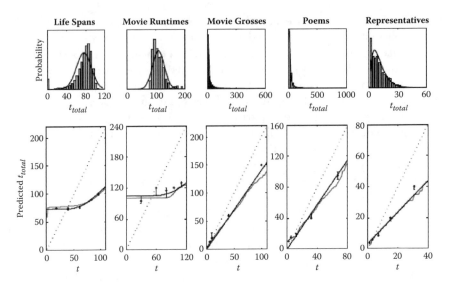

Figure 7.7   People use different prior distributions when making predictions about different quantities. The upper panels show the empirical distribution of the total duration or extent, t_{total}, for five different everyday phenomena. The values of t_{total} are the hypotheses h to be evaluated, and these distributions are the appropriate priors. The first two distributions (human life spans and movie runtimes) are approximately Gaussian, the next two (the gross of movies and the length of poems) are approximately power–law, and the last (length of terms of members of the U.S. House of Representatives) is approximately Erlang. Best fitting parametric distributions are plotted in black. In the lower panels, black dots show subjects' median predictions for t_{total} when given a single observed sample t of a duration or extent in each of five domains (the data d used when applying Bayes' rule). Judgments are consistent with Bayesian predictions using the empirical prior distribution shown in the upper panel (gray lines), and the best fitting parametric prior (black lines). Predictions based on a single uninformative prior (dotted lines), which results in the simple rule of predicting that something will persist exactly as long as it has persisted so far, are not consistent with these judgments. Adapted from Griffiths and Tenenbaum (2006).

total? The resulting predictions should be based on people's prior knowledge about these domains, and should reflect the differences in the distributions for these two domains. Studying everyday inductive leaps of this kind provides the opportunity to explore the constraints on human inductive inferences using naturalistic tasks that are easily reproduced in a laboratory setting. The fact that these inferences are made from only a small amount of data (in this case, just one data point—how long something has lasted or how much money it has made so far) means that we can measure the effects of prior knowledge directly.

By examining inductive inferences in domains where we know the statistics that should inform the prior, we can examine how well people's prior knowledge is calibrated to their environment. In other settings, we can use the Bayesian framework to explore the consequences of using different kinds of prior knowledge, and work backward from people's judgments to identify possible constraints. Although most work in this area has focused on memory and probabilistic reasoning, a similar methodology can be applied to other kinds of inductive problems. For example, one way to explore inductive biases in language learning is to examine what simulated learners with different priors might be able to extract from corpora of the speech that adults produce when interacting with children. An analysis of this kind for the problem of word segmentation—learning the words that appear in continuous speech—suggests that assumptions about the nature of the interaction between words can have a significant effect on how well a simulated learner recovers the correct words from an unsegmented corpus (Goldwater, Griffiths, & Johnson, 2006). Extending these formal analyses and connecting them to the results of word segmentation experiments with children and adults comprise a promising direction for future research.

Designing Experiments to Reveal Biases

The second approach to studying inductive biases involves developing laboratory methods specifically designed to provide information about the constraints that guide people's inductive inferences. This approach takes inspiration less from the tradition of computational models of cognition, and more from methods like *mechanism design* in theoretical economics (Hurwicz, 1973). The basic idea behind mechanism design is to structure an interaction between agents in a way that provides them with incentives to produce a particular kind of behavior. For example, an auction can be structured so that every bidder should bid the true value that he or she assigns to the prize, revealing information that might be concealed in a more conventional auction (Vickrey, 1961). Mechanism design proceeds from the assumption that the bidders are rational in their behavior and when making choices try to maximize the gain provided by those choices. This makes it possible to predict their behavior in different situations. By analogy, assuming that learners are Bayesian agents can allow us to design tasks intended to reveal their inductive biases.

One line of work that uses this idea grew out of analyzing the properties of a class of models of language evolution by "iterated learning" (Kirby, 2001). These models are based on the idea that every speaker of a language learns that language from another speaker, who had to learn it from somebody else in turn. Formally, we can imagine a sequence of learners, each of whom receives data from the previous learner, forms a hypothesis from those data, and then generates new data that are passed to the next learner. Griffiths and Kalish (2005, 2007) analyzed the consequences of iterated learning in the case where learners form hypotheses by applying Bayes' rule and then sampling a hypothesis from the resulting posterior distribution, and generate data by sampling from the likelihood function associated with that hypothesis. In this case, the probability that a learner selects a particular hypothesis will converge to the prior probability that the learners assign to that hypothesis as the length of the sequence increases, regardless of the hypothesis selected by the first learner. As the length of the sequence increases, the influence of the first learner thus gradually diminishes, until all such sequences converge to the same distribution over hypotheses—the prior. This result has significant implications for the connection between the biases of individual learners and linguistic universals, as it indicates that the priors that guide language learning will ultimately determine the languages spoken by a population (Griffiths & Kalish, 2007; Kirby, Dowman, & Griffiths, 2007). However, it also goes beyond language evolution, applying to iterated learning with any kind of hypotheses and data. The fact that iterated learning converges to the prior suggests a simple procedure for explore human inductive biases: Implement iterated learning in the laboratory with human learners, and examine which hypotheses survive.

A series of recent experiments have provided results suggesting that iterated learning can be used to reveal the inductive biases of human learners. Figure 7.8 shows the results of an experiment in iterated function learning, where the hypotheses concerned the form of a function causally relating two variables, and the data were values of these variables (Kalish, Griffiths, & Lewandowsky, 2007). In this experiment, we ran 32 "families" of learners (i.e., sequences of nine learners, each learning from the previous learner). These families were divided into four groups based on the nature of the function used to train the first learner in each family—positive linear, negative linear, nonlinear, or just a random set of values for y. We found that iterated learning had remarkably consistent consequences, with the last learner in 28 of the 32 families producing the same positive linear function by the end of the experiment despite the variation in the function used to train the first learner (the other four were producing negative linear functions). This is consistent with previous experiments in function learning suggesting that people

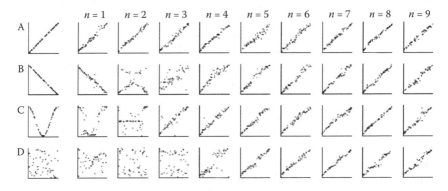

Figure 7.8   Iterated learning as a method for identifying inductive biases. The leftmost panel in each row shows the set of samples from a function seen by the first learner in a sequence. The (x,y) pairs were each presented as the lengths of two bars on a computer screen. During training, participants predicted the length of one bar from the other before seeing the second bar as feedback. The second panel in each row shows the predictions produced by the first learner in a test phase where participants made predictions of y for a range of x values without receiving feedback. These predictions were then used as the training data for the second learner, who produced the predictions shown in the third column. The other panels show the data produced by each generation of learners, each being trained from the predictions produced by the previous learner. Each row shows a single sequence of nine learners, drawn at random from eight "families" of learners run with the same initial data. The rows differ in the functions used to generate the data shown to the first subject. In each case, iterated learning quickly converges to a linear function with positive slope, consistent with findings indicating that human learners are biased toward this kind of function. Adapted from Kalish, Griffiths, and Lewandowsky (2007).

have an inductive bias favoring linear functions with a positive slope (Brehmer, 1971, 1974; Busemeyer et al., 1997). We have subsequently obtained similar results using an iterated generalization task based on the category structures studied by Shepard, Hovland, and Jenkins (1961), finding that the structures people find easiest to learn quickly dominate (Griffiths, Christian, & Kalish, 2006).

Again, this approach is in its infancy, but has promise as a way to discover the inductive biases of human learners. Its main advantage over fitting models assuming different priors is that it is nonparametric—it does not require any assumptions about the form of the prior on the part of the modeler. This is important in domains where the stimuli or hypotheses are complex, making it hard to formally describe the prior in a way that would not be an oversimplification. The results shown in Figure 7.8 illustrate this: It is clear that the prior is one that favors positive linear functions, even though we might not know exactly how to define a prior over the space of functions that people are considering. If we want to explore inductive biases for aspects of natural languages, the structure of categories, and networks of causal relationships, this capacity to deal with complexity could prove extremely valuable.

CONCLUSION

I began this chapter with the question of what makes people so good at generalization. The example of function learning shows that one simple answer—richer hypothesis spaces—is not sufficient to produce good generalization. The bias–variance trade-off helps to explain why this is, showing that generalization errors are affected by both the bias of a learning algorithm and the variability in its answers across data sets, and richer hypothesis spaces reduce bias at the cost of increasing variance. Richer hypothesis spaces need to be complemented by inductive biases that constrain inferences from small amounts of data. Bayes' rule provides a way to state these biases—through the prior distribution over hypotheses—and to define graded degrees of plausibility over rich hypothesis spaces. Analyzing people's inferences in these terms gives us at least two ways to explore human inductive biases: by comparing Bayesian models with different priors to human behavior, and by designing experiments explicitly intended to reveal the priors of learners.

Although my focus in this chapter has been on revealing inductive biases, a critical question that this raises is where those biases come from. The Bayesian framework provides a natural answer to this question, through a class of models known as *hierarchical Bayesian models* (Tenenbaum, Griffiths, & Kemp, 2006). The basic idea behind a hierarchical Bayesian model is that the knowledge that we draw upon in solving inductive problems is represented at many levels, and that Bayesian inference can be applied at any of these levels. For example, in learning words, a child might learn what specific words mean, but also what kinds of things words are likely to describe, and in learning causal relationships we might not only identify specific relationships that exist but also make inferences about the kinds of mechanisms that are likely to mediate between cause and effect. Hierarchical Bayesian models make it possible to extract the principles that are relevant to many inductive inferences within a domain, and use these principles to constrain future inferences. Essentially, people can learn the prior distributions that characterize their environment, and use this knowledge to improve their inferences. By using Bayesian models to chart the inductive biases that guide people's inferences in different domains, we can begin to explore whether this kind of approach can also account for their origins.

NOTES

1. Despite the intimidating description of searching through an infinite hypothesis space to find the best fitting function, this reduces to the familiar problem of linear regression, where appropriate powers of x are used as predictors, and has a simple closed-form solution (e.g., Bishop, 2006).
2. This very real phenomenon is partly exacerbated by the fact that not just priors but also likelihoods depend on location, with the marine layer resulting in a high probability of clouds even when rain is unlikely along the coast of California.
3. Again, although this might seem complicated, it reduces to a simple algebra problem (Bishop, 2006). It is also possible to compute the predictions of a Bayesian model when averaging over the posterior distribution, which provides another way of controlling complexity and leads to some sophisticated solutions to this kind of function learning problem (Mackay, 2003).

REFERENCES

Anderson, J. R. (1990). *The adaptive character of thought*. Hillsdale, NJ: Lawrence Erlbaum.

Anderson, J. R., & Milson, R. (1989). Human memory: An adaptive perspective. *Psychological Review, 96*, 703–719.

Anderson, J. R., & Schooler, L. J. (1991). Reflections of the environment in memory. *Psychological Science, 2*, 396–408.

Bishop, C. M. (2006). *Pattern recognition and machine learning*. New York: Springer.

Brehmer, B. (1971). Subjects' ability to use functional rules. *Psychonomic Science, 24*, 259–260.

Brehmer, B. (1974). Hypotheses about relations between scaled variables in the learning of probabilistic inference tasks. *Organizational Behavior and Human Decision Processes, 11*, 1–27.

Busemeyer, J. R., Byun, E., DeLosh, E. L., & McDaniel, M. A. (1997). Learning functional relations based on experience with input-output pairs by humans and artificial neural networks. In K. Lamberts & D. Shanks (Eds.), *Concepts and categories* (pp. 405–437). Cambridge, MA: MIT Press.

Chomsky, N. (1965). *Aspects of the theory of syntax*. Cambridge, MA: MIT Press.

Cox, R. T. (1961). *The algebra of probable inference*. Baltimore, MD: Johns Hopkins University Press.

DeLosh, E. L., Busemeyer, J. R., & McDaniel, M. A. (1997). Extrapolation: The sine qua non of abstraction in function learning. *Journal of Experimental Psychology: Learning, Memory, and Cognition, 23*, 968–986.

Domingos, P. (2000). A unified bias-variance decomposition and its applications. In *Proceedings of the 17th international conference on machine learning* (pp. 231–238). Stanford, CA: Morgan Kaufmann.

Elman, J. L., Bates, E. A., Johnson, M. H., Karmiloff-Smith, A., Parisi, D., & Plunkett, K. (1996). *Rethinking innateness: A connectionist perspective*. Cambridge, MA: MIT Press.

Fodor, J. A. (1980). On the impossibility of acquiring more powerful structures. In M. Piattelli-Palmarini (Ed.), *Language and learning: The debate between Jean Piaget and Noam Chomsky*. London: Routledge and Kegan Paul.

Friedman, J. H. (1997). On bias, variance, 0/1 loss, and the curse-of-dimensionality. *Data Mining and Knowledge Discovery, 1*, 55–77.

Geisler, W. S., Perry, J. S., Super, B. J., & Gallogly, D. P. (2001). Edge co-occurrence in natural images predicts contour grouping performance. *Vision Research, 41*, 711–724.

Geman, S., Bienenstock, E., & Doursat, R. (1992). Neural networks and the bias-variance dilemma. *Neural Computation, 4*, 1–58.

Goldwater, S., Griffiths, T. L., & Johnson, M. (2006). Contextual dependencies in unsupervised word segmentation. In *Proceedings of COLING/ACL 2006*. Retrieved November 3, 2009, from http://www.aclweb.org/anthology/P/P06/

Griffiths, T. L., Christian, B. R., & Kalish, M. L. (2006). Revealing priors on category structures through iterated learning. In *Proceedings of the 28th annual conference of the Cognitive Science Society*. Mahwah, NJ: Lawrence Erlbaum.

Griffiths, T. L., & Kalish, M. L. (2005). A Bayesian view of language evolution by iterated learning. In B. G. Bara, L. Barsalou, & M. Bucciarelli (Eds.), *Proceedings of the 27th annual conference of the Cognitive Science Society* (pp. 827–832). Mahwah, NJ: Lawrence Erlbaum.

Griffiths, T. L., & Kalish, M. L. (2007). A Bayesian view of language evolution by iterated learning. *Cognitive Science, 31*, 441–480.

Griffiths, T. L., & Tenenbaum, J. B. (2006). Optimal predictions in everyday cognition. *Psychological Science, 17*, 767–773.

Hastie, T., Tibshirani, R., & Friedman, J. (2001). *The elements of statistical learning: Data mining, inference, and prediction*. New York: Springer.

Helmholtz, H. von. (1866/1962). Concerning the perceptions in general. In *Treatise on physiological optics* (Vol. 3, Trans. J. P. C. Southall). New York: Dover.

Hume, D. (1739/1978). *A treatise of human nature*. Oxford: Oxford University Press.

Hurwicz, L. (1973). The design of mechanisms for resource allocation. *American Economic Review, 63*, 1–30.

Inhelder, B., & Piaget, J. (1958). *The growth of logical thinking from childhood to adolescence*. London: Routledge and Kegan Paul.

James, G., & Hastie, T. (1997). *Generalizations of the bias/variance decomposition for prediction error*. Stanford, CA: Department of Statistics, Stanford University.

Jaynes, E. T. (2003). *Probability theory: The logic of science*. Cambridge: Cambridge University Press.

Kalish, M., Lewandowsky, S., & Kruschke, J. (2004). Population of linear experts: Knowledge partitioning and function learning. *Psychological Review, 111*, 1072–1099.

Kalish, M. L., Griffiths, T. L., & Lewandowsky, S. (2007). Iterated learning: Intergenerational knowledge transmission reveals inductive biases. *Psychonomic Bulletin and Review, 14*, 288–294.

Kant, I. (1781/1964). *Critique of pure reason*. London: Macmillan.

Kearns, M., & Vazirani, U. (1994). *An introduction to computational learning theory*. Cambridge, MA: MIT Press.

Kirby, S. (2001). Spontaneous evolution of linguistic structure: An iterated learning model of the emergence of regularity and irregularity. *IEEE Journal of Evolutionary Computation, 5*, 102–110.

Kirby, S., Dowman, M., & Griffiths, T. L. (2007). Innateness and culture in the evolution of language. *Proceedings of the National Academy of Sciences, 104*, 5241–5245.

MacKay, D. (1995). Probable networks and plausible predictions: A review of practical Bayesian methods for supervised neural networks. *Network: Computation in Neural Systems*, 6, 469–505.

MacKay, D. J. C. (2003). *Information theory, inference, and learning algorithms*. Cambridge: Cambridge University Press.

Marr, D. (1982). *Vision*. San Francisco: W. H. Freeman.

McKenzie, C. R. M., & Mikkelsen, L. A. (2000). The psychological side of Hempel's paradox of confirmation. *Psychonomic Bulletin and Review*, 7, 360–366.

McKenzie, C. R. M., & Mikkelsen, L. A. (2007). A Bayesian view of covariation assessment. *Cognitive Psychology*, 54, 33–61.

Minsky, M. L., & Papert, S. A. (1969). *Perceptrons*. Cambridge, MA: MIT Press.

Neal, R. M. (1992). Connectionist learning of belief networks. *Artificial Intelligence*, 56, 71–113.

Oaksford, M., & Chater, N. (1994). A rational analysis of the selection task as optimal data selection. *Psychological Review*, 101, 608–631.

Oaksford, M., & Chater, N. (2001). The probabilistic approach to human reasoning. *Trends in Cognitive Sciences*, 5, 349–357.

Oaksford, M., Chater, N., & Grainger, R. (1999). Probabilistic effects in data selection. *Thinking and Reasoning*, 5, 193–243.

Oaksford, M., Chater, N., Grainger, R., & Larkin, J. (1997). Optimal data selection in the reduced array selection task (RAST). *Journal of Experimental Psychology: Learning, Memory, and Cognition*, 23, 441–458.

Robert, C. P. (1994). *The Bayesian choice: A decision-theoretic motivation*. New York: Springer.

Rogers, T., & McClelland, J. (2004). *Semantic cognition: A parallel distributed processing approach*. Cambridge, MA: MIT Press.

Rosenblatt, F. (1958). The perceptron: A probabilistic model for information storage and organization in the brain. *Psychological Review*, 65, 386–408.

Rumelhart, D., & McClelland, J. (1986). On learning the past tenses of English verbs. In J. McClelland, D. Rumelhart, & the PDP Research Group (Eds.), *Parallel distributed processing: Explorations in the microstructure of cognition* (Vol. 2). Cambridge, MA: MIT Press.

Rumelhart, D. E., Hinton, G. E., & Williams, R. J. (1986). Learning representations by back-propagating errors. *Nature*, 323, 533–536.

Shepard, R. N. (1987). Towards a universal law of generalization for psychological science. *Science*, 237, 1317–1323.

Shepard, R. N., Hovland, C. I., & Jenkins, H. M. (1961). Learning and memorization of classifications. *Psychological Monographs*, 75 (13, Whole No. 517).

Tenenbaum, J. B., & Griffiths, T. L. (2001). Generalization, similarity, and Bayesian inference. *Behavioral and Brain Sciences*, 24, 629–641.

Tenenbaum, J. B., Griffiths, T. L., & Kemp, C. (2006). Theory-based Bayesian models of inductive learning and reasoning. *Trends in Cognitive Science*, 10, 309–318.

Tibshirani, R. (1996). *Bias, variance, and prediction error for classification rules*. Toronto, Canada: Statistics Department, University of Toronto.

Vapnik, V. N. (1995). *The nature of statistical learning theory*. New York: Springer.

Vickrey, W. (1961). Counterspeculation, auctions, and competitive sealed tenders. *Journal of Finance*, 16, 8–27.

Wason, P. C. (1966). Reasoning. In B. Foss (Ed.), *New horizons in psychology*. Harmondsworth, UK: Penguin.

8

Representing American Sign Language Classifier Predicates Using Spatially Parameterized Planning Templates

MATT HUENERFAUTH

INTRODUCTION

*T*his chapter addresses the concept of *generalization* primarily from a linguistic and engineering standpoint. We examine this issue from the perspective of the field of natural language processing, which explores how computer software can be created to automatically understand or generate information in the form of human languages. Our research program focuses on the creation of software that can generate animations of American Sign Language (ASL); specifically, we have examined how to best design software for translating from English sentences into animations of a virtual human character performing ASL. Our motivation for building this software is to make information more accessible to people who are deaf. A majority of deaf 18-year-olds in the United States have an English reading level below that of a typical 10-year-old student, and so machine translation software that could translate English text into ASL animations could significantly improve these individuals' access to information, communication, and services.

This chapter explores how the choice of representation for the linguistic structure of a specific construction in a language can have an impact on our ability to build software to generate that construction. Specifically, this chapter will focus on computational linguistic software for generating animations of a kind of ASL sentence called a *classifier predicate* (CP), a phenomenon in which signers use special hand movements to indicate the location and movement of invisible objects in space around their bodies (to represent entities under discussion). Because CPs are frequent in ASL and necessary for conveying many concepts, we have developed an English-to-ASL machine translation architecture that includes a classifier predicate generator. Previous English-to-ASL machine translation projects have been unable to generate CPs, and they were thus limited in the type of ASL sentences they could produce.

A major goal of our research is to ensure that the design of our English-to-ASL software is scalable—that is, we want to design the software so that a programmer's time is used as efficiently as possible while he or she is developing the English-to-ASL system. We would like the software to be able to produce the largest number of possible ASL sentences with the minimal amount of programming effort. To support such a scalable implementation of our system, computational ASL representations had to be developed that support the *generalization* of the structure of classifier predicates and other ASL phenomena. The CP generator in our system represents the structure of CPs using a set of templates that are parameterized on the spatial and linguistic features of the entities that they discuss (i.e., features of the entities in the sentence will "fill in the blanks" in the templates we have designed—when that template is used to produce an ASL animation for a particular English sentence). These templates are built from a set of reusable animation subcomponents that calculate motion parameters for the ASL performance based upon a three-dimensional (3D) model encoding how entities under discussion are associated with locations in space around the animated signing character.

Because a theme of this chapter is to examine how the *representation* of information can support *generalization* in different fields, we will begin by discussing the common representations used in the field of natural language processing. We will explore how the term *generalization* takes on two different meanings in the field—depending on whether one is considering the issue from a "classical" or a modern "statistical" perspective in the field of natural language processing. Finally, the chapter will discuss the specific representations we have used in our software for ASL classifier predicates.

REPRESENTATIONS IN NATURAL LANGUAGE PROCESSING

A major question for any area of computer science is how to represent the data that will be processed by the software under development. For simple applications, information may be represented as bits (1s and 0s), numbers, characters, or strings; however, for more complex tasks, it is often necessary to design "data structures"—combinations of basic units of data—into frameworks that enable information to be organized and accessed in a more convenient form. In the field of natural language processing, researchers have developed their own data structures, which often mimic the ways in which languages are represented in the field of linguistics. Broadly speaking, NLP software has been developed using one of two major approaches: Classical-NLP and Statistical-NLP. The representations of language used by computer scientists (i.e., the data structures) have differed for each of these two approaches.

Classical-NLP was more common in the field prior to the mid-1990s. In this design approach, a team of linguistically knowledgeable developers construct large libraries of language-specific information to guide their software. For example, they may create large electronic dictionaries (called *lexicons*) that contain a listing of all the words in a language (e.g., English or Spanish) with important information about how those words can be used (e.g., part of speech) and what they mean (e.g., some kind of semantic representation). In order to build software that could understand sentences in a human language, the information in such a lexicon would be needed. Similarly, the syntax of a language is often represented as *grammar rules* that encode how categories of words (e.g., nouns, verbs, or adjectives) can be combined to form entire phrases and sentences. Finally, the meanings of words and phrases can also be encoded in various forms; for instance, there are some NLP semantic representations that are similar to formal logic sentences (e.g., first-order predicate logic).

Since the mid-1990s, Statistical-NLP has become an increasingly common design approach in the field. In this approach, a large sample of text in some human language is analyzed by linguists to mark important information in the text (e.g., they may label the part of speech of each word in a document). This linguistically annotated text is then used as "training data" for a machine-learning algorithm that learns the structure of the language under consideration. For example, the software may look for patterns in how certain words tend to co-occur or how the part of speech of a word can be predicted by the words around it. The statistical models of the language created by these algorithms can later be used to analyze or generate a new *previously unseen* text. In the Statistical-NLP approach, human language is often represented in a more numerical manner. For example, after analyzing a large sample of "training" text, machine-learning software may produce a large table of numerical probabilities on the likelihood of specific words following other specific words. A possible application of such a probability table would be within software in mobile telephones to predict the next word in a sentence based on the previous several words that have been typed. This word predication software can save the user from having to type every word in a sentence on a small telephone keypad.

GENERALIZATION AND NATURAL LANGUAGE PROCESSING

The term *generalization* has different meanings within the two different NLP approaches. In Classical-NLP, the human developers who build linguistic software make generalizations about the structure of a human language (e.g., English or Chinese) when they construct lexicons, grammar rules, or other forms of NLP software that use these resources (e.g., a grammar-checking component for a word processor document that uses a lexicon and grammar rules for the language it is checking). Thus, in this approach, *humans* are making generalizations about a human language's words and grammar rules when they design software. In Statistical-NLP, the machine-learning algorithm (the computer software that analyzes the large sample of text annotated by linguists) makes generalizations about the structure of the language from examples that appear in its training data. Thus, *computer software* is making generalizations about language when statistically looking for patterns in large samples of text.

Choosing a good representation for the information about a language's words, syntax structure, and semantics can support the generalization process that occurs in either approach. To illustrate this point, the remainder of this chapter will focus on a specific example: the design of computer software for generating animations of sentences in American Sign Language. This discussion will demonstrate how selecting the proper representation for a certain type of ASL sentence (i.e., a *classifier predicate*) can facilitate the work of software developers who are designing rules that describe how to automatically produce a variety of ASL sentences of this type.

BACKGROUND AND MOTIVATIONS FOR OUR RESEARCH ON ASL SOFTWARE

During the critical language acquisition years of childhood, a deaf individual requires sufficient exposure to an accessible language input (like a sign language, which is conveyed visually) to enable the acquisition of a first language. From this foundation, the acquisition of literacy in a spoken and written language can later be facilitated. Unfortunately, many deaf individuals do not have an opportunity to fully acquire a first language in this manner, and many have below-average levels of literacy in a written language. In fact, studies have shown that the majority of deaf high school graduates in the United States have only a fourth-grade English reading level (Holt, 1993). This means that students age 18 and older have a reading level more typical of a 10-year-old student. Unfortunately, many strategies for making elements of the hearing world accessible to the deaf (e.g., television closed captioning or teletype telephone services) assume that the user has strong English literacy skills. Because many deaf people who have difficulty reading English possess stronger fluency in ASL, an automated English-to-ASL machine translation system can make more information and services accessible in situations where English captioning text is at too high a reading level or where a live interpreter is unavailable.

Previous English-to-ASL machine translation systems have used 3D graphics software to animate a virtual human character to perform ASL output. Generally, a script written in a basic animation instruction set controls the character's movement. To accomplish this, machine translation systems must translate English text into a script directing the character to perform ASL. Previous projects have either used word-to-sign dictionaries to produce English-like manual signing output, or they have incorporated some rules for how to translate English sentence structures into ASL structures to generate ASL output (Huenerfauth, 2003; Sáfár & Marshall, 2001; Speers, 2001; Zhao et al., 2000). Although most of this ASL machine translation work is still preliminary, there is promise that a machine translation system will one day be able to translate many kinds of English-to-ASL sentences, although some particular ASL phenomena—those involving complex use of the signing space—have proven difficult for traditional machine translation approaches. This chapter will present our software design for generating these expressions.

THE FOCUS OF OUR RESEARCH: ASL CLASSIFIER PREDICATES

ASL signers use the space around them for several grammatical, discourse, and descriptive purposes. During an ASL conversation, constructions called *classifier predicates* allow signers to use their hands to position, move, trace, or reorient an imaginary object in the space in front of them to indicate the location, movement, shape, contour, physical dimension, or some other property of a corresponding real-world entity under discussion (DeMatteo, 1977; Liddell, 1977; Mandel, 1977; Supalla, 1978, 1982, 1986). Classifier predicates of movement and location (CPMLs) convey the movement and location of these objects (generally without indicating their specific size or shape). A CPML consists of a semantically meaningful handshape and a 3D hand movement path. The handshape is chosen from a closed set based on characteristics of the entity described (whether it is a vehicle, human, animal, etc.) and what aspect of the entity the signer is describing (surface, position, motion, etc.).

For example, the English sentence "The car drove past the cat" could be expressed in ASL using two classifier predicates. First, a signer would move a hand in a *hooked* V handshape (see Figure 8.1) forward and slightly downward to a point in space in front of his or her torso where an imaginary miniature cat could be envisioned. Next, a hand in a *number 3* handshape would trace a path in space past the "cat" as if it were a car driving past the "cat." Generally, *hooked* V handshapes are used for animals, and *number 3* handshapes for vehicles. The third handshape shown in Figure 8.1 is called a *number 1* handshape, and it is generally used to represent upright human figures. There are many other handshapes used during classifier predicates not included in this figure.

The ability of classifier predicates to visually represent a 3D scene makes them particularly difficult to generate using traditional computational linguistic methods. For our ASL machine translation system to produce this pair of classifier predicates, we use a spatial model depicting how the scene is arranged, including the locations of the cat and the car. Previous ASL machine translation systems have largely omitted classifier predicate expressions from their

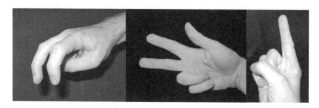

Figure 8.1   Some handshapes used during classifier predicates: *hooked* V, *number 3*, and *number 1*.

coverage. However, many English concepts lack a fluent ASL translation without them. Further, classifier predicates are common in ASL; signers produce a classifier predicate one to 17 times per minute, depending on genre (Morford & MacFarlane, 2003). So, systems that cannot produce classifier predicates can only produce ASL of limited fluency.

REPRESENTATIONS AND GENERALIZATION IN OUR ASL SOFTWARE

We discussed above how the work of NLP researchers can be broadly categorized as falling within a Classical-NLP or Statistical-NLP design approach. Although there are advantages to having an automatic algorithm discern the structure of a language, Statistical-NLP approaches often require very large amounts of linguistically annotated samples of the human language under consideration. These resources may be unavailable and expensive to build for many languages. (It is very human-labor-intensive to accurately and consistently annotate the linguistic information in a large sample of text in some language.) For various reasons, it is quite difficult to build ASL resources necessary for Statistical-NLP approaches (Huenerfauth, 2006), and so our work (and most other computational work on sign language) uses Classical-NLP.

Because of this Classical-NLP approach, the "generalization" that occurs in our research is performed by a team of human linguistic developers who are implementing an ASL system. We have designed new representations for ASL sentences that enable programmers to design only a *small number* of "building blocks" that can be composed together to characterize the structure of a *large number* of ASL sentences. A good representation helps us to encode the grammatical structure of ASL in a way that will help us to make generalizations across specific ASL sentences and to take advantage of these generalizations to encode the structure of the language in a succinct manner. It is important to note that representations that are "good" from a computer science perspective could differ from cognitive models that humans may use to generalize linguistic data in their minds during language acquisition.

Human software designers must keep in mind the set of all possible grammatically correct ASL sentences, and then they must write a finite set of rules that direct the software how to produce correct ASL sentences (without accidentally allowing it to produce any incorrect ones). These rules are typically fill-in-the-blank templates that allow words in the software's dictionary (of a particular part of speech or particular subtype) to be used to produce a sentence. If the rules are incorrectly written, then they might allow combinations of words in a grammatically incorrect order. If the rules are written in too restrictive a manner, then they may not allow the system to produce all possible ASL sentences.

When designing a candidate set of grammar rules to account for all possible sentences in a language, a linguist may sometimes write a grammar that is called *undergenerative*—meaning that there is no possible way to derive some sentences in the language using the set of grammar rules currently under consideration. Other grammars may be *overgenerative*—meaning that the set of rules allows us to derive strings of words that are not possible sentences in the language that the linguist is attempting to model. The grammar rules should define the set of strings that are correct, grammatical sentences by encoding generalizations of the structure across all sentences in that language. There is a link between how "generative" a grammar is and the concept of *generalization* examined in this book. In many cases, an undergenerative grammar is not generalizing enough about how words may be combined to produce grammatical sentences (i.e., it may also be missing some necessary rules), and an overgenerative grammar is often generalizing too much (i.e., it may decide that some word combinations are correct sentences in the language when they actually are not).

Even before a computational linguist writes a set of rules for how to produce the sentences in some language, they must first select a *formalism* (i.e., a format of representation) to use for writing their rules. Different grammar formalisms may allow a linguist designing a grammar for a language to encode particular kinds of restrictions on the grammar rules that specify when they can be applied. Thus, some formalisms may make it easier for the linguist to encourage or to prevent particular generalizations over the set of sentences in the language. A good grammar formalism will give the linguist enough control without forcing him or her to specify too many restrictions (that might prevent the grammar from succinctly encoding the sentences of the language).

To illustrate how the choice of a linguistic representation can support generalization during the design of natural language processing software, this chapter will discuss the formalisms we have used to encode the structure of ASL classifier predicate sentences in our software. Some ways of representing these sentences would make it difficult to generalize enough when capturing their underlying structure, and some representations would make it difficult to restrict generalization sufficiently so that we only encode the structure of correct, grammatical ASL sentences. We will discuss how our design choices have facilitated the successful creation of our system.

OVERVIEW OF OUR SOFTWARE: 6-STEP PROCESS

We have developed a prototype software system for producing animations of a virtual human character performing American Sign Language classifier predicates; these ASL sentences are translations of English sentences that discuss the movement and locations of a set of people or objects. Our software uses a 6-step process for translating English sentences about 3D scenes into ASL sentences. The steps are as follows:

1. Analyze an English sentence.
2. Create a list of objects discussed in the sentence.
3. Visualize a 3D scene.
4. Map the scene to the signing space.
5. Plan the classifier predicate sentences.
6. Create 3D animation output.

This chapter will focus on the computational linguistic work in step 5, but to give the reader a sense of the overall system, we will discuss the surrounding steps of the translation process.

Step 1: Analyzing an English Sentence to Identify Important Information

The input to the system in step 1 is the text of an English sentence that should be translated into ASL. Although many computational linguistic researchers have developed software for analyzing the structure of an English sentence, identifying the main verb in a sentence, and identifying other linguistic details in a sentence, the automatic analysis of English sentences was not a focus of our research. So, for our prototype system, we have merely simulated the work of step 1. Our software is given an analyzed English sentence that contains the following information: the text of an English sentence discussing the movement or location of some people or objects, with the main verb of the sentence identified, and with the main noun phrases in the sentence (that refer to the people and objects) also identified. From our earlier example, "The car drove past the cat," the main verb of the sentence is *drove*, and the important nouns include the *car* and the *cat*.

Step 2: Creating a List of Objects Discussed in the Sentence

Given the analyzed English sentence with the main verb and important noun phrases identified, our system maintains a list of the set of objects that are discussed in that sentence. In our software, we refer to each item in this list as a *discourse entity*, each of which represents a particular person, object, or concept currently being discussed in the sentence. Although there are various pieces of information that may be useful to record about each object, there is one "state" of the object particularly important for the classifier predicate–planning process that occurs in step 5. We keep track of a true-false value as to whether each object is currently "topicalized"—the meaning and purpose of this value will be discussed in the "Example of a Classifier Predicate Template" section. The true-false value of this property may change over time during the ASL sentence-planning process.

Step 3: Visualizing a 3D Scene to Be Described in ASL

Human ASL signers who perform classifier predicates use their spatial knowledge and reasoning to visualize the elements of the scene they are discussing, and so English-to-ASL translation software also benefits from a 3D representation of the scene from which it could calculate the movement paths of classifier predicates. Our system uses *scene visualization software* to analyze an English text describing the motion of real-world objects and build a 3D graphical model of how the objects mentioned in the text are arranged and move (Huenerfauth, 2006). Scene visualization is a problem studied by several researchers, and there are multiple systems that can build a 3D model based on an English text, including the AnimNL system (Badler et al., 2000) and the WordsEye system (Coyne & Sproat, 2001).

One challenge for scene visualization systems is that English sentences are often ambiguous about the details of the spatial arrangement of objects that they discuss. When we say, "The car drove past the cat," we don't necessarily know whether the car was approaching from the left or right, nor what angle it was approaching from. The scene visualization system will often need to select one of these options when producing the 3D model, and it may not have sufficient information to make this decision. If there are errors in the way in which the scene visualizer arranges the objects in the 3D model, this error will be propagated through the later "steps" of the process and may become apparent in the classifier predicate animation that is produced. (If the scene visualizer decides that the *car* is to the left of the *cat*, then the classifier predicate that the virtual signer will perform will also indicate this arrangement.) Although dividing the English-to-ASL translation task into stages allows us to identify subproblems that could be solved using software created by other researchers, the use of a multistage design means that mistakes made in the early stages will likely propagate through the rest of the system.

Step 4: Mapping the 3D Scene to the Signing Space

Once an animated 3D model of the scene has been produced, it can be used in our English-to-ASL system in the following way: (a) The scene will be miniaturized (and possibly rotated), (b) the objects in the scene will be made transparent, and (c) the scene will be "overlaid" onto the space in front of the ASL signing character (see Figure 8.2). Thus, the scene visualization software produces a computer model (a 3D scene) of how some objects are arranged in space, and this model is miniaturized and placed in front of the animated signing character. The color or other precise visual details of the cat and the car are not important for the system to be

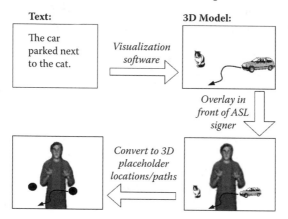

Figure 8.2 Use of scene visualization in American Sign Language (ASL) machine translation.

correct—this information does not affect the performance of classifier predicates of movement and location.

For each object that has been mapped into the space in front of the signer, we record the following information:

- A 3D location (center of mass) of the object in the scene.
- A 3D orientation of the object (i.e., how the object is tilted or turned in 3D space).
- A link to the discourse entity (in the list from step 2) representing this object.
- A set of true-false values indicating whether the object is a human, an animal, a vehicle, or some other category. (This final set of information determines which handshape the signer should use to indicate the object during a classifier predicate. For example, vehicles are typically represented by the *number* 3 handshape shown in Figure 8.1.)

Step 5: Planning the ASL Classifier Predicate Process

In step 5, our software plans a set of ASL sentences to be performed that convey how the people or objects described in the original English sentences move through space. During this step of the process, the system must make choices based on the grammatical requirements of ASL. To facilitate this process, we have designed a novel format for rules representing the structure of ASL classifier predicates. These rules act like templates that specify in general how different types of classifier predicates should be performed. These templates are used by the system to produce specific sentences that describe how a particular object moves through space in a particular way.

We have already implemented an initial set of rules (using this format) for a small subset of ASL classifier predicates (as a proof of concept). These rules access information contained in the discourse entity list (from step 2) and the 3D mapping of objects onto the space in front of the signer (from step 4). This information is used to plan the movements of the signer's hands and body to perform grammatically correct ASL classifier predicate sentences. Before discussing step 5 of our system in more detail, we will first discuss the final step (step 6) of our software so that it is clear what the output of step 5 should be.

Step 6: Producing an ASL Animation

The output of step 5 is a timeline of the performance of the parts of the virtual human signer's body. The entire "pose" of our animated human character's body can be specified using a small set of numerical parameters: the 3D location where the signer's eyes are aimed, the 3D location where the signer's forehead is tilted, the 3D location and orientation in space for each of the signer's hands, the shape for each hand, and so on. Thus, the goal of step 5 is to build a timeline for how these values change over time during the ASL sentences to be performed. In step 6, this "script" for the movement of the animated character is used to generate an actual animation output to be displayed on the computer screen. This chapter does not discuss the 3D graphic and animation details of step 6; more details may be found in Huenerfauth (2006) and Huenerfauth, Zhou, Gu, and Allbeck (2007, 2008).

REPRESENTATIONS OF ASL CLASSIFIER PREDICATES: STEP 5 IN MORE DETAIL

Our approach to representing and generating animations of ASL classifier predicates is based upon a linguistic model proposed by Liddell (2003a, 2003b) in which ASL classifier predicates are stored as a large set of templates in a list. They are called *templates* because each represents how a whole *class* of classifier predicates could be performed, and one must "fill in the blanks" in the template to produce a specific ASL classifier predicate. For example, there may be one template representing classifier predicates expressing that a car is parked at a particular 3D point in space; when this template is turned into an actual classifier predicate, then the 3D coordinate of the car would be "filled in" to the template to produce a complete ASL sentence. The template records information that is the same across all performances (e.g., the handshape during classifier predicates showing a car should be the *number 3* handshape; see Figure 8.1).

Our system contains a list of classifier predicate templates that represent types of classifier predicate performances that the virtual human signer can perform. For example, there is a template for showing the location of an animal, showing a motion path for an upright-walking human, or showing how a vehicle parks near some other objects. A template will specify a handshape for the signer to use when performing a classifier predicate showing the movement of a specific type of object. For instance, as mentioned, the template for animal locations uses the *hooked* V handshape, but the template for a motorized vehicle uses the *number 3* handshape. Generally, the template does not specify the exact motion path for the classifier predicate because this value is calculated based on the particular 3D spatial location and orientation of the object being described. The 3D location and orientation information from the scene visualization process (step 3) and the mapping of the 3D scene onto the space in front of the signer (step 4) is used to determine how the signer's hands should move through space. Thus, the 3D information is what we "fill in" to the template when we want to generate a specific sentence.

Each classifier predicate template is linked to a set of English motion verbs that may be translated into ASL using this template. For example, ASL classifier predicates showing the movement of a vehicle object may be linked to the English verb *drive*. During the generation process in step 5 of the software, the system selects a template to use (based on the English verb identified in step 1). Next, the locations, orientations, and specific movement paths of objects in a 3D space around the signer are used to fill the remaining parameters of the template and produce a full specification of how to perform the classifier predicate.

Sections of a Classifier Predicate Template

All of the templates used by our software to represent the structure of ASL classifier predicates contain the following sections. The examples shown in this chapter are simplified versions of the classifier predicate templates used in our system; a more complete description of our representation appears in Huenerfauth (2006).

- **Parameters** are a list of variables that the template will access and modify. These variables may represent objects currently under discussion (like the *car* or *cat* that were mentioned in the original English sentence). These variables may also include parts of the signer's body (such as the left or right hand).
- **Preconditions** are requirements that have to be satisfied in order for this classifier predicate sentence to be performed by the virtual signing character. During the planning process, the software can insert additional actions prior to the performance of this sentence in order to satisfy some of these requirements.
- **Actions** are the basic units of output animation that are associated with this template (it specifies the values for the locations and shape of the parts of the signer's body during the timeline of the performance).
- **Effects** are changes to the values of some variables that result from per- forming this particular classifier predicate. (Examples are discussed in the next section.)

Example of a Classifier Predicate Template

The next two sections will discuss the classifier predicate template shown in Figure 8.3. This template can be used by our software to produce an animation of a signer performing a classifier predicate to show the location of an object using the handshape for stationary animals (the *hooked* V handshape). In the "car drove past the cat" example that has been mentioned in this chapter, our software could use the template in Figure 8.3 to generate the classifier predicate that shows the location of the cat (prior to showing the movement of the car past the cat). The meaning and purpose of the various portions of the template in Figure 8.3 will be explained below.

The template shown in Figure 8.3 includes parameters, preconditions, actions, and effects. These parts of the template are used to represent important informa- tion during the planning process. In the parameters section of Figure 8,3, *de0* is a variable representing some discourse entity in the list from step 2 (e.g., some *cat* whose location will be shown using a classifier predicate).

The precondition *isAnimal(de0)* ensures that the discourse entity *de0* is an ani- mal. This allows the system to restrict the use of this classifier predicate so that it is only used to show the location of objects that are animals. Otherwise, the software might incorrectly use this classifier predicate to show the location of other kinds

LOCATE-STATIONARY-ANIMAL

Parameters:	Discourse Entity:	de0
	Resources List:	resource_list0
Preconditions:	(hasDom resource_list0)	
	(hasEg resource_list0)	
	(isAnimal de0)	
	(hasGhost de0)	
	(topicalized de0)	
Actions:	(setLocation	target: (location dom)
		function: downward_arc_to_location
		source: (location (ghost de0)))
	(setOrientation	target: (orientation dom)
		function: get_to_final_orientation
		source: (orientation)ghost de0))
		alignment: top_backpalm_front_knuckles
	(setHandshape	target: (handshape dom)
		function: get_to_final_handshape
		source: hooked_v_handshape)
	(setLocation	target: (location eg)
		function: get_to_final_location
		source: (location (ghost de0)))
Effects:	(topicalized de0)	
	(identified de0	
	(position de0)	

Figure 8.3   An ASL classifier predicate template for showing the location of an animal.

of objects. Only "animal" objects should be shown in 3D space using the *hooked V* handshape.

Finally, the precondition *isTopicalized(de0)* ensures that *de0* is already an object that is the topic of conversation. Before a signer can use his hand to show the location of an animal object in 3D space around him, the specific animal whose location is being shown must already clearly be the topic of conversation. The signer can accomplish this by first performing a noun phrase that refers to this animal prior to performing the classifier predicate that shows its location in space. For example, the signer could perform the noun phrase *cat* prior to performing an animal location classifier predicate. Then, it would be clear to whoever sees this animation that the signer is going to show the location of a cat. Thus, the precondition *isTopicalized(de0)* allows the software to encode this grammatical requirement of ASL—if an object is about to be described by a classifier predicate, then it must be clear what object you are discussing.

Inside of the "Actions" field of Figure 8.3, values are assigned to the locations, orientations, and handshapes of the various parts of the signer's body. There are various parts of the signer's body whose movement may be specified in the "Actions" field of the template, including "dominant_hand," "nondominant_hand," "eye_gaze," "head_tilt," or "eye_brow." For most signers, their right hand is their dominant hand, and their left hand is their nondominant one. Typically, our software uses a location or orientation value for an object that has been

TOPICALIZATION-PHRASE

Parameters:	Discourse Entity: de0
Preconditions:	(none)
Actions:	Perform noun phrase referring to the entity de0.
	The eye-gaze should look at the audience.
	The eye-brows should be raised during the noun phrase.
Effects:	isTopicalized de0)

Figure 8.4 An ASL template for performing a noun phrase for an object under discussion.

mapped to the 3D space around the signer to assign a value to each part of the body. In this case, the location of the object under discussion is used to calculate where the signer's hand should go during the classifier predicate for showing the location of the animal object in 3D space. The orientation of the hand is also based on the entity being described, and its handshape will be a *hooked* V (again, used for animals).

The effects field contains true-false values that should be set to *true* when this template is used to produce an animation action. Although Figure 8.3 does not contain any items in the "Effects" field, the template shown in Figure 8.4 does. When our software encounters the precondition *isTopicalized(de0)* in the "Locate-Stationary-Animal" template, if the object to be described is not currently the topic of the conversation, then the software must find a way to make it so. One way for the software to accomplish this is to trigger another animation action before the classifier predicate in which the signer will perform a noun phrase referring to the object. This will have the effect of making the object a topic of conversation. We can see how the "Topicalization-Phrase" template has the following effect: *isTopicalized(de0)*. Thus, our software can trigger this template to perform its action first, and then the precondition for the "Locate-Stationary-Animal" template will be satisfied.

OUR CLASSIFIER PREDICATE REPRESENTATION SUPPORTING GENERALIZATION

The representation used in our software has been shown to be part of a 6-step process for generating ASL classifier predicates, and an example of the representation has been shown in Figure 8.3. This section will examine how the design of this representation has supported the process of *generalization*—specifically, how the representation has facilitated the work of human software programmers who are building an English-to-ASL translation system that can produce a wide variety of ASL sentences. The programmers must be able to make generalizations about common types of ASL sentences so that they can build the software in a modular "building-block" approach; the goal is to create English-to-ASL software that can produce as many types of ASL sentences as possible without having to explicitly write a template for every possible sentence. A single template must be able to produce a variety of ASL classifier predicate animations. With this goal of supporting generalization, there are three desired properties that our representation must have: (a) abstraction, (b) composability, and (c) specificity.

Our software contains a large number of templates for different kinds of ASL classifier predicates, but it does not contain a template for every possible sentence that it might produce. This is why it is important that our representation uses *abstraction*—each template represents an entire class of ASL classifier predicates. When certain information is used to "fill in the blanks" in the template, then it becomes a specific ASL classifier predicate sentence. In the example shown in Figure 8.3, the template itself did not include the 3D coordinates for where the signer's hand should go during the classifier predicate. Instead, it would use the 3D coordinates of the "cat" placeholder that was mapped to the 3D space in front of the signer. When this 3D information was added to the template, then a fully specified script is produced that tells the virtual signing character how to move its body to perform a classifier predicate that communicates the location of the animal. Thus, the 3D information from the scene visualization process (that determined how to map objects onto the space in front of the signer) can be used to produce many different ASL classifier predicate performances without requiring the programmer to write a different template for every possible 3D location and orientation of objects in the scene. The same template shown in Figure 8.3 could be used to produce ASL classifier predicates that show the location of "cat" objects in other 3D locations in space or show the location of other kinds of animal objects.

Another feature of our representation that facilitates generalization is the *composability* of the templates. We have seen that in order to satisfy the preconditions of one template, the system may need to trigger additional actions (whose effects satisfy the preconditions of later templates). In the example shown in Figures 8.3 and 8.4, the "Topicalization-Phrase" template was used to "topicalize" the object under discussion before performing a classifier predicate about it. In fact, the "Topicalization-Phrase" template could perform a similar function for many different sentences—thus, it is a "building block" that can be reused in a modular manner during the classifier predicate–planning process. Thus, our templates can be used and recombined in many different ways to produce different kinds of ASL classifier predicate performances; this ability to be reused means that a human programmer building an English-to-ASL system can write a small amount of programming code but enable the software to produce a wide variety of ASL classifier predicate animations.

Although the properties of abstraction and composability allow a small number of templates to produce a wide variety of ASL classifier predicate animations, this generalization must be limited in some way. Otherwise, the components may promote overgeneralization—that is, the templates may be combined by the software to produce animation performances that are not actually grammatically correct ASL classifier predicates. For example, the software might incorrectly use a classifier predicate with the wrong handshape to refer to some object, or it might perform two classifier predicates sequentially without the appropriate signs in between them. For this reason, our representation also includes the property of *specificity*. Our templates must restrict the situations in which they can be used so that the software produces only grammatically correct ASL classifier predicates. The primary way in which this occurs in the example in Figures 8.3 and 8.4 is through the use of true-false tests in the "Preconditions" portion of the template. For example, the "Locate-Stationary-Animal" template includes a precondition that requires the object it is describing to be an "animal." This requirement ensures that the software does not accidentally use this classifier predicate (with a *hooked* V handshape) to refer to objects that are not animals. Another example in Figure 8.3 is the precondition that the *de0* object being described by the template has already been "topicalized" prior to the classifier predicate being performed.

IMPLEMENTATION PROGRESS

To illustrate how the design sketched in this chapter can be used to successfully implement a classifier predicate animation system, we have built a prototype of the classifier predicate generator of our English-to-ASL system (Huenerfauth, 2006; Huenerfauth et al., 2007, 2008). This prototype consists of the linguistic data structures and processing architecture, and it has sufficient lexical and grammatical resources to support a limited linguistic repertoire of ASL classifier predicates. A pilot evaluation study was conducted in which native ASL signers evaluated the output of the system in comparison to several baselines (Huenerfauth, 2005, 2006; Huenerfauth et al., 2008). This pilot study indicated that the overall software design of the system was capable of generating animations of ASL sentences that participants felt were grammatical, understandable, and natural appearing (Huenerfauth, 2006). The descriptions of the classifier predicate template formalism shown in this chapter were simplified to illustrate key issues relating to generalization for the purposes of this chapter. A more complete discussion of the technical aspects of the system and its design may be found in Huenerfauth (2006) and Huenerfauth et al. (2008).

CONCLUSION

This chapter has focused on how the choice of representation for a linguistic construction in a language can have a major impact on the ease with which generalizations about that language can be made—and, consequently, the ease with which developers can create natural language processing software for that language. By way of example, this chapter has examined a representation of the structure of classifier predicates, a construction in ASL whose 3D spatial properties required a representation unlike those traditionally used for written languages. We have described a 6-step process for translating English text into ASL classifier predicates. The use of a templated design that is abstract, composable, and specific successfully allowed us to build software in which a single template could be used to generate a much larger number of ASL classifier predicate performances.

ACKNOWLEDGMENTS

I would like to thank my collaborators at the Center for Human Modeling and Simulation at the University of Pennsylvania: Liming Zhao, Erdan Gu, and Jan Allbeck. I would like to thank Mitch Marcus, Martha Palmer, and Norman Badler for their advice and support. This work has been supported by a grant from the U.S. National Science Foundation (Award No. 0520798, "SGER: Generating Animations of American Sign Language Classifier Predicates," Universal Access Program, 2005) and by a grant from the Siemens Corporation ("Generating Animations of American Sign Language," Go PLM Grant Program, Siemens Automation & Discovery, UGS PLM Software).

REFERENCES

Badler, N., Bindiganavale, R., Allbeck, J., Schuler, W., Zhao, L., Lee, S., et al. (2000, March). Parameterized action representation and natural language instructions for dynamic behavior modification of embodied agents. In *Proceedings of the AAAI Spring Symposium*. Menlo Park, CA: Association for the Advancement of Artificial Intelligence.

Coyne, R., & Sproat, R. (2001). WordsEye: An automatic text-to-scene conversion system. In *Proceedings of ACM SIGGRAPH 2001* (pp. 487–496). Retrieved November 8, 2009, from http://portal.acm.org/toc.cfm?id=383259&type=proceeding&coll=portal &dl=ACM&idx=SERIES382&part=series&WantType=Proceedings&title=Internati onal%20Conference%20on%20Computer%20Graphics%20and%20Interactive%20 Techniques&CFID=3706057&CFTOKEN=14294579

DeMatteo, A. (1977). Visual analogy and the visual analogues in American Sign Language. In L. A. Friedman (Ed.), *On the other hand: New perspectives on American Sign Language* (pp. 109–136). New York: Academic Press.

Holt, J. (1993). *Demographic,* Stanford Achievement Test: 8th edition for deaf and hard of hearing students: Reading comprehension subgroup results. American Annals of the Deaf., 138, pp. 172–175.

Huenerfauth, M. (2003). *Survey and critique of ASL natural language generation and machine translation systems* (Technical Report MS-CIS-03-32). Philadelphia: Department of Computer and Information Science, University of Pennsylvania.

Huenerfauth, M. (2004). A multi-path architecture for machine translation of English text into ASL animation. In *Proceedings of the HLT-NAACL Student Workshop*. Retrieved November 8, 2009, from http://portal.acm.org/citation.cfm?id=1614038

Huenerfauth, M. (2005). American Sign Language generation: Multimodal NLG with multiple linguistic channels. In *Proceedings of the Association for Computational Linguistics 43rd annual meeting, Student Research Workshop*. Retrieved November 8, 2009, from http://www.aclweb.org/anthology/P/P05/P05-1000.pdf

Huenerfauth, M. (2006). *Generating American Sign Language classifier predicates for English-to-ASL machine translation*. Unpublished doctoral dissertation, Department of Computer and Information Science, University of Pennsylvania.

Huenerfauth, M., Zhou, L., Gu, E., & Allbeck, J. (2007, June 23–30). Design and evaluation of an American Sign Language generator. In *Proceedings of the 45th annual meeting of the Association for Computational Linguistics, Workshop on Embodied Language Processing*, Prague, Czech Republic. Retrieved November 8, 2009, from http://www.aclweb.org/anthology/W/W07/W07-1907.pdf

Huenerfauth, M., Zhou, L., Gu, E., and Allbeck, J. (2008). Evaluation of American Sign Language generation by native ASL signers. *ACM Transactions on Accessible Computing, 1*(1), .

Liddell, S. (1977). *An investigation into the syntactic structure of ASL.* Unpublished doctoral dissertation, University of California, San Diego.

Liddell, S. (2003a). *Grammar, gesture, and meaning in American Sign Language.* Cambridge: Cambridge University Press.

Liddell, S. (2003b). Sources of meaning in ASL classifier predicates. In K. Emmorey (Ed.), *Perspectives on classifier constructions in sign languages, Workshop on Classifier Constructions, La Jolla, San Diego, California* (pp. 249–257). Mahwah, NJ: Lawrence Erlbaum.

Liu, Y. (2003). *Interactive reach planning for animated characters using hardware acceleration.* Unpublished doctoral dissertation, Department of Computer and Information Science, University of Pennsylvania.

Mandel, M. (1977). Iconic devices in American Sign Language. In L. A. Friedman (Ed.), *On the other hand: New perspectives on American Sign Language* (pp. 57–107). New York: Academic Press.

Morford, J., & MacFarlane, J. (2003). Frequency characteristics of American Sign Language. *Sign Language Studies, 3*(2), 213–225.

Sáfár, É., & Marshall, I. (2001). The architecture of an English-text-to-sign-languages translation system. In G. Angelova (Ed.), *Proceedings of recent advances in natural language processing* (pp. 223–228). Amsterdam: John Benjamins.

Speers, d'A. L. (2001). *Representation of American Sign Language for machine translation.* Unpublished doctoral dissertation, Department of Linguistics, Georgetown University.

Supalla, T. (1978). Morphology of verbs of motion and location. In F. Caccamise & D. Hicks (Eds.), *Proceedings of the Second National Symposium on Sign Language Research and Teaching* (pp. 27–45). Silver Spring, MD: National Association for the Deaf.

Supalla, T. (1982). *Structure and acquisition of verbs of motion and location in American Sign Language.* Unpublished doctoral dissertation, University of California, San Diego.

Supalla, T. (1986). The classifier system in American Sign Language. *Noun Phrases and Categorization, Typological Studies in Language, 7,* 181–214.

Zhao, L., Kipper, K., Schuler, W., Vogler, C., Badler, N., & Palmer, M. (2000). A machine translation system from English to American Sign Language. In *Proceedings of the Association for Machine Translation in the Americas.* Berlin: Springer.

9

Generalization in Higher Order Cognition
Categorization and Analogy as Bridges to Stored Knowledge

KIMERY LEVERING and KENNETH J. KURTZ

Without effort, he had learned English, French, Portuguese, Latin. I suspect, nevertheless, that he was not very capable of thought. To think is to forget a difference, to generalize, to abstract. In the overly replete world of Funes, there were nothing but details.

— ***Funes, the Memorious,*** **by Jorge Borges**

*J*orge Borges tells a fictional story about a man with the extraordinary ability to remember specific details of everything that happened to him. This ability came at the detriment of experiencing each instance of an object, person, or category as completely distinct. Every time he saw a dog (even the same dog), he was incapable of drawing inferences based on his past experiences because he saw each instance as a different entity. Such an extreme case, although unlikely, elucidates the importance of abstraction and generalization in how one interprets the world. These mechanisms organize objects and events into useful concepts and categories, allowing us to understand our environment and extend predictions to new experiences. Without this ability, everyday occurrences would lack coherence and a grounding in terms of what could be learned and generalized.

In this chapter we aim to convey why generalization is so integral to the process of interpreting the world around us. Although we will address a number of specific ways in which generalization is used to develop and apply knowledge, it is valuable to first define in a broad sense what generalization means from the perspective of the psychological study of human higher order cognition. We use the term *generalization*, first, to refer to cases in which general knowledge about objects, events, or concepts is abstracted over a set of instances; and, second, to refer to cases in which existing knowledge (generic, but also potentially specific) is accessed and applied to guide the interpretation of a target instance. These purposes are clearly interrelated. Generalized knowledge must be present to guide interpretation of the world and guided interpretation plays a role in mediating the formation of general knowledge.

To provide an overview of the chapter's organization, we begin our discussion by defining key terms and establishing a set of foundational issues. We then discuss in some detail how generalization to new instances can be based on commonalities in (a) category membership, or (b) relational structure. In each of these cases, we review theory and research aimed at understanding how, and to what extent, an experience becomes represented abstractly and the circumstances under which properties of abstract concepts are transferred to new experiences. We describe research demonstrating the circumstances under which generalization is more or less likely to occur. Although the nature of our discussion includes the presumption that *similarity* is the primary mediating factor in generalization, we also attempt to incorporate alternate perspectives such as the theory- or knowledge-based view of categorization (Murphy & Medin, 1985).

THE FOUNDATIONS

Because we frequently use the terms *representation* and *similarity* throughout this chapter, it is important to briefly establish what we mean. There is not a clear consensus in cognitive psychology about exact definitions for these terms, so for purposes of clarity, some subtle complexities will be overlooked (for more in-depth analysis of these topics, suggested readings include Gentner & Medina, 1998; Goldstone, 1994; Hahn & Chater, 1997; Markman, 1999; Medin, Goldstone, & Gentner, 1993; Murphy, 2002; Schyns, Goldstone, & Thibaut, 1998).

Representation

As we move through life, we are constantly taking in information about the world around us, not only so we know how to act or respond in a given moment, but also so we can learn and remember information for later retrieval. In order to do all these things, we *represent* both general and specific forms of information in our minds. Later in the chapter we will talk more about specific theories of representation, but in a general sense, a representation can be viewed as a mental model, system, or data structure composed of elements corresponding to content encoded from entities in the world. There is rarely a perfect match between this representation and the actual world. Instead, it is widely thought that the creation, activation, and use of representations are infused with *constructive* processing that is mediated, subjective, and interpretative. For example, certain properties of an object might be represented as more central based on the goals of the individual or the nature of contrast categories (Levering & Kurtz, 2006; Schyns et al., 1998).

Similarity

Generalization or transfer of learning is closely linked to the presence of some form of representational similarity. To the extent that two entities are similar, they share certain properties or affiliations. One way we can talk about similarity is in terms of the physical, objective matching or mismatching of features that exist in the world. For example, a line that is 5 inches long might be considered more similar to a line that is 6 inches long than to one that is 25 inches long. A blue car might be considered more similar to a teal car than an orange car, all else being equal. Although this is one way of assessing similarity, it turns out that in practice people's idea of similarity is often more complex and subjective. In many cases physical dimensions are unable to accurately encompass the rich representations and relationships inherent in our conceptual system. One example of this is that learning to place two objects in the same category does not change anything about their actual form, but makes the objects more psychologically similar (Goldstone, Lippa, & Shiffrin, 2001; Kurtz, 1996; Livingston, Andrews, & Harnad, 1998). Similarity has also been shown to be quite flexible and subject to influence from context. Medin et al. (1993) demonstrated that people list different and even contradictory features about a specific object depending on the context of other objects provided (see Tversky, 1977, for foundational work on similarity in context).

A number of methods have been established for evaluating the psychological or representational relationship between stimuli or concepts. One frequently used method called *multidimensional scaling* (Torgerson, 1952) creates a representational solution using a set of derived dimensions. This process begins by employing some measure of how proximal a set of items are to one another. A common method for this is to show a group of participants all possible pairs from a stimulus set and have them rate each pairwise similarity. From this information, the "psychological distance" between each pair of examples can be represented in a multidimensional space using a small number of derived dimensions that optimally capture the full set of relationships. These psychological dimensions need not be meaningfully defined, but materialize a posteriori from the data and serve as tools for describing representational organization. Similarity between concepts and, thus, the likelihood of generalization can be derived from their psychological distance—measured as a function of metric distance along these created dimensions. For example, Shepard (1987) argued for a universal law of generalization at the core of human cognition stating that the probability that two objects will have the same consequence decays exponentially as their metric psychological distance increases (see also Tenenbaum & Griffiths, 2001).

Tversky's (1977) contrast model challenges the idea of similarity being based on metric distances between points in space. Instead, Tversky presented an approach that computes similarity based on matching and mismatching features. The similarity of two objects is calculated by subtracting the features of each object not shared by the other (differences) from the features shared by them both (commonalities). Adjustable weights for each feature make it possible to differentially assign levels of salience. The contrast model does not assume that similarity is fixed in relation to other objects (weighting of features is dependent on the task), thereby accounting for some cases of asymmetrical similarity and contextual influence.

Role of Theory

Some theorists have rejected the idea that similarity is able to fully account for conceptual organization and generalization. Much of this argument centers on the critique of similarity being unconstrained (the degree of similarity depends on the features considered and how they are weighted) or lacking explanatory power (see Goldstone, 1994). Instead, the coherence underlying concepts may be organized around knowledge or theories grounded in causal relationships (Murphy, 2002; Murphy & Medin, 1985). Such intuitive theories about conceptual domains can provide meaningful constraints on the features that people construct, attend to, and encode. These constraints can drive not only the nature of conceptual organization, but also inferences about unknown properties and generalization to new examples.

Gentner and Markman (1997) proposed that differences between similarity-based and theory-based accounts of concept representation can potentially be reconciled if similarity is understood to operate not only on features but also on relationships between features. As we will soon discuss, organizing concepts around *structural* similarity has the potential to account for the types of relations that the theory view holds as central to representation. In this chapter, we will tend to consider generalization in terms of similarity, in regard first to features and then to structure. Although we also refer to the theory-based view, we will not focus on it because it is largely unspecified in its own right and the construct of similarity serves, at the very least, as a useful guideline or heuristic for applying generalizations.

CATEGORY-BASED GENERALIZATION

Although it is often taken for granted, comprehending the world around us involves solving a potentially continuous set of information-processing problems. We are constantly confronted with objects and events that we need to understand and make predictions about using preexisting knowledge. One tool that helps us understand our environment involves recognizing and using information about category membership. Imagine that while walking down the street, you encounter an animal that you have never seen before and cannot identify. Being able to realize that it is a type of dog (as opposed to, say, a wolf, fox, etc.) will help you to correctly interpret the situation and predict possible behaviors or outcomes—even if you have never encountered that particular dog, or even that entire type of dog, before.

Transfer of information based on category membership can be thought of as involving three possible stages. A necessary first stage is the abstraction across a group of examples to form a category-level representation (e.g., *dog*). This category can be extended to include a new case (e.g., a specific dog approaching you on the street) based on certain qualifications required for membership. From this classification, properties of the target instance can be inferred based on knowledge of preexisting members of the category or abstract knowledge of the category itself (e.g., *friendly*). In this section, we address each of these aspects of category-based generalization. First, we present the current theoretical frameworks for explaining category representations. The nature of these representations determines the form of category-level knowledge and, thus, the basis for membership decisions and inferences. We then review specific category-learning experiments that demonstrate some properties of categories that facilitate generalization to new examples. Last, we address how category knowledge can be generalized to produce inductive inferences about entire categories as opposed to reasoning about specific instances.

Theories About the Nature of Category Representation

Several competing classification theories and models have been proposed that make assumptions about the representational structure or nature of categories. An important distinction between these representational theories is in the degree of abstraction posited at the level of category knowledge. These assumptions drive predictions about whether and how generalization over instances occurs—as well as about what novel examples will be considered members of a learned category. That which establishes a category and makes it coherent is generally understood to be the same as the basis used to place new members into the category and to infer traits based on category membership (though see Armstrong, Gleitman, & Gleitman, 1983).

The earliest theories of category representation (e.g., rule based and prototype) tended to view category knowledge as consisting of abstract information that summarizes the central tendency across examples. Rule-based theories and models hypothesize that category representations consist of one or more rules or definitions that can be learned from experience (Bourne, 1982; Nosofsky, Palmeri, & McKinley, 1994). An example is the rule "If an animal has wings, flies, and eats bugs, it is a bird." Originally, rules were considered necessary and sufficient conditions for membership, although more complex models have been developed to deal with limitations arising from this assumption (for example, it is known that people consider some category members to be better than others and that some categories have members that are, in some way, exceptions). In the rule-based view, never-before-seen examples are evaluated relative to the rule, and those that satisfy it are considered members. If an object is encountered that is known to have wings, fly, and eat bugs, it will activate the category for *bird*. Importantly, abstraction across category members involves only those features addressed by the rule and thus takes on a focal quality unlike overall similarity (as in Shepard, 1987; Tversky, 1977).

Prototype theory, grounded in the theoretical and empirical work of Rosch and Mervis on family resemblance (1975), also views categories as being represented by abstract category-level knowledge. Instead of a rule, a person's idea of a category consists of a statistical representation that summarizes common properties across all learned exemplars (see Hampton, 1993; Homa, et al., 1973; Minda & Smith, 1998; Posner & Keele, 1968; and for a critical view, Medin & Schaffer, 1978; Nosofsky, 1992). In natural categories, this is typically thought of as a prototype that possesses properties present in most members of the category, although they need not be necessary or sufficient for membership. In artificial category-learning experiments, a prototype usually consists of feature averages along relevant dimensions across all members of the group. Regardless of how the prototype is defined or derived, a new category member is identified by its similarity to that prototype. An object would be considered a bird because it possesses those properties most common to the bird category. Evidence for this view initially came from a series of studies (Rosch & Mervis) showing that when asked to list attributes of natural categories, people were generally in agreement, and the degree of attribute match was a successful predictor of judged typicality. Further evidence emerges from studies demonstrating superior recognition or classification of instantiations of physical averages of artificial categories, even when those specific items were not shown during training (e.g., Posner & Keele).

An alternate view that has gained substantial popularity takes category representations to consist of a memory for each example of the category that has been experienced (Brooks, 1978; Kruschke, 1992; Medin & Schaffer, 1978; Nosofsky, 1986). In the extreme form of this view, a category is no more or less than a combination of these examples. For instance, your category of *bird* may be represented solely by memories of specific birds you have experienced. A novel instance is considered a category member based on the summed metric similarity to each item within the category relative to items in contrast categories. An object will be considered a bird if it is highly similar to one or all examples within your category representation of bird. It is important to note that this way of viewing category representation, by definition, *does not* necessitate the generation or activation of abstract category-level knowledge; activation of a category is solely by way of attention-weighted similarity to individual category members. As a consequence, if there is a category member (*penguin*) that is dissimilar to the rest of the category (*bird*), the category might be generalized to include a new example (*puffin*) that is highly similar to that member, even if its features do not match those of the majority of other category members.

There is experimental evidence that this type of representation is used, at least in certain situations. In an artificial learning task, Allen and Brooks (1991) explicitly told participants a rule that could successfully distinguish between categories, but when given new examples that were or were not members of the category, their ability to classify them was influenced significantly by the similarity of the test item to the specific training items. Brooks, Norman, and Allen (1991) demonstrated this sensitivity to exemplars with preexisting, ecological categories. They had doctors view slides of different types of skin diseases labeled with their diagnosis and had them rate how typical each was of its disease category. In a test phase the doctors viewed slides without labels and classified them as being in one of the three categories. This set of slides included some that had been previously studied and others that had not been studied but were in the same categories as studied examples. These untrained examples either were or were not superficially similar to the studied slides. Brooks et al. found that although the doctors did have abstract rules for classification, they were more accurate at classifying slides that were superficially similar to a studied slide.

Formal models based on assumptions derived from exemplar-specific and abstraction-oriented (rule-based, prototype) theories have been developed that can account for classic category-learning phenomena (Kruschke, 1992; Love, Gureckis,

& Medin, 2004; Nosofsky, 1986). Several models of category learning have also been introduced that integrate assumptions about representation and/or processing through a hybrid approach (e.g., Erickson & Kruschke, 1998; Nosofsky et al., 1994; Vandierendonck, 1995). In Nosofsky et al.'s RULEX model, instances are considered members of a category if they either satisfy stored category-level rules *or* activate the representation of specific exceptions to these rules. Vandierendonck proposed a model in which, depending on the availability of exemplar and category source information, generalization can be based on similarity to stored examples (referred to as *primary generalization*) or similarity to abstracted category information (referred to as secondary generalization). Erickson and Kruschke's ATRIUM model includes a module that works to detect unidimensional rules and one that associates individual exemplars with their category label.

Although similarity to reference points (i.e., specific exemplars or abstractions) provides one explanation of how knowledge can be transferred via category membership, it has been shown that in certain circumstances, coherence of a category may occur without similarity between its members (see Rips, 1989). Good examples of this are goal-derived categories such as "things to take out of the house in case of a fire" in which the members (e.g., children, photos, and money) are not similar in terms of broad overlap of features but nonetheless form a sensible category (Barsalou, 1983). The theory view is able to account for this because category organization is thought to reflect in part an explanatory principle common to all members (Murphy & Medin, 1985). New examples belong to the category not based on their level of similarity to other members or to a category average, but according to their fit to the conceptual basis or goal for membership. Along these lines, when people are asked to sort a group of items into categories, this organization is often strongly determined by prior knowledge about the features of the items (Ahn & Medin, 1992; Kaplan & Murphy, 1999). Kim and Ahn (2002) showed that clinicians' representations of mental disorders were organized around rich causal theories (not similarity) that also guided classifications of new mental disorder cases and inferences drawn about each case. It has also been shown that in supervised category-learning tasks involving meaningful features, learning is accelerated when those features and relationships between them coincide with previous knowledge (evidence reviewed in Murphy, 2002). In this view, generalization across examples occurs in part because there is an underlying explanatory basis for thinking of them as being related or similar, not necessarily based on feature matches (Murphy & Medin, 1985).

In order to present a complete analysis of the nature of category representation, it may be necessary to incorporate mechanisms accounting for aspects of both similarity and theory-like knowledge. A recently introduced computational model of category learning, DIVA, offers novel assumptions about the role of both in making classification decisions (Kurtz, 2007). In DIVA, each category is represented by a statistical model of the regularities that hold among members. When a new example is encountered, the model recodes the input and then tries to decode or reconstruct the original information in terms of each possible category. Instead of basing classification of a new item on its attention-weighted similarity to stored reference points, DIVA bases a decision on the relative ability of each category to account for (successfully recode and decode) its properties. The model has a unique ability to incorporate statistical category information and task constraints into the interpretation of the data. DIVA maintains exemplar sensitivity without explicitly storing each example and abstracts rule-like or statistical information without storing an explicit prototype or rule. As a basis for generalization, DIVA organizes categories around simple or complex statistical regularities that hold within categories and that differentiate between contrast categories. Established categories are generalized to new cases according to the extent to which these regularities are found to hold. Inferential and construal processes are built directly into the categorization process because the mechanism for assessing membership depends on constructing a representation of the target instance in terms of each category.

Category Properties That Facilitate Generalization of New Examples

Abstracted category-level knowledge is useful only in interpreting a novel experience when a category is generalized or extended to include it. An unknown animal encountered on the street must be recognized as a member of the *dog* category before dog-like properties can be inferred and dog-like predictions can be made about it. This type of category-to-example generalization is studied in two ways in the laboratory—through inquiring about inferences made from existing natural categories or by observing the acquisition and subsequent transfer of novel artificial category knowledge. In this section we focus on artificial category-learning experiments because the simple nature of the stimuli (usually visual shapes that vary along three or four binary dimensions) makes it easier to explore what types of learned category structures or members facilitate generalization to new examples. We first describe a typical category-learning experiment and how generalization is typically observed and measured. We then go on to present findings from the category-learning literature that demonstrate specific factors shown to facilitate the generalization of a category to new examples.

Typical Classification Tasks
In a typical artificial classification learning experiment, examples from novel categories (usually two) are presented one at a time in a random order, and participants are asked to decide which category is the correct one. In a supervised classification task, they are given feedback as to whether or not their answer is correct. Although they are guessing at first, over time they tend to learn the category distinction. In experiments of this sort, generalization is tested after classification training by introducing transfer items— items from the same domain that have not yet been seen. Generalizing to a new example occurs when one considers a new example to be an instance of the learned category. Testing novel instances is one of the only ways to make sure that some coherent and abstract concept of the category has been formed and that individual members have not simply been memorized.

By teaching participants novel categories, researchers have the advantage of being able to manipulate specific properties of the task, stimuli, and category structure in order to assess the role of each in one's ability to acquire a concept and apply it to new examples. Several factors have been isolated and identified as contributing to the ability of a category to extend or generalize to new examples. In broad terms, the factors that make a category more generalizable are those that promote ease of focus on common qualities of the objects within the category. The more a category representation is abstracted to include shared properties and disregard others, the more judgments of similarity will be determined based on those defining features.

Breadth of the Category   The number of unique instances that comprise a category has an effect on the probability that a new example will be treated as a member of that category. Learning a large range of category members will more likely lead to an abstraction of the category that facilitates generalization to new examples (Homa, 1978; Homa, Sterling, & Trepel, 1981; Smith & Minda, 1998). Homa (1978) trained subjects on categories composed of few or many random-dot patterns and then observed their tendency to consider new unseen examples as members of the categories. He found that transfer to these new dot patterns was greatly enhanced by increasing the number of learned category members. This is most likely due to the fact that presenting few examples encourages memorization of those specific examples, whereas presenting many examples encourages some form of category abstraction (Smith & Minda). Homa et al. (1981) found that when only a few examples were included in a training set, generalizations were more likely to be made when a new example was very close to one or more of those trained examples. When many examples were included, generalization was primarily based on similarity to the central tendency of the category. More examples increase the variability within a category, and this has been found to have a direct impact on the generalization of that category (Homa & Vosburgh, 1976). In other words, the larger the range of possible values along relevant feature dimensions, the more likely a new value will be considered for membership in that category.

Nature of Coherence   Another important influence on the probability of transfer to new examples is the nature and degree of coherence within a generalizing category. For example, smaller, less differentiated categories that can be better accounted for by exemplar models are less likely to be generalized than larger, more differentiated categories. Also, categories that are linearly separable are more likely to generalize to new examples than those that are not (Smith, Murray, & Minda, 1997). Two category sets are said to be linearly separable when they can be partitioned by a single linear boundary when all examples are plotted in multidimensional stimulus space.

The extension of a category representation to include new examples is also strongly affected by its specific structure and that of other categories in the classification task. A category that coheres based on the presence of one feature (unidimensional) will only generalize to a subset of new examples that possess that feature. For category structures like this, representation is likely to be more abstract; information about individual examples could be lost, and people could still perform accurately on the task (by just remembering a rule). In the case of a category structure that coheres by being highly similar to a prototype, abstraction will be more likely based around that prototype and generalization may depend on an item's similarity to that prototype. Categories consisting of members that do not have any consistent featural regularities or correlations will promote the use of memorization. In these cases, the only generalization possible would be based on similarity to those examples.

Extent of Training   The extent of training on a particular category greatly influences the ability to generalize to new examples. It has been suggested that across the time course of learning a category, one can employ different strategies with distinct consequences. For example, Smith and Minda (1998) found evidence that as a category is learned, processing may transition from being based initially on reference to a prototype to eventually being based on access to specific examples. A prediction that follows is that early in learning a category, one is more likely to overgeneralize (have too low a threshold for extending the category to new examples), but that later in learning, generalization may occur only when a new example is highly similar to specific learned examples.

Related research has investigated differences in representation between experts and novices in established domains (medicine, physics, etc.). In general, as expertise increases, the likelihood that categorization occurs based on similarity to exemplars also increases (this is also known as *case-based reasoning*). Rosch, Mervis, Gray, Johnson, and Boyes-Braem (1976) proposed that as experience with specific examples within a class grows, the more likely the examples will be stored or represented distinctly, and therefore the need for a prototype or abstraction for the category becomes less useful. For example, highly experienced doctors are more likely to diagnose patients based on their similarity to specific past examples and not to some central tendency of all experienced examples (Brooks et al., 1991). In fact, it is possible to overlearn a category if too much training has occurred. Especially in the case of categories with few training examples, overtraining leads to a representation that is exceedingly sensitive to these particular examples. The idea of the category becomes less about an abstracted concept and more about the specific examples that make up the category. This can lead to undergeneralization because the category is not extended to include new examples unless they are highly similar to those trained examples, despite a possibly coherent internal category structure.

Familiar Versus Novel Instantiations of Features   Brooks and Hannah (2006) asked participants to learn a family resemblance-based category structure of novel creatures. They demonstrated that transfer to a novel instance was more likely when a relevant feature was perceptually similar to trained examples despite the fact that novel instantiations of the feature were informationally equivalent. They were able to find this difference even when the common features of both categories were explicitly told to the participants. From these results they proposed that generalization to new examples depends on both abstract feature rule representations (e.g., "has a tail") and perceptual similarity to physically instantiated features of learned category members ("has a furry gray tail"). Although one's general concept of a bird might explicitly include the premise that they have two legs, a new object will not be considered a bird unless it possesses *certain* types of legs.

General Versus Specific Information A set of research suggests that the ability to generalize depends on whether you are thinking of a new stimulus in terms of an individual object or in terms of being in a group. Whittlesea, Brooks, and Westcott (1994) investigated situations in which one has knowledge of both category-level principles and information about particular members of the category. They had people learn many examples of nonsense words, once while looking at the whole item (induced viewing item as independent of a category), and again looking specifically at typical features (induced viewing item as an instantiation of a category). After they had acquired these two types of information, they were given a transfer task. Conditions of the transfer task focused the participants on either their general knowledge of typical category features or their specific knowledge of the item. They concluded that when participants were given a transfer task that focused attention on typical features, they were more likely to generalize than when they were focused on information that defined each specific item (even if that item included typical category information). In the case of the latter, participants were more likely to invoke item- and context-specific knowledge that did not facilitate generalization.

Inferences From Category Membership

In the previous sections, we have discussed specific theories about category representation and some category and target properties that influence category membership decisions. In this section, we discuss the phenomenon in which properties about a particular category member are inferred or predicted based on information about category membership. Once we know that an encountered animal is a dog, we might assume that it chases cats, even if we have never seen it do so. We base this prediction on the fact that we know of other dogs who display this behavior or because we simply know this to be true of dogs in general. Despite the fact that people make category-driven inferences all the time and it is commonly considered to be the primary objective of categorization (Anderson, 1991), it is perhaps the least studied aspect of category-based generalization.

Inference From Category Knowledge Feature predictions based on category-level knowledge have been studied in the lab (e.g., Ross & Murphy, 1996) using posttraining feature inference tasks (i.e., given a target described by the presence of certain features and/or category membership, what value is most likely on missing information?). A recent surge of research has been conducted in which people learn category knowledge through an inference task. In such an inference task, instead of displaying entire feature sets and asking for the category label (as in classification tasks), the category label and some of the feature set are displayed and participants are asked to predict the missing feature value. Despite commonalities between classification and inference learning, it has been shown that depending on the task, people learn at different speeds and in different ways, and end up with different representations (Yamauchi & Markman, 1998). For example, in inference tasks, people tend to pay more attention to relationships between items within a category instead of the items themselves and adopt a representation based on family resemblance (Anderson, Ross, & Chin-Parker, 2002). People also tend to learn more about common features and the relationship between them (internal structure) instead of focusing on a small number of diagnostic features as in classification learning (Ahn & Medin, 1992; Chin-Parker & Ross, 2002; Medin, Wattenmaker, & Michalski, 1987).

Inferences From Knowledge About Similar Categories or Other Items Within a Category   One of the consequences of thinking of two categories or category members as similar is that a specific property known to apply to one is more likely to be considered a property of the other. For example, if you know that hair from a horse contains a certain kind of protein, you might predict that hair from zebras or donkeys contains that same kind of protein. This process of induction is thought to arise based on the similarity of the source and the target categories. The importance of category-level similarity can be seen in Gelman and Markman's (1986) finding that membership in a category was more important than perceived featural similarity in determining inductive inference, even for young children. They had participants learn properties of two visually presented objects (e.g., "A bat feeds its babies milk" and "A flamingo feeds its babies chewed food") and then gave them a new object (a raven) that was perceptually similar to one of the objects (the bat) and categorically similar to the other object (the flamingo). Participants were asked to predict which of the two learned properties was true of the new visually presented object. They found that children as young as 4 years old were more likely to base their inductions on the categorically similar object than the perceptually similar object (however, see also Sloutsky & Fisher, 2004).

Rips (1975) investigated the specific mechanisms behind induction by asking participants to draw conclusions about a target from properties given about a source. For example, he used a task in which participants saw a predicate like "Robins have sesamoid bones." These predicates purposely involved information that would not be a part of their existing knowledge representation. The task was to judge what percentage of members of another category (e.g., blue jays) would have that same property. Rips (1975) discovered that one's willingness to extend a given category's property to a new category or instance was determined by two factors. One factor was the similarity of the given category to the target category; people were more likely to extend a property to a similar than a dissimilar category. For example, when given the predicate "*Robins* have sesamoid bones," people would be more willing to say that *blue jays* had sesamoid bones than *pelicans* because blue jays are thought to be more similar to robins. The other factor was the typicality of the given predicate category (but not the target category). For example, people were more likely to extend the sesamoid bone property from a robin than from an ostrich. This was presumably due to the intuition that a more typical member of the category *bird* (robin) would be more likely to possess a trait that applied to the whole category of bird than an atypical member (ostrich).

Osherson, Smith, Wilkie, Lopez, and Shafir (1990) developed a slightly different task that included a set of two premises and a conclusion and had participants rate their confidence in the argument. For example, the researchers would provide the argument "*Mosquitoes* use the neurotransmitter dihedron; *ants* use the neurotransmitter dihedron; therefore, *bees* use the neurotransmitter dihedron." The premises and conclusions were all in the same domain, and either they were at the same category level (as in the example) or else the conclusion referred to a superordinate, higher level category to the premises (i.e., *insect* is a superordinate category to *mosquito*). One determinant of confidence was again identified as similarity, but they more specifically defined typicality as the level of *coverage* of the premise category. They used this term to refer to how well the premises were distributed over the smallest category that would include all items in the problem. In our example, coverage would be the extent to which mosquitoes and ants covered the category of insects. The more coverage of a particular set of premises, the more likely the property would be extended to include the category in the conclusion. Osherson et al. developed a formal model to account for this and other phenomena in category-based induction (see also Medin, Coley, Storms, & Hayes, 2003; Sloman, 1993).

Problems That Can Arise Through Category-Based Generalization

Although it is easy to think of instances when generalization is helpful in making inferences that could not have been made otherwise, it is clear that the mechanisms behind generalization can also result in erroneous conclusions. If a category representation involves the conception that category members possess a certain property, a new example may be believed to have that property, even if they do not. For example, it may be presumed that a penguin is able to fly because it belongs to the category *bird* and most of the examples within this category can fly. Research on the overapplication of category-based inference is most prominent in the social cognition literature on stereotypes. Despite the fact that racial or social categories rarely provide a reliable basis for drawing inferences, category activation is often automatic and has the potential to influence false conclusions or biased interpretations based on properties considered common within that category (Bodenhausen & Macrae, 1998; Dijksterhuis & Knippenberg, 1996).

Problems can also arise when a new example possesses many properties common to a certain category but does not actually belong in the category. Because a bat has wings, flies, and eats bugs, it could be mistaken as a member of the category *bird* despite the fact that it is actually not a bird. This overapplication of category knowledge is more likely to occur when category knowledge is very abstract and not grounded in specific examples (Homa et al., 1981).

GENERALIZATION BASED ON ANALOGICAL COMPARISON

We have focused on how similarity can facilitate transfer of information to a novel case. Up to this point, similarity between previous knowledge (a source) and something novel (a target) has largely been based on taxonomic similarity (i.e., categories based on overlapping sets of independent features). Now we introduce the ways in which a bridge can be formed between a target and prior knowledge through similarity of sets of represented relationships (*structural* similarity). Although we discuss these types of similarity separately, rarely are structural and surface similarity between cases mutually exclusive. Gentner and Medina (1998) described similarity in terms of a continuum from that based on *mere appearance* (feature overlap with little relational overlap), to *literal similarity* (both relational and feature overlap), to *pure analogy* (relational overlap with very little feature overlap). Although generalization may be promoted by similarity in any sense, generalization based on structure can be especially useful in providing a link between importantly alike yet dissimilar domains. For example, our solar system and an atom have little feature overlap, but they are structurally consistent (e.g., both involve smaller objects rotating around a larger object, and both involve some sort of force keeping them together). Because they share relational structure despite arbitrary differences in specifics, these two cases can be considered analogous (Gentner, 1983). By recognizing the structural similarity between two analogous entities and comparing them, information about one can be generalized to the other. By comparing a solar system and an atom, we can generate the prediction that electrons furthest from the nucleus have the weakest pull towards that nucleus. We refer to this type of generalization as *analogical inference* because information about one situation is used to infer the presence of the same *type* of property in the analogous case. Although analogy can serve as a very powerful tool in interpretation, reasoning, and problem solving, spontaneous analogical transfer is often difficult to elicit.

This section will largely be a discussion about two processes that are necessary in making generalizations based on analogical comparison—focusing on the conditions under which transfer is most facilitated. We first address how a useful analogy comes to mind or is retrieved based on some cue from the current problem or situation. Differences between retrieval from a single case source or from a generic knowledge structure abstracted from multiple cases will be discussed. Second, we describe a theoretical account of how elements of a target are mapped onto a source analog after it is retrieved. This mapping leads to the projection of candidate inferences based on the structural alignment of compared cases.

Retrieval of Source Information

In some cases, one is explicitly led to consider a problem in terms of an analogous situation. For example, someone might suggest to you that electricity can be thought of as being like a flowing river (Gentner & Gentner, 1983). However, more commonly, this kind of explicit connection is not available, so it is necessary to spontaneously activate source information based solely on cues from the target. This is a particularly difficult task when the source and the target are from different domains. Our cognitive systems tend to rely on surface information as a means of reminding, often failing to notice and use potential analogies based on relations between those features (e.g., Gentner, Ratterman, & Forbus, 1993; Goldstone & Sakamoto, 2003; Holyoak & Koh, 1987; Novick, 1988; Ross, 1989; though see also Blanchette & Dunbar, 2000, 2001).

A classic example of failure to relate and thus transfer across problems that share common relational structure is a series of experiments by Gick and Holyoak

(1980, 1983). They gave participants a military story about a general who was trying to attack a fortress surrounded by mines. In the story, the general solved this problem by splitting his troops up into small groups that attacked from various sides, converging on the fortress. Participants were subsequently given a problem that was highly analogous to the story about the general. In this problem (Duncker, 1945), participants have to think of how radiation could be used to destroy a cancerous tumor without destroying the healthy cells around it. A solution to the problem is analogous to that in the military example: Small amounts of radiation should be administered from different directions in order to preserve the surrounding tissue but still destroy the cancer. Interestingly, when given the highly analogous story prior to solving the problem, only 30% were able to come up with the correct solution (compared to 10% of a control group that was able to come up with the correct solution without having read the story about the general). However, when a hint was given after an unsuccessful answer (Gick & Holyoak, 1983), 92% were able to provide the correct solution. This implies that people were simply unable to retrieve the first problem or solution as being relevant to the current problem. Once they were able to do so, they had little difficulty mapping the source to the target to get the correct solution.

Several factors have been shown to facilitate the retrieval of a relevant source, given a structurally similar target. For one, analogical retrieval has been shown to benefit from abstraction of a source. Just as we saw with categorization, the process of abstraction by definition disregards specific details and highlights more general, potentially transferable aspects of one case. For example, Clement, Mawby, and Giles (1994) found that people are more likely to retrieve an analogical match if the examples are written using generic relational words rather than concrete, domain-specific terms. Abstract symbols have also been shown to transfer to novel domains significantly better than concrete ones (Sloutsky, Kaminski, & Heckler, 2005). This may occur because concrete source representations are more perceptually rich than their generic form. Superficial features of a representation have been shown to compete with relational structure for attention (Goldstone & Sakamoto, 2003); salient perceptual features of a concrete source might distract from noticing more subtle relational qualities.

Because analogy has such a potential to facilitate learning (especially in an educational setting), research has been directed at discovering what types of structure-sensitive abstraction facilitate analogical retrieval. Gick and Holyoak (1983) explored several possible ways of creating an abstraction from the previously described general story in order to facilitate transfer to the radiation problem. They found that neither explicitly stating the principle of convergence nor presenting a diagram demonstrating those principles facilitated transfer. However, they did find that when presenting two source analog stories instead of one, participants were much more likely to later generate the correct solution to a structurally related target. Since then, it has been established that although analogical transfer can occur from one instance to another, retrieving a source based on more than one case is a key determinant of successful transfer, especially if the multiple source analogs are highly dissimilar (Gick & Holyoak, 1983; Goldstone & Sakamoto, 2003; Loewenstein, Thompson, & Gentner, 1999). When two or more cases are encountered, it appears that a structurally sensitive abstraction (often referred to as a *schema*) is formed by preserving relational commonalities and disregarding presumably nondefining differences (Catrambone & Holyoak, 1989). A similarity-based retrieval mechanism is thought to activate an appropriate schema as a consequence of some level of structural match with a target.

The primary mechanism behind the formation of a schema is, more specifically, the *comparison* of multiple cases. In fact, it has been found that the more thoroughly a participant is encouraged to compare cases, the greater the transfer will be (Gentner, Loewenstein, & Thompson, 2003; Kurtz, Miao, & Gentner, 2001). This process of comparison leads one to focus on causal or relational elements of two or more stories and ignore surface properties (Hummel & Holyoak, 1997). Another suggestion is that comparison improves one's ability to articulate relations that they share and this type of articulation is what facilitates analogical retrieval (Gick & Holyoak, 1983; Loewenstein et al., 1999). Although comparison has traditionally been employed by having two source problems along with their solutions, Kurtz and Loewenstein (2007) showed that comparing two target problems (without solutions) also facilitated analogical transfer of a solution from a provided source—thereby demonstrating that online (i.e., at the time of problem-solving) enhancement of the problem representation promotes spontaneous analogical retrieval.

Mapping a Source Onto a Target

Once a specific source is retrieved and recognized as being a helpful tool for generalization, its components must be compared and understood in relation to the corresponding target. This process is called *mapping*, and the specific nature of the mapping determines the inferences that can be drawn based on the source. Gentner (1983, 1989) and colleagues have developed a rich and productive account of comparison processes called *structure-mapping theory* (including a computational model; see Falkenheiner, Forbus, & Gentner, 1989). Within this approach, cases or situations are assumed to be represented in the mind as structured systems of symbolic predicates. Predicates can be both attributes about an object (e.g., *red*) and also relations of objects (e.g., *collide*) and/or lower order relations. According to structure-mapping theory, when a source representation is being generalized to a target, elements in the source are mapped onto the objects in the target that share similar relational structure via an alignment process. For example, when comparing the solar system and the atom, *sun* and *planets* might map onto *nucleus* and *electrons* because each pair shares a similar relationship (e.g., the later revolves around the former). Constraints on the mapping process include the following: Each matching object or feature relationship must have matching arguments, and any one element in one representation must match no more than one element in the other. The degree of structural consistency as well as the systematicity (depth of relational structure) have been shown to drive the mapping process (Markman & Gentner, 2000) and the inferential process that follows (Markman, 1997). MAC/FAC is a computational model (Forbus, Gentner, & Law, 1995) of how a structurally insensitive search mechanism can be combined with a structurally sensitive mapping engine to account for the available psychological evidence on similarity-based retrieval for structured content (i.e., stories, scenes, situations, events, and complex objects).

Making Inferences About the Target Based on Information About the Source

After retrieval and mapping, information about a target can be predicted or inferred from the source. For example, say that you know that water flowing through a pipe will decrease its flow when there is constriction in a particular section. By mapping this situation onto the case of electricity, you could generate the prediction that, like water flow, electrical current is affected by resistance along a circuit. In other words, the information about water flow can be generalized to electricity. Depending on the analogy that is retrieved or applied, different inferences can be made (Gentner & Gentner, 1983). For example, although electricity can be thought of as analogous to flowing water, it can also be thought of as analogous to a crowd moving through a corridor, and depending on which analogy is activated and mapped, one might come up with different predictions about its behavior.

A possible issue that can arise with extending an analogy or schema is knowing how far to take it. How do we select which relations to pay attention to or generalize and which to ignore? Knowing that electricity and water flow are structurally related can certainly be helpful in understanding some of the basic relationships between the objects in the system, but generalizing too far can result in erroneous conclusions. It would be a mistake to assume, for example, that if a wire in an electrical system is severed, electrical current would spill out into the room and cover the floor. In the structure-mapping framework, projected analogical inferences are considered to be mere candidates. There is some evidence that the validity of these candidate inferences is not assumed until a process of explicit evaluation reveals an appropriate level of applicability (Gentner & Markman, 1997).

PUTTING THE PIECES TOGETHER

Analogical and category-based inferences have largely been treated as different entities—as we have done in this chapter. In truth, these are most likely two pieces of the same puzzle, and they may involve some of the same mechanisms (see also Gentner & Markman, 1997). For example, although most research in the categorization literature talks about categories based around features, some research has focused on relational categories—those that cohere around principles of relational similarity (see Gentner & Kurtz, 2005). In a relational category like *barrier*, members fulfill some relation (i.e., blocking something) and may include instances like *prison bars*, *raging river*, or even *lack of education*, which have few, if any, surface features in common (Kurtz & Gentner, 2001). For categories like this, generalization to a novel item depends on its ability to satisfy a specified relational structure; just as in the case of analogy. In fact, this type of category is very similar to the notion of a schema constructed across multiple analogous cases. As we have discussed, forming a category is thought to consist (at least in part) of extracting some sort of commonality between members—which is exactly what a schema is thought to be. Further, just as activating a category representation can provide useful information about unknown intrinsic properties of a novel instance, activating a category consisting of abstract relational information (or schema) may be the vehicle for extending a generalization to an analogous situation. For instance, there is research suggesting that experts in a domain categorize members of that domain according to abstract structural principles and use these categories in order to find solutions to new problems (Chi, Feltovich, & Glaser, 1981). Evidence of this sort suggests the possibility that analogical-based inferences may be mediated by the same sort of representations and processes as those underlying categorization.

CONCLUSIONS

Based on research in categorization and analogy, we can draw several broad conclusions about the processes by which generalization occurs and, more specifically, the conditions that facilitate generalization. First, an existing representation of prior knowledge must be present to form a source of information from which to generalize. As we have learned, this existing representation can be in the form of an individual case, or an abstraction of multiple cases cohering around either (or both) surface or structural similarity. Although we have made no specific claims about how classes of multiple items are formed or represented, we have seen evidence that, in general, the more abstract the representation, the better that representation will generalize. After a representation has been created, it must be successfully retrieved while encountering a new case. This is believed to occur based on some form of similarity (surface or structural) between the novel item and existing knowledge. The higher the degree of similarity, the more likely that information will be transferred to the new case. After a connection and comparison have been made between a target and existing knowledge, inferences can be made about unknown properties of the new case. The extent to which this prior knowledge is applied can be determined not only by the nature of its representation and the degree to which it is thought of as similar to the present case, but also by reasoning processes grounded in theory and knowledge.

REFERENCES

Ahn, W., & Medin, D. L. (1992). A two-stage model of category construction. *Cognitive Science, 16*, 81–121.

Allen, S. W., & Brooks, L. R. (1991). Specializing the operation of an explicit rule. *Journal of Experimental Psychology: General, 120*, 3–9.

Anderson, A. L., Ross, B. H., & Chin-Parker, S. (2002). A further investigation of category learning by inference. *Memory and Cognition, 30*, 119–128.

Anderson, J. R. (1991). The adaptive nature of human categorization. *Psychological Review, 98*, 409–429.

Armstrong, S., Gleitman, L. R., & Gleitman, H. (1983). What some concepts might not be. *Cognition, 13*, 263–308.

Barsalou, L. W. (1983). Ad hoc categories. *Memory & Cognition, 11*, 211–227.

Blanchette, I., & Dunbar, K. (2000). How analogies are generated: The role of structural and superficial similarity. *Memory & Cognition, 28*, 108–124.

Blanchette, I., & Dunbar, K. (2001). Analogy use in naturalistic settings: The influence of audience, emotion, and goals. *Memory & Cognition, 29*, 730–735.

Bodenhausen, G. V., & Macrae, C. N. (1998). Stereotype activation and inhibition. In R. S. Wyer (Ed.), *Stereotype activation and inhibition: Advances in social cognition* (Vol. 11). Mahwah, NJ: Lawrence Erlbaum.

Bourne, L. E. (1982). Typicality effects in logically defined categories. *Memory & Cognition, 10*, 3–9.

Brooks, L. R. (1978). Non-analytic concept formation and memory for instances. In E. Rosch & B. B. Lloyd (Eds.), *Cognition and categorization* (pp. 169–211). Hillsdale, NJ: Lawrence Erlbaum.

Brooks, L. R., & Hannah, S. D. (2006). Instantiated features and the use of "rules." *Journal of Experimental Psychology: General, 135*, 133–151.

Brooks, L. R., Norman, G. R., & Allen, S. W. (1991). Role of specific similarity in a medical diagnosis task. *Journal of Experimental Psychology: General, 120*, 278–287.

Catrambone, R., & Holyoak, K. J. (1989). Overcoming contextual limitations on problem-solving transfer. *Journal of Experimental Psychology: Learning, Memory, and Cognition, 15*, 1147–1156.

Chi, M. T. H., Feltovich, P., & Glaser, R. (1981). Categorization and representation of physics problems by experts and novices. *Cognitive Science, 5*, 121–152.

Chin-Parker, S., & Ross, B. R. (2002). The effect of category learning on sensitivity to within-category correlations, *Memory & Cognition, 30*, 353–362.

Clement, C. A., Mawby, R., & Giles, D. E. (1994). The effects of manifest relational similarity on analog retrieval. *Journal of Memory & Language, 33*, 396–420.

Dijksterhuis, A., & Knippenberg, A. (1996). The knife that cuts both ways: Facilitated and inhibited access to traits as a result of stereotype activation. *Journal of Experimental Social Psychology, 32*, 271–288.

Duncker, K. (1945). On problem-solving. *Psychological Monographs, 58*(Whole No. 70).

Erickson, M. A., & Kruschke, J. K. (1998). Rules and exemplars in category learning. *Journal of Experimental Psychology: General, 127*, 107–140.

Falkenheiner, B., Forbus, K., & Gentner, D. (1989). The structure-mapping engine: Algorithm and examples. *Artificial Intelligence, 41*, 1–63.

Forbus, K. D., Gentner, D., & Law, K. (1995). MAC/FAC: A model of similarity-based retrieval. *Cognitive Science, 19*, 141–205.

Gelman, S. A., & Markman, E. M. (1986). Categories and induction in young children. *Cognition, 23*, 183–209.

Gentner, D. (1983). Structure mapping: A theoretical framework for analogy. *Cognitive Science, 7*, 155–170.

Gentner, D. (1989). The mechanisms of analogical learning. In S. Vosniadou & A. Ortony (Eds.), *Similarity, analogy, and thought* (pp. 199–241). New York: Cambridge University Press.

Gentner, D., & Gentner, D. R. (1983). Flowing waters or teeming crowds: Mental models of electricity. In D. Gentner & A. L. Stevens (Eds.), *Mental models* (pp. 99–129). Hillsdale, NJ: Lawrence Erlbaum.

Gentner, D., & Kurtz, K. J. (2005). Relational categories. In W. Ahn, R. L. Goldstone, B. C. Love, A. B. Markman, & P. Wolff (Eds.), *Categorization inside and outside of the lab: Festschrift in honor of Douglas L. Medin*. Washington, DC: American Psychological Association.

Gentner, D., Loewenstein, J., & Thompson, L. (2003). Learning and transfer: A general role for analogical encoding. *Journal of Educational Psychology, 95*, 393–408.

Gentner, D., & Markman, A. (1997). Structure mapping in analogy and similarity. *American Psychologist, 52*, 45–56.

Gentner, D., & Medina, J. (1998). Similarity and the development of rules. *Cognition, 65,* 263–297.

Gentner, D., Ratterman, M. J., & Forbus, K. D. (1993). The roles of similarity in transfer: Separating retrievability from inferential soundness. *Cognitive Psychology, 25,* 524–575.

Gick, M. L., & Holyoak, K. J. (1980). Analogical problem solving. *Cognitive Psychology, 12,* 306–355.

Gick, M. L., & Holyoak, K. J. (1983). Schema induction and analogical transfer. *Cognitive Psychology, 15,* 1–38.

Goldstone, R. L. (1994). The role of similarity in categorization: Providing a groundwork. *Cognition, 52,* 125–157.

Goldstone, R. L., Lippa, Y., & Shiffrin, R. M. (2001). Altering object representations through category learning. *Cognition, 78,* 27–43.

Goldstone, R. L., & Sakamoto, Y. (2003). The transfer of abstract principles governing complex adaptive systems. *Cognitive Psychology, 4,* 414–466.

Hahn, U., & Chater, N. (1997). Similarity and rules: Distinct? Exhaustive? Empirically distinguishable? *Cognition, 65,* 197–230.

Hampton, J. A. (1993). Prototype models of concept representation. In I. Van Mechelen, J. Hampton, R. Michalski, & P. Theuns (Eds.), *Categories and concepts: Theoretical views and inductive data analysis* (pp. 67–95). New York: Academic Press.

Holyoak, K. J., & Koh, K. (1987). Surface and structural similarity in analogical transfer. *Memory & Cognition, 15,* 332–340.

Homa, D. (1978). Abstraction of ill-defined form. *Journal of Experimental Psychology: Human Learning and Memory, 4,* 407–416.

Homa, D., Cross, J., Cornell, D., Goldman, D., & Schwarz, S. (1973). Prototype abstraction and classification of new instances as a function of number of instances defining the prototype. *Journal of Experimental Psychology, 101,* 116–122.

Homa, D., Sterling, S., & Trepel, L. (1981). Limitations of exemplar-based generalization and the abstraction of categorical information. *Journal of Experimental Psychology: Human Learning and Memory, 7,* 418–439.

Homa, D., & Vosburgh, R. (1976). Category breadth and the abstraction of prototypical information. *Journal of Experimental Psychology: Human Learning and Memory, 2,* 322–330.

Hummel, J. E., & Holyoak, K. J. (1997). Distributed representations of structure: A theory of analogical access and mapping. *Psychological Review, 104,* 427–466.

Kaplan, A. S., & Murphy, G. L. (1999). The acquisition of category structure in unsupervised learning. *Memory & Cognition, 27,* 699–712.

Kim, N. S., & Ahn, W. K. (2002). Clinical psychologists' theory-based representations of mental disorders predict their diagnostic reasoning and memory. *Journal of Experimental Psychology: General, 131,* 451–476.

Kruschke, J. K. (1992). ALCOVE: An exemplar-based connectionist model of category learning. *Psychological Review, 99,* 22–44.

Kurtz, K. J. (1996). Category-based similarity. *Proceedings of the 18th annual conference of the Cognitive Science Society* (pp. 790–796). Hillsdale, NJ: Lawrence Erlbaum.

Kurtz, K. J. (2007). The divergent autoencoder (DIVA) model of category learning. *Psychonomic Bulletin & Review, 14,* 560–576.

Kurtz, K. J., & Gentner, D. (2001). Kinds of kinds: Sources of category coherence. In J. D. Moore & K. Stenning (Eds.), *Proceedings of the 23rd annual conference of the Cognitive Science Society* (pp. 522–527). Mahwah, NJ: Lawrence Erlbaum.

Kurtz, K. J., & Loewenstein, J. (2007). Converging on a new role for analogy and retrieval: When two problems are better than one. *Memory & Cognition, 35,* 334–341.

Kurtz, K. J., Miao, C., & Gentner, D. (2001). Learning by analogical bootstrapping. *Journal of the Learning Sciences, 10,* 417–446.

Levering, K. R., & Kurtz, K. J. (2006). Influence of learning to distinguish categories on graded structure. In R. Sun (Ed.), *Proceedings of the 28th annual conference of the Cognitive Science Society* (pp. 1681–1686). Mahwah, NJ: Lawrence Erlbaum.

Livingston, K. R., Andrews, J. K., & Harnad, S. (1998). Categorical perception effects induced by category learning. *Journal of Experimental Psychology: Learning, Memory, and Cognition, 24,* 732–753.

Loewenstein, J., Thompson, L., & Gentner, D. (1999). Analogical encoding facilitates knowledge transfer in negotiation. *Psychonomic Bulletin & Review, 6,* 586–597.

Love, B. C., Medin, D. L., & Gureckis, T. M. (2004). SUSTAIN: A network model of category learning. *Psychological Review, 111,* 309–332.

Markman, A. B. (1997). Constraints on analogical inference. *Cognitive Science, 21,* 373–418.

Markman, A. B. (1999). *Knowledge representation.* Mahwah, NJ: Lawrence Erlbaum.

Markman, A. B., & Gentner, D. (2000). Structure mapping in the comparison process. *The American Journal of Psychology, 113,* 501–538.

Medin, D. L., Coley, J. D., Storms, G., & Hayes, B. K. (2003). A relevance theory of induction. *Psychonomic Bulletin & Review, 10,* 517–532.

Medin, D. L., Dewey, G. I., & Murphy, T. D. (1983). Relationships between item and category learning: Evidence that abstraction is not automatic. *Journal of Experimental Psychology: Learning, Memory, and Cognition, 9,* 607–625.

Medin, D. L., Goldstone, R. L., & Gentner, D. (1993). Respects for similarity. *Psychological Review, 100,* 254–278.

Medin, D. L., & Schaffer, M. M. (1978). Context theory of classification learning. *Psychological Review, 85,* 207–238.

Medin, D. L., & Schwanenflugel, P. J. (1981). Linear separability in classification learning. *Journal of Experimental Psychology: Human Learning and Memory, 7,* 355–368.

Medin, D. L., Wattenmaker, W. D., & Michalski, R. S. (1987). Constraints and preferences in inductive learning: An experimental study of human and machine performance. *Cognitive Science, 11,* 299–339.

Minda, J. D., & Smith, J. P. (1998). Prototypes in the mist: The early epochs of category learning. *Journal of Experimental Psychology: Learning, Memory, and Cognition, 24,* 1411–1436.

Murphy, G. L. (2002). *The big book of concepts.* Cambridge, MA: MIT Press.

Murphy, G. L., & Medin, D. L. (1985). The role of theories in conceptual coherence. *Psychological Review, 92,* 289–316.

Nosofsky, R. M. (1986). Attention, similarity, and the identification-categorization relationship. *Journal of Experimental Psychology: General, 115,* 39–57.

Nosofsky, R. M. (1988). Exemplar-based accounts of relations between classification, recognition, and typicality. *Journal of Experimental Psychology: Learning, Memory, and Cognition, 14,* 700–708.

Nosofsky, R. M. (1992). Exemplars, prototypes and similarity rules. In A. Healy, S. Kosslyn, & R. Shiffrin (Eds.), *From learning theory to connectionist theory: Essays in honor of W. K. Estes* (Vol. 1, pp. 149–168). Hillsdale, NJ: Lawrence Erlbaum.

Nosofsky, R. M., Palmeri, T. J., & McKinley, S. C. (1994). Rule-pus-exception model of classification learning. *Psychological Review, 101,* 53–79.

Novick, L. R. (1988). Analogical transfer, problem similarity, and expertise. *Journal of Experimental Psychology: Learning, Memory, and Cognition, 14,* 510–520.

Osherson, D. N., Smith, E. E., Wilkie, O., Lopez, A., & Shafir, E. (1990). Category-based induction. *Psychological Review, 97,* 85–200.

Posner, M. I., & Keele, S. W. (1968). On the genesis of abstract ideas. *Journal of Experimental Psychology, 77,* 353–363.

Rehder, G., & Hastie, R. (2001). Causal knowledge and categories: The effects of causal beliefs on categorization, induction, and similarity. *Journal of Experimental Psychology: General, 130,* 323–360.

Rips, L. J. (1975). Inductive judgments about natural categories. *Journal of Verbal Learning and Verbal Behavior, 14,* 665–681.

Rips, L. J. (1989). Similarity, typicality and categorization. In S. Vosniadou & A. Ortony (Eds.), *Similarity and analogical reasoning* (pp. 21–59). Cambridge: Cambridge University Press.

Robinson, A. J., & Pascalis, O. (2004). Development of flexible recognition memory in human infants. *Developmental Science, 7,* 527–533.

Rosch, E., & Mervis, C. B. (1975). Family resemblance: Studies in the internal structure of categories. *Cognitive Psychology, 7,* 573–605.

Rosch, E., Mervis, C. B., Gray, W., Johnson, D., & Boyes-Braem, P. (1976). Basic objects in natural categories. *Cognitive Psychology, 8,* 382–439.

Ross, B. H. (1989). Distinguishing types of superficial similarities: Different effects on the access and use of earlier problems. *Journal of Experimental Psychology: Learning, Memory, & Cognition, 15,* 456–468.

Ross, B. H., & Kennedy, P. T. (1990). Generalizing from the use of earlier examples in problem solving. *Journal of Experimental Psychology: Learning, Memory, & Cognition, 16,* 42–55.

Ross, B. H., & Murphy, G. L. (1996). Category-based predictions: Influence of uncertainty and feature associations. *Journal of Experimental Psychology: Learning, Memory, and Cognition, 22,* 736–753.

Schyns, P. G., Goldstone, R. L., & Thibaut, J. (1998). The development of features in object concepts. *Behavioral and Brain Sciences, 21,* 1–54.

Shepard, R. N. (1987). Toward a universal law of generalization for psychological science. *Science, 237,* 1317–1323.

Shepard, R. N., Hovland, C. I., & Jenkins, H. M. (1961). Learning and memorization of classifications. *Psychological Monographs: General and Applied, 75*(13, Whole No. 517).

Sloman, S. A. (1993). Feature-based induction. *Cognitive Psychology, 25,* 231–280.

Sloutsky, V. M., & Fisher, A. V. (2004). When learning and development decrease memory: Evidence against category-based induction. *Psychological Science, 15,* 553–558.

Sloutsky, V. M., Kaminski, J. A., & Heckler, A. (2005). *Psychonomic Bulletin and Review, 12,* 508–513.

Smith, J. D., & Minda, J. P. (1998). Prototypes in the mist: The early epochs of category learning. *Journal of Experimental Psychology, 24,* 1411–1436.

Smith, J. D., Murray, M. J., & Minda, J. P. (1997). Straight talk about linear separability. *Journal of Experimental Psychology: Learning, Memory, and Cognition, 23,* 659–680.

Tenenbaum, J. B., & Griffiths, T. L. (2001). Generalization, similarity, and Bayesian inference. *Behavioral and Brain Sciences, 24,* 629–640.

Torgerson, W. S. (1952). Multidimensional scaling: I. Theory and method. *Psychometrika, 17,* 401–419.

Tversky, B. (1977). Features of similarity. *Psychological Review, 84,* 327–352.

Vandierendonck, A. (1995). A parallel rule activation and rule synthesis model for generalization in category learning. *Psychonomic Bulletin & Review, 2,* 442–459.

Whittlesea, B. W. A., Brooks, L. R., & Westcott, C. (1994). After the learning is over: Factors controlling the selective application of general and particular knowledge. *Journal of Experimental Psychology: Learning, Memory, and Cognition, 20,* 259–274.

Yamauchi, T., & Markman, A. B. (1998). Category learning by inference and classification. *Journal of Memory and Language, 39,* 124–148.

Section 4

Educational and Training Approaches to Generalization

10

Computer Learning Environments With Agents That Support Deep Comprehension and Collaborative Reasoning

ARTHUR C. GRAESSER, DAVID LIN, and SIDNEY D'MELLO

*A*nimated conversational agents play a central role in some visions of advanced learning environments. Imagine a virtual world that has a close correspondence with everyday scenarios and problems, with human-like cyber agents that interact with students and help them learn by holding a conversation in natural language. The cyber agents may take on different roles: mentors, tutors, peers, players in multiparty games, or avatars in the virtual worlds. The students communicate with the agents through speech, keyboard, gesture, touch-panel screen, or conventional input channels. In turn, the agents express themselves with speech, facial expression, gesture, posture, and other embodied actions. In essence, students and agents have face-to-face conversations in the context of authentic situations and problems. The students are highly engaged in their interactions with the agents in the virtual worlds because the system dynamically adapts to their cognitive, emotional, and motivational states. The entire system is also embedded in a game environment in which the students score points to the extent that their speech and actions reflect mastery of the material. These are serious games—games that help the students acquire important academic and technical content.

This vision of virtual worlds with agents is not science fiction. Outstanding examples of virtual environments with agents are those developed at the University of Southern California, funded by the U.S. Army, National Science Foundation (NSF), and other agencies. The Mission Rehearsal system (Gratch et al., 2002) has dozens of agents in a combat scenario. The user interacts with a commander at a war scenario in spoken language and tries to help the entire company solve a crisis. In Tactical Iraqi (Johnson & Beal, 2005), the student speaks to soldiers and civilians in an Iraqi village that has been attacked and needs assistance. The student learns both the language and the culture during dozens of hours of training. He or she learns by holding spoken dialogues in natural language and by scoring points in a serious game with authentic situations and problems. These award-winning virtual environments are major milestones that could be achieved only by interdisciplinary teams of researchers working on projects over a sustained period of time.

The Mission Rehearsal and Tactical Iraqi systems have not yet been sufficiently tested on learning gains, transfer, and generalization. However, there are theoretical and empirical reasons for being optimistic that they will be successful. There are at least four major reasons:

1. *Similarity helps transfer.* The higher the similarity between the training context and the test situation, the better the transfer of performance, representations, and strategies (Anderson, Reder, & Simon, 1996; Bransford, Brown, & Cocking, 2000). The virtual realities are very rich perceptually and socially, and the training scenarios are carefully selected to have a close correspondence with real-world problems.

2. *Tutoring helps learning.* One-on-one human tutoring is among the most effective methods of helping students learn (Graesser & Person, 1994). Meta-analyses show learning gains of .42 sigma (effect size in standard deviation units) compared to classroom controls and other suitable controls (Cohen, Kulik, & Kulik, 1982). There are many potential reasons for the effectiveness of one-on-one tutoring (Graesser, Person, & Magliano, 1995), most notably that the tutor adapts to the learner's cognitive states (Van Lehn et al., 2007) and emotions (Lepper & Henderlong, 2000).

3. *Agents model good learning strategies.* Students learn from observing others who model good behavior (Bandura, 1986). Students rarely have the opportunity to observe other students exhibiting good learning strategies in the classroom and other typical settings in school systems. Agents not only enact these strategies but also can think aloud while they do so (McNamara, Levinstein, & Boonthum, 2004).

4. *Games are engaging.* Games are extremely engaging, so there will be an increase in training time if serious content is woven into the games (Gee, 2003; Johnson & Beal, 2005; Malone & Lepper, 1987). Time on task is, of course, predictive of learning gains and presumably transfer (Taraban, Rynearson, & Stalcup, 2001).

It is important to acknowledge that many forms of computer-based training have been shown to facilitate learning. This gives us additional reasons to be optimistic about the effectiveness of virtual environments with agents. The outcome variables have varied widely in existing assessments of learning technologies. The assessments have included tests of retention for shallow knowledge, answers to questions that tap deep knowledge (e.g., causal explanations, or justifications of claims), problem-solving performance, and the transfer of knowledge or skill to different but related contexts. Meta-analyses have revealed that computerized learning environments fare well compared to classroom instruction (Dodds & Fletcher, 2004; Wisher & Fletcher, 2004); the effect sizes (i.e., sigma, comparing treatment to control conditions) are .39 for conventional computer-based training, .50 for multimedia, and 1.08 for intelligent tutoring systems. At this point in the science, there are precious little data on learning gains from learning environments with virtual reality and serious games, so research is needed in these arenas. Learning gains are routinely reported in published studies, but there often are incomplete data on usage (attrition), engagement (including how much the learners like the system), study time, system development time, and development costs. But just as important, from the standpoint of this edited volume, there has been insufficient attention to segregating test items that involve retention of explicit training material versus transfer of knowledge, skills, and strategies to new contexts. Therefore, the matter of generalization needs more focused analyses in all classes of learning technologies.

This chapter describes some of the agent-based learning technologies that we have developed in the Institute for Intelligent Systems at the University of Memphis. All of these projects have assessed these technologies with respect to learning gains, and most of them have assessed transfer of knowledge. We will take a very close look at transfer in AutoTutor, an intelligent tutoring system that helps college students learn technical topics (such as physics) by holding a conversation in natural language. As we describe these projects, we will offer some conclusions about the status of transfer and generalization in learning technologies with agents.

AGENT-BASED LEARNING TECHNOLOGIES

Embodied animated conversational agents have become increasingly popular in learning technologies (Atkinson, 2002; Baylor & Kim, 2005; Cole et al., 2003; Graesser, Jackson, & McDaniel, 2007; Johnson, Rickel, & Lester, 2000; McNamara et al., 2004; Moreno & Mayer, 2004; Reeves & Nass, 1996). These agents speak, point, gesture, walk, and exhibit facial expressions. Some are built in the image of humans, whereas others are animals or cartoon characters. The potential power of these agents, from the standpoint of Learning Environments (LEs), is that they can mimic face-to-face communication with human tutors, instructors, mentors, peers, or people who serve other roles. Single agents can model individuals with different knowledge, personalities, physical features, and styles. Ensembles of agents can model social interaction. Both single agents and ensembles of agents can be carefully choreographed to mimic virtually any activity or social situation: curiosity, inquiry learning, negotiation, interrogation, arguments, empathetic support, helping, and so on. Researchers can have precise control over what the agents say, how they say it, and what conditions trigger specific actions. Therefore, agent technologies are having a revolutionary impact on social science research.

Animated conversational agents could conceivably have a negative impact on learning. For example, the agent might create cognitive overload, a split-attention effect, or a distraction from other information on the display that has higher importance (Moreno & Mayer, 2004). An agent might be so realistic that the student has overly high expectations regarding its intelligence (Norman, 1994; Shneiderman & Plaisant, 2005). Such concerns can be mitigated only by systematic empirical research that tests theoretical models that intersect social psychology and the learning sciences. For example, we might explore what impact the personality and attractiveness of the agent have on learning and transfer. We can explore whether students learn best from agents that are similar to them. The results of the studies are sometimes counterintuitive. Available research suggests that it is the content of what is expressed, rather than the aesthetic quality of the speech or face, that is most important in predicting learning (Graesser, Moreno, et al., 2003). Research suggests that it is possible to create social presence from simple facial icons with expressions (☺)—a minimalist form of the persona effect (Reeves & Nass, 1996).

Researchers in the Institute for Intelligent Systems have developed several learning environments with animated conversational agents. The remainder of this chapter describes some of these systems, their goals, and learning outcomes in the empirical studies that have been conducted. We will hereafter refer to these agents as *animated pedagogical agents* because they were designed for the purpose of improving learning. Most of these agents have a direct pedagogical role as a tutor or instructor. Others are members of a social ensemble of agents, taking on the role as a student or conversational partner with a tutor or instructor. In either case, researchers designed the agents in a fashion that was theoretically motivated by pedagogical theories.

AutoTutor

AutoTutor was the first pedagogical agent developed and tested at the University of Memphis (Graesser, Chipman, Haynes, & Olney, 2005; Graesser, Wiemer-Hastings, Wiemer-Hastings, Kruez, & the Tutoring Research Group, 1999). AutoTutor is an intelligent tutoring system that helps students learn by holding a conversation in natural language. AutoTutor's dialogues are organized around difficult questions that require reasoning and explanations. The primary method of scaffolding good student answers is through *expectation- and misconception-tailored dialogue*. Both AutoTutor and human tutors (Graesser et al., 1995) typically have a list of anticipated good answers (called *expectations*; e.g., "Force equals mass times acceleration") and a list of anticipated *misconceptions* associated with each main question. AutoTutor guides the student in articulating the expectations through a number of dialogue moves: *pumps* (e.g., "What else?"), *hints*, and *prompts* for specific information. As the learner expresses information over many turns, the list of expectations is eventually covered and the main question is scored as answered. Another conversation goal is to correct the misconceptions that are manifested in the student's talk. When the student articulates a misconception, AutoTutor acknowledges the error and corrects it. Another conversational goal is to be adaptive to what the student says. AutoTutor adaptively responds to the student by giving short *feedback* on the quality of student contributions (positive, negative, or neutral) and by *answering* the student's questions. The answers to the questions are retrieved from glossaries or from paragraphs in textbooks via intelligent information retrieval.

It is beyond the scope of this chapter to describe the mechanisms of AutoTutor that drive the conversation. It suffices to say that AutoTutor attempts to hold a mixed-initiative dialogue that mimics the conversational patterns of human tutors. This is now possible by virtue of recent advances in computational linguistics (Jurafsky & Martin, 2000), statistical representations of world knowledge (Landauer, McNamara, Dennis, & Kintsch, 2007), and discourse processes (Graesser, Gernsbacher, & Goldman, 2003).

The pedagogical framework of AutoTutor was inspired by three bodies of theoretical, empirical, and applied research. The first is explanation-based constructivist theories of learning (Aleven & Koedinger, 2002; Chi, de Leeuw, Chiu, & LaVancher, 1994; McNamara, 2004). These theories postulate that learning is deeper and more effective when the learner must actively generate explanations, justifications, and functional procedures than when they are merely given information to study. The second is intelligent tutoring systems that adaptively respond to student knowledge at a fine-grained level (Anderson, Corbett, Koedinger, & Pelletier, 1995; VanLehn et al., 2002). These tutors give immediate feedback to learner's actions and guide the learner on what to do next in a fashion that is sensitive to what the system believes the learner knows. The third is empirical research that has documented the collaborative constructive activities that routinely occur during human tutoring (Chi, Siler, & Jeong, 2004; Chi, Siler, Jeong, Yamauchi, & Hausmann, 2001; Fox, 1993; Graesser et al., 1995). The patterns of discourse uncovered in naturalistic tutoring were directly imported into the dialogue management facilities of AutoTutor.

One version of AutoTutor on introductory computer literacy covers the topics of hardware, the operating system, and the Internet. Each of these topics has six challenging questions that require about a paragraph of information (3 to 7 sentences) in an ideal answer. The questions require answers that involve inferences and deep reasoning, such as "Why?" "How?" "What if?" "What if not?" and "How is X similar to Y?" An example question about the operating system is "When you turn on the computer, how is the operating system first activated and loaded into RAM?" A typical exchange has 50 to 100 turns to answer a single challenging question. In this version of AutoTutor, the students give spoken input, whereas students typed their contributions into the keyboard in earlier versions. We use the commercially available Dragon Naturally Speaking™ (version 6) speech recognition system for speech-to-text translation.

The AutoTutor interface has three major windows, as shown in Figure 10.1, in the version with speech recognition. Window 1 (top of screen) is the main question that stays on the computer screen throughout the conversation with the question. Window 2 (left middle) is the animated conversational agent that speaks the content of AutoTutor's turns. Window 3 (right middle) either is blank or has auxiliary diagrams. In addition to these interface components, there are two buttons on the keyboard that the learner presses to start speaking and stop speaking.

Each turn of AutoTutor in the conversational dialogue has three information slots (i.e., units, constituents). The first slot of most turns is feedback on the quality

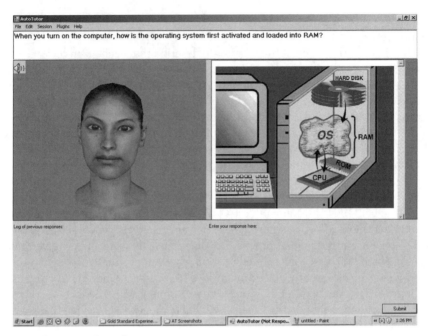

Figure 10.1   Interface of AutoTutor.

of the learner's last turn. This feedback is positive (*very good*, or *yeah*), neutral (*uh huh*, or *I see*), or negative (*not quite*, or *not really*). The second slot advances the interaction with prompts for specific information, hints, assertions with correct information, corrections of misconceptions, or answers to student questions. The third slot is a cue for the floor to shift from AutoTutor as the speaker to the learner. For example, AutoTutor ends each turn with a question or a gesture to cue the learner to do the talking. Discourse markers (*and also, okay*, or *well*) connect the utterances of these three slots of information.

The conversations managed by AutoTutor are sufficiently smooth that students can get through the session with minimal difficulties (Person, Graesser, & the Tutoring Research Group, 2002). In fact, the dialogue is sufficiently tuned so that a bystander who observes tutorial dialogue in print cannot tell whether a particular turn was generated by AutoTutor or by an expert human tutor of computer literacy (Person et al., 2002). A series of studies were conducted that randomly sampled AutoTutor's turns. Half of the turns were generated by AutoTutor, and half were substituted by a human expert tutor on the basis of the dialogue history. Bystander participants were presented these tutoring moves and asked to decide whether each was generated by a computer or a human. Signal detection analyses revealed that the bystanders had zero d' scores in making these discriminations. In this sense, AutoTutor passed the bystander Turing test for individual tutoring turns. Of course, a bystander can eventually tell whether a sequence of turns was part of a dialogue with AutoTutor versus a human tutor. The dialogue is far from perfect because AutoTutor does not have the depth of language comprehensions that humans do. But AutoTutor is surprisingly close.

Versions of AutoTutor   Several versions of AutoTutor have been developed since 1997, when the initial NSF project was funded. Most versions of AutoTutor have animated conversational agents with facial expressions, synthesized speech, and gestures. These full versions have been compared with alternative versions with voice only, text only, and various combinations of modalities in presenting AutoTutor's dialogue messages (Graesser, Moreno, et al., 2003). The fully animated conversational agent has shown advantages in promoting learning over alternative modalities under some conditions, particularly for deeper levels of learning (Atkinson, 2002; Moreno, Mayer, Spires, & Lester, 2001). However, as mentioned, available research on AutoTutor suggests that it is the verbal content of the tutor's messages that most robustly explains learning gains (Graesser, Moreno, et al., 2003).

A version of AutoTutor called AutoTutor-3D guides learners on using interactive simulations of physics microworlds (Graesser, Chipman, et al., 2005; Jackson, Olney, Graesser, & Kim, 2006). For example, an example question in conceptual physics is "When a car without headrests on the seats is struck from behind, the passengers often suffer neck injuries. Why do passengers get neck injuries in this situation?" For each of the physics problems, we developed an interactive simulation world in 3D Studio Max. The world included the people, objects, and spatial setting associated with the problem. The student can manipulate parameters of the situation (e.g., mass of objects, speed of objects, and distance between objects) and then ask the system to simulate what will happen. They can cognitively compare their expected simulated outcome with the actual outcome after the simulation is completed. Moreover, they are prompted to describe what they see. Their actions and descriptions are evaluated with respect to covering the expected principles in an ideal answer. In order to manage the interactive simulation, AutoTutor gives hints and suggestions, once again scaffolding the learning process with dialogue. Thus, AutoTutor combines interactive simulation with mixed-initiative dialogue.

We are currently working on a version of AutoTutor that is sensitive to the student's emotions. AutoTutor is augmented with sensing devices and signal-processing algorithms that classify affective states of learners. Emotions are classified on the basis of dialogue patterns during tutoring, the content covered, facial expressions, body posture, and speech intonation (D'Mello, Craig, et al., 2005; D'Mello, Craig, & Graesser, 2006). The primary emotions that occur during learning with AutoTutor are frustration, confusion, boredom, and flow (engagement), whereas surprise and delight occasionally occur (Graesser, D'Mello, et al., 2008). We plan on investigating whether learning gains and learner impressions of AutoTutor are influenced by dialogue moves of AutoTutor that are sensitive to the learner's emotions. For example, if the student is extremely frustrated, then AutoTutor presumably should give a good hint or prompt that directs the student in a more positive learning trajectory. If the student is bored, AutoTutor should give more engaging, challenging, and motivating problems. If the student is very absorbed and satisfied, then AutoTutor should be minimally directive.

Learning Gains With AutoTutor   The learning gains of AutoTutor have been evaluated in 15 experiments conducted during the last 9 years. Assessments of AutoTutor on learning gains have shown effect sizes of approximately .8 standard deviation units in the areas of computer literacy (Graesser, Lu, et al., 2004) and Newtonian physics (VanLehn et al., 2007). These evaluations place previous versions of AutoTutor somewhere between an untrained human tutor (Cohen et al., 1982) and an intelligent tutoring system (Corbett, 2001). The assessments of learning gains from AutoTutor have varied between 0 and 2.1 sigma (a mean of .8), depending on the learning performance measure, the comparison condition, the subject matter, and the version of AutoTutor. Approximately a dozen measures of learning have been collected in these assessments on the topics of computer literacy and physics, including (a) multiple-choice questions on shallow knowledge that tap definitions, facts, and properties of concepts; (b) multiple-choice questions on deep knowledge that tap causal reasoning, justifications of claims, and functional underpinnings of procedures; (c) essay quality when students attempt to answer challenging problems; (d) a cloze task that has subjects fill in missing words of texts that articulate explanatory reasoning on the subject matter; and (e) performance on problems that require problem solving.

Assessments of learning uncovered a number of findings that were either provocative or very illuminating (see Graesser, Lu, et al., 2004; VanLehn et al., 2007).

1. *AutoTutor versus reading a textbook.* Learning gains with AutoTutor are superior to those from reading a textbook on the same topics for an equivalent amount of time. However, this gap gets smaller to the extent that the textbook content is restricted to the content that directly corresponds to the problems covered by AutoTutor. Therefore, it is important to guide the learner's attention to the most relevant text when he or she reads.
2. *Reading a textbook versus doing nothing.* Learning gains are zero in both of these conditions when the tests tap deeper levels of comprehension. This provocative result is compatible with the results of comprehension calibration studies (Maki, 1998) that report a very low correlation ($r = .27$) between college students' perceptions of how well they are comprehending and their actual comprehension measured by objective tests. Readers need difficult problems that challenge their *illusions of comprehension* when they read at shallow levels; challenging problems encourage them to have deeper standards of comprehension.
3. *AutoTutor versus expert human tutors.* One recent evaluation of physics tutoring compared learning gains of AutoTutor with the gains of accomplished human tutors via computer-mediated communication. These learning gains were equivalent for students with a moderate degree of physics knowledge. In contrast, the expert human tutors prevailed when the students had low physics knowledge and the dialogue was spoken.
4. *Deep versus shallow tests of knowledge.* The largest learning gains from AutoTutor have been on measures of deep reasoning rather than measures of shallow knowledge (e.g., definitions of terms, lists of entities, properties of entities, and recognition of explicit content).
5. *Zone of proximate development.* AutoTutor is most effective when there is an intermediate gap between the learner's prior knowledge and the ideal

answers of AutoTutor. AutoTutor is not particularly effective in facilitating learning in students with high domain knowledge and when the material is too much over the learner's head.

One way of analyzing the learning gains is to compare the normal conversational AutoTutor with different comparison conditions. We computed mean effect sizes for these contrasts on multiple-choice questions that tapped deep reasoning. An example of a deep-reasoning question in physics is presented below.

As a truck moves along the highway at constant speed, a nut falls from a tree and smashes into the truck's windshield. If the truck exerts a 1,000 N force on the nut, what is the magnitude of the force that the nut exerts on the truck?

A. 1,000 N
B. Less than 1,000 N
C. N (the nut does not exert a force on the truck)
D. Greater than 1,000 N (because the nut hit the truck, it exerts a greater force on the truck than the truck exerts on the nut)

The conversational AutoTutor has (a) a .80 effect size (sigma) compared with pretests, reading a textbook, or doing nothing; (b) a .22 sigma compared with reading textbook segments directly relevant to the AutoTutor problems; (c) a .07 sigma compared with reading a script that answers the questions posed by AutoTutor; (d) a .13 sigma compared with AutoTutor presenting speech acts in print instead of the talking head; (e) a .08 sigma compared with expert human tutors in computer-mediated conversation; and (f) a –.20 sigma compared with a version of AutoTutor that is enhanced with interactive 3D simulations (i.e., the interactive simulations are better).

Transfer and Generalization   Our definition of *generalization* consists of the application of principles, procedures, solutions to problems, and conceptual structures to relevant new situations. In essence, there is transfer from one set of learning activities to appropriate new activities. It is widely acknowledged in cognitive science that transfer and generalization can be very difficult or nearly impossible when the surface characteristics are different between training and transfer problems and when the correspondences are not highlighted (Forbus, Gentner, & Law, 1995; Gick & Holyoak, 1980; Hayes & Simon, 1977). For example, Hayes and Simon's classical study showed that college students experienced zero transfer between successive problems that were solved when the problems were structurally isomorphic but varied in surface features. Gick and Holyoak reported that students needed instruction to focus on comparisons between Dunker's radiation problem and a story analogue before the story facilitated solving the problem. Gentner's research has emphasized the importance of making explicit comparisons between problems before transfer is maximized (Forbus, Gentner, & Law, 1995).

We have conducted detailed analyses of transfer and generalization when students learn physics with AutoTutor (Van Lehn et al., 2007). Our analyses have contrasted coarse-grained and fine-grained analyses. In coarse-grained analyses, there is a comparison between training problems and transfer problems that vary in surface similarity with the training problem. For illustration, Table 10.1 shows a comparison between a near-transfer problem and a far-transfer problem. The training problem would be predicted to facilitate the near-transfer problem more than the far-transfer problem, even though they have the same set of principles (expectations) and the same structure.

Our assessments of AutoTutor did not show facilitation for far-transfer problems (Jackson, Ventura, Chewle, Graesser, & the Tutoring Research Group, 2004; Van Lehn et al., 2007) when compared with a *scripted minilesson* condition in which they read solutions to the same problems that are solved with AutoTutor. The authors also failed to show better facilitation in near-transfer than far-transfer problems. This appears to be bad news from the standpoint of having a learning environment that promotes far transfer. However, this conclusion appears to be limited to coarse-grained analyses, a comparatively insensitive method of assessing transfer. Differences emerged only when we performed fine-grained analyses.

The fine-grained analyses involve partistic scoring of solutions rather than wholistic performance on the problem as a whole. Each problem has a set of expectations and misconceptions, as discussed earlier. Once the problems are decomposed in this fashion, we can pitch these expectations (and misconceptions) in a more generic form that allows comparisons between problems. There are more abstract principles that correspond to the expectations in the training, near-transfer, and far-transfer problems. For example, the following principles underlie the three problems in Table 10.1.

1. The magnitudes of the forces exerted by A and B on each other are equal.
2. If A exerts a force on B, then B exerts a force on A in the opposite direction.
3. The same force will produce a larger acceleration in a less massive object than a more massive object.

TABLE 10.1   Training, Near-Transfer, and Far-Transfer Physics Problems

Training Problem

If a lightweight car and a massive truck have a head-on collision, upon which vehicle is the impact force greater? Which vehicle undergoes the greater change in its motion? Defend your answer.

Near-Transfer Problem

A huge ocean liner traveling due east collides with a small yacht traveling due west. During the collision, the front end of the yacht is smashed in, causing the yacht to sink and the passengers to evacuate to their lifeboat. The ocean liner merely suffered a dent. What is true of the relationship between the force of the ocean liner on the yacht and the force of the yacht on the ocean liner?

Far-Transfer Problem

A 30 kg child receives her first A+ on a spelling test and, overcome with joy, jumps up and down on her 200 kg desk. This desk is very strong and does not move while the child jumps on it. Does the child exert a force on the desk? Does the desk exert a force on the child? Justify both your answers.

Similarly, there are the following abstract forms of the misconceptions.

1. A lighter or smaller object exerts no force on a heavier or larger object.
2. A lighter or smaller object exerts less force on other objects than a heavier or larger object.
3. The force acting on a body is dependent on the mass of the body.
4. Heavier objects accelerate faster for the same force than lighter objects.
5. Action and reaction forces do not have the same magnitude.

After we decompose the problems into abstract principles and misconceptions, we can analyze how accurately the student performs on each of these decomposed units throughout the course of pretest, training, and posttest. We have indeed tracked 60 principles and misconceptions across the following events: 4 pretest essay questions, 26 multiple-choice questions, 10 training problems (AutoTutor versus comparison conditions), 4 posttest essay questions, 4 far-transfer essays, and 26 multiple-choice questions. Any given principle P_i is relevant to some but not all of these 74 events. Similarly, any given misconception M_j is relevant to some but not all of these 74 events. We observe how well the individual student performs on each principle (or misconception) over the course of relevant events. For example, suppose there are 4 relevant events in each of the following 5 phases of testing and training: pretest essay, pretest multiple choice (MC), training, posttest essay, and posttest MC. The student receives a 1 if the behavior is correct in an event and a 0 if not correct. A student with the following history would exhibit all-or-none learning, with learning emerging in the third training problem:

All-or-none learning = [(0000)(0000)(0011)(1111)(1111)]

The following history would exhibit no learning because the likelihood of a correct response is only 25% in each of the five stages:

No learning = [(0010)(1000)(0100)(0100)(0010)]

The following history consists of variable learning because the learner does better, on the average, in the posttests than the pretests, but never ends up being consistently perfect toward the end.

Variable learning = [(0010)(1000)(0101)(1110)(1011)]

There is also refresher learning, when the learner gets reminded of the correct answers during pretests, as illustrated below.

Refresher learning = [(0001)(1111)(1111)(1111)(1111)]

It should be apparent that this partistic, fine-grained analysis offers a more precise framework for investigating learning processes and products.

VanLehn et al. (2007) conducted a fine-grained analysis on the physics principles and misconceptions. They computed the proportion of relevant events in which correct performance was manifested for the specific principles and misconceptions. The good news was that (a) these fine-grained measures showed significant learning gains from the pretests to the posttests, and (b) the AutoTutor condition had better scores at posttest than the control conditions when we performed a sign test on the means for multiple dependent measures. For example, the far-transfer principle proportions were .275 and .213 for AutoTutor and control conditions, respectively, whereas the corresponding far-transfer misconception proportions were .078 versus .095. The disappointing news, however, is that only a few of the differences were statistically significant when we examined each dependent variable separately.

We are currently conducting additional fine-grained analyses on the particular principles and misconceptions. We are interested in the sequential patterns and consistency of performance over time and over contextual fluctuations. We are interested in what training or testing conditions influence particular principles and misconceptions. It may be that some classes of principles are amenable to learning by a conversational AutoTutor and some by 3D simulation, whereas other classes of principles are best acquired by reading or didactic instruction. We believe these detailed analyses have merit, but the proof of the pudding awaits further research.

The SEEK Web Tutor

Current standards for science education assume that *critical thinking* is an essential component for understanding in science (American Association for the Advancement of Science, 1993). Critical thinking about science requires learners to actively evaluate the truth and relevance of information, to think about the quality of information sources, to trace the likely implications of evidence and claims, and to ask how the information is linked to the learner's goals and larger conceptual frameworks (Halpern, 2002; Linn, Davis, & Bell, 2004). Critical thinking is needed to achieve deeper levels of learning that involve causal reasoning, integration of the components in complex systems, and logical justifications of claims. A *critical stance* presupposes that the quality of the information is potentially suspect and requires close scrutiny with respect to its truth, relevance, and other dimensions of quality. A critical stance toward scientific information is especially important in the Internet age. The Internet furnishes millions of Web pages on any topic imaginable, yet there is no control over the quality of the scientific information presented over the Internet. Learners need a critical stance in their arsenal of self-regulated learning strategies (Azevedo & Crowley, 2004) in this age of information pollution from the public and media.

We developed a Web tutor to scaffold the acquisition of a critical stance to science learning. The Web tutor is called SEEK (for Source, Evidence, Explanation, and Knowledge) (Graesser, Wiley, et al., 2007; Wiley, 2001). The SEEK Tutor was designed to improve college students' critical stance while they search for information on the Internet. The learners search through Web pages on the topic of plate

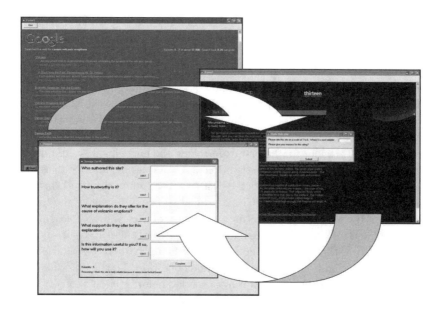

Figure 10.2   Seek Web Tutor.

tectonics. Some of the Web sites are reliable information sources on the topic, whereas others have erroneous accounts of earthquakes and volcanoes. The goal assigned to the students in our experiments was to search the Web for the purpose of writing an essay on what caused the eruption of the volcano Mt. St. Helens.

The SEEK Tutor fosters a critical stance with three main facilities. First, there is a Hint button on the Google search engine page that contains suggestions on how to effectively guide students' search. This page was a mock Google page with titles and URLs for Web sites. Half of the sites are reliable, including sites from the National Aeronautics and Space Administration (NASA), the Public Broadcasting Station (PBS), and *Scientific American*. Half are unreliable sites that explain volcanoes and earthquakes by appealing to the stars, the moon, and oil drilling. Whenever the learner clicks on the Hint button, there are spoken messages that give reminders of the goal of the task (i.e., writing an essay on the causes of the Mt. St. Helens eruption) and suggestions on what to do next (i.e., reading Web sites with reliable information). One version of the SEEK Tutor has a talking head, but the studies we conducted were on a version that had voice only.

The second facility to foster critical stance are *pop-up ratings* that ask students to evaluate the expected reliability of the information in a site. Students provide a rating and a rationale for their rating. The pop-up rating and justification appear after the students first view a particular Web site for 20 seconds. The third facility consists of a *pop-up journal* that has five questions about the reliability of the site that the learner just visited. These questions were designed to address some of the core aspects of critical stance: Who authored this site? How trustworthy is it? What explanation do they offer for the cause of volcanic eruptions? What support do they offer for this explanation? Is this information useful to you, and if so, how will you use it? Each question has a Hint button that can be pressed to evoke spoken hints (at least 20 auditory statements per question) to guide the learners on answering each question. The pop-up journal is launched whenever the learner exits one of the Web sites. It forces the learner to think about each of the five core aspects of critical stance and also to articulate verbally the reasons for his or her ratings.

We conducted two experiments that evaluated the impact of the SEEK Tutor in acquiring a critical stance (Graesser, Wiley, et al., 2007). College students explored the Web sites for 50 minutes with the goal of writing an essay on the causes of the eruption of Mt. St. Helens. In the first experiment, the participants were randomly assigned to either the SEEK Tutor condition or a Navigation condition that had no training on critical stance. We expected that the 50-minute training of the SEEK Tutor would be effective in enhancing a critical stance, influencing the learner's exploration of the Web sites, evaluating the quality of the Web sites, learning the content of plate tectonics, and articulating the causes of the volcano in the essay. To the extent that the Tutor is effective, there should be better performance in the SEEK Tutor condition than the Navigation condition. On the other hand, it is also conceivable that much more training is needed before students can effectively plan, monitor, and strategically apply a critical stance to science learning. In a second experiment, we augmented these two conditions with a set of instructions and example Web sites that more thoroughly described and illustrated critical stance in the context of an Atkins diet. In essence, our goal was to pack in as much training on critical stance as we could in approximately 70 minutes and compare it to a condition in which there was no training on critical stance.

We were surprised to learn that 70 minutes of intense training on critical stance had very little impact on college students, even when we assessed the impact of the SEEK Tutor (with instructions) on dozens of measures of study processes and learning. The SEEK Tutor did not improve learners' ability to detect reliable information sources, as manifested by their ratings and rank orderings of Web sites on reliability. The Tutor had no impact on the amount of study time they allocated to reliable versus unreliable sites. The SEEK Tutor had no significant impact on a statement verification task in which they rated the truth or falsity of 30 statements about plate tectonics, including true statements, false plausible statements, misconceptions, and ridiculous distractors. The essays that college students wrote on the causes of the Mt. St. Helens eruption did not have more core ideas and fewer misconceptions if they had the SEEK Tutor with Instructions than if they had no training at all on critical stance. Indeed, after assessing dozens of measures, there was only one measure that showed a benefit of the SEEK Tutor: Students had more expressions in the essay with language about causal explanations (such as "cause" and "explanation") compared to controls. The Tutor with Instructions did affect the language in their essays, which is a reassuring manipulation check, but had virtually no influence on the learning processes and results.

It appears that there will need to be much more training and scaffolding from the SEEK Tutor before robust effects emerge on the application of critical stance to Web learning. Simply put, very little can be accomplished in one hour of online training. One wonders whether 20 hours of the SEEK Tutor on multiple topics and problems would produce deep learners of science who have a more penetrating critical stance.

Human Use Regulatory Affairs Advisor (HURAA)

HURAA is a comprehensive learning environment on the Web with didactic lessons, a document repository, hypertext, multimedia (including an engaging video), lessons with concrete scenarios to assess case-based reasoning, query-based information retrieval, and an animated agent that serves as a navigational guide (Graesser, Hu, Person, Jackson, & Toth, 2004; Hu & Graesser, 2004). Trainees learn the U.S. federal policies and regulations on the ethical use of human subjects in research. The goals of HURAA were to train high-ranking military personnel on research ethics in a small amount of time (less than an hour) and to provide a repository of up-to-date information on research ethics that can be retrieved by learner questions.

The animated conversational agent, appearing in the upper left of the Web page, serves as a navigational guide to the trainee. It makes suggestions on what to do next and answers the trainee's questions. Below the agent are the major learning modules. Introduction and Historical Overview provide didactic instruction, including an engaging video. The Lessons module presents trainees with case scenarios, and they are to evaluate whether the cases violate one of seven critical ethical issues (e.g., informed consent, favorable risk–benefit ratio, or independent review). Thus, the trainees actively apply the didactic knowledge (which is potentially inert; Bransford et al., 2000) to case-based reasoning. Explore Issues and Explore Cases both allow further training on particular cases and issues, whereas Decision Making provides further testing. Search IRB Documents allows the learner to search for information in a large repository of documents through natural language queries. Generally, speaking, the recommendation is for the trainees to proceed in the sequential order of these modules. However, the navigational guide can recommend skipping modules, depending on the trainee's cognitive profile. The more active learners can immediately access any of the modules at any point in the learning session. There also is a repository of information they can access in the lower left of the screenshot: Glossary, Archives & Links, Bibliography, and so on. All of these learning modules can be expanded as information accumulates over time.

Case-based scenario training is one of the foundational principles of learning in cognitive science and education (Ashley, 1990; Kolodner, 1993; Sweller & Cooper, 1985). Each scenario in HURAA provides a text description of a particular experiment that was problematic with respect to one or more of seven ethical issues. Thus, there is a Case Scenario (S) × Critical Ethical Issue (I) matrix that specifies whether each scenario S_i did or did not have a problem with ethical issue I_j. The trainees are asked to rate potential problems with these scenarios. The trainee's ratings are continuously being compared with the ideal SI matrix. Discrepancies between trainee decisions and actions and the SI matrix are used to guide feedback to the learner (i.e., when there were false alarms and misses) and also to select the next scenario for training. Scenarios are dynamically selected in a fashion that optimizes the repair of their false alarms and misses.

HURAA was evaluated in experiments that contrasted it with conventional computer-based instruction containing the same content. There were two pieces of good news in evaluations of the system on over a dozen measures of retention, reasoning, and inquiry. First, memory for core concepts was enhanced by HURAA compared to the conventional Web software; the effect sizes varied between .56 and 1.19 sigma (mean = .78) (Hu & Graesser, 2004). Second, HURAA's answers to learner questions in the information retrieval facilities were impressive; 95% of the answers were judged as relevant by the learner, and 50% were judged as being informative (Graesser, Hu, et al., 2004). However, HURAA had no significant increment for many measures compared with the control condition. In particular, there was no improvement in case-based reasoning, as measured by the accuracy in identifying ethical problems in new cases and in the response time in making these judgments. There was no improvement in the speed of accessing information when trainees were given difficult questions that required information search. There was no improvement in the trainees' perceptions of the system with respect to interest, enjoyment, amount learned, and ease of learning.

Our evaluation of the HURAA leads to some conclusions that are similar to our evaluation of the SEEK Tutor. One hour of training is not sufficient to train adults on reasoning strategies and applying their knowledge to new cases. It clearly takes substantially more training than one hour to actively transfer one's knowledge to new situations. In contrast, one hour of training did show improvements in the articulation of causal language in the SEEK Tutor and the recall of key concepts in the HURAA. These results underscore the importance of assessing learning, retention, and transfer with multiple measures. The results also suggest that extensive training is needed before we can expect changes in reasoning, strategies, and application of knowledge to new situations.

Ensembles of Agents: iSTART and iDRIVE

Ensembles of agents can be designed to exhibit good learning strategies and social interactions. It is very difficult, if not impossible, to train teachers and tutors to apply specific pedagogical techniques. This is because years of normal social interaction and conversation are often incompatible with ideal pedagogical methods (Person, Kreuz, Zwaan, & Graesser, 1995). However, it is possible to design pedagogical agents to have such precise forms of interaction. And, of course, the agents do not get weary, irritated, and snippy. Researchers at the University of Memphis have designed two systems in which students learn by observing and interacting with ensembles of agents: the Interactive Strategy Trainer for Active Reading and Thinking (iSTART) and Instruction With Deep-Level Reasoning Questions in Vicarious Environments (iDRIVE).

iSTART is an automated strategy trainer that helps students become better readers by constructing self-explanations of the text (McNamara et al., 2004). It uses groups of animated conversational agents to scaffold these strategies. The primary goal of iSTART is to help adolescent and college students learn meta-comprehension strategies that support deeper comprehension while they read. It combines the power of self-explanation in facilitating deep learning (Chi et al., 1994) with content-sensitive, interactive strategy training (Palincsar & Brown, 1984). iSTART interventions teach readers to self-explain using five reading strategies: *monitoring comprehension* (i.e., recognizing comprehension failures and the need for remedial strategies), *paraphrasing* explicit text, making *bridging inferences* between the current sentence and prior text, making *predictions* about the subsequent text, and *elaborating* the text with links to what the reader already knows.

The animated agents of iSTART provide three phases of training. The Introduction Module provides instruction on self-explanation and reading strategies. There is a trio of animated agents (an instructor and two students) who cooperate with each other, provide information, pose questions, and provide explanations of the reading strategies. After the presentation of each strategy, the trainees complete brief multiple-choice quizzes to assess their learning. Next comes the Demonstration Module, where two Microsoft Agent characters (Merlin and Genie) demonstrate the use of self-explanation in the context of a science passage and the trainee identifies the strategies being used. The final phase is Practice, where Merlin coaches and provides feedback to the trainee while the trainee practices self-explanation using the repertoire of reading strategies. For each sentence in a text, Merlin reads the sentence and asks the trainee to self-explain it by typing a self-explanation. The system interprets the trainee's contributions using recent advances in computational linguistics. Merlin gives feedback and sometimes asks the trainee to modify unsatisfactory self-explanations.

Studies have evaluated the impact of iSTART on both reading strategies and comprehension for thousands of students in K through 12 and college (McNamara, O'Reilly, Best, & Ozuru, 2006). The 3-phase iSTART training (approximately 3 hours) has been compared with a control condition that didactically trains students on self-explanation, but without any vicarious modeling and any feedback via the agents. After training, the participants are asked to self-explain a transfer text (e.g., on heart disease) and are subsequently given a comprehension test in the form of open-ended questions, short-answer questions, and multiple-choice tests. The results have revealed that strategies and comprehension are facilitated by iSTART, with impressive effect sizes (1.0 sigma or higher) for strategy use and for comprehension. Therefore, after approximately 3 hours of training, we do begin to see some impact on the mastery and application of comprehension strategies.

The results have revealed that the facilitation by iSTART depends on world knowledge and general reading ability. For example, readers with low prior knowledge of reading strategies benefit primarily at the level of the explicit text base, whereas those with high prior knowledge of reading strategies benefit primarily on tests of bridging inferences. These findings are in line with Vygotsky's (1978) theory of the zone of proximal development, as we discovered in our research with AutoTutor. iSTART can help students to achieve a level of comprehension that is closest to their proximal level of development, or the highest level they can achieve with appropriate scaffolding.

The iDRIVE system has duets of animated agents train students to learn science content by modeling deep-level reasoning questions in question–answer dialogues. A student agent asks a series of deep questions about the science content, and the teacher agent immediately answers each question. There is evidence that learning improves when learners have the mind-set of asking deep questions ("Why?" "How?" "What if?" and "What if not?") that tap causal structures, complex systems, and logical justifications (Craig, Gholson, Ventura, Graesser, & the Tutoring Research Group, 2000; Driscoll et al., 2003; King, 1994; Mayer, 2005; Rosenshine, Meister, & Chapman, 1996). However, the asking of deep questions does not come naturally (Graesser, McNamara, & VanLehn, 2005; Graesser & Olde, 2003), so the process needs to be modeled by agents or humans. The iDRIVE system models the asking of deep questions with dialogues between animated conversational agents. Learning gains on the effectiveness of iDRIVE on question asking, recall of text, and multiple-choice questions have shown effect sizes that range from .56 to 1.77 compared to a condition in which students listen to the monologue on the same content without questions.

CLOSING COMMENTS

Animated pedagogical agents are destined to have a major impact on learning environments of the future. Researchers have only begun to scratch the surface on their potential. Individual agents can have an endless number of dialogue styles, strategies, personalities, and physical features. They can be matched to the cognitive, personality, emotional, and social profiles of individual learners in an endless number of ways. The agents can exhibit the activities of good learners in addition to the activities of good teachers. There are also an endless number of agent ensembles that can be choreographed to implement promising theories of social interaction. The agents can tirelessly train learners for hundreds of hours on many topics and in many contexts. This is apparently necessary, according to the research presented in this chapter, for an adequate transfer and generalization of knowledge and strategies. Very little is accomplished in a one-hour training session.

The role of technology in education and training has had its critics. In particular, Cuban (1986, 2001) documented that technology has historically had a negligible impact on improvements in education. He pointed out that radio and television did not have much of an impact on education, even after initial hopes and promises that they would revolutionize the educational landscape. Cuban has similarly argued that computers have had a negligible impact on education, in part because teachers have not adequately integrated them into the curriculum. It is our contention, however, that agent-based learning technologies will ultimately prevail and revolutionize the educational enterprise. Agents are like humans, and humans provide the best education that we know. Available empirical research supports the claim that some agents are almost as good as accomplished human tutors. And who knows what the future may bring as the science of pedagogical agents evolves. The agents just might end up being better.

ACKNOWLEDGMENTS

The research on AutoTutor was supported by the National Science Foundation (SBR 9720314, REC 0106965, REC 0126265, ITR 0325428, and REESE 0633918), the Institute of Education Sciences (IES; R305H050169), and the U.S. Department of Defense (DoD) Multidisciplinary University Research Initiative (MURI) administered by the Office of Naval Research (ONR) under Grant No. N00014-00-1-0600. Any opinions, findings, and conclusions or recommendations expressed in this material are those of the authors and do not necessarily reflect the views of the NSF, IES, DoD, or ONR.

REFERENCES

Aleven, V., & Koedinger, K. R. (2002). An effective metacognitive strategy: Learning by doing and explaining with a computer-based cognitive tutor. *Cognitive Science, 26,* 147–179.

American Association for the Advancement of Science. (1993). *Benchmarks for science literacy: Project 2061.* New York: Oxford University Press.

Anderson, J. R., Corbett, A. T., Koedinger, K. R., & Pelletier, R. (1995). Cognitive tutors: Lessons learned. *Journal of the Learning Sciences, 4,* 167–207.

Anderson, J. R., Reder, L. M., & Simon, H. A. (1996). Situated learning and education. *Educational Researcher, 25,* 5–11.

Ashley, K. D. (1990). *Modeling legal argument: Reasoning with cases and hypotheticals.* Cambridge, MA: MIT Press.

Atkinson, R. K. (2002). Optimizing learning from examples using animated pedagogical agents. *Journal of Educational Psychology, 94,* 416–427.

Azevedo, R., & Cromley, J. G. (2004). Does training on self-regulated learning facilitate students' learning with hypermedia? *Journal of Educational Psychology, 96,* 523–535.

Bandura, A. (1986). *Social foundations of thought and action: A social cognition theory.* Englewood Cliffs, NJ: Prentice Hall.

Baylor, A. L., & Kim, Y. (2005). Simulating instructional roles through pedagogical agents. *International Journal of Artificial Intelligence in Education, 15,* 95–115.

Bransford, J. D., Brown, A. L., & Cocking, R. R. (Eds.). (2000). *How people learn.* Washington, DC: National Academy Press.

Chi, M. T. H., de Leeuw, N., Chiu, M., & LaVancher, C. (1994). Eliciting self-explanations improves understanding. *Cognitive Science, 18,* 439–477.

Chi, M. T. H., Siler, S. A., & Jeong, H. (2004). Can tutors monitor students' understanding accurately? *Cognition and Instruction, 22,* 363–387.

Chi, M. T. H., Siler, S. A., Jeong, H., Yamauchi, T., & Hausmann, R. G. (2001). Learning from human tutoring. *Cognitive Science, 25,* 471–533.

Cohen, P. A., Kulik, J. A., & Kulik, C. C. (1982). Educational outcomes of tutoring: A meta-analysis of findings. *American Educational Research Journal, 19,* 237–248.

Cole, R., van Vuuren, S., Pellom, B., Hacioglu, K., Ma, J., Movellan, J., et al. (2003). Perceptive animated interfaces: First steps toward a new paradigm for human computer interaction. *Proceedings of the IEEE, 91,* 1391–1405.

Corbett, A. T. (2001). Cognitive computer tutors: Solving the two-sigma problem. In *User modeling: Proceedings of the Eighth International Conference* (UM 2001, pp. 137–147). Berlin: Springer.

Craig, S. D., Gholson, B., Ventura, M., Graesser, A. C., & the Tutoring Research Group. (2000). Overhearing dialogues and monologues in virtual tutoring sessions: Effects on questioning and vicarious learning. *International Journal of Artificial Intelligence in Education, 11*, 242–253.

Cuban, L. (1986). *Teachers and machines: The classroom use of technology since 1920.* New York: Teachers College.

Cuban, L. (2001). *Oversold and underused: Computers in the classroom.* Cambridge, MA: Harvard University Press.

D'Mello, S. K., Craig, S. D., Gholson, B., Franklin, S., Picard, R., & Graesser, A. C. (2005). *Integrating affect sensors in an intelligent tutoring system.* In Affective Interactions: The Computer in the Affective Loop Workshop at 2005 International Conference on Intelligence Users Interfaces (pp. 7–13) New York: AMC Press.

D'Mello, S. K., Craig, S. D., & Graesser, A. C. (2006). Predicting affective states through an emote-aloud procedure from AutoTutor's mixed-initiative dialogue. *International Journal of Artificial Intelligence in Education, 16*, 3–28.

Dodds, P., & Fletcher, J. (2004). Opportunities for new "smart" learning environments enabled by next-generation Web capabilities. *Journal of Educational Multimedia and Hypermedia, 13*, 391–404.

Driscoll, D. M., Craig, S. D., Gholson, B., Ventura, M., Hu, X., & Graesser, A. C. (2003). Vicarious learning: Effects of overhearing dialog and monolog-like discourse in a virtual tutoring session. *Journal of Educational Computing Research, 29*, 431–450.

Forbus, K., Gentner, D., & Law, K. (1995). MAC/FAC: A model of similarity-based retrieval. *Cognitive Science, 19*, 141–205.

Fox, B. (1993). *The human tutorial dialogue project.* Hillsdale, NJ: Lawrence Erlbaum.

Gee, J. (2003). *What video games have to teach us about learning and literacy.* New York: Palgrave Macmillan.

Gick, M. L., & Holyoak, K. J. (1980). Analogical problem solving. *Cognitive Psychology, 12*, 306–355.

Graesser, A. C., Chipman, P., Haynes, B. C., & Olney, A. (2005). AutoTutor: An intelligent tutoring system with mixed-initiative dialogue. *IEEE Transactions in Education, 48*, 612–618.

Graesser, A. C., D'Mello, S. K., Craig, S. D., Witherspoon, A., Sullins, J., McDaniel, B., & Gholson, B., (2008). The Relationship between Affective States and Dialogue Patterns during interactions with AutoTutor. *Journal of Interactive Learning Research, 19*(2), 293–312.

Graesser, A. C., Gernsbacher, M. A., & Goldman, S. (Eds.). (2003). *Handbook of discourse processes.* Mahwah, NJ: Erlbaum.

Graesser, A. C., Hu, X., Person, P., Jackson, T., & Toth, J. (2004). Modules and information retrieval facilities of the Human Use Regulatory Affairs Advisor (HURAA). *International Journal on eLearning, 3*, 29–39.

Graesser, A. C., Jackson, G. T., & McDaniel, B. (2007). AutoTutor holds conversations with learners that are responsive to their cognitive and emotional states. *Educational Technology, Educational Technology, 47*, 19–22.

Graesser, A. C., Lu, S., Jackson, G. T., Mitchell, H., Ventura, M., Olney, A., et al. (2004). AutoTutor: A tutor with dialogue in natural language. *Behavioral Research Methods, Instruments, and Computers, 36*, 180–193.

Graesser, A. C., McNamara, D. S., & VanLehn, K. (2005). Scaffolding deep comprehension strategies through Point&Query, AutoTutor, and iSTART. *Educational Psychologist, 40*, 225–234.

Graesser, A. C., Moreno, K., Marineau, J., Adcock, A., Olney, A., & Person, N. (2003). AutoTutor improves deep learning of computer literacy: Is it the dialog or the talking head? In U. Hoppe, F. Verdejo, & J. Kay (Eds.), *Proceedings of artificial intelligence in education* (pp. 47–54). Amsterdam: IOS Press.

Graesser, A. C., & Olde, B. A. (2003). How does one know whether a person understands a device? The quality of the questions the person asks when the device breaks down. *Journal of Educational Psychology, 95,* 524–536.

Graesser, A. C., & Person, N. K. (1994). Question asking during tutoring. *American Educational Research Journal, 31,* 104–137.

Graesser, A. C., Person, N. K., & Magliano, J. P. (1995). Collaborative dialogue patterns in naturalistic one-to-one tutoring. *Applied Cognitive Psychology, 9*(359), 1–28.

Graesser, A. C., Wiemer-Hastings, K., Wiemer-Hastings, P., Kreuz, R., & the Tutoring Research Group. (1999). AutoTutor: A simulation of a human tutor. *Journal of Cognitive Systems Research, 1,* 35–51.

Graesser, A. C., Wiley, J., Goldman, S. R., O'Reilly, T., Jeon, M., & McDaniel, B. (2007). SEEK Web Tutor: Fostering a critical stance while exploring the causes of volcanic eruption. *Metacognition and Learning, 2*(2–3), 89–105.

Gratch, J., Rickel, J., Andre, E., Cassell, J., Petajan, E., & Badler, N. (2002). Creating interactive virtual humans: Some assembly required. *IEEE Intelligent Systems, 17,* 54–63.

Halpern, D. F. (2002). *An introduction to critical thinking* (4th ed.). Mahwah, NJ: Erlbaum.

Hayes, J. R., & Simon, H. A. (1977). Psychological differences among problem isomorphs. In J. Castellan, D. B. Pisoni, & G. Potts (Eds.), *Cognitive theory* (Vol. 2). Hillsdale, NJ: Erlbaum.

Hu, X., & Graesser, A. C. (2004). Human Use Regulatory Affairs Advisor (HURAA): Learning about research ethics with intelligent learning modules. *Behavioral Research Methods, Instruments, and Computers, 36,* 241–249.

Jackson, G. T., Olney, A., Graesser, A. C., & Kim, H. J. (2006). AutoTutor 3D simulations: Analyzing user's actions and learning trends. In R. Son (Ed.), *Proceedings of the 28th annual meetings of the Cognitive Science Society* (pp. 1557–1562). Mahwah, NJ: Erlbaum.

Jackson, G. T., Ventura, M. J., Chewle, P., Graesser, A. C., & the Tutoring Research Group. (2004). The impact of Why/AutoTutor on learning and retention of conceptual physics. In J. C. Lester, R. M. Vicari, & F. Paraguacu (Eds.), *Intelligent tutoring systems 2004* (pp. 501–510). Berlin: Springer.

Johnson, W. L., & Beal, C. (2005). Iterative evaluation of a large-scale intelligent game for language learning. In C. Looi, G. McCalla, B. Bredeweg, & J. Breuker (Eds.), *Artificial intelligence in education: Supporting learning through intelligent and socially informed technology* (pp. 290–297). Amsterdam: IOS Press.

Johnson, W. L., Rickel, J., & Lester, J. (2000). Animated pedagogical agents: Face-to-face interaction in interactive learning environments. *International Journal of Artificial Intelligence in Education, 11,* 47–78.

Jurafsky, D., & Martin, J. H. (2000). *Speech and language processing: An introduction to natural language processing, computational linguistics, and speech recognition.* Upper Saddle River, NJ: Prentice Hall.

King, A. (1994). Guiding knowledge construction in the classroom: Effects of teaching children how to question and how to explain. *American Educational Research Journal, 31,* 338–368.

Kolodner, J. (1993). *Case-based reasoning.* San Mateo, CA: Morgan Kaufman.

Landauer, T., McNamara, D. S., Dennis, S., & Kintsch, W. (Eds.). (2007). Handbook on latent semantic analysis. Mahwah, NJ: Erlbaum.

Lepper, M. R., & Henderlong, J. (2000). Turning "play" into "work" and "work" into "play": 25 years of research on intrinsic versus extrinsic motivation. In C. Sansone & J. M. Harackiewicz (Eds.), *Intrinsic and extrinsic motivation: The search for optimal motivation and performance* (pp. 257–307). San Diego, CA: Academic Press.

Linn, M. C., Davis, E. A., & Bell, P. (Eds.). (2004). *Internet environments for science education*. Mahwah, NJ: Lawrence Erlbaum.

Maki, R. H. (1998). Test predictions over text material. In D. J. Hacker, J. Dunlosky, & A. C. Graesser (Eds.), *Metacognition in educational theory and practice* (pp. 117–144), Mahwah, NJ: Lawrence Erlbaum.

Malone, T. W., & Lepper, M. R. (1987). Making learning fun: A taxonomy of intrinsic motivations for learning. *Cognitive Science, 5*(4), 333–369.

Mayer, R. E. (2005). *Multimedia learning*. Cambridge, MA: Cambridge University Press.

McNamara, D. S. (2004). SERT: Self-explanation reading training. *Discourse Processes, 38*, 1–30.

McNamara, D. S., Levinstein, I. B., & Boonthum, C. (2004). iSTART: Interactive strategy trainer for active reading and thinking. *Behavioral Research Methods, Instruments, and Computers, 36*, 222–233.

McNamara, D. S., O'Reilly, T., Best, R., & Ozuru, Y. (2006). Improving adolescent students' reading comprehension with iSTART. *Journal of Educational Computing Research, 34*, 147–171.

Moreno, R., & Mayer, R. E. (2004). Personalized messages that promote science learning in virtual environments. *Journal of Educational Psychology, 96*(1), 165–173.

Moreno, R., Mayer, R. E., Spires, H. A., & Lester, J. C. (2001). The case for social agency in computer-based teaching: Do students learn more deeply when they interact with animated pedagogical agents? *Cognition and Instruction, 19*, 177–213.

Norman, D. A. (1994). How might people interact with agents? *Communication of the ACM, 37*(7), 68–71.

Palincsar, A. S., & Brown, A. (1984). Reciprocal teaching of comprehension-fostering and comprehension-monitoring activities. *Cognition and Instruction, 1*, 117–175.

Person, N. K., Graesser, A. C., & the Tutoring Research Group. (2002). Human or computer? AutoTutor in a bystander Turing test. In S. A. Cerri, G. Gouarderes, & F. Paraguacu (Eds.), *Intelligent tutoring systems 2002* (pp. 821–830). Berlin: Springer.

Person, N. K., Kreuz, R. J., Zwaan, R., & Graesser, A. C. (1995). Pragmatics and pedagogy: Conversational rules and politeness strategies may inhibit effective tutoring. *Cognition and Instruction, 13*, 161–188.

Reeves, B., & Nass, C. (1996). *The media equation: How people treat computers, televisions, and new media like real people and places*. Cambridge: Cambridge University Press.

Rosenshine, B., Meister, C., & Chapman, S. (1996). Teaching students to generate questions: A review of the intervention studies. *Review of Educational Research, 66*, 181–221.

Shneiderman, B., & Plaisant, C. (2005). *Designing the user interface: Strategies for effective human–computer interaction* (4th ed.). Reading, MA: Addison-Wesley.

Sweller, J., & Cooper, M. (1985). The use of worked examples as a substitute for problem solving in learning algebra. *Cognition and Instruction, 2*, 59–89.

Taraban, R., Rynearson, K., & Stalcup, K. A. (2001). Time as a variable in learning on the World-Wide Web. *Behavior Research Methods, 33*(2), 217–225.

VanLehn, K., Graesser, A. C., Jackson, G. T., Jordan, P., Olney, A., & Rose, C. P. (2007). When are tutorial dialogues more effective than reading? *Cognitive Science, 31*(1), 3–62.

VanLehn, K., Lynch, C., Taylor, L., Weinstein, A., Shelby, R. H., Schulze, K. G., et al. (2002). Minimally invasive tutoring of complex physics problem solving. In S. A. Cerri, G. Gouarderes, & F. Paraguacu (Eds.), *Intelligent tutoring systems, 2002, 6th International Conference* (pp. 367–376). Berlin: Springer.

Vygotsky, L. S. (1978). *Mind and society: The development of higher mental processes.* Cambridge, MA: Harvard University Press.

Wiley, J. (2001). Supporting understanding through task and browser design. *Proceedings of the 23rd annual conference of the Cognitive Science Society* (pp. 1136–1143). Hillsdale, NJ: Lawrence Erlbaum.

Wisher, R. A., & Fletcher, J. D. (2004). The case for advanced distributed learning. *Information & Security, 14,* 17–25.

11

How Does Cognition Get Distributed? Case Studies of Making Concepts General in Technical and Scientific Work

ROGERS HALL, KÄREN WIECKERT,
and KENNETH WRIGHT

INTRODUCTION

*T*his chapter approaches generalization as an activity that people do together. We start by looking back at studies of distributed cognition, raise some broad questions about processes of distribution as they relate to making things general, and then use materials drawn from ethnographic and cognitive case studies to explore activities of generalizing. The broad questions are as follows:

- How does cognition get distributed?
- How do people, working together, make technical or scientific concepts general?
- How do these activities work as environments for learning and development?

These questions presuppose a framework in which cognition is specific to historical periods (Wartofsky, 1983) and dependent upon cultural artifacts and conventions in situations of actual use (Engestrom, Miettinen, & Punamaki, 1999). This approach to cognition (and generalization) may not be familiar to readers operating under a different received view. For example, the second question—how are concepts *made* general (Jurow, 2004)—appears to reverse a view common in cognitive science that general concepts exist outside human activities and are acquired, either accurately or not, on the basis of individual experience. Under this received view, generalization (the organizing topic of this volume) is an outcome of individual experience and thinking, a basic process of cognition and the stuff of knowledge. But if cognition is distributed over artifacts and social groups (Hutchins, 1995), how, when, and where should we think about generalization?

GENERALIZING AND DISTRIBUTING COGNITION

The word *distributed* hides part of the problem, because it is an adjective, past tense, and a modifier of already existing cognition. It is as if some aspects of cognition were distributed, but others were not. For conceptual domains that are learned as people participate in cultural activity (Hall, 2005), one cannot find cognition that is not distributed over people and things.[1] If we also want to understand how cognition gets to be this way, then we need to study distributing cognition. The word *distributing* is a verb, operating in an ongoing present, and shifts our attention to studies of how cognition, including the generalizing of concepts, is produced historically out of human activity.

It is not possible to review the literature on distributed cognition in this chapter, but Hutchins' book, *Cognition in the Wild* (1995), provides several important insights that are worth remembering at the outset. Hutchins conducted a comparative analysis of navigation in U.S. Navy (USN) and Micronesian contexts, arguing in the end that each used different representational systems to take advantage of the same computational constraints (i.e., fixing the position of a vessel on the surface of the earth). Way finding, particularly in the case of the USN, was not a solo cognitive performance, but instead was accomplished by functional systems made up of people and historically specific, representational artifacts (e.g., a gyrocompass and navigational chart). These representational technologies provided an infrastructure for coordinated, team activities of way finding. When everything worked smoothly, new generations of navigators learned to fix the ship's position by participating in team way finding where their "horizon of observation" included activities of more knowledgeable practitioners, doing different jobs in a routine division of labor. But when representations supporting this distributed, functional system broke down (e.g., the USN carrier that Hutchins was studying lost power to gyrocompass and steering while steaming into a harbor), way finding did not (could not) stop. Instead, members of the navigational team were able to discover a new division of labor by noticing and exploiting regularities in the coordinated structure of each other's activity—in effect, reorganizing the functional system and using different technologies to overcome the disruption (Hutchins, 2006).

While the ship eventually rested safely at anchor, the solution to navigating without routine instruments discovered by these navigators

> was not saved in the system. The conditions for the reproduction of this piece of knowledge are quite rare. The participants who were directly involved in this event eventually separated from the Navy without ever encountering this situation again. One of them went on to a position aboard a civilian oil tanker,

> so perhaps the knowledge constructed in this event will someday be reproduced in a different organizational setting. (Hutchins, 1995, p. 351)

The cases used to illustrate processes of distributing cognition in this chapter have a very different quality. Over the past decade, we have studied groups working on projects in field entomology, architectural design, conservation planning, biostatistics, and clinical medicine (Hall, 1999; Hall, Wright, & Wieckert, 2007). We videotaped typical chunks of their work, acted as participant observers (when possible) in that work, and interviewed people about their activities. We also collected working and published documents from these groups, so were able to follow their progress on open problems over time. In all of our cases, project groups sought new ways of working more productively, often borrowing methods or model structures from published papers of other work groups and sometimes inviting specialists from other disciplines to help them create or refine new methods (Hall, Stevens, & Torralba, 2002). In this sense, and unlike the USN case analyzed by Hutchins,[2] the work groups we studied were bringing new team members on board and changing their work practices simultaneously. These ethnographic and cognitive studies of learning at work provide rich empirical material for asking how cognition gets distributed.

Our analysis of distributing cognition focuses on three levels of analysis. At a microgenetic level, what Hutchins (1995, pp. 372–374) called "the conduct of activity," people participate in moment-to-moment interaction where they find problems, compare alternative courses of action, and reach agreements about what they might do next. At this level, we focus closely on speakers' and hearers' turn-structured talk, gesture, gaze, and the visible use and production of symbolic or graphical representational forms. We analyze video and audio recordings using methods similar to those developed in conversation analysis (Jordan & Henderson, 1995; Sacks, 1992; Schegloff, 1991) with explicit attention to representational forms (Goodwin, 2000). At an ontogenetic level, what Hutchins (1995) called "the development of practitioners," people learn by participating in project activities where they make contributions based on their personal knowledge and history of experience. Over a wider time scale (from moments to years), individual's contributions are evaluated, sometimes edited, and selectively incorporated into the work of other project participants. At this level, we focus on an individual's contributions both in project meetings (analysis of video recordings) and in working documents produced as part of project activities. In making inferences about what individuals know or have learned, we also use interviews, typically conducted over documents and video excerpts selected from previous work sessions, in which we ask people about their personal understandings and history. At a sociogenetic level (Cole, 1996), what Hutchins (1995) called "the development of practice," people working together develop expectations about how representations will be used and labor divided over a still wider time scale (months to years), and these expectations both constrain and provide resources for individual development (ontogenesis) and for the conduct of activity (microgenesis). At this level, we focus on work group products like publications, archives of research material, routine methods or procedures, and the staffing of research projects (e.g., recruiting a new member with particular methodological skills). Our analysis at this level uses both biographical interviews (e.g., about the history of a work group in relation to individual careers) and archival records of individual and group production (e.g., vitae and project reports).

Processes of distributing cognition involve relations between different levels of analysis. For example, in a study of how language changes with increasing currency use and schooling among indigenous people in New Guinea, Saxe and Esmonde (2005) described cross-level relations as follows:

> [I]ndividuals' microgenetic constructions in collective practices are moments in the sociogenetic reconstruction and propagation of [representational] forms and functions. Thus microgenetic constructions take form in relation to processes of sociogenesis. Such microgenetic and sociogenetic constructions are also moments in ontogenetic trajectories, taking form in relation to individuals' prior understandings and affording the possibility of new developmental trajectories. (p. 210)

When a group's conventional way of working is disrupted, as in the navigational crisis reported by Hutchins (1995), discovery or innovation at the microgenetic level can produce new ways of accomplishing that work. If these innovations are adopted as conventional resources in the group's work practices (sociogenesis, not observed in Hutchins' case), they in turn create a new environment for individual learning (ontogenesis). Our studies explore these cross-level relations as processes of distributing cognition in technical and scientific work groups.

In the following sections, we present descriptive findings on processes through which scientific and technical work groups go about changing what they know and can do. Under conditions where stable group practices have been disrupted or suspended in order to find new ways to work, we examine three processes that make up distributing cognition (there may be others) across different levels of analysis. First is narrative assembly of future work in conversation (at a microgenetic level, though the history of individuals and work groups are important here). Second is using parables to position coworkers or clients in alternative ways of working (at an ontogenetic or biographical level of analysis). Third is building infrastructure by analogical reasoning (at a sociogenetic level of analysis, in collective practices). Each process will be described more fully as the chapter proceeds and grounded in empirical material drawn from one or more of our ethnographic and cognitive case studies.

NARRATIVE ASSEMBLY OF FUTURE
WORK (BUGHOUSE CASE)

We studied a team of field entomologists at the BugHouse (all place and participant names are pseudonyms) working on the taxonomy of forest insects, with a particular focus on termites. These scientists sought to classify termites on the basis of "chemical fingerprints" found in a waxy residue on insects' exoskeletons. As shown in Figure 11.1, this involved capturing termites in geographically precise locations in the soil and detritus making up the forest floor (lower left). After characterizing

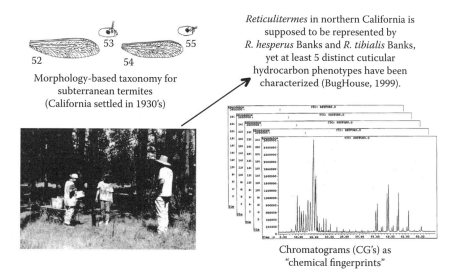

Morphology-based taxonomy for
subterranean termites
(California settled in 1930's)

Reticulitermes in northern California is
supposed to be represented by
R. hesperus Banks and *R. tibialis* Banks,
yet at least 5 distinct cuticular
hydrocarbon phenotypes have been
characterized (BugHouse, 1999).

Chromatograms (CG's) as
"chemical fingerprints"

Figure 11.1   Classifying termites at the BugHouse: A team of field entomologists captures termites in a forested region of California (lower left), then compares hydrocarbons found in a waxy residue on these insects' exoskeletons (chromatograms at lower right) to revise species taxonomy originally established using body morphology (upper left).

the type and abundance of hydrocarbons found on the exoskeletons of samples of captured termites (graphs of chemical abundance, called *chromatograms* or *chemical profiles*, shown in Figure 11.1, lower right), BugHouse researchers analyzed chemical differences in relation to other field and laboratory data to make claims about new termite species, the ecology of termite colonies in turning over wood in the forest, and the evolutionary history of these insects in the continental United States. This group actively questioned the taxonomy of termites in northern California, revisiting taxa that were thought settled in the 1930s on the basis of body morphology (Figure 11.1, upper left).

As part of this research project, investigators at the BugHouse were constantly on the lookout for new methods of analyzing the chemical fingerprints their group was known for, in hopes of advancing a novel approach to insect taxonomy. In our multiyear, ethnographic, and cognitive case study of work at the BugHouse, we attended several meetings in which senior investigators scheduled consulting time with a statistician, Bill, who worked at the same federal research station.

In one such meeting, routine work at the BugHouse had been suspended to consult with Bill about new ways to analyze differences between chromatograms (Hall et al., 2002). In that consultation one of the senior entomologists, Gary, proposed that the group might borrow a method of cluster analysis (phylogenetic analysis using parsimony, or PAUP) from evolutionary biologists, in order to identify groups or taxa of termites related by their capacity for secreting particular hydrocarbons. During conversational exchanges concerning cluster analysis, we find interesting examples of distributing cognition by narrative assembly of alternative ways of working in the future (see also Ochs, Jacoby, & Gonzales, 1994).

We describe a 3-part conversational exchange that occurred during Gary's proposal that the BugHouse team borrow methods of cluster analysis. Each part of the exchange was structured as a narrative (i.e., relating events in temporal order, where the meaning intended by speakers depends upon that order; see Labov, 1972). In the meeting, Mark, Bill, and then Gary each contributed different narratives that, as the conversation progressed, were used to assemble a reasonable (by Bill's expert advice) way of using cluster analysis to find insect groups. Each narrative put cluster analysis, field and laboratory labor by team members, insects, and data together in order to make claims about termite taxonomy. In the first narrative (Figure 11.2, top panel), Mark (the BugHouse team leader) told a story that bound together field worker activity and cluster analysis, addressed to the statistician (Bill) as someone who might decide to do this work. Mark's narrative was structured in time and space as a sequence of activities, moving down the east coast of the United States, collecting termites and making field observations in a biogeographic survey that Bill (addressed as *you*) might do. At the end of his narrative, Mark positioned Bill as someone choosing what to do next: "What would you do there? Cluster analysis?" Cluster analysis followed the survey and, in Mark's proposed use, would *confirm* termite groups already seen in field observations. As the conversation continued, there was more evidence that Mark expected to use cluster analysis to confirm structures already seen in the field.

As the conversation continued (Figure 11.2, center panel), Bill (the statistician) would have none of Mark's leading narrative. In sharp contrast, Bill's use of *you* referred exclusively to the entomologists, removing himself from their activities altogether. His narrative also reorganized BugHouse activity in relation to cluster analysis over time: Researchers made inferences about termite groups while still in the field (i.e., *before* any chemical analysis), they chose cluster analysis *after* these discoveries, and cluster analysis would find clusters *whenever* it was done. By following Mark's proposal, the BugHouse team would use cluster analysis to confirm insect groups observed in the field. But in Bill's counternarrative, cluster analysis generates structures regardless of whether they are meaningful in the domain of analysis—as he later led Mark to understand, "That's its job." Bill's narrative and criticism were bad news for the BugHouse, and this led Gary jokingly to ask (with ensuing laughter by other team members, not shown here) why they chose to talk with Bill at all, because he was advising them (yet again) to avoid relying on statistical methods in place of their biological knowledge.

Gary, the entomologist who originally proposed borrowing cluster analysis from others' publications as a new method, later offered a repair of Mark's original narrative (Figure 11.3, bottom panel). In Gary's proposal, they would instead reserve graphs of chemical abundance as numbered data, in a way that was independent of field observations. As he spoke, Gary formed a "jar" with his hand, placed chemistry data into this gestural container, and then hid the container (his held gesture) below the table, out of sight for Bill and other members of the BugHouse team. Gary and the BugHouse team (a "we" exclusive of Bill) would use cluster analysis to *discover* possible insect groups using chemistry data that were independent of field observations. As the conversation continued, and with Bill's enthusiastic agreement,

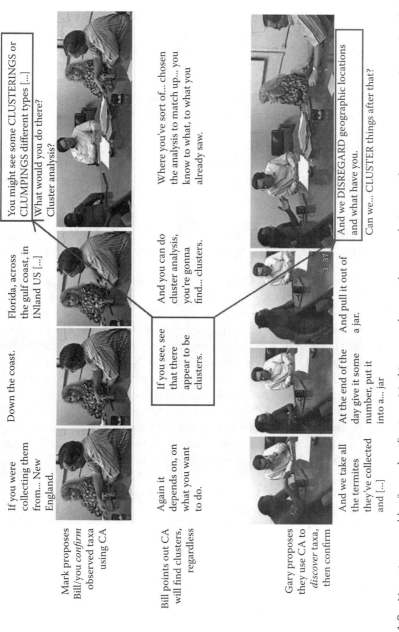

Figure 11.2 Narrative assembly of new classifications: Mark's proposal to use cluster analysis to *confirm* termite groups observed in the field (upper panel) was deconstructed by the consulting statistician (Bill, middle panel). In a conversational repair, a senior entomologist (Gary, lower panel) proposed using cluster analysis to *discover* termite groups, using field observations later for confirmation.

they decided to use these other field data (geographic location, fighting behavior, and morphology) to confirm insect groups discovered using cluster analysis.

Returning to our argument about how narratives assemble future work, the three panels in Figure 11.2 show two alternative ways of using cluster analysis. Mark (and Bill in the next speaker position) would use cluster analysis to *confirm* insect groups seen in the field. In Gary's alternative, they would use cluster analysis over chemistry data to *discover* candidate insect groups, which they could later confirm (or disconfirm) using other field data. The advice of the consulting statistician (Bill) deconstructed Mark's narrative and affirmed Gary's repair, relocating cluster analysis to play a different epistemic role in the work of the BugHouse (i.e., discovery versus confirmation). In summary, the BugHouse research group invited Bill to help find new ways of working, the history of their project was suspended while they had the conversation, and they produced multiple, narrative versions of how to work in the future. As the meeting progressed, the epistemic role of a borrowed statistical method hung in the balance, and they eventually agreed to use cluster analysis to discover new insect groups.

USING PARABLES TO EVALUATE ALTERNATIVE WAYS OF WORKING (BUGHOUSE AND STREAMS CASES)

Another process of distributing cognition that we have studied is using parables to evaluate choices about alternative ways of working in the future. This is something done primarily by statistical consultants, in our data. As part of their consulting practice, statisticians typically work across multiple client research projects. Along these consulting trajectories, statisticians acquire and reuse a variety of representational forms (Figure 11.3; see also Tuomi-Grohn & Engestrom, 2003; Wenger, 1998). Parables—by which we mean structural analogies that offer clients a choice among alternatives with clear evaluative or moral consequences—are one of the representational forms that statisticians carry around with them.

Bill used parables regularly in his consulting, as in the following example from his work with the BugHouse team.[3] Again concerning whether structures discovered using cluster analysis had any intrinsic meaning, Bill said to Mark,

Bill: Um, it's like you can have definite clusters. Uh like, the analogy I've used a lot of times, that's, it may not very, be very good. But you have the A, B, O blood groups. Which are DEFINITE ... diff— different groups, uh ...

Mark: Don't get O blood. 'Cause they call you all the time for more.

Bill: Yes. Uh, but, but if you go to apply for a driver's license in California, it's totally irrelevant. You know it doesn't, you know, there, there are DEFINITE groups, but it has NOTHING to do with getting a driver's license. So it has to do with what are you trying to do. I mean, what what's the question?

Before Bill could even complete the parable, Mark took up the position of a harried donor of type O blood, asked repeatedly for donations. But Bill was building

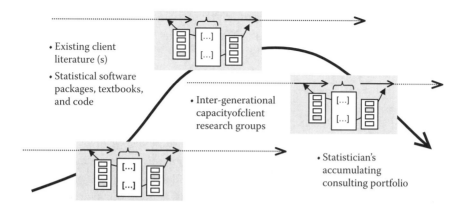

- Existing client literature (s)
- Statistical software packages, textbooks, and code
- Inter-generational capacityofclient research groups
- Statistician's accumulating consulting portfolio

Figure 11.3 Statistical consultants work across client research projects (from Hall, Wright, & Wieckert, 2007). Along a consulting trajectory that spans multiple research projects (heavy arrow), a statistician makes contributions, both in conversation and in other media, to research clients and their projects. Alternative ways of working are considered in each consultation (nodes along consulting trajectory), and statisticians use parables to influence client choices among these alternatives.

a very different position for Mark as recipient and subject of the parable. What Bill intended was critical of Mark and his group, because the remainder of the parable positioned Mark as a user of discovered clusters that had no relevance to his research question. By analogy to issuing driver's licenses on the basis of blood type, Mark would distinguish between insect taxa on the basis of clusters that were biologically irrelevant. In this way, parables told by statisticians serve an evaluative purpose, depending on which position the clients chooses.

In another of Bill's consulting projects, the client (Pam, a conservation biologist modeling a mountain watershed; see Hall et al., 2007, for details) asked for Bill's help in using statistical tests to create an objective definition of biodiversity. In this sense, she hoped to make her models more defensible for use in a litigious regulatory context (e.g., whether to restrict foresting or human residential development in watershed areas with endangered species). Pam was considering the use of statistical tests to exclude species from her model, even though for many species, she did not have budget to collect adequate distributional data. After commiserating about her funding situation, Bill compared her problem to that of researchers attempting to map the home range of animals.

Bill: It's a LITTLE bit like uh, um I always go back to home ranges. People have all these data points for the home range.... So someone.... You have a data point over here ... and uh, so they'll do a minimum ... minimum convex polygon. And all of sudden you, enclosed like this.

Pam: Three times the area. ((*Laughing*))

Bill: And someone'll say, well, they've got a better idea.... And so they develop, they have some algorithm that will get rid of this stuff, to make it look more like what they would have drawn by eye in the first place. So it begs

the question. You see a scatter of points, why not just, you know, draw it
like that? And do it by hand. That uses your biological [knowledge.

Pam: [It's repeatable though. (2 sec) But yeh.

Bill: Use your biological knowledge. You KNOW maybe there's a waterhole right
in here? They have to have, so you can USE all that information.

Pam initially heard Bill's analogy to researchers devising home range algorithms
as a (somewhat mocking) criticism of researchers whose algorithms vastly overes-
timate range, and she evidently shared this criticism (i.e., agreement and laughter
in her first turn, above). But Bill's advice, completed in the form of a parable, positioned Pam along with home range researchers, using algorithms (or, by analogy,
statistical tests) to make decisions about phenomena that violated their own biological knowledge. Again, Bill offered a client (as he did with Mark at the BugHouse)
a position in a parable with clear evaluative consequences.

A final example from an interview with Bill concerned advice he gave to clients
trying to borrow methods or statistical techniques from others' published papers
(a common occurrence in Bill's work). Asked about his approach in these cases,
Bill said,

Bill: And so we always have to back 'em up, and it's … for some people it's real awk-
ward. Cause they just don't want—they figure it's none of our business.

Interviewer: Um hmm.

Bill: And uh, because others have been doing it this way for years. And then uh …
we usually answer that with—Well, if your kid said, well Johnny's got
an Uzi, and you know, his parents let him have an Uzi, you know?

Interviewer: ((*Laughter*))

Bill: And all the kids in the block have Uzi's, you know, doesn't mean you should
give your kids—and here you're doing science, you know?

Interviewer: Um hmm.

Bill: Come on! Uh, just humor us a little bit, and pretend like you—you're gonna
tell us … the why.

Although we never found Bill using the Uzi parable with a client, he did serve on an
internal review committee for research conducted and published in the research
station. So in addition to his consulting portfolio, Bill saw a variety of researchers
trying to borrow statistical methods from other groups or previous publications.
Again, researchers (his clients and coworkers) were positioned as protagonists in a
parable, in this case as children seeking ever more spectacular toys for use in their
play activities. Bill acted through the parable as a skeptical parent, regarding not
only guns and statistical methods, but also the character and adequacy of scientific
explanation demonstrated by client investigators.

BUILDING INFRASTRUCTURE BY ANALOGICAL REASONING (FLU CASE)

Finally, we turn to a process of distributing cognition that was prefigured in Bill's Uzi parable and common across our case studies of statistical consulting. Research clients regularly borrowed methods or models from other groups or from published literature, as Gary (BugHouse) and Pam (Streams) were doing in the cases described above. Borrowing structure by analogy to prior work happens both at individual and collective levels of thinking and action (see also Dunbar, 1995), with the result that research groups build new layers of representational infrastructure for working differently in the future. We illustrate the multilevel character of analogy with the flu case, in which researchers working on infectious disease borrowed methods from prior publications to estimate how many children were hospitalized with influenza in county hospitals.

The researchers wanted to borrow a *capture–recapture estimate* (CRE), originally developed in animal studies to estimate the size of populations that were too large, elusive, or expensive to count exhaustively. CRE is usually explained[4] by asking a reader to imagine a pond full of fish, where the number of fish is unknown and, in practice, uncountable. Using a screen (or net), you pull out some number of fish and mark them (e.g., capture and mark 29 fish). You then let the marked fish go back into the pond, where they distribute themselves uniformly among the unmarked fish. Later using a second screen (or net), which does not need to be of the same size, you capture a second group of fish (e.g., 34 fish captured by the second screen). If 11 of the 34 fish caught by the second screen had already been marked, you can estimate how many fish are in the pond with an algebraic proportion ($N = (n1 \times n2)/m2 = (29 \times 34)/11 = 90$; see Table 11.1). CRE users make several important assumptions: There is independent probability of capture, the population is closed (no animals or children escape), and the marking or diagnosis used is valid and durable (e.g., fish stay marked, and children get and keep their diagnosis).

Flu case researchers wanted to use two influenza screens, one prospective and expensive (active enrollment of sick children), and the other retrospective but

TABLE 11.1 Capture–Recapture Estimation (CRE) Using Peterson's Method for the Number of Children Hospitalized With Influenza in County Hospitals

		Prospective Screen (4 Days)		
		Enrolled	Missed	
Retrospective Screen (7 Days)	Enrolled	a = m2	b	n2 = (a + b)
	Missed	c	z	
		n1 = (a + c)		N = a + b + c + z
				N = (n1 × n2) / m2

Note: Estimated number of cases missed by both systems: $z = (b \times c) / a$. The prospective screen is active (4 days, enrolling children at hospital intake) and expensive, whereas the retrospective screen is passive (7 days, chart review) and relatively cheap. "Enrolling" a child is like marking a captured fish with a diagnosis of influenza. (From Alberto's published study.)

cheaper (passive review of hospital charts), to estimate the number of children hospitalized with influenza during the annual influenza season. But as they discovered, using CRE to count populations in epidemiology can be controversial for at least two reasons. First, if state or federal sponsors are paying for two screens to count the same children, and both screens are expensive, why should they pay for both? Instead, why can't researchers get one of the screens right and eliminate the weaker one? Sponsors ask these kinds of questions, so researchers need to explain that CRE leverages undercounting from two independent screens: The combination of two imperfect screens is better than either alone, *because* they make independent counts. Second, consider the quantity, z, in the lower-right cell of Table 11.1. This represents children captured by neither screen, yet researchers using CRE will estimate how many of these children there are. Some sponsors do not want to consider or allocate funds to things that no one has ever seen (Anderson & Fienberg, 2000). In this sense, flu researchers borrowed not only the method but also the controversies (criticisms and justifications) attending that method.

Figure 11.4 shows two scenes from a conversation in which a member of the Flu team (Alberto, left image) and the consulting statistician (Ted, right image) worked through the assumptions and structure of the CRE method. Each had a stack of annotated documents under his elbow. Alberto started with a partial manuscript and printout from a statistical software package (STATA, his coding efforts were in progress). Beneath these were publications Alberto used as sources for borrowing the method. These included articles using CRE in the epidemiology literature

Alberto aligns a table from his in-progress manuscript with his own STATA printout. In a layer beneath these documents are publications from which Alberto borrows the structure of CRE calculations. Ted's marked up copies of these publications are in a stack under his left elbow. Nancy (Flu PI) has directed Alberto to Ted.

Alberto calls out observed screening values to Ted, who enters these in his own STATA code to "bootstrap" confidence intervals for the in-progress CRE estimate. Alberto leaves the consulting meeting with Ted's code, which he edits later when finishing the manuscript with co-authors. Ted can publish the code.

Figure 11.4 Building infrastructure by analogical reasoning: Early in the consulting meeting (left image), the client (Alberto) showed his provisional results to the statistician (Ted), in a layer of documents built up from prior publications (bottom of Alberto's stack), software code that implemented calculations described in these publications, and a table of provisional results (in left image, Alberto points at tabled values). Later in the consulting meeting (right image), Ted typed Alberto's observed values into his own version of software code, then compared his results with those obtained by Alberto.

(e.g., a study of pneumonia in children) and a heavily cited paper on uses of CRE in the wider field of epidemiology (Hook & Regal, 1995). Ted (the statistician) had a different set of annotated documents and publications under his elbow, most sent to him by Alberto before the meeting. Ted had also written his own STATA code, which was quite sophisticated by comparison with Alberto's code.

Reviewing these scenes in terms of the cognitive science literature on analogical inference and learning (Gentner, 1983; Gick & Holyoak, 1983, 1987), there is a lot going on above the level of the individual. Analogical inference and learning are usually thought to consist of four individual cognitive processes. First, the reasoner must *notice* or access the analogy. For example, faced with a difficult target problem in mathematics, a reasoner might notice this is similar to a source problem with a known solution, and they might then retrieve the source problem and solution. Second, the reasoner constructs a *mapping* between source and target problems, considering different ways in which they could be placed in correspondence. This produces structurally different mappings and possible solutions to the target problem. Third, the reasoner *evaluates* alternative mappings and the analogical inferences they would support, choosing a mapping that is most promising for finding a target problem solution. Fourth and finally, the reasoner *consolidates* what has been learned through the completed analogy by storing it in memory, where it can be retrieved and used to solve future problems. Spontaneous noticing of an analogy is known to be difficult for individual reasoners (Gick & Holyoak, 1983, 1987), and there is a sizable literature on laboratory studies of mapping, evaluation, and consolidation (Gentner, 2002). As Gentner put it in the conference leading to this edited book, humans have memories like rodents, which are dominated by surface similarity, but their inference and mapping engines are like supercomputers (D. Gentner, personal communication, August, 2006).

In the flu case, Alberto did not notice the analogy—instead, Nancy (the leader of the Flu research group) noticed that CRE methods were used by other epidemiologists and suggested Alberto pursue this lead. Nancy also found out that Ted (the statistician) had worked on CRE methods for his dissertation, almost 20 years earlier. Thus, Nancy drew together source publications and statistical expertise (Ted) to consider the analogy in a consulting meeting that she did not attend. In this sense, noticing and mapping—components of analogy that have been understood as matters of individual cognitive processing—involved participants from across a complex division of labor in the surrounding organization (e.g., Nancy and Ted are senior faculty in different departments; Alberto was a physician and graduate student at the time of our study). Furthermore, in the Flu case, processes of analogical reasoning went on for several weeks, not for several minutes, as would be the case in typical experimental settings. In an effort to borrow CRE for counting children hospitalized with influenza, analogical reasoning extended well beyond the consulting meeting in both participants and time. Representations used to pursue and complete the analogy were also quite varied, including published research reports, text and tables for Alberto's in-progress manuscript, hand-drawn illustrations of conventional distributions, demonstrations of how to calculate statistical estimates with simplified number sets, and independently written versions of computer code. Some representations (as material objects) persisted over time and were reused

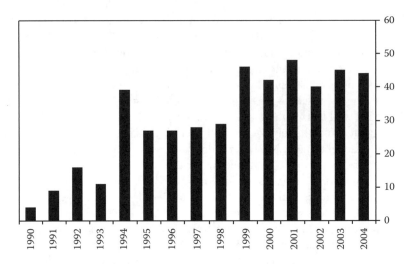

Figure 11.5 Alberto's depiction of the spread of CRE in health sciences publications listed by the National Library of Medicine (articles using CRE from 1990 to 2004), used in a seminar talk about the Flu project given to clinical researchers in infectious diseases.

for other research studies. For example, as shown to the right in Figure 11.4, Ted typed parameters into his STATA code as Alberto called out screening values, in order to generate confidence intervals on the resulting counts. Alberto left the meeting with Ted's code, which he later edited and used with other members of the flu team to publish an article estimating the number of children with influenza in county hospitals. Alberto repeated this reuse cycle for a second article that incorporated data from other states (published 12 months after their original article). Thus, the STATA code traveled, was edited and reused by the research team, and eventually was consolidated as a resource for the Flu research group. One part of distributing cognition across multiple levels of analysis, the STATA code drew from Ted's experience as an identified CRE and STATA expert (ontogenesis), provided resources for conversation in the consulting meeting (microgenesis), was later edited and reused by Alberto for multiple data sets (ontogenesis), and was eventually consolidated as a new method by the Flu research group (sociogenesis). Ted also retained his code and told us he might use it again or publish it, in a STATA journal that is widely used by practitioners (he had done so in other cases). In this sense, elements of a mapping structure worked out in conversation both implemented a particular case of analogical inference (Alberto's study of childhood influenza rates) and became infrastructural resources that began to circulate in different professional settings (epidemiology and biostatistics) as we followed the Flu case over time (Figure 11.3).

While the structure of CRE and its material implementation were being distributed, thinking and action by individuals were also highly consequential. During the consulting meeting, Alberto and Ted substantively disagreed over how CRE should be used in this study. Because the prospective screen operated only 4 days a week during the flu season, but the retrospective screen operated 7 days a week (i.e., continuously), Alberto assumed they could use only matched calendar days for each screen (i.e., 4 matching days, each week). In his draft manuscript, on the table during the consult, Alberto wrote,

> Since the [prospective screen] limited surveillance to 4 days per week and the [retrospective screen] uses the entire week, cases will be limited to those who were hospitalized during the same period of time for both systems.

Based on our analysis of the entire consultation and subsequent interviews, we conclude that Alberto believed nonmatching calendar days would violate the CRE assumption of a closed population (i.e., some children might not be available to the 4-day screen).

Ted challenged Alberto's assumption about matched calendar days, proposing instead that he use all days from both screens because the method "doesn't care" if screens have different probabilities of capture. This would increase the size of counts, perhaps allowing Alberto to break out child flu rates by age group (something he could not do using only matched days). Alberto followed Ted's proposal closely but gave no sign of agreement. Instead, he[5] narrated an extreme case in which the screens shared only one matched day each week.

Alberto: I wou—I I thought about that uh a little bit, that it was a little difficult to me to understand for example, you're uh if they, if there were no data for 4 days, just one day.
Ted: Yeah.
Alberto: And the other system would be working the whole, the whole week. Do you think it would be still possible to apply?
Ted: Sure.
Alberto: Mm.

Alberto's mapping of CRE assumptions (i.e., use only matching calendar days) in this extreme case would lead to uninterpretable results. But Ted was casually positive ("Sure") about using the method with all available screening days. Ted mapped the number of days per week during which each screen operated onto the sample size captured by each screen (i.e., screen or "trap" sizes), not onto the CRE assumption of a closed population. As Ted went on to argue (turns not shown), because the CRE method did not require that screens have equal probability of capture (i.e., 4 versus 7 days, or even 1 versus 7 days), each screen could be used both to assess and to extend the count of the other screen (i.e., through the algebraic proportion in Table 11.1).

In subsequent conversations with the Flu team, the statistician's advice to use all days was subjected to close scrutiny, particularly by authors working for the federal agency that funded screens used in the study (we were not invited to these meetings, but asked what happened in interviews). As Ted (the statistician) put it in our debrief interview, he did an adequate job of "salesmanship" to overcome concerns about matching days. He also addressed concerns that using CRE might bring negative attention to the screening systems, which despite being very expensive still undercounted cases of child influenza. Alberto confirmed this tension in a separate debrief interview, noting that there were "two kinds of epidemiologists"—those willing to adopt CRE as an improvement over screens that undercount, and those who preferred to base findings and health policy only on cases that could be directly counted. In this sense, the evaluation of the analogical mapping was sensitive to issues and controversies both inside and outside the Flu research group.

Alberto used all data from the 4-day (prospective) and 7-day (retrospective) screen in his first published article, which appeared in print 14 months after the consulting meeting. Alberto and his colleagues adopted Ted's advice about meeting CRE assumptions, and as a result, they obtained more precise estimates of the number of children hospitalized with flu than would have been possible using only the more sensitive (4-day) screen or using CRE with only matching calendar days. But their adoption of the CRE method was extended even further by Ted's advice.

In the final paragraph of their first published article, Alberto and the Flu team proposed extending the approach taken in their study of county children to a national influenza surveillance system for U.S. adults. Relaxing the constraint of matched calendar days and embracing the extreme case Alberto originally contributed as a problem for interpretation (1 versus 7 days), they proposed using the more expensive (and accurate) prospective screening procedures only one day a week. This would make maximally efficient use of limited funds for influenza screening. Thus, what Alberto originally proposed as a "bug" in the consulting meeting (his extreme case was a challenge to Ted's advice) later became a "feature" in the published article. What started as a case of analogical cross mapping (i.e., of CRE assumptions) played out in negotiations over several weeks, with potential significance for influenza surveillance systems that operate at a national level.

DISCUSSION

We started this chapter with an argument that generalization—making technical or scientific concepts more broadly useful across situations—is an activity that people do together. Important aspects of generalization, we have argued, are the outcome of processes of distributing cognition. In two cases, we have shown how technical or scientific concepts (cluster analysis in the BugHouse case, and capture–recapture estimation in the Flu case) are borrowed, used, and reused by people working together in research groups. We have described three processes that contribute to distributing cognition, each operating at a different level of analysis. These include using narratives to assemble future work, using parables to position coworkers or clients in alternative ways of working, and building representational infrastructure by analogical reasoning. Narrative assembly operates at the time scale of face-to-face interaction, during conversations between coworkers who have suspended existing practice to consider working differently. Alternative ways of working produced in these conversations are compared, sometimes using parables that offer subject positions with strongly evaluative consequences for choices that clients must make among alternatives. Parables contributed by statistical consultants (in our cases) can be seen as tools of the trade that are acquired over biographical time, carried along consulting trajectories, and used repeatedly with clients. Analogy provides structural material for working in new ways, and alternative mappings of that structure can become the intended topic of parables told by specialists and advisors. Analogy and parable, in this sense, create a new set of possible uses of technical or scientific concepts and contribute to generalization. Processes of analogical reasoning may also operate in substantial ways at a collective level of analysis, in the sense that noticing a potential analogy and mapping structural relations between source and target are accomplished by different members of a work team, over time scales longer than typical in experimental studies of individual analogical inference, and with materials that are quite diverse (e.g., multiple source publications, and multiple coding efforts to replicate published results). We now return to our leading questions.

How Does Cognition Get Distributed?

These three processes are a partial answer to the first of our leading questions. The partial answer is messy, certainly messier than an account in which individuals find and solve problems, then union their results together as a team, all moving forward with the same productive understanding. Just as studies of distributed cognition have revealed a complex structure of tasks, supporting technologies, and distributions of labor in work teams, our efforts to study how people change these structures (e.g., distributing cognition) add new layers of structural complexity and pose new questions. For example, we have described processes that operate at different levels of analysis regarding change and development, but how are these levels articulated so that change is possible? As Lemke (2001) argued, part of the answer involves different time scales at which things are changing, particularly when routine work organization has been disrupted (as in Hutchins' [1995] navigational crisis) or suspended to find ways of working differently (the cases reported in this chapter). We might expect structures that change at a faster rate always to unfold dynamically within stable constraints provided by structures that change more slowly. In this nested time scales model, conversations between research team members that play out in seconds to minutes (microgenesis) reflect stable understandings brought to interaction by individual participants. Similarly, individuals learn to participate and so change their thinking (ontogenesis) in relatively stable collective practices. But what happens when work groups have sustained conversations about changing collective practice and then adopt changes (sociogenesis)? Processes operating at a more rapid time scale (e.g., narratives produced through talk-in-interaction, and creating and editing representational forms) evidently are required to reorganize new collective practices or routines, and these set expectations for what individuals are to know or do in the future (see Saxe & Esmonde, 2005).

When we follow processes of distributing cognition, we encounter new questions about scale and change. For example, how do processes of narrative assembly, which unfold quickly in interactions at a microgenetic level, make present and sensibly use or transform past work practices of the group (a sociogenetic level)? Similarly, how do these uses of history in the moment, and agreements on how the group might work differently in the future, become new forms of distributed cognition (past tense, a stable accomplishment) in the future? We are working on these questions, focusing on interaction within and across work groups and on the history of these groups, using comparative case studies (Hall et al., 2007).

How Do People, Working Together, Make Technical or Scientific Concepts General?

Processes of distributing cognition also provide a window onto activities through which people work together to make technical or scientific concepts general, and we turn to that broad question next. Looking back over how CRE was adopted in Alberto's study, it appears that Ted's advice about meeting the assumptions of the method had important consequences for Alberto's study and his group's proposals for future research and public health policy. Whereas Alberto's original assumption of matching calendar days (mapped to the CRE assumption of a closed population) limited the number of children available for estimation, Ted's advice to use all days instead mapped screening days to the size of samples taken by each screen. These samples needed to be statistically independent of each other, but they did not need to be of the same size. After further conversation and "salesmanship," Alberto and his more senior colleagues adopted Ted's advice. They made more precise estimates of the true number of children hospitalized with flu, but they also proposed a surveillance strategy, using the more expensive, prospective screen on a single day and running the less expensive (and less sensitive) retrospective screen continuously (7 days). What Alberto originally offered as an extreme case that would make CRE difficult to interpret ended up as a proposal for a new, national surveillance system for adult influenza. Clearly the Flu research group used CRE in new situations and studies, and in this sense, their efforts make CRE "more general" through processes we have called *distributing cognition*. But what is the nature of generality under distribution?

Based on our analysis of case material, statistical concepts and methods are actively distributed over time, places, and people. In this sense, concepts could be said to be "more general" because they are used more widely and in new ways over time. We now consider three types of generality that appear to be operating in these cases, using material from the Flu case as an illustration. Because Alberto was already in the process of borrowing CRE methods before meeting with Ted, the "career" (our term) of CRE in epidemiology was being extended through a cycle of analogical reuse even without Ted's help. This is, we argue, a mundane but widespread and important way of making a technical concept (X) general:

> *Type 1, Spread*: The collection of projects using X increases with each group that publishes a study in which a claim rests on X as an ally in some way.

This view of generality is nicely illustrated by a graphic that Alberto produced to present his research to other researchers of infectious diseases (Figure 11.5). The bar chart shows an advancing career for CRE in health sciences, and it has the interesting feature that Alberto will, himself, become a data point if his efforts in the Flu research group are successful.

Type 1 generality increases as a concept spreads to new users. But as we found, Alberto had an overly narrow understanding of CRE assumptions (i.e., use only matching calendar days), a restriction that was eventually relaxed by Ted's advice to use all days. The CRE method became both more appropriate and powerful in the published arguments of Alberto and his coauthors. Ted's advice extended the reach of CRE in this study, beyond what Alberto was already doing. This, we argue, is a second and more expansive sense of making a concept general:

> *Type 2, Transform Local Work*: The claims of the research group using X become stronger or more precise because of the way X is fitted to their work (e.g., stronger inferences from sample to population).

Finally, as evident in the last paragraph of Alberto's in-press article, what he originally contributed as a critical challenge to Ted's advice (i.e., combining screens that operate for 1 and 7 days) not only was shown to be possible, in an exchange that was critical to improving Alberto's understanding of CRE assumptions, but also was extended to a proposal for a national influenza surveillance system for adults. Thus, not only did the CRE method provide greater reach in the study completed by Alberto and his colleagues (Type 2, above), but also it became a model for a new screen (adult influenza) and a recommendation to the wider field for how to make "best use" of limited financial and human resources in "essential surveillance activities" (both quotes from the final paragraph of Alberto's published study). This is a third, still more expansive sense of making concepts general:

> *Type 3, Transform Concept*: As X is fitted to a client's local project, it undergoes a transformation that changes its available meanings in the future.

Although these three types present different views of the nature of generality under distribution (i.e., concepts spread, work is transformed, and the concept itself is transformed), they are not mutually exclusive and may operate simultaneously.

How Do These Activities Work as Environments for Learning and Development?

We return finally to our broad question about how distributing cognition, as an activity that is structured at different levels of analysis, serves as an environment for learning and teaching. In contrast to Bill's Uzi parable about the tensions of consulting, Ted (in interview) gave a hopeful account when asked if Alberto's use of the CRE method "has a future" that is larger than his particular study. Ted initially focused on Alberto's trajectory, then recalled an earlier, similar case:

> And you know from my point of view, um, if for instance Alberto stays around and becomes Nancy's go-to guy for capture–recapture [CRE] analyses, that's wonderful. And, you know one moment that was particularly satisfying for me, one of my ex-students came to me with a problem that required an interrupted time series analysis, which I explained to him and helped him do. And then a couple of years later I was listening to one of our [clinical] students who said

he was doing an interrupted time series analysis which he had been taught how to do by the first student. And, I said YES! You know. It's wonderful. To the extent that one can position oneself at the beginning of an avalanche of knowledge. That's what teaching is really all about. It's not that I don't enjoy doing analyses for other people, but it's much more fun if you can teach them to do it themselves and have ... and if they can then transmit this further, that's cooler yet. (Interview)

Ted's response leads us to ask how three processes of distributing cognition—narrative assembly, using parables, and borrowing structure by analogy—fit together as an environment for learning and teaching. Having looked closely at the conceptual structure of Ted's conversation with Alberto in the consulting meeting, Ted teaches and Alberto learns about appropriate uses of the CRE method. Symmetrically, Ted must learn enough about Alberto's project and its organizational context to give advice in the meeting, but also to persevere with good "salesmanship" in the face of persistent skepticism by other, more senior members of the flu research group. The learning outcomes include a stronger analysis for Alberto, at an individual level, and an implemented method for using CRE to count cases of child flu for the larger research group. Alberto does, indeed, become a "go-to guy" in at least two group publications (though Ted is a coauthor on both), and the Flu research group ends up in a position to make recommendations for a national influenza surveillance system. In documenting this kind of learning, in and through processes of distributing cognition, we have attempted to unpack interactive and historical aspects of what Ted called an "avalanche of knowledge." In addition to providing partial answers to our starting questions, we hope to have encouraged further, systematic investigation of how cognition gets distributed in scientific and technical work groups, as well as in contexts of formal instruction.

ACKNOWLEDGMENTS

Research reported in this chapter was supported by NSF grants (ESI-94552771 and REC-0337675) to Rogers Hall. We thank folks at the Center for Advanced Study in the Behavioral Sciences (CASBS), in Palo Alto, California, where this chapter was written and vigorously discussed, particularly Don Brenneis, Andy diSessa, and Keith Lehrer. The Spencer Foundation provided partial fellowship support to Hall while at CASBS.

NOTES

1. Greeno and the Middle School Mathematics Through Applications Project Group (1998) made a similar argument about a broader understanding of "situated cognition."
2. Later studies by Hutchins and colleagues have been conducted with scientific work groups (e.g., Becvar, Hollan, & Hutchins, 2005); also see Goodwin (1994, 1995).

3. Transcript conventions include the following: Turns at talk are labeled with identified speakers. Onset of [overlapping talk is shown with left brackets. EMPHATIC utterances are shown in upper case. ((*Activity descriptions*)) appear within double parentheses and in italics.

4. See European Programme for Intervention Epidemiology Training (n.d.) for a typical example.

5. Alberto speaks English as a second language, and we have transcribed his talk as accurately as possible here.

REFERENCES

Anderson, M., & Fienberg, S. E. (2000). Partisan politics at work: Sampling and the 2000 Census. *Political Science and Politics*, 33(4), 795–799.

Becvar, L. A., Hollan, J., & Hutchins, E. (2005). Hands as molecules: Representational gestures as cognitive artifacts for developing theory in a scientific laboratory. *Semiotica*, 156(1/4), 89–112.

Cole, M. (1996). *Cultural psychology: a once and future discipline*. Cambridge, MA: Harvard University Press.

Dunbar, K. (1995). How scientists really reason: Scientific reasoning in real-world laboratories. In R. J. Sternberg & J. Davidson (Eds.), *Mechanisms of insight* (pp. 365–395). Cambridge, MA: MIT Press.

Engestrom, Y., Miettinen, R., & Punamaki, R. L. (1999). *Perspectives on activity theory*. New York: Cambridge University Press.

European Programme for Intervention Epidemiology Training. (N.d.). *Course programme 2006*. Retrieved November 14, 2009, from http://www.epiet.org/course/coursep2006.html

Gentner, D. (1983). Structure-mapping: A theoretical framework for analogy. *Cognitive Science*, 7(2), 155–170.

Gentner, D. (2002). Analogical reasoning, psychology of. In *Encyclopedia of cognitive science* (Vol. 1, pp. 106–112). London: Nature Publishing Group.

Gick, M. L., & Holyoak, K. J. (1983). Schema induction and analogical transfer. *Cognitive Psychology*, 15, 1–38.

Gick, M. L., & Holyoak, K. J. (1987). The cognitive basis of knowledge transfer. In S. M. Cormier & J. D. Hagman (Eds.), *Transfer of learning: Contemporary research and applications* (pp. 9–46). Orlando, FL: Academic Press.

Goodwin, C. (1994). Professional vision. *American Anthropologist*, 96(3), 606–633.

Goodwin, C. (1995). Seeing in depth. *Social Studies of Science*, 25, 237–274.

Goodwin, C. (2000). Practices of seeing, visual analysis: An ethnomethodological approach. In T. van Leeuwen & C. Jewitt (Eds.), *Handbook of visual analysis* (pp. 157–182). Thousand Oaks, CA: Sage.

Greeno, J. G., & Middle School Mathematics Through Applications Project Group. (1998). The situativity of knowing, learning, and research. *American Psychologist*, 53(1), 5–26.

Hall, R. (1999). *Case studies of math at work: Exploring design-oriented mathematical practices in school and work settings* (Final report to the National Science Foundation, No. RED–9553648). Washington, DC: National Science Foundation.

Hall, R. (2005). Reconstructing the learning sciences. *Journal of the Learning Sciences*, 14(1), 139–155.

Hall, R., Stevens, R., & Torralba, A. (2002). Disrupting representational infrastructure in conversations across disciplines. *Mind, Culture, and Activity*, 9(3), 179–210.

Hall, R., Wright, K., & Wieckert, K. (2007). Interactive and historical processes of distributing statistical concepts through work organization. *Mind, Culture, and Activity*, *14*(1–2), 103–127.

Hook, E. B., & Regal, R. R. (1995). Capture-recapture methods in epidemiology: Methods and limitations. *Epidemiologic Reviews*, *17*, 243–264.

Hutchins, E. (1995). *Cognition in the wild*. Cambridge, MA: MIT Press.

Hutchins, E. (2006). *Imagining the cognitive life of things*. Unpublished manuscript (Department of Cognitive Science, University of California, San Diego).

Jordan, B., & Henderson, A. (1995). Interaction analysis: Foundations and practice. *Journal of the Learning Sciences*, *4*, 39–104.

Jurow, A. S. (2004). Generalizing in interaction: Middle school mathematics students making mathematical generalizations in a population modeling project. *Mind, Culture, and Activity*, *11*(4), 279–300.

Labov, W. (1972). The transformation of experience in narrative syntax. In W. Labov (Ed.), *Language in the inner city* (pp. 354–396). Philadelphia, PA: University of Pennsylvania Press.

Lemke, J. (2001). The long and the short of it: Comments on multiple timescale studies of human activity. *Journal of the Learning Sciences*, *10*(1–2), 17–26.

Ochs, E., Jacoby, S., & Gonzales, P. (1994). Interpretive journeys: How physicists talk and travel through graphic space. *Configurations*, *1*, 151–171.

Sacks, H. (1992). *Lectures on conversation* (Vols. 1 and 2, Ed. Gail Jefferson). Oxford: Blackwell.

Saxe, G. B., & Esmonde, I. (2005). Studying cognition in flux: A historical treatment of "fu" in the shifting structure of Oksapmin mathematics. *Mind, Culture and Activity*, *12*(3–4), 171–225.

Schegloff, E. A. (1991). Conversation analysis and socially shared cognition. In L. B. Resnick, J. L. Levine, & S. D. Teasley (Eds.), *Perspectives on socially shared cognition* (pp. 150–171). Washington, DC: American Psychological Association.

Tuomi-Grohn, T., & Engestrom, Y. (2003). *Between school and work: New perspectives on transfer and boundary crossing*. Amsterdam: EARLI.

Wartofsky, M. (1983). The child's construction of the world and the world's construction of the child: From historical epistemology to historical psychology. In F. S. Kessel & A. W. Siegel (Eds.), *The child and other cultural inventions* (pp. 188–215). New York: Praeger.

Wenger, E. (1998). *Communities of practice: Learning, meaning and identity*. Cambridge: Cambridge University Press.

12

Generalization in Language Learning
The Role of Structural Complexity

CYNTHIA K. THOMPSON

INTRODUCTION

*T*his chapter considers the role of structural complexity in language learning and generalization in persons with agrammatic aphasia, a language disorder resulting from stroke. Structural complexity is discussed first on theoretical grounds, followed by a summary of studies examining recovery patterns in agrammatism.

Generalization

Prior to proceeding with discussion of complexity and how it impacts generalized language learning, it is necessary to briefly discuss generalization itself. What is generalization? What is the role of generalization in language learning? Can learning occur without generalization? Behavioral definitions of generalization detail two basic types: stimulus generalization and response generalization, processes originally observed and studied under tightly controlled laboratory conditions (Keller & Schonfeld, 1950; Skinner, 1953). Discussed in the early behavioral literature in terms of stimulus gradients, stimulus generalization concerns the extent to which stimuli can be varied but, nonetheless, result in the same response. For example, experimental research shows that responses (such as a button press), conditioned to occur to pure tone stimuli of a particular frequency, can be elicited when the frequency of the stimulus is altered, and the extent to which it can be altered defines the stimulus gradient. In the domain of language, stimulus gradients are relevant to learning labels for objects and actions. For example, the gradient for *dog* includes all types of dogs; the gradient for *go* includes all of the ways that we get somewhere (run, walk, drive, fly, etc.). Response generalization, on the other hand, concerns extensions of learned responses to new ones. This requires development of relevant representations and computations and their subsequent application to create new forms. Generalized use of syntactic structure and grammatical inflection with novel words are examples of response generalization in the domain of language.

Both stimulus and response generalization are integral to language learning and, indeed, are indices of it. When a child language learner learns to associate a particular object or entity, for example, with a word such as *dog*, applying the label only to certain four-legged animals but not to others, the child has in behavioral terms learned a stimulus gradient for dog. In cognitive terms, the child has learned sets of features that constitute *dog*, and thereby learns a category for *dog*. Further, it is learned that the gradient has boundaries and that when the boundaries are crossed, the label is no longer relevant. Only when the child has been exposed to stimulus gradients that differentiate dogs from other animals does the child learn when to use the proper label. That is, the child learns which features go with *dog*, and which features differentiate *dog* from other four-legged animals.

Similarly, learning action names involves developing a stimulus gradient for each word and establishing boundaries that differentiate one word from another. For example, both *buy* and *sell* are actions that involve the transfer of money, but there are features that discriminate them from one another, which must be learned. In behavioral terms, a child learns these actions by developing stimulus gradients for them.

In the morphosyntactic domain, response generalization is a critical feature of learning. Denoting verb tense in English, for example, for regular past tense, requires adding a grammatical morpheme to the base form. In language learning, the child learns this "rule" by exposure to the language. In other words, the linguistic representation for tense is instantiated, and the computations required for its formation are learned. In early stages of language learning, it is well known that children often "overgeneralize" when learning how to inflect verbs for tense, applying regular verb inflection to irregular verbs (e.g., *runned* or *goed*). Eventually, once language learning is complete, the learner comes to know when overt inflection is, or is not, required. This learning involves a process of generalization (as well as discrimination), an integral process underlying language learning.

AGRAMMATISM

Agrammatic aphasia is a symptom complex, seen in the context of Broca's aphasia, which selectively affects the grammatical structure of sentences. Sentences produced are largely structurally impoverished, simple, active constructions. Comprehension of these forms is generally spared; however, difficulty arises when computation of complex sentences is required. There are three primary deficits in agrammatism. First, verbs often are omitted, and, in turn, verb arguments (or the participant roles selected by the verb) are deleted in sentences (Bastiaanse & van Zonneveld, 2005; Kim & Thompson, 2000, 2004; Thompson, 2003; Zingeser & Berndt, 1990). Second, grammatical morphemes (particularly verb inflections) are substituted or omitted (see Menn & Obler, 1990, for review; and see Caramazza &

Hillis, 1989; Faroqi-Shah & Thompson, 2007). Third, word order deficits are prevalent. In production, noun phrases (NPs) and other material often are misordered around the verb, and comprehension breaks down for noncanonical sentences, that is, for sentences that are not in subject–verb–object (in English) order (see Caplan & Hildebrandt, 1988; Grodzinsky, 1986; Schwartz, Linebarger, Saffran, & Pate, 1987; and many others). Because of these selective deficits, agrammatism has garnered the attention of psycholinguists and neurolinguists alike. Agrammatic aphasia occurs in the context of a mature language system; therefore, understanding how the grammar is fractionated as well as how it recovers provides insight into how language is normally represented and processed. In particular, studying language learning (relearning) and generalization patterns in aphasia provides a window into the workings of the normal language system.

STRUCTURAL COMPLEXITY

The sentence structural work discussed here is informed by models of sentence comprehension and production, as well as by relevant linguistic theories and principles. Models of sentence comprehension and production postulate levels of processing, which involve (minimally) access to a rich array of lexical information and integration of that information into structural relationships at the sentence level, anchored by conceptual or message-level and phonological processes. Although most models of production and comprehension ascribe to these minimal distinctions and processes, they tend to vary in terms of levels of interdependence among these (and in more finely detailed) processes. For example, some models (Bock and Levelt, 1994, 2002; Levelt, 1993, 1999) suggest serial construction of sentences from the conceptual level to the phonological level (and vice versa), whereas others consider interaction among these levels (e.g., Dell, 1986; Dell & Sullivan, 2004; Stemberger, 1995). Furthermore, the models are largely underspecified with regard to processes operating at each level. Nevertheless, these models have been used successfully to facilitate understanding of aphasic deficits and for examining generalization patterns (see, for example, Caramazza & Miceli, 1991; Mitchum & Berndt, 1994). In addition, they are particularly useful for understanding complexity, which can be considered at all levels, from the message to phonological instantiation.

This chapter deals with complexity at two levels: the functional level, where lemmas (preword concepts) and associated grammatical information are accessed; and the positional level, where sentence frames are derived based on information from the functional level. Information required to express the propositions of interest, including the number and type of propositions, aligned with the number and type of verbs selected, is determined at the functional level. Verb subcategorization and argument structure assignment play a key role at the functional level. For example, verbs that require a direct object subcategorize for a noun phrase in the object position (i.e., V NP as in "*Follow* the leader"). In turn, argument structure is assigned. Grammatical morphology also is represented and accessed at the functional level. For example, verb inflection (person, number, and tense features) is selected indirectly by the verb. In addition, grammatical encoding occurs at the functional level, which drives phrase structure operations and the order in which elements appear in sentences at the positional level (i.e., canonical versus noncanonical order). Grammatical morphology, required for concatenating lexical material, also is selected at the functional level and drives positional level processing. Indeed, as discussed above, lexical material (particularly verbs and verb-related material) is often deleted from agrammatic speech, grammatical morphology is omitted or substituted, and word order problems in both production and comprehension are prevalent, indicating possible malfunction of the functional and/or positional levels (Bastiaanse, Hugen, Kos, & van Zonneveld, 2002; Caplan & Hanna, 1998; Gibson, 1998; Yngve, 1960).

Linguistic theories and principles such as those from government binding, the principles and parameters (P&P) frameworks, and the minimalist program (Chomsky, 1986, 1995, 1998; Marantz, 1995; also see Adger, 2003), which have counterparts in other mainstream linguistic theories (e.g., generalized phrase structure grammar, or GPSG [Gazdar, Klein, Pullam, & Sag, 1985], and lexical functional grammar, or LFG [Bresnan, 1982], among others), also can be exploited in order to forward understanding of sentence complexity. The principles most relevant to understanding language breakdown and recovery in agrammatism discussed here have support from both normal and disordered speakers and listeners, showing that they impact language production and comprehension. Lexical concepts can be conceptualized as features organized in the form of local trees (Kegl, 1995), and the process of grammatical encoding is a unification operation of the selected lexical concepts, which results in a well-formed syntactic tree. Local trees combine with other (lexically headed) local trees to form the underlying syntactic representation of sentences, generally akin to the canonical order of words in a language. Any deviation from this order at the surface level (for either comprehension or production) has been linked to processing complexity (e.g., Garnsey, Tanenhaus, & Chapman, 1989; and many others). In comprehension, surface forms of noncanonical sentences must make contact with their canonical form in order for sentences to be interpreted correctly. In production, this is conceptualized in terms of operations to transform canonical to noncanonical surface configurations, thereby changing the linear order of elements in the sentence. At an abstract linguistic level, this rearrangement is captured by the concept of *movement*, more recently referred to as *move* (Chomsky, 1995; see below for further discussion). Such an account, which separates an underlying form from its surface realization, underlies one aspect of complexity; when the two differ, sentence complexity is increased. Below, I briefly discuss linguistic constructs central to the concepts of canonical order and movement, as well as evidence supporting the centrality of these concepts to normal and disordered sentence processing and production and to complexity in language learning and generalization.

Canonical Sentence Processing and Production

Information Structure of Verbs

Verbs play a central role in sentence processing and production, because without them sentences are ungrammatical. Use of (and hence knowledge of) verbs includes information about the types of participants (arguments) encoded within the verb's lexical representation. Formal linguistic accounts classify verbs based on the number and type of arguments that they encode and the thematic roles assigned to these arguments (e.g., Grimshaw, 1990; Levin & Rappaport Hovav, 1995). For example, intransitive verbs such as *run* (an unergative intransitive) encode only one argument (with the thematic role of agent), as in the following: "The boy *runs*": (NP [$_{VP}$ V]). Other verbs, such as *chase*, take two arguments, a chaser (someone doing the chasing [agent]) and a chasee (someone or something being chased [theme]), and still other verbs take three arguments, such as *put* (e.g., "The boy *put* the book on the shelf"), which assigns the thematic roles of agent, theme, and goal.

Verbs also are classified based on the way that arguments can be arranged. The three-argument verb *put*, for example, has just one possible arrangement of its arguments, whereas the three-argument verb *give* has two; for example, it can be expressed as a double object construction as in "The boy gave the girl the cake" or a prepositional construction as in "The boy gave the cake to the girl." Furthermore, some verbs have obligatory arguments, whereas others select for arguments that are optional. For example, three-argument verbs such as *put* and two-argument verbs such as *fix* must have all arguments present in the syntax in order to form grammatical sentences. Sentences such as "*The woman put the flowers" or "*The woman fixed" are ungrammatical. Conversely, three-argument verbs like *send* or *donate* and two-argument verbs such as *eat* can be realized in sentences with missing arguments, even though the arguments are part of the verb's representation. That is, sentences such as "The woman donated the paintings" and "The woman ate" are grammatical.

Some verbs also encode movement or other semantic or syntactic detail. For example, the verb *melt* is an unaccusative intransitive (one-argument verb). However, rather than an *agent*, the verb assigns the thematic role of *theme* to its single argument, which must move from its base-generated position (the object position) to the subject position in sentences in order for them to be grammatical (so that case can be assigned), as in, for example, "The ice $_{THEME}$ *melts*": (____ [$_{VP}$ V NP]) (Burzio, 1986; Levin & Rappaport Hovav, 1995; Perlmutter, 1978). Similarly, psych verbs, a class of two-argument verbs, differ from other two-argument verbs with regard to the type of argument that they assign. Rather than assigning an agent–theme *thematic grid*, psych verbs assign the thematic roles of experiencer and theme. Interestingly, there are two types of psych verbs—those in which the experience occupies the subject position, and those in which it occupies the object position. For example, for the verb *admire*, the experience is in the subject position, as in "The children *admired* the clown"; whereas for the verb *amuse*, the experiencer is in the object position, as in "The clown *amused* the children." Both theoretically and psycholinguistically, sentences with psych verbs in which the experiencer is in the object position are more complex, more difficult to process, and less preferred than psych verbs in which the experiencer takes the subject position (see Belleti & Rizzi, 1998; Pesetsky, 1995; also see Ferreira, 1994).

Complexity Hierarchies of Verbs
Complexity can be described in terms of the argument structure properties of verbs. This includes the number of

arguments that a verb encodes, the number of argument combinations or arrangements a verb allows, whether or not the arguments are obligatory or optional, and whether or not there is a direct mapping of arguments onto the surface position of sentences.

A large range of empirical studies find that when a particular verb is accessed for either production or comprehension, so too are its argument structure properties (e.g., Bock, 1995; Bock & Levelt, 1994; Levelt, 1999; Shapiro, Brookins, Gordon, & Nagel, 1991, 1993; Trueswell & Kim, 1998). For example, a verb's thematic representation affects real-time processing of sentences (e.g., Shapiro, Nagel, & Levine, 1993; see also MacDonald, Pearlmutter, & Seidenberg, 1995). For normal listeners, reaction times are correlated with verb argument structure density—speeded up for less dense verbs and slowed down for more dense ones. Agrammatic aphasics show similar patterns (Shapiro & Levine, 1990; Shapiro et al., 1993). These data indicate that when verbs are encountered in sentences, the entire argument structure entry of the verb is activated together with the verb, and when the argument structure entries of verbs become more complex, greater processing resources are required.

Production also is affected by argument structure complexity. This is particularly apparent in agrammatic aphasia. It has been well documented that many individuals with Broca's aphasia show greater difficulty producing verbs as compared to nouns, whereas the opposite patterns are prevalent in persons with anomic and other fluent-type aphasias (Miceli, Silveri, Romani, & Caramazza, 1989; Miceli et al., 1984; Zingeser & Berndt, 1990). Furthermore, the number of syntactic arguments associated with the verb and corresponding participant roles influence verb production in patients across languages, including Dutch, English, German, and Hungarian (deBleser & Kauschke, 2003; Jonkers & Bastiaanse, 1996, 1998; Kegl, 1995; Kemmerer & Tranel, 2000; Kim & Thompson, 2000, 2004; Kiss, 2000; Thompson, Lange, Schneider, & Shapiro, 1997). Simple verbs (i.e., one-argument verbs) are easier to produce than two- or three-argument verbs (deBleser & Kauschke, 2003; Jonkers & Bastiaanse, 1996, 1998; Kemmerer & Tranel; Kim & Thompson, 2000, 2004; Kiss, 2000; Luzzatti et al., 2002; Thompson, Lange, et al., 1997). In addition, verbs that assign nonagentive thematic roles (e.g., unaccusative verbs, such as *fall*) increase production difficulty for agrammatic aphasic speakers, likely because of their argument structure properties (Bastiaanse & van Zonneveld, 2005; Kegl; Lee & Thompson, 2004; Thompson, 2003). Interestingly, when examining production patterns in agrammatism, unaccusative verbs that do not have a direct mapping of their thematic roles onto sentence positions are more difficult to produce than those that do; for example, *fall*-type verbs are more difficult than *run*-type verbs (Bastiaanse & van Zonneveld; Lee & Thompson; Luzzatti et al.). This same pattern holds when examining the production pattern of psych verbs. Sentences with *admire* verbs are easier to produce than those with *amuse* verbs in agrammatic aphasia, likely because in *admire*-type verbs, the experiencer and theme map directly onto the subject and object positions, respectively. However, in *amuse*-type verbs, the experiencer occupies the object position, rendering *amuse*-type verbs more complex than *admire*-type psych verbs (Thompson & Lee, 2009; see also Thompson,

2003, for discussion of the argument structure complexity hypothesis). This is not to suggest that other factors also do not play a role in verb complexity, including frequency and familiarity (Kemmerer & Tranel, 2000), imageability (Bird, Franklin, & Howard, 2000), and semantic factors (Breedin, Saffran, & Schwartz, 1998; Kim & Thompson, 2004); however, the focus here is on argument structure complexity. I, therefore, will not detail here with how other variables impact sentence processing and production in agrammatism.

Verb production deficits are undoubtedly tied to sentence production ability. For example, failure to access the full array of verb arguments diminishes the lexical material available for insertion into sentence frames. Berndt, Mitchum, Haendiges, and Sandson (1997) examined verb production in individuals with aphasia and found that verb retrieval deficits significantly correlated with sentence production deficits. They also found that when verbs were provided to individuals with verb retrieval deficits, most patients were able to produce "better formed" sentences. Marshall, Pring, and Chiat (1998) also described a patient who was unable to name verbs or produce well-formed sentences, but when this patient was provided with verbs, sentence production ability improved.

Sentence Building   Theoretical accounts of sentence formation indicate that sentences are developed through phrase structure–building operations. In the minimalist program (Chomsky, 1995), this is accomplished via a syntactic operation, *merge*, in which two categories merge to yield a higher order category, and a series of merge operations builds the syntactic structure. Simply put, a lexical item (e.g., a verb) is selected from the lexicon and combines with another selected item to form a higher order category such as a verb phrase (VP). Because of their argument structure properties, verbs play a particularly important role in this process.

Figure 12.1 demonstrates how this occurs in a sentence such as "The thief chased the artist"—a simple, active, canonical sentence with one verb. V (e.g., *chase*) merges with a determiner phrase (DP) to yield V', and the role of theme is assigned to the direct object argument, *the artist*. V' then merges with another DP to form a verb phrase, and the agent role is assigned to the subject, *the thief*. The VP then merges with higher nodes in the syntactic tree. These operations are similar in sentences with more than one verb or proposition, but the derived sentences are more complex.

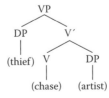

Figure 12.1   Schematic representation of *merge* within the verb phrase (VP). DP = determiner phrase; and V = verb.

Functional Categories

Another problem seen in agrammatism is difficulty producing grammatical morphemes, or functional category members. Patients often present with patterns of omission and/or substitution of both bound (e.g., person, number, and tense markers) and freestanding grammatical morphemes (e.g., complementizers, such as *if*, *that*, and *whether*; determiners; and auxiliary verbs), resulting in production of grammatically ill-formed sentences (Benedet, Christiansen, & Goodglass, 1998; Faroqi-Shah & Thompson, 2003; Rochon, Saffran, Berndt, & Schwartz, 2000; Saffran, Berndt, & Schwartz, 1989). The following excerpts, taken from a patient with agrammatic aphasia telling the story of Cinderella, illustrate these deficits.

> Cinderella uh ... scrubbing and uh ... hard worker, really. Scrubbing uh uh working. Stepmother ... ugly. No dress ... break dress and now what? Well anyway ... dance, yes ... OK ... I don't know. Dancing and shoe and majic girl. Uh ... I don't know but happily ever after! That's it.

The nature of these deficits, however, is not completely clear. For example, there are reasons to believe that inflectional affixes and function words are under the control of unique operations. Dissociations noted in aphasic individuals' ability to produce bound morphemes and function words support this notion (Arabatzi & Edwards, 2002; Izvorski & Ullman, 1999; Miceli et al., 1989; Rochon et al., 2000). Further, dissociations in inflectional affixes are common, for example, between tense and agreement markers (Cholewa & deBleser, 1996; Faroqi-Shah & Thompson, 2004; Friedmann & Grodzinsky, 1997; Menn & Obler, 1990; Miceli & Mazzucchi, 1990; and many others). One theory advanced to accommodate these dissociations is the tree-pruning hypothesis (TPH; Friedmann, 2001, 2002; Friedmann & Grodzinsky; Hagiwara, 1995). Based on the syntactic tree, the TPH suggests that functional categories projecting from higher nodes in the tree are more at risk than those projecting from lower nodes. Although impairment may occur at any level, deficits at all levels above the impaired node will be affected. Accordingly, as shown in Figure 12.2, if the deficit is below agreement (Agr'), then all functional category nodes above it will be impaired, including the tense (T') and complementizer (C') nodes.

Data supporting the TPH have come from Hebrew, Palestinian Arabic (Friedmann, 2002; Friedmann & Grodzinsky, 1997), and Spanish agrammatic speakers (Benedet et al., 1988). Friedmann and Grodzinsky described a Hebrew-speaking agrammatic aphasic patient who showed intact representation of lower nodes on the tree (i.e., the agreement phrase [AgrP]), but selective impairment in higher ones (i.e., the tense phrase [TP]). This pattern coincides with predictions based on *agree* (Bhatt, 2005; Chomsky, 2001, 2004) that subject–verb agreement involves a local syntactic relationship, whereas tense involves intersentential referential dependencies, rendering tense more vulnerable than agreement.

The TPH, however, has been challenged by research showing impairments that do not follow this hierarchy—in Korean (Lee, 2003), German (Burchert, Swoboda-Mill, & deBleser, 2005; Wenzlaff & Clahsen, 2004), English (Lee, Milman, & Thompson, 2008), and other languages (Menn & Obler, 1990). Lee et al. studied

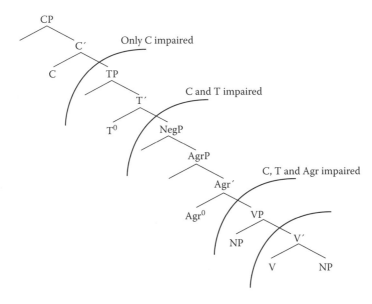

Figure 12.2   Illustration of ways that the syntactic tree can be "pruned" according to the tree-pruning hypothesis, which assumes a split IP. Functional category members C (complementizers), T (tense), or Agr (agreement) may be impaired or underspecified. When a node is impaired, all nodes above the "pruned" one will also be impaired.

four English-speaking agrammatic patients with spared complementizer phrase (CP) but impaired inflection phrase (IP), that is, complementizers were spared, but verb tense and agreement were impaired. Furthermore, tense was not more impaired than agreement. In addition, error analysis showed substitutions, rather than omission, for both inflected forms, suggesting difficulty with implementation of morphological rules, rather than difficulty at the level of syntactic representation. Lee and colleagues' patients also showed impaired comprehension (viz., grammaticality judgment), which was affected more so for verb inflection than for complementizers and other clausal structures (see Dickey, Milman, & Thompson, 2008). Similar performance patterns were noted in the patients studied by Burchert et al. (2005), Lee, and Wenzlaff and Clahsen, and in some cases, deficits were specific to tense. In all patients, both production and comprehension of inflected verbs were impaired, suggesting a central deficit (Burchert et al., 2005). These patterns suggested failure to specify IP-related morphosyntactic features, rather than a syntactically related deficit. Another similar view is that morphology is an independent grammatical component, which interprets bundles of concatenated syntactic features. Under this theory (i.e., distributed morphology; Halle & Marantz, 1993; see also Harley & Noyer, 1999), the morphological component operates separately from the syntactic component, but it takes the results of syntactic computations (hierarchical phrase structures and feature bundles) as input for its computations. These computations have their own properties and combinatoric structure, selecting which syntactic features will be spelled out and which ignored (via language-specific impoverishment rules) in morphological insertion transactions.

Complexity of Functional Categories   Functional category complexity has been considered by the TPH. Accordingly, higher nodes are more complex than lower nodes. Consider the following sentences:

1. They wonder *if* the boy is tickling the girl.
2. The boy tickl*ed* the girl.
3. The boy tickle*s* the girl.

The complementizer, *if*, in (1) as well as morphemes marking verb tense and agreement in (2) and (3), respectively, are functional category members. Considering the syntactic tree, the TPH suggests that (1) is more complex than either (2) or (3) because complementizers occupy higher nodes in the tree than tense or agreement. Furthermore, (2) is more complex than (3), again because tense is higher in the tree than agreement, at least according to Pollock (1989).

   Predicting patterns of learning and generalization within and across these structures based on the TPH would suggest that training production of complementizers should improve tense and agreement. However, complementizers have a different role in sentences than verb inflection. Complementizers introduce a complement (subordinate) clause, whereas verb inflection specifies temporal and other verb detail. Thus, the linguistic nature of the two types of grammatical morphemes differs. Indeed, the underlying linguistic representation and computations involved in generating a sentence like (1) differ markedly from those for sentences like (2) and (3). Therefore, we do not predict generalization between these structures, even though the two forms are functional category members and one takes a higher position in the tree than the other. Furthermore, generalization from training tense and agreement should not influence complementizers.

   Predicting generalization between verb tense and agreement using the syntactic tree also has been attempted. Accordingly, the prediction is that generalization should occur from higher to lower nodes. Using Pollock's (1989) tree, generalized learning should occur from tense to agreement, but not from agreement to tense, because tense occupies a higher node than agreement. One problem with this conceptualization is that there is little agreement in the literature with regard to the position in the tree that these grammatical morphemes occupy. Contrary to Pollock, some theorists place agreement higher than tense (Ouhalla, 1990). Still others argue that the two morphemes occupy the same node (Bobaljik & Thráinsson, 1998) and that the position they take in the tree is language specific.

   One other consideration in developing complexity hierarchies of grammatical morphemes concerns the morphological features (rather than syntactic detail) that they instantiate. Consider, for example, the morphemes -*s* and -*ed* and their corresponding features (see Text Box 12.1). On the face of it, these morphemes appear to be similarly marked. However, in English, past tense is underspecified for person and number features. That is, all persons and numbers take -*ed* (e.g., *I walked*, *he walked*, and *they walked*; cf. *I walk*, *he walks*, and *they walk*) (see Halle & Marantz, 1993, viz., distributed morphology theory). Thus, even though syntactic features for both tense and agreement are specified in the grammar, in

---

TEXT BOX 12.1

-s: agreement (person, number) and present tense
-ed: agreement (person, number) and past tense

---

the case of English past tense, the actual "piece of inflection" is only specified for tense (see Sauerland, 1997). On these grounds, English *-s* is more specified than English *-ed*, because *-s* conveys present tense as well as agreement features, including separate person and number features. Complexity can, therefore, be considered in terms of feature specification, and on these grounds agreement is more complex than tense.

One last consideration with regard to functional categories is that auxiliary verbs—freestanding morphemes, which also are difficult for agrammatic aphasics—also instantiate both tense and agreement, leaving only aspectual morphology to the main verb (e.g., *am walking*, *is walking*, and *was walking*). In the context of distributed morphology, Halle (1997) proposed a complexity hierarchy for these forms based on auxiliaries marked for feature specifications (see Text Box 12.2).

In summary, the extant data indicate that higher nodes are not necessarily more impaired than lower ones in agrammatism. Thus, the TPH is likely not the best way to develop complexity hierarchies relevant to language (relearning) and generalization in agrammatism. Rather, complexity in the domain of functional categories may be better motivated by morphological, rather than syntactic, considerations.

Generating Noncanonical Sentences

Consider the following sentences:

4. The thief chased the artist. (Active)
5. The artist$_i$ was chasedt_i by the thief. (Passive)
6. It was the artist$_i$ who(m)$_i$ the thief chasedt_i. (Object cleft)

All three sentences convey the same proposition that a thief chased an artist; however, the structure of the three sentences is different. What are the crucial differences? One crucial difference is that (5) and (6) are noncanonical, thus, as

---

TEXT BOX 12.2

am	<-->	[+1, –PL, +PRES, +FINITE]
is	<-->	[–PL, +PRES, +FINITE]
was	<-->	[–PL, +FINITE]
are	<-->	[+PRES, +FINITE]
were	<-->	[+FINITE]
be	<-->	_____ (= elsewhere)

discussed above, they are both more complex than sentence (4) because there is not a one-to-one correspondence between their base-generated (underlying) form and their surface form. Based on linguistic theory, these constructions involve movement of structures from their canonical (base-generated) position. Sentences (5) and (6) also are different from one another in that they involve different types of movement. Sentence (5) above is derived from NP-movement, whereas (6) involves wh-movement. Importantly, both types of movement are difficult for agrammatic aphasics to comprehend and produce.

Wh-Movement Wh-movement, involved in sentences like (6), involves displacement of the direct object (or internal argument of the verb) from its underlying position to a different position in the sentence. Simply put, the direct object moves to occupy a position prior to the verb and leaves behind a trace or copy (denoted as t above, and see below) of the moved object.[1] Once the object is moved, it is linked (coindexed) with the position from which it was derived (denoted by subscripted $_i$ above, and see below) and inherits the thematic role originally assigned to the object position. There are several types of sentences in the English language that involve wh-movement, including object clefts as in (6) above and object relatives and object-extracted wh-questions (see [7] and [8], below, respectively).

7. The man saw the artist$_i$ who$_i$ the thief chasedt_i. (Object relative)
8. Who$_i$ has the thief chasedt_i? (Object-extracted wh-question)

Importantly, movement occurs in an embedded clause in object cleft (6) and object relative clause constructions (7), whereas it occurs in the matrix (main) clause in wh-questions (8), because simple object-extracted wh-questions do not involve embedding. Thus, although sentences (6), (7), and (8) are structurally related in that they all involve wh-movement, object clefts and object relatives can be considered more complex than wh-questions based on depth of embedding (Yngve, 1960; also see Chomsky & Miller, 1963; Miller & Isard, 1964). There also are crucial differences between object clefts and object relatives. First, the number of propositions differs. Object relatives as in (7) involve two propositions as compared to only one in object clefts as in (6). Object relatives have two lexical verbs, one in the main clause (i.e., *saw*) and one in the embedded clause (i.e., *chase*), whereas object clefts have a copular verb (*was*) in the main clause and a lexical, two-argument verb in the embedded clause.[2] Thus, the merge operations (discussed above) are more complex for object relatives because of the additional linguistic material in the main clause. Further, recent linguistic theory holds that the surface subjects of sentences move from their base-generated position in the VP to the subject position (see Koopman & Sportiche, 1991, for discussion of the VP internal subjects hypothesis). For example, in the matrix clause of object relative structures (e.g., "The man saw the artist"), the subject (*the man*) moves from its position in the VP to the subject position. Conversely, in the main clause of object cleft constructions (e.g., "It was the artist"), the subject is represented by a pronoun (*it*), which is generated in and remains in the surface position; thus, no subject movement is required, and it lacks a thematic role because the copula cannot assign one.

These differences render object relatives to be more complex than object clefts. In summary, sentences (6), (7), and (8) are linguistically related because they all involve wh-movement. However, (7) is more complex than (6), and both (6) and (7) are more complex than (8). In our experiments, discussed below, we find that these distinctions are relevant to learning and generalization. That is, training more complex structures such as object relatives engenders generalization to object clefts and object wh-questions. But training simpler object wh-questions does not improve object clefts or object relatives.

NP-Movement   NP-movement is involved in the formation of English passives and subject-raising constructions as in sentence (5), above, and sentence (9), below:

9. The thief$_i$ seemst_i to have chased the artist. (Subject raising)

NP-movement occurs because, in their underlying form, both sentence types have an empty subject position (Ø), as shown in sentences (10) and (11). This is because passive verbs (i.e., *chased*) and raising verbs (i.e., *seems*) take only one internal argument and, therefore, do not assign an external thematic role to the subject position (Haegeman, 1994). Because all grammatical English sentences must have subjects, the internal argument moves to the subject position.

10. φ chased the artist by the thief. (Underlying form of the passive)
11. φ seems the thief to have chased the artist. (Underlying form of subject-raising structures)

There are, however, crucial differences between the two NP-movement structures. In passives (10), an object NP is moved to the subject position of the same clause, whereas in raising structures (11), the subject NP is raised from a lower clause to a higher one, resulting in an embedded sentence. In addition, in sentence (11) there are two verbs, the raising verb *seems* and the two-argument verb *chased*. Thus, subject-raising structures can be considered more complex than passive sentence structures.

Wh-Versus NP-Movement   As established above, both wh- and NP-movement structures involve displacement of sentence elements in order to develop their surface form. Crucially, however, there are important differences between the two, primarily concerned with the position in the sentence that the moved element occupies following movement. In wh-movement, the moved element occupies a nonargument position (in formal linguistics, this is the specifier position of the complementizer phrase). In NP-movement, the moved element lands in an argument position (the specifier position of the inflection phrase). Skipping the details here, there is a greater distance between the moved element and the trace or copy site for wh-movement structures than for NP-movement. Relatedly, wh-movement crosses clausal boundaries, whereas NP-movement does not. These properties add a level of complexity to wh-movement structures, which is not inherent in NP-movement forms. For illustration, see (12) and (13):

12. The artist was chased [trace site] by the thief.
13. It was the artist who the thief chased [trace site].

The concept of movement has important implications for human sentence processing as well as production (see, e.g., Garnsey et al., 1989; Hickok, Canseco-Gonzalez, Zurif, & Grimshaw, 1993; Sussman & Sedivy, 2003; Tanenhaus, Carlson, & Seidenberg, 1985; Zurif, Swinney, Prather, Solomon, & Bushell, 1993). For example, Zurif et al. tested unimpaired as well as aphasic participants' ability to process sentences with movement (called *filler gap sentences* in psycholinguistic research) using a cross-modal priming (CMP) task. Participants were required to make a lexical decision (i.e., decide if a visually presented string of letters is a word or a nonword) while listening to sentences such as "Which doctor did the supervisor call to help with the emergency?" Crucially, a lexical decision was required at certain points in the sentence, for example, before and after the verb *call*. In addition, some of the real word letter strings were semantically related to the moved sentence constituent, which doctor (e.g., *patient*), and some were not (e.g., *current*). Results showed that lexical decision times (i.e., reaction times) were faster for semantically related words as compared to unrelated words (i.e., a semantic priming effect was found) at both test points. However, reaction times were even faster after the verb as compared with before the verb (i.e., at the gap, or trace or copy, site), suggesting sensitivity to the origin of the moved sentence constituent. A similar pattern of gap filling also has been shown in studies using eye-tracking while-listening paradigms with both agrammatic aphasic and normal listeners (Dickey, Choy, & Thompson, 2007; Sussman & Sedivy; Thompson & Choy, 2009). Some CMP studies, however, have found a semantic priming effect both before and after the verb, but no difference between reaction times at the two probe sites for Broca's aphasic listeners, suggesting an insensitivity to movement (but see Blumstein et al., 1998; Thompson & Choy). Dickey and Thompson (2004) also found that untreated aphasic patients with agrammatism were unable to reject anomalous sentences with movement such as "The girl wore the shirt that her mother fried for her." However, following training of sentences with wh-movement, patients showed a normal pattern in which they were able to reject these sentences.

Summary

In summary, all sentences are similarly formed through phrase structure–building operations, and the argument structure of selected verbs as well as the number of selected verbs influence sentence-building complexity. Grammatical sentences also require access to and use of proper grammatical morphology. In addition, some sentences are noncanonical; that is, the word order of their surface form is derived by moving sentence elements from their underlying position to other positions in the sentence, rendering them more complex than canonical sentences. In some cases, movement crosses clausal boundaries (i.e., from a lower clause to a higher one), creating a greater distance between the moved element and its original site, and clausal embedding results, which further influences sentence complexity. Importantly, these complexity variables affect human sentence processing.

I now turn to discussion of the findings derived from treatment studies examining recovery of sentence production and comprehension in agrammatic aphasia. Results of these studies show that the complexity of structures trained affects recovery. In addition, they help to clarify the complexity metrics that are important to consider in order to promote generalization in language learning (relearning). Specifically, training more complex structures facilitates generalization to less complex forms. Crucially, however, such generalization is enjoyed only among structures that are linguistically related to one another—that is, when structures share similar underlying linguistic properties and processing routines, generalization occurs; but when they do not, generalized learning is limited or lacking.

OVERVIEW OF TREATMENT STUDIES AND FINDINGS

We have conducted three sets of studies examining the effects of training complex versus simple sentence structures and examining the generalization patterns resulting from training. These include studies controlling the (a) argument structure density of verbs contained in both noncanonical and canonical sentences, (b) grammatical morphology in active canonical sentences, and (c) movement operations involved in deriving the surface form of noncanonical sentences.

Promoting Generalization by Controlling the Complexity of Verb Argument Structure

Given the discussion above pertaining to the argument structure density of verbs and the fact that this density impacts sentence processing and production, we undertook three studies in which we controlled the argument structure complexity of the verbs in sentences entered into training. This involved training selected structures and testing generalization to sentences with verbs of lesser (or greater) complexity. Our working hypothesis was that training sentences with more complex three-argument verbs would improve sentences with less complex one- or two-argument verbs. In our 1993 study (Thompson, Shapiro, & Roberts, 1993) we trained agrammatic aphasic participants to produce object-extracted wh-questions with either three-argument verbs such as "What did the boy give to his mother?" or two-argument verbs such as "What did the boy eat?" Skipping the details, we trained these forms using *treatment of underlying forms* (TUF), a training protocol that involves a series of steps concerned with the identification and naming of verbs and their thematic roles, and the way that verb arguments move from their base position to the surface position to derive wh-questions (see Thompson, 2008, for training protocols). Participants received a maximum of 20 treatment sessions focused on one of the two structures. Results showed that participants trained to produce questions with three-argument verbs acquired these structures, and, in addition, they showed generalized improvement on untrained, simpler structures with two-argument verbs. The opposite pattern, however, was not observed; that is, training questions with two-argument verbs did not generalize to three-argument verbs structures. We attributed these effects to the complexity relation between the two verb types.

In two other studies, we also trained sentences with verbs controlled for argument structure density (Schneider & Thompson, 2003; den Ouden, Fix, Parrish & Thompson, 2008). All three studies involved training participants to produce simple active (canonical) sentence forms with three-argument verbs and testing generalized production of untrained sentences with two- and one-argument verbs. In addition, in Schneider and Thompson (2003) some participants were trained on two-argument verbs and generalization was tested to sentences with three-argument verbs. Across studies, 13 agrammatic aphasic patients participated (seven in Schneider & Thompson, 2003, and six in the current study). Results showed that all participants trained on sentences with three-argument verbs acquired the trained forms. In addition, sentences with two- and one-argument verb, which were correctly named during baseline, improved without direct training. For these verbs, sentence production was near 100% correct by the end of treatment. Interestingly, however, none of the participants who received treatment on structures with two-argument verbs improved sentence production with three-argument verbs. Furthermore, none of the subjects showed improved naming of untrained verbs of any type, and in turn, the ability to produce sentences with these verbs was not affected, indicating that treatment improved access to arguments, which impacted sentence production, for both trained and untrained verbs, but it did not improve access to untrained verb naming per se. This latter effect likely reflects the fact that verbs, controlled for argument structure, do not have featural overlap, as do nouns (see Kiran & Thompson, 2003).

Given these findings, it is possible to consider complexity in treatment of other verb types, that is, those that do not have a direct mapping of thematic roles onto the surface position in sentences. For example, training sentences with unaccusative verbs that generate themes in the subject position (e.g., "The boy$_{(THEME)}$ fell") or psych verbs with a nonagentive subject and experiencer object (e.g., "The clown amused the boy$_{(EXPERIENCER)}$") would be predicted to improve sentences with agentive intransitives (e.g., "The boy$_{(AGENT)}$ winked") and subject–experiencer psych verbs ("The boy$_{(EXPERIENCER)}$ admired the clown"), respectively. Although this pattern has not been tested, it is worthy of investigation.

Generalization by Controlling Complexity of Functional Category Members

Few treatments have been developed or experimentally tested for overcoming patterns of omission and/or substitution of functional category members, either bound or freestanding grammatical morphemes, which result in grammatically ill-formed sentences in agrammatism. As noted above, grammatical morphemes like complementizers and tense or agreement markers are within the class of functional categories.

We recently tested the effects of training complementizers (e.g., *if, that,* and *whether*), verb tense (regular past +*ed*), and agreement (third person singular +*s*) in sentence contexts in 12 participants with agrammatic aphasia (Thompson et al., 2006). Using a modified TUF approach, the three structures were trained, one at a time, in counterbalanced order across participants. Results showed that all participants improved on trained forms following stable baseline, both on a production probe task and in narratives. However, generalization from complementizers to tense or agreement (i.e., from CP to IP structure) did not occur. Furthermore, training tense or agreement did not influence complementizers, indicating that complementizers and verb inflections are not functionally related, even though both are members of the same grammatical category.

More successful generalization was noted between tense and agreement, although not all participants showed the same pattern. That is, agreement-to-tense generalization occurred in six of eight participants; whereas tense-to-agreement generalization was noted in only one subject. These findings suggest that the two inflected forms are related to one another, but that agreement may be more complex than tense because this was the dominant generalization pattern. In future studies, we propose to train grammatical morphology by controlling the features of verb inflections, that is, instantiation of agreement (person and number) and tense features.

Promoting Generalization by Controlling Movement Properties in Noncanonical Sentences

Most of our work examining patterns of generalization in language learning and the role of complexity has derived from manipulating wh-movement and NP-movement structures (Ballard & Thompson, 1999; Jacobs & Thompson, 2000; Thompson, Ballard, & Shapiro, 1998; Thompson, Shapiro, et al., 1997). Across studies a robust finding is that sentences entered into treatment are acquired when treatment is provided and remain significantly above baseline performance levels through follow-up phases. Further, the generalization patterns show that training wh-movement constructions results in significantly increased production and comprehension of untrained wh-movement sentences (i.e., training object clefts improves wh-question production and comprehension). However, generalization from wh-movement to NP-movement forms does not occur. That is, training sentences such as object clefts and/or object wh-questions does not improve subject-raising or passive sentences.

Similarly, training NP-movement structures (such as subject raising) improves untrained NP-movement structures (such as passives), but this training does not affect sentences with wh-movement. This lack of cross-movement-type generalization from wh- to NP-movement, and vice versa, is not surprising in that the syntactic computations involved in the two structures are quite different, as described above. Notably, however, within the classes of wh- and NP-movement sentences, a complexity effect emerges in learning and generalization. That is, participants trained on more complex sentence types show better generalization than those trained on less complex ones.

Complexity in Treatment of Wh-Movement
In two studies, we directly examined the complexity effect (Thompson et al., 1998; Thompson, Shapiro, Kiran, & Sobecks, 2003), testing the training and generalization effects of wh-movement structures. Participants were trained to produce (and comprehend) object relative clause structures (e.g., "The man saw the artist who the thief chased"), object clefts (e.g., "It was the artist who the thief chased"), and/or wh-questions (e.g., "Who did the thief chase?") in counterbalanced order. During treatment, generalization to untrained structures was tested. Results of the first study (Thompson et al., 1998) showed that when treatment was applied to object clefts, object cleft production increased significantly above baseline levels. In addition, wh-question production emerged, with no treatment provided, and similar learning curves were noted for both constructions. Conversely, participants who received initial treatment focused on wh-questions showed no generalization to object clefts. Rather, these structures required direct treatment. Similar results were found in our later study (Thompson et al., 2003). Training object relatives resulted in generalization to untrained object clefts and wh-questions, whereas training wh-questions did not improve untrained object relatives or clefts. Furthermore, when object clefts were entered into treatment, generalization was not observed to object relatives (see Figure 12.3).

In summary, across studies examining the generalization effects of training wh-movement constructions, over 80% of participants trained to produce complex wh-movement structures, involving movement within an embedded clause, showed successful generalization to simpler structures with movement in the

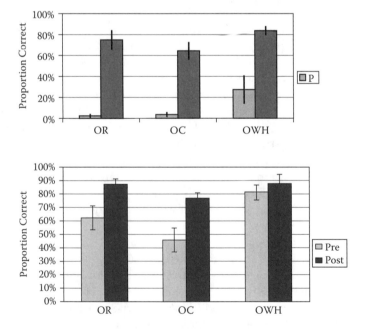

Figure 12.3 Pre- and postproduction (top) and comprehension (bottom) data by sentence type for participants receiving TUF. OR = object relative; OC = object cleft; and OWH = object wh-questions.

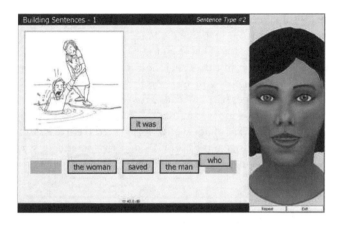

Figure 12.4 Sample step of Sentactics program for training object cleft structures (building sentences).

main clause (i.e., wh-questions). In contrast, less than 15% of individuals trained to produce wh-questions showed generalization to more complex structures with embedded clauses.

Given these findings, we recently developed and tested a fully automated computer-based version of TUF, with the goal of providing an accessible, easy-to-use, and cost-effective alternative to clinician-administered TUF (Choy, Holland, Cole, & Thompson, in press). The program, *Sentactics®*, trains object relative clause structures using a series of steps identical to those provided by human clinicians delivering TUF (see Figure 12.4, showing a sample template used for one of the training steps). Six adults with agrammatic Broca's aphasia (five males), resulting from a single stroke, participated in the study. Participants used Sentactics® twice weekly for one-hour sessions, for a maximum of 20 sessions (or until a criterion of 80% correct was achieved). Computer-generated comprehension and production probes were administered prior to and following training to test acquisition of trained forms as well as generalization to linguistically related object cleft and object wh-question structures.

Results showed that all participants improved in their ability to produce and comprehend both trained and untrained sentence types. Production of object relatives changed from a mean of 0% pretreatment to 90% posttreatment. In addition, participants showed statistically significant improvement in production of untrained object cleft and wh-question structures. The comprehension data for object relatives also showed significant improvement from pre- to posttreatment, with pretreatment performance at chance and posttreatment performance significantly above chance. Similarly, for the untrained object cleft structures, performance improved from chance at pretreatment to above chance following treatment.

Complexity in Treatment of NP-Movement

We have found a similar pattern of training and generalization within and across NP-movement structures. That is, training more complex NP-movement structures (i.e., subject-raising constructions) results in improved production and comprehension of less complex NP-movement structures (i.e., passive sentences), but the opposite pattern has not been noted (see Thompson, Shapiro, et al., 1997). We presently are studying learning and generalization in three sentences types: subject-raising structures, passives, and active sentences with unaccusative verbs. Like raising structures and passives, active sentences with unaccusative verbs entail NP-movement. Thus, based on structural complexity, we predict the following generalization patterns: subject raising to passives and unaccusative forms, and passives to unaccusatives. However, we do not expect generalization from active sentences with unaccusative verbs to passives or subject-raising sentences. To date, our findings support these predictions.

Discussion of Treatment Findings

Patterns of learning derived across studies indicate that treatment results in more pronounced effects when it is initiated on complex structures rather than simpler ones. The reverse approach—that is, beginning treatment with structures that are less complex and progressively increasing the complexity of material entered into treatment—appears to be less effective, even though it is embraced in traditional language intervention approaches. Based on these data, we coined the term *complexity account of treatment efficacy* (CATE; Thompson et al., 2003, also see Thompson, 2003). Crucially, however, it appears that treatment of complex structures improves less complex structures only when they are linguistically linked to trained structures. As noted above, there are important differences between the linguistic constructs discussed here: Verbs differ in their argument structure detail, functional categories differ in terms of the role that they play in sentences, and noncanonical structures with movement differ with regard to the type of movement involved and other detail. Nevertheless, the precise linguistic constructs that need to be considered in developing complexity metrics is not completely clear. It appears, however, that in the case of verbs both the number and type of arguments play a role. When considering functional categories, whether or not they are selected as part of verb argument structure detail, for example in the case of complementizers, or whether they are inflected on verbs appears to make a difference. Finally, the type of movement involved in sentences as well as whether or not movement occurs in an embedded clause play a role. Notably, our findings are not completely in line with the complexity metric established by the TPH. From a treatment perspective, the TPH suggests that training individuals with agrammatism to successfully produce elements that occupy higher nodes in the syntactic tree—for example, CP structures such as object clefts or wh-questions and complementizers—would result in accessibility to elements that occupy lower nodes such as passive sentences, verb inflection, and sentences with unaccusative verbs (see Friedmann, Wenkert-Olenik, & Gil, 2000). However, our data do not support this conceptualization. CP structures do not generalize to IP structures; that is, object clefts and object wh-questions do not generalize to passives, and complementizers do not generalize to verb tense and agreement. Further, persons with aphasia who improve on wh-movement still show impairments on lower structures, including verb inflections (i.e., agreement and tense) and unaccusative verbs (Dickey & Thompson, 2007; Thompson, Shapiro, et al., 1997). On the complexity account (i.e., CATE), such generalization patterns would not be predicted because the underlying linguistic properties differ across structures.

The sentence generalization patterns noted also cannot be explained by nonlinguistic accounts of complexity. It could be argued, for example, that syntactically more complex forms differ from simpler forms in that they require greater processing resources. And treating more resource-demanding sentences improves general sentence-processing and production ability (e.g., the ability to hold sentence elements in memory and simultaneously compute linguistic operations, grammatically encode sentences for production, and assemble phonological information). Therefore, it is possible that the noted generalization effects resulted because more complex forms are generally longer than simpler ones (i.e., object–relative clause constructions that we used for training included eight words; wh-questions included only five words). However, this interpretation would also predict wh- to NP-movement generalization. That is, the object cleft and passive structures that we have studied were quite similar in length (eight and seven words, respectively), yet we found no generalization from one form to the other. In addition, on some accounts, the former require greater processing demands than the latter. That is, wh-movement structures are essentially unbounded (and cross-clausal boundaries) and NP-movement structures are quite constrained (Berwick & Weinberg, 1984), as discussed above. We, therefore, conclude that the lack of generalization from wh- to NP-movement structures is because the two types of movement are fundamentally unrelated.

Similarly, it could be argued, based on a resource account, that training complementizers would generalize to verb tense and agreement. But, again, this was not the pattern seen in the data.

Clinical Relevance

Complexity in treatment of sentence production and comprehension has important clinical implications. First, as noted above, generalized production and comprehension of untrained sentences occur to a greater extent by training complex items as compared to simple ones. This treatment outcome is crucial because generalization has become a gold standard in treatment research. Without it, the efficacy of treatment can be questioned.

Another clinically relevant finding is that the number of training sessions required for acquisition and generalization of target structures differs when complex versus simple linguistic material is entered into treatment. For example, in Thompson et al. (1998), participants who began treatment with complex structures required a mean of 13 sessions to reach criterion (i.e., 80% correct production and comprehension of target structures), whereas those trained from simple to complex structures required a mean of 34 sessions. Similarly, participants in Thompson et al. (2003), trained from complex to simple or from simple to complex forms, required 12 and 28 sessions, respectively. At the end of treatment, all participants were able to produce and comprehend all structures, but those receiving treatment on complex forms required fewer treatment sessions to do so, because treatment was required on only one sentence type. This observation is particularly important given the current health care climate in the United States. Even though individuals with chronic aphasia show language improvement when provided with treatment, most patients receive only a few weeks of therapy, usually shortly after the aphasia-inducing event. Given this, it is important that clinicians provide treatment that results in the greatest improvement in the shortest amount of time.

CONCLUSION

Our findings suggest that optimal generalization across sentence structures results when the underlying linguistic properties of sentences are shared. When the underlying properties differ across structures, generalization does not occur. Further, we find that when the structural complexity of sentences is controlled, treatment focused on more complex forms results in cascading generalization to simpler forms. The complexity effect, although counterintuitive and unconventional, holds much promise for maximizing treatment gains. Traditional treatment approaches for sentence deficits in aphasia have espoused beginning treatment at the level of the patient's language ability. Therefore, the starting point generally involves training simple structures (Bandur & Shewan, 2001; Crystal, 1984; Schwartz, Saffran, Fink, Myers, & Martin, 1994; Shewan & Kertesz, 1984). Training complex structures ensues only if and when simpler structures are improved. Our findings show, however, that when placed in proper complexity hierarchies, training complex material not only improves the comprehension and production of complex sentences, but also simultaneously improves simpler structures. It is argued that there are a number of syntactic variables that need to be considered in developing complexity hierarchies, including the number of propositions (e.g., the number of verbs), the argument structure properties of verbs, the depth of embedding the type of syntactic dependencies within sentences, and the distance over which these dependencies are computed. However, we note that further experimental work is needed in order to completely understand how different aspects of complexity might influence generalization patterns in language learning and recovery in aphasia. Indeed, the more we learn about the variables that are most important for building complexity metrics, the more precise we can be about the selection of treatment targets, and the more individuals with aphasia will benefit from treatment.

ACKNOWLEDGMENT

This work was supported by the National Institutes of Health, National Institute on Deafness and Other Communication Disorders (R01 DC01948 and R21 DC007377).

NOTES

1. The trace or copy is an abstract marker that denotes the place of origin of a moved sentence element in order to maintain the structural relation between the surface form of a sentence and its underlying form. The *trace* was used in Chomsky's principles and parameters (i.e., government binding theory; Chomsky, 1986) and replaced by *copy* in the minimalist program (Chomsky, 1995). Although the details of the two theories differ, the basic function of trace and copy are the same.
2. A lexical verb is a member of the open class of verbs, which assign thematic roles and form the primary verb vocabulary of a language. Closed-class verbs (e.g., the copula) do not assign thematic roles (Crystal, 1984; Quirk, Greenbaum, Leech, & Svartvik, 1985).

REFERENCES

Adger, D. (2003). *Core syntax: A minimalist approach*. New York: Oxford University Press.

Arabatzi, M., & Edwards, S. (2002). Tense and syntactic processes in agrammatic speech. *Brain and Language, 80*(3), 314–327

Ballard, K. J., & Thompson, C. K. (1999). Treatment and generalization of complex sentence structures in agrammatism. *Journal of Speech, Language, and Hearing Research, 42*, 690–707.

Bandur, D. L., & Shewan, C. M. (2001). Language oriented treatment: A psycholinguistic approach to aphasia. In R. Chapey (Ed.), *Language intervention strategies in aphasia and related neurogenic communication disorders* (4th ed., pp. 629–662). Philadelphia, PA: Lippincott Williams & Wilkins.

Bastiaanse, R., Hugen, J., Kos, M., & van Zonneveld, R. (2002). Lexical, morphological and syntactic aspects of verb production in Dutch agrammatic aphasics. *Brain and Language, 80*, 142–159.

Bastiaanse, R., & van Zonneveld, R. (2005). Sentence production with verbs of alternating transitivity in agrammatic Broca's aphasia. *Journal of Neurolinguistics, 18*, 57–66.

Belleti, A., & Rizzi, L. (1998). Psych-verbs and q-theory. *Natural Language & Linguistic Theory, 6*, 291–352.

Benedet, M. J., Christiansen, J. A., & Goodglass, H. (1998). A cross-linguistic study of grammatical morphology in Spanish- and English-speaking agrammatical patients. *Cortex, 34*, 309–336.

Berndt, R., Mitchum, C., & Haendiges, A. (1996). Comprehension of reversible sentences in "agrammatism": A meta-analysis. *Cognition, 58*, 289–308.

Berndt, R., Mitchum, C., Haendiges, A., & Sandson, J. (1997). Verb retrieval in aphasia: I. Characterizing single word impairments. *Brain and Language, 56*, 68–106.

Berwick, R. C., & Weinberg, A. S. (1984). *The grammatical basis of linguistic performance: Language use and acquisition*. Cambridge, MA: MIT Press.

Bhatt, R. (2005). Long distance agreement in Hindi-Urdu. *Natural Language & Linguistic Theory, 23*, 757–807.

Blumstein, S. E., Byma, G., Kurowski, K., Hourihan, J., Brown, T., & Hutchinson, A. (1998). On-line processing of filler-gap construction in aphasia. *Brain and Language, 61*, 149–168.

Bird, H., Howard, D., & Franklin, S. (2002). Why is a verb like an inanimate object: Grammatical category and semantic category deficits. *Brain and Language, 72*, 246–309.

Bobaljik, D. B., & Thráinsson, H. (1998). Two heads aren't always better than one. *Syntax*, *1*, 37–71.

Bock, J. K. (1995). Sentence production: From mind to mouth. In J. Miller & P. Eimas (Eds.), *Handbook of perception and cognition: Speech, language, and communication* (Vol. 11, pp. 181–216). New York: Academic Press.

Bock, J. K., & Levelt, W. J. M. (1994). Language production: Grammatical encoding. In M. Gernsbacher (Ed.), *Handbook of psycholinguistics* (Vol. 29, pp. 945–984). New York: Academic Press.

Bock, K., & Levelt, W. J. M. (2002). Language production: Grammatical encoding. In G. T. M. Altmann (Ed.), *Psycholinguistics* (Critical Concepts in Psychology No. 5, pp. 405–452). London: Routledge.

Breedin, S. D., Saffran, E. M., & Schwartz, M. F. (1998). Semantic factors in verb retrieval: An effect of complexity. *Brain and Language*, *63*, 1–31.

Bresnan, J. (ed.) (1982). *The mental representation of grammatical relations*, The MIT Press, Cambridge, Ma.

Burchert, F., Swoboda-Moll, M., De Bleser, R. (2005). Tense and agreement dissociations in German agrammatic speakers: Underspecification vs. hierarchy. *Brain and language*, *94*, 188–199.

Burzio, L. (1986). *Italian syntax: A government-binding approach*. Dordrecht, the Netherlands: Reidel.

Caplan, D., & Hanna, J. (1998). Sentence production by aphasic patients in a constrained task. *Brain and Language*, *63*, 184–218.

Caplan, D., & Hildebrandt, N. (1988). Specific deficits in syntactic comprehension. *Aphasiology*, *2*, 255–258.

Caramazza, A., & Hillis, A. E. (1989). The disruption of sentence production: Some dissociations. *Brain and Language*, *36*, 625–650.

Caramazza, A., & Miceli, G. (1991). Selective impairment of thematic role assignment in sentence processing. *Brain and Language*, *41*, 402–436.

Cholewa, J., & deBleser, R. (1996). Further neurolinguistic evidence for morphological fractionation within the lexical system. *Journal of Neurolinguistics*, *9*, 95–111.

Chomsky, N. (1986). *Barriers* (Linguistic Inquiry Monograph No. 13). Cambridge, MA: MIT Press.

Chomsky, N. (1995). *The minimalist program*. Cambridge, MA: MIT Press.

Chomsky, N. (1998). Some observations of economy in generative grammar. In P. Barbosa, D. Fox, P. Hagstrom, M. McGinnis, & D. Pesetsky (Eds.), *Is the best good enough? Optimality and competition in syntax* (pp. 115–127). Cambridge, MA: MIT Press.

Chomsky, N. (2001). Derivation by phrase. In M. Kenstowicz (Ed.), *Ken Hale: A life in language*. Cambridge, MA: MIT Press.

Chomsky, N. (2004). Beyond explanatory adequacy. In A. Beletti (Ed.). *Structures and beyond: The cartography of syntactic structures* (Vol. 2). Oxford: Oxford University Press.

Chomsky, N., & Miller, G. A. (1963). Introduction to the formal analysis of natural languages. In R. D. Luce, R. R. Bush, & E. Galanter (Eds.), *Handbook of mathematical psychology* (Vol. 2, pp. 269–321). New York: Wiley.

Crystal, D. (1984). *Linguistic encounters with language handicap*. New York: Basil Blackwell.

deBleser, R., & Kauschke, C. (2003). Acquisition and loss of nouns and verbs: Parallel or divergent patterns? *Journal of Neurolinguistics*, *16*, 213–229.

Dell, G. (1986). A spreading activation theory of retrieval in sentence production. *Psychological Review*, *93*, 283–321.

Dell, G. S., & Sullivan, J. M. (2004). Speech errors and language production: Neuropsychological and connectionist perspectives. In B. H. Ross (Ed.), *The psychology of learning and motivation* (pp. 63-108). San Diego, CA: Elsevier.

Dickey, M. W., Choy, J., & Thompson, C. K. (2007). Real-time comprehension of wh-movement in aphasia: Evidence from eyetracking while listening. *Brain and Language, 100,* 1–22.

Dickey, M. W., Milman, L. H., & Thompson, C. K. (2008). Judgment of functional morphology in agrammatic aphasia. *Journal of Neurolinguistics, 21,* 35–65.

Dickey, M. W., & Thompson, C. K. (2004). The resolution and recovery of filler-gap dependencies in aphasia: Evidence from on-line anomaly detection. *Brain and Language, 88,* 108–127.

Dickey, M. W., & Thompson, C. K. (2007). The relation between syntactic and morphological recovery in agrammatic aphasia: A case study. *Aphasiology, 21,* 604–616.

Faroqi-Shah, Y., & Thompson, C. K. (2003). Effect of lexical cues on the production of active and passive sentences in Broca's and Wernicke's aphasia. *Brain and Language, 85,* 409–426.

Faroqi-Shah, Y., & Thompson, C. K. (2004). Semantic, lexical, and phonological influences on the production of verb inflections in agrammatic aphasia. *Brain and Language, 89*(3), 484–498.

Faroqi-Shah, Y., & Thompson, C. K. (2007). Verb inflections in agrammatic aphasia: Encoding of tense features. *Journal of Memory and Language, 56,* 129–151.

Ferreira, F. (1994). Choice of passive voice is affected by verb type and animacy. *Journal of Memory and Language, 33,* 715–736.

Friedmann, N. (2001). Agrammatism and the psychological reality of the syntactic tree. *Journal of Psycholinguistic Research, 30,* 71–90.

Friedmann, N. (2002). Question production in agrammatism: The tree pruning hypothesis. *Brain and Language, 80,* 160–187.

Friedmann, N., & Grodzinsky, Y. (1997). Tense and agreement in agrammatic production: Pruning the syntactic tree. *Brain and Language, 56,* 397–425.

Friedmann, N., Wenkert-Olenik, D., & Gil, M. (2000). From theory to practice: Treatment of agrammatic production in Hebrew based on the tree pruning hypothesis. *Journal of Neurolinguistics, 13,* 250–254.

Garnsey, S., Tanenhaus, M., & Chapman, R. (1989). Evoked potentials and the study of sentence comprehension. *Journal of Psycholinguistic Research, 18,* 51–60.

Gazdar, G., Klein, E., Pullam, G., & Sag, I. (1985). *Generalized phrase structure grammar.* Cambridge, MA: Harvard University Press.

Gibson, E. (1998). Linguistic complexity: Locality of syntactic dependencies. *Cognition, 68,* 1–76.

Grimshaw, J. (1990). *Argument structure.* Cambridge, MA: MIT Press.

Grodzinsky, Y. (1986). Language deficits and syntactic theory. *Brain and Language, 27,* 135–159.

Haegeman, L. (1994). *Introduction to Government and Binding Theory.* 2nd. edn. Oxford: Blackwell.

Hagiwara, H. (1995). The breakdown of functional categories and the economy of derivation. *Brain and Language, 50,* 92–116.

Halle, M. (1997). On stress and accent in Indo-European. *Language, 73*(2), 275–313.

Halle, M., & Marantz, A. (1993). Distributed morphology and the pieces of inflection. In K. Hale & S. J. Keyser (Eds.), *The view from Building 20: Essays in linguistics in honor of Sylvain Bromberger* (pp. 111–176). Cambridge, MA: MIT Press.

Harley, H., & Noyer, R. (1999). Distributed morphology. *Glot International, 4*(4), 3–9.

Hickok, G., Canseco-Gonzalez, E., Zurif, E., & Grimshaw, J. (1993). Modularity in locating wh-gaps. *Journal of Psycholinguistic Research, 21,* 545–561.

Izvorski, R., & Ullman, M. T. (1999). Verb inflection and the hierarchy of functional categories in agrammatic anterior aphasia. *Brain and Language, 69*(3), 288–291.

Jacobs, B., & Thompson, C. K. (2000). Cross-modal generalization effects of training non-canonical sentence comprehension and production in agrammatic aphasia. *Journal of Speech, Language, and Hearing Research, 43,* 5–20.

Jonkers, R., & Bastiaanse, R. (1996). The influence of instrumentality and transitivity on action naming in Broca's and anomic aphasia. *Brain and Language, 55,* 37–39.

Jonkers, R., & Bastiaanse, R. (1998). How selective are selective word class deficits? Two case studies of action and object naming. *Aphasiology, 12,* 245–256.

Kegl, J. (1995). Levels of representation and units of access relevant to agrammatism. *Brain and Language, 50,* 151–200.

Keller, F. S., & Schonfeld, W. N. (1950). *Principles of psychology: A systematic text in the science of behavior.* New York: Appleton-Century-Crofts.

Kemmerer, D., & Tranel, D. (2000). Verb retrieval in brain damaged subjects: I. Analysis of stimulus, lexical, and conceptual factors. *Brain and Language, 73,* 347–392.

Kim, M., & Thompson, C. K. (2000). Patterns of comprehension and production of nouns and verbs in agrammatism: Implications for lexical organization. *Brain and Language, 74,* 1–25.

Kim, M., & Thompson, C. K. (2004). Verb deficits in Alzheimer's disease and agrammatism: Implications for lexical organization. *Brain and Language, 88,* 1–20.

Kiran, S., & Thompson, C. K. (2003). Effects of exemplar typicality on naming in aphasia. *Journal of Speech, Language, and Hearing Research, 46,* 608–822.

Kiss, K. (2000). Effects of verb complexity on agrammatic aphasics' sentence production. In R. Bastiaanse & Y. Grodzinsky (Eds.), *Grammatical disorders in aphasia* (pp. 123–151). London: Whurr.

Koopman, H., & Sportiche, D. (1991). The position of subjects. *Lingua, 85,* 211–258.

Lee, J., Milman, L. H., & Thompson, C. K. (2008). Functional category production in English agrammatism. *Aphasiology, 22*(7–8), 893–905.

Lee, M. (2003). Dissociations among functional categories in Korean agrammatism. *Brain and Language, 84,* 170–188.

Lee, M., & Thompson, C. K. (2004). Agrammatic aphasic production and comprehension of unaccusative verbs in sentence contexts. *Journal of Neurolinguistics, 17,* 315–330.

Levelt, W. J. M. (1993). Language use in normal speakers and its disorders. In G. Blanken, J. Dittman, H. Grimm, J. Marshall, & C. W. Wallesh (Eds.), *Linguistic disorders and pathologies* (pp. 1–15). Berlin: Walter de Gruyter.

Levelt, W. J. M. (1999). Producing spoken language: A blueprint of the speaker. In C. Brown & P. Hagoort (Eds.), *The neurocognition of language* (pp. 83–122). New York: Oxford University Press.

Levin, B., & Rappaport Hovav, M. (1995). *Unaccusitivity: At the syntax-lexical semantics interface.* Cambridge, MA: MIT Press.

Luzzatti, C., Raggi, R., Zonca, G., Pistarini, C., Contardi, A., & Pinna, G. D. (2002). Verb-noun double dissociation in aphasic lexical impairments: The role of word frequency and imageability. *Brain and Language, 81,* 432–444.

MacDonald, M., Pearlmutter, N., & Seidenberg, M. (1995). The lexical nature of syntactic ambiguity resolution. *Psychological Review, 101,* 676–703.

Marantz, A. (1995). The minimalist program. In G. Webelhuth (Ed.), *Government and binding theory and the minimalist program.* London: Basil Blackwell.

Marshall, J. C., Pring, T., & Chiat, S. (1998). Verb retrieval and sentence production in aphasia. *Brain and Language, 63,* 159–183.

Menn, L., & Obler, L. (1990). *Agrammatic aphasia: Cross language narrative sourcebook.* Baltimore: John Benjamins.

Miceli, G., & Mazzucchi, A. (1990). Agrammatism in Italian: Two case studies. In L. Menn & L. Obler (Eds.), *Agrammatic aphasia: A cross-language narrative sourcebook* (pp. 717–816). Philadelphia: John Benjamins.

Miceli, G., Silveri, M. C., Romani, C., & Caramazza, A. (1989). Variation in the pattern of omissions and substitutions of grammatical morphemes in the spontaneous speech of so-called agrammatic patients. *Brain and Language, 36,* 447–492.

Miller, G. A., & Isard, S. (1964). Free recall of self-embedded English sentences. *Information and Control, 7,* 292–303.

Mitchum, C., & Berndt, R. (1994). Verb retrieval and sentence construction: Effects of targeted intervention. In M. Riddoch & G. Humphreys (Eds.), *Cognitive neuropsychology and cognitive rehabilitation* (pp. 317–348). Hillsdale, NJ: Lawrence Erlbaum.

Ouhalla, J. (1990). Sentential negation, relativised minimality and the aspectual status of auxiliaries. *The Linguistic Review, 7,* 183–231.

Perlmutter, D. (1978). Impersonal passives and the unaccusative hypotheses. In *Proceedings of the fourth annual meeting of the Berkeley Linguistics Society* (pp. 159–189). Berkeley: University of California.

Pesetsky, D. (1995). *Zero syntax.* Cambridge, MA: MIT Press.

Pollock, J. Y. (1989). Verb movement, universal grammar, and the structure of IP. *Linguistic Inquiry, 20*(3), 365–424.

Quirk, R., Greenbaum, S., Leech, S., & Svartvik, J. (1985). *A comprehensive grammar of the English language.* London: Longman.

Riley, E. A., den Ouden, D. B., Lukic, S., & Thompson, C. K. (2009). Neuroplasticity and recovery from aphasia: Treatment-induced recovery of verbs and sentence production. Paper presented at the *Academy of Aphasia. Boston, October, 2009.*

Rochon, E., Saffran, E. M., Berndt, R. S., & Schwartz, M. F. (2000). Quantitative analysis of aphasic sentence production: Further development and new data. *Brain and Language, 72,* 193–218.

Saffran, E. M., Berndt, R. S., & Schwartz, M. F. (1989). The quantitative analysis of agrammatic production: Procedure and data. *Brain and Language, 37,* 440–479.

Sauerland, U. (1997). *The late insertion of Germanic inflection.* Unpublished manuscript. Retrieved November 15, 2009, from http://ling.auf.net/lingBuzz/000097

Schneider, S., & Thompson, C. K. (2003). Verb production in agrammatic aphasia: The influence of semantic class and argument structure properties on generalization. *Aphasiology, 17,* 213–241.

Schwartz, M. F., Linebarger, M., Saffran, E. M., & Pate, D. (1987). Syntactic transparency and sentence interpretation in aphasia. *Language and Cognitive Processes, 2,* 85–113.

Schwartz, M. F., Saffran, E. M., Fink, R. B., Myers, J. L., & Martin, N. (1994). Mapping therapy: A treatment programme for agrammatism. *Aphasiology, 8,* 19–54.

Shapiro, L. P., Brookins, B., Gordon, B., & Nagel, N. (1991). Verb effects during sentence processing. *Journal of Experimental Psychology, 17,* 983–996.

Shapiro, L., & Levine, B., (1990). Verb processing during sentence comprehension in aphasia. *Brain and Language, 38,* 21–47.

Shapiro, L. P., Nagel, H. N., & Levine, B. A. (1993). Preferences for a verb's complements and their use in sentence processing. *Journal of Memory and Language, 32,* 96–114.

Shewan, C. M., & Kertesz, A. (1984). Effects of speech and language treatment on recovery from aphasia. *Brain and Language, 23,* 272–299.

Skinner, B. F. (1953). *Science and human behavior.* New York: McMillan.

Stemberger, J. (1995). An interactive activation model of language production. In A. Ellis (Ed.), *Progress in the psychology of language* (Vol. 1, pp. 143–186). London: Erlbaum.

Sussman, R. S., & Sedivy, J. C. (2003). The time-course of processing syntactic dependencies: Evidence from eye movements. *Language and Cognitive Processes, 18,* 143–161.

Tanenhaus, M. K., Carlson, G. N., & Seidenberg, M. S. (1985). Do listeners compute linguistic representations? In D. R. Dowty, L. Kartunnen, & A. Zwicky (Eds.), *Natural language parsing: Psychological, computational, and theoretical perspectives* (pp. 359–408). Cambridge: Cambridge University Press.

Thompson, C. K. (2003). Unaccusative verb production in agrammatic aphasia: The argument structure complexity hypothesis. *Journal of Neurolinguistics, 16*, 151–167.

Thompson, C. K. (2007). Complexity in Language Learning and Treatment. American *Journal of Speech and Language Pathology, 16*, 3–5.

Thompson, C. K. (2008). Treatment of syntactic and morphological deficits in agrammatic aphasia: Treatment of underlying forms. In R. Chapey (Ed.), *Language intervention strategies in aphasia and related neurogenic communication disorders* (5th ed., pp. 734–753). Philadelphia: Lippincott Williams & Wilkins.

Thompson, C. K., Ballard, K. J., & Shapiro, L. P. (1998). The role of complexity in training wh-movement structures in agrammatic aphasia: Optimal order for promoting generalization. *Journal of the International Neuropsychological Society, 4*, 661–674.

Thompson, C. K., & Choy, J. (2009). Pronominal resolution and gap filling in agrammatic aphasia: Evidence from eye movements. *Journal of Psycholinguistic Research, 38*(3), 255–283.

Thompson, C. K., Choy, J. J., Holland, A., & Cole, R. (in press). Sentactics®: Computer-automated treatment of underlying forms. *Aphasiology*.

Thompson, C. K., Lange, K. L., Schneider, S. L., & Shapiro, L. P. (1997). Agrammatic and non-brain damaged subjects' verb and verb argument structure production. *Aphasiology, 11*, 473–490.

Thompson, C. K., & Lee, M. (2009). Psych-verb production in agrammatic aphasia. *Journal of Neurolinguistics, 22*(4), 354–369.

Thompson, C. K., Milman, L., Dickey, M. W., O'Connor, J. E., Bonakdarpour, B., Fix, S. C., et al. (2006). Functional category production in agrammatism: Treatment and generalization effects. *Brain and Language, 99*, 79–81.

Thompson, C. K., Shapiro, L. P., Ballard, K. J., Jacobs, B. J., Schneider, S. L., & Tait, M. (1997). Training and generalized production of wh- and NP-movement structures in agrammatic aphasia. *Journal of Speech, Language, and Hearing Research, 40*, 228–244.

Thompson, C. K., Shapiro, L. P., Kiran, S., & Sobecks, J. (2003). The role of syntactic complexity in treatment of sentence deficits in agrammatic aphasia: The complexity account of treatment efficacy (CATE). *Journal of Speech, Language, and Hearing Research, 46*, 591–607.

Thompson, C. K., Shapiro, L. P., & Roberts, M. (1993). Treatment of sentence production deficits in aphasia: A linguistic-specific approach to wh-interrogative training and generalization. *Aphasiology, 7*, 111–133.

Trueswell, J., & Kim, A. (1998). How to prune a garden-path by nipping it in the bud: Fast priming of verb argument structure. *Journal of Memory and Language, 39*, 102–123.

Wenzlaff, M., & Clahsen, H. (2005). Finiteness and verb-second in German agrammatism. *Brain and Language, 92*, 33–44.

Yngve, V. H. (1960). A model and an hypothesis for language structure. *Proceedings of the American Philosophical Society, 104*, 444–466.

Zingeser, L., & Berndt, R. S. (1990). Retrieval of nouns and verbs in agrammatism and anomia. *Brain and Language, 39*, 14–32.

Zurif, E., Swinney, D., Prather, P., Solomon, J., & Bushell, C. (1993). On-line analysis of syntactic processing in Broca's and Wernicke's aphasia. *Brain and Language, 45*, 448–464.

Section 5

Technological Approaches to Generalization

13

Generalization in Human–Computer Interaction Research

JOANNA MCGRENERE, ANDREA BUNT, LEAH
FINDLATER, and KARYN MOFFATT

INTRODUCTION

Generalization is a key concept in the field of human–computer interaction (HCI), a field that is concerned with creating usable and useful interactive technology for humans. We begin this chapter with an outline of the role of generalization in the central methods used in HCI, in particular the design and evaluation methods. Next, we provide a survey of two of our research projects that challenge the desired goal of generalization in HCI. The first project addresses the problem of feature richness in software applications and strives to find personalized interface solutions as a means of combating overgeneralized interface designs. The second project focuses on designing technology for people with aphasia, a speech and language impairment, and illustrates the difficulties in achieving generalization in design for highly variable populations. We conclude by highlighting linkages between the two projects and noting that although a tension exists between the goals of generalization and personalization, they can also be seen as complementary within HCI research.

We note that our use of the term *generalization* in this chapter is quite different than its use in other chapters in this book. Whereas others tend to look at the ability of an individual to generalize or transfer learning, we are looking at how the design of interactive software is generalized to meet a broad target user population. Near the end of our chapter, however, we do identify research opportunities for improving interface design to allow users to generalize, or transfer their learning, from one interface to another.

GENERALIZATION IN HUMAN–COMPUTER INTERACTION

Human–computer interaction is a discipline concerned with the design, evaluation, and implementation of interactive computing systems for human use, and with the study of major phenomena surrounding them (Hewett et al., 1996). Fundamentally, HCI focuses on designing systems while fully taking into account what tasks users need and want to accomplish; the strengths and limitations of human sensory perceptual, motor, and cognitive abilities; and the technology available or envisioned. HCI is a highly multidisciplinary field; the two founding disciplines were computer science and psychology, but it is much broader today, including sociology, anthropology, mechanical and industrial engineering, and others.

Fundamental to HCI are its methods. In fact, one way to view HCI is as a basket of methods that one needs to choose from judiciously for any given technology design problem. At the broadest level is a method known as *user-centered design*, which refers to *iteratively* designing, implementing, and evaluating interactive systems with input from actual users throughout the design cycle (see Figure 13.1). The general goal is to gradually design and evaluate a system, making iterative advances, rather than to risk a single stage of design, fully implement (build in software) the system, and then evaluate that system with real users only to find out that the months of implementation were wasted because of a critical flaw in the design concept. Leaving user involvement to the very end is the norm in traditional approaches to software engineering (such as the waterfall method; Royce, 1970). It is common in HCI research to prototype, or to simulate, an interactive software system. The goal is to build only the fidelity (robustness) of system required to evaluate the design elements under consideration. For example, in early design, paper-and-pencil mockups are often used as low-fidelity systems to solicit preliminary user feedback. These are relatively inexpensive to create and can clarify important dimensions such as task support before doing any programming, which is relatively expensive. High-fidelity prototypes, by contrast, are ones that do run in software and support at least a core set of tasks. Figure 13.2 shows the progression from a low- to a high-fidelity prototype of one of our projects, the Enhanced with Sound and Images (ESI) Planner, a multimodal daily planner, which is described in greater detail later in this chapter. There are also several medium-fidelity prototyping techniques as well.

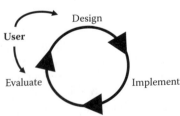

Figure 13.1   Design, implementation, and evaluation are the key stages in the iterative design cycle. User-centered design espouses strong involvement of users at the design and evaluation stages.

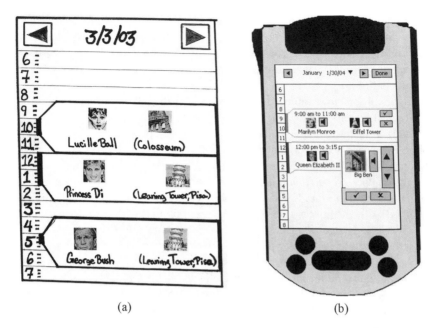

Figure 13.2   Low- and high-fidelity prototypes of the ESI Planner. (a) The low-fidelity prototype is a pencil-and-paper mockup. (b) The high-fidelity prototype was written in the Java programming language and runs on an iPAQ mobile device.

Of the three iterative stages in user-centered design, HCI is primarily concerned with generalization as it applies to the design and evaluation stages, and more specifically to methods used in these stages; typically, these methods heavily involve real target users. As we will describe, generalization in the design stage is the process of moving from the individual user data to general system requirements. Generalization in the evaluation stage is the process of determining the extent to which an evaluation of particular users doing specific tasks will apply to the broader target population of users and expected tasks. Below, we highlight selected methods used in the design and evaluation stages and elaborate on the generalization of those methods. Generalization in implementation methods is a focus in software engineering research, and will not be discussed any further here.

Generalization in the Design Phase

In early iterations of the design stage, whether it be for the creation of an altogether new interactive system or the redesign of an existing one, it is common to solicit input from target users. Frequently used methods for doing so include interview studies (such as focus groups, questionnaires, or one-on-one interviews), observational studies (such as ethnography, or a more applied variant known as *contextual inquiry*), and participatory design. The goal is to understand human practice with respect to an envisioned or existing system. For example, if the objective is to redesign existing electronic daily planners, one could interview individuals who have bought but abandoned such electronic planners to understand their specific needs and the barriers of use that led to abandonment. Alternatively, one could observe a small number of users over several days and record how they interact with their traditional paper-and-pencil-based planner. Or one could actively involve a number of potential target users to participate in its design and the decision-making process. Ideally one uses multiple methods, integrating the results, as each method has its own strengths and weaknesses.

Based on the individual user data collected in such predesign studies, one goes through the process of data analysis and synthesis, where data are reduced and abstracted. The output is sometimes a set of personas and scenarios, and task analysis is always done. A *persona* is a description of a user archetype that can serve as a guide in the design process (Cooper, 1999). It is a representation of an individual that embodies the characteristics of a target user population. Each persona usually amounts to a 1–2-page description that includes information such as education, goals, skills, attitudes, job description, and personal details such as name, education, marital status, and favorite sport to bring the character to life. Alternatively, a scenario is an informal narrative description (Carroll, 2000) that describes human activities in a story format to help clarify human needs. It typically does not reference any particular information technology so that many possible design solutions can be considered. The set of personas and scenarios help with the task analysis, which is a more formal process for identifying the specific tasks that need to be accomplished with the system. The tasks are usually prioritized and ranked according to their degree of importance to the system. These then feed specifically into technology requirements that drive the next iterative prototype.

Generalization in the design phase is thus achieved by moving from specific, individual data that are collected through a host of methods to a set of general system requirements (see Figure 13.3). For this process to work effectively, it is important that the original set of users included in the predesign study be representative of the broader target user population. Ideally they should be representative in that they cover a sufficient spectrum of the types of users who will be using the intended system in terms of any relevant dimensions, which often include computer experience, domain knowledge, and motor, sensory, and cognitive abilities. In reality, processes to gather precise empirical data about a target user population are often somewhat

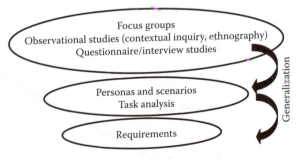

Figure 13.3   Selected HCI design methods. Generalization is the process of moving from specific individual data to general system requirements.

ad hoc in HCI, and so the degree to which the actual users involved in design (and evaluation) represent the true target population is often an issue. Further, including sufficient representative users can be a challenge in HCI research, especially when the diversity of the target population is large. The risk of not working with representative users is that the requirements generated will fit only a subset of the target population. We elaborate on this again later in this chapter.

Generalization in the Evaluation Phase

Evaluation is the second stage of the user-centered design process in which generalization plays a key role in HCI research. Evaluation takes place when there is a system, often in prototype form, to assess. As with the design stage, there are a host of evaluation methods that can be used. Informal qualitative methods, such as focus groups and one-on-one unstructured interviews, are common with low-fidelity prototypes. With higher fidelity prototypes, laboratory experiments are the norm; field experiments are comparatively rare. Laboratory experiments support the well-known scientific method where hypotheses are tested: Independent variables are manipulated, subjects complete a series of tasks, and dependent variables are measured. Field experiments are analogous except that, as the name suggests, they are conducted in a field setting.

Generalization in evaluation is often broken down into two dimensions: external validity and ecological validity. *External validity* refers to the applicability of the evaluation results to the broader target population. This is similar to what was described above for the generalization of the design methods. If the users involved in the evaluation are not representative of the true target user population, it is unclear that the results will generalize. *Ecological validity* refers to the applicability of the evaluation results to the target tasks, context, and setting. Laboratory studies typically suffer from low ecological validity because the high degree of control needed for precise measurement strips away much of the representativeness of the tasks and context. Field studies often have much higher ecological validity but suffer from less precise variable control and measurement, and they can be more difficult to conduct than lab studies. This highlights the fact that there are many trade-offs at play when choosing a method, and to truly understand a phenomenon one needs to triangulate across multiple different studies that use different methods (McGrath, 1995).

To conclude this section, generalization plays a critical role in HCI research. It is always important to understand the extent to which the design and evaluation methods used will apply to the broader target population, task, and setting in which the system will be used. A key concept in HCI is *implications for design*, which embodies the notion of generalization. More specifically, HCI researchers are expected to explicitly describe and discuss how their results of involving users will translate into design recommendations that apply to the broader population. Although generalization is a goal of HCI research, there are often associated challenges or disadvantages. In the upcoming sections, we discuss two of our research projects, each of which is impacted by generalization. In addition to highlighting the role of generalization within these projects, to provide context, we also summarize several specific research subprojects conducted to date.

RESEARCH PROJECT 1: PERSONALIZATION OF GRAPHICAL USER INTERFACES

Using appropriate design and evaluation methods does not guarantee success. One chronic design problem today is the overgeneralization of previously specific tools. This happens when an interactive technology that was initially designed to serve a relatively specific purpose evolves from one version to the next to meet increasingly diverse needs, as well as changing technological environments. For example, the word processor initially supported simple text document creation, but is now a complex tool, not only for document creation but also for page layout, Web publishing, and communication. Aggregating task requirements across a broad target population and over time has led to very feature-rich software,[1] a phenomenon that has also been referred to more negatively as "software bloat" (Kaufman & Weed, 1998).

Our research project on personalization is, in part, addressing the problem of overgeneralization. We argue that there is a need to have interface designs that better meet the needs of individuals, that is, that are more personal rather than broad in their attempts to satisfy the needs of a large population. However, balancing the collective needs of the target population with the individual users' needs is a challenge, and there is no easy solution. Research in command usage has shown that users use only a small subset of the total set of commands available, and even users doing similar tasks have only a small overlap in their command vocabulary (Greenberg, 1993; McGrenere & Moore, 2000). Thus, the most straightforward potential solution to overly feature-rich software, namely, removing a set of unused features,[2] is not viable without inconveniencing some users. The interface needs to be personalized to different users who use different feature subsets.

The specific goal in our project has been to make the set of features available to an individual user better match that user's needs. Our focus has been on features accessible through the menu and toolbars, although our work could be extended to other graphical user interface widgets.

Research on personalization has mainly centered around two opposing approaches. An *adaptive approach* is a system-controlled approach whereby the system tries to figure out what the user needs and then personalizes the interface accordingly. At the other end of the spectrum is the *adaptable approach*, which is a user-controlled approach, whereby the user adapts or customizes the interface appropriately for his or her needs. The adaptive (system-controlled) approach is intended to save the user the inconvenience and knowledge required to do the customization; however, in practice, it often leaves the user feeling a loss of control in that there is insufficient transparency and predictability to the changing interface (Shneiderman & Maes, 1997). The adaptable approach, by contrast, keeps the user in control, but most users choose not to customize because of the effort involved and the complexity of many customization facilities (Mackay, 1990,

1991). In between these two approaches lies the *mixed-initiative approach*, which attempts to leverage the strengths of the other approaches while mitigating their weaknesses. It does this by having the system and the user work together, that is, sharing the initiative in creating a personalized interface. Understanding how to make the user–system sharing efficient and effective is a difficult problem.

An orthogonal approach is a *level-structured* or *layered approach* whereby the interface has several layers and the user can choose within which layer to work (Shneiderman, 1997, 2003). Classically, these layers are fixed in terms of the features they contain. The goal is to start off the user in a minimal layer, and then have the user advance to more complex layers based on the user's learning and needs. Although this approach is intuitive, it has yet to be put into real practice. Questions that remain are how to determine a reasonable number of layers, and which features should be contained in each layer.

The three subprojects we outline below explore the trade-offs of adaptive, adaptable, mixed-initiative, and layered designs for achieving personalization.

Three Personalization Subprojects

Comparison of Adaptable and Adaptive Designs
In our first subproject, we sought to understand the benefits of a two-layer interface in which one interface (the personal interface) is easy to customize, and the second interface (the full interface) is always available such that the user can, with a single button press, switch back and forth between the two interfaces (McGrenere, Baecker, & Booth, 2007). This design, which we call *multiple interfaces*, is intended to support easy personalization and mitigate users' fear of "losing" features (McGrenere & Moore, 2000). It is a hybrid between a classical layered approach and an adaptable (user-controlled) approach. We prototyped this design as the front end to Microsoft Word 2000 (MSWord), as shown in Figure 13.4, and compared it during a 6-week field experiment to the native adaptive (system-controlled) "smart menus" from MSWord.[3] Our evaluation included 20 participants: 10 who were feature keen, and 10 feature shy. Roughly speaking, this feature profiling reflects the user's desire for a full-featured versus feature-reduced interface. Results showed that both a user's feature profile (feature keen vs. feature shy) and the interface type to which they were exposed (adaptable multiple interfaces vs. adaptive smart menus) impacted their feelings of satisfaction and control over MSWord. While using the adaptive smart menus interface, feature-shy users felt significantly less satisfied and less in control compared to feature-keen users, but after continued use of the adaptable multiple-interfaces design, there was no difference between the two groups of users for either satisfaction or sense of control. This means that using our adaptable design brought feature-shy users' satisfaction and sense of control up to the same level experienced by the feature-keen users. Multiple interfaces also had positive effects on interface learnability and navigation, and this design was preferred overall by the majority of participants (both feature keen and shy). Thus, we showed that our two-layer model, where one of the interfaces was easy to personalize, had significant advantages over the specific adaptive smart menus native to MSWord.

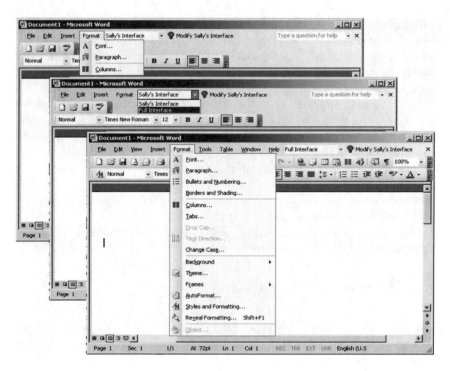

Figure 13.4   The two-layer interface of MSWord. In the first screen, the user opens the Format menu in the Personal Interface. In the second screen, the user invokes the toggle and will select the Full Interface. In the third screen, the user reopens the Format menu.

Comparison of Mixed-Initiative and Adaptable Designs   In our second subproject, we extended our multiple-interfaces design with a mixed-initiative component, which allows the user and the system to work together to achieve a personalized interface. The *mixed-initiative customization assistance* (MICA) system, shown in Figure 13.5, makes user-specific customization recommendations once the user initiates customization (Bunt, Conati, & McGrenere, 2007). Unlike MSWord's smart menus, which automatically personalize the interface, users remain in control of personalizing their interfaces, and are free to follow or ignore any of the recommendations as they see fit. The main goal of MICA recommendations is to help the user to construct an *efficient* personal interface, one where the user will not be "tripping over" unused or infrequently used features. In general, having a personal interface that contains only one's frequently used features, and leaving one's infrequently used features to be accessed from the full interface, yields the most efficient interface. In addition to frequency of use, MICA also balances two other factors to determine customization recommendations: user expertise with each given feature and layout of the interface (positioning of the features relative to one another). Expertise reflects the time it takes to select a feature from the toolbar or menu (i.e., does the user know exactly where the feature is, or does she or he need to search for it?), which does correlate with frequency of use. Layout is more subtle; if, for example, adding a feature causes a

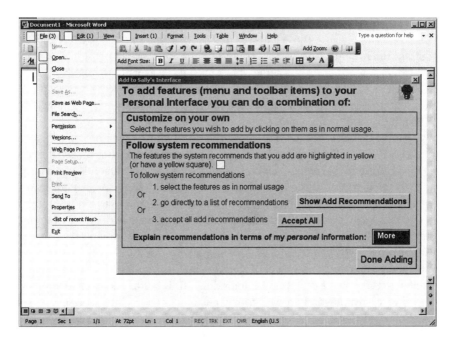

Figure 13.5 MICA's mixed-initiative customization support. When the user initiates customization, she or he is told that the features highlighted in yellow (shown as white boxes in the figure) are recommended and that a detailed explanation of the recommendations can be obtained by clicking on the More button, if desired.

whole new menu to be added, it can slow down the visual search time for many of the other features. In a lab experiment with 12 participants, we compared MICA to an equivalent adaptable-only version of the multiple-interface design that did not provide any adaptation suggestions. Results showed that MICA was strongly preferred to the adaptable-only alternative, that tasks were completed faster with MICA, and that, in general, participants spent less time customizing with MICA. Although participants made roughly the same number of customizations in the two conditions, the recommendations appeared to positively impact *which* features the participants chose to add. For example, participants using MICA included more of their frequently used features in their personal interfaces and did not include as many infrequently used features, relative to the non-MICA participants. Thus, the strong support of our mixed-initiative approach to user customization indicates that it is a viable direction and worth further investigation.

Comparison of a Personalized Layered Interface to a Full Interface   In

a third subproject, we shifted gears to take a somewhat deeper look at learning. The main measure of performance studied in lab experiments is speed, for example, speed to access menu items in an adaptive interface design. We argue that this is insufficient. A feature-reduced personalized interface is likely to increase *findability*, the speed of finding the remaining available features, because there are fewer to choose from in the interface. However, there may be a detrimental effect on the user's *awareness*, that is, his or her ability to learn the full feature set of the interface, because those features not available in the personalized interface are often somewhat or fully hidden from the user. Thus, we hypothesized a trade-off between initial feature learning and longer term learning of the full feature set (Findlater & McGrenere, 2007). In a lab experiment with 30 participants, we found that using a minimal personalized interface layer for Microsoft PowerPoint XP resulted in better findability than using the full application interface layer. However, participants who initially used the minimal interface before transitioning to the full interface layer exhibited reduced awareness of advanced features compared to those participants who worked in the full interface layer from the outset. Demonstrating this trade-off shows that although personalization can be beneficial, it can also come at a cost. More research is required to understand how this cost may vary based on the different methods of personalizing. For example, a system like MICA that recommends features may be less detrimental to the user's awareness of the advanced features.

Bringing the three subprojects together, the first showed that users prefer to personalize their own interfaces, compared to a fully system-controlled approach, and will take advantage of an easy-to-use customization facility. The second subproject showed that the system can relatively unobtrusively help users with this task (because it can be onerous even with a well-designed interface). The third subproject showed that although working in a personalized interface has benefits, it may also negatively impact the user's overall knowledge of the application.

Generalization in the Personalization Project

To conclude this section on personalization, we have argued that the generalization of user needs, resulting in part by applying HCI design and evaluation methods, has led to complex, heavily featured interfaces that have become the norm in the marketplace today. Our research has shown that personalized interfaces can help mitigate problems associated with such complexity. In particular, a mixed-initiative, multiple-interface design is the most promising personalization approach, but we caution that awareness of the full feature set may be impacted.

Future work in our personalization project will involve investigating how our study results and interface solutions generalize to different types of users and applications. Here we highlight three levels: (a) within the same application, but to different users or tasks; (b) across different versions of the same application or across applications within the same class; and, finally, (c) across application classes. We provide example research questions and directions for each of these levels.

At the first level (within the same application), we are interested to know how the findability–awareness trade-off will impact different kinds of learners. It is likely that exploratory learners will be more willing to occasionally look through the full interface layer instead of staying largely fixed within the minimal layer (recall that in our multiple interfaces design, users can freely toggle back and forth between layers). Thus, the detrimental impact on awareness of a multilayered design may be lessened for exploratory learners.

At the second level (across different versions of the same application or applications within the same class), we are interested to know how personalized interface designs might support transitioning, that is, helping users to generalize their knowledge from one context to another. For example, a user may have to transition from version *X* of a word processor to version *X+1* as a result of an upgrade. One could imagine having an initial interface layer in version *X+1* that exactly matches the user's familiar personal interface from version *X*. The user could work comfortably in his or her personal interface in the new version, whereas a mixed-initiative dialogue might assist the user to adjust that personal interface based on new relevant features in version *X+1*. A related example covers a user transitioning from Word Processor Brand A (WPA) to Word Processor Brand B (WPB), perhaps because of a job change. It might be possible to start the user in WPB with an initial interface layer that looks identical to the user's familiar interface in WPA, and thereby support a more gradual transition. Transitioning support may lessen some users' apprehension about upgrading their software or having to learn new applications.

Last, with respect to the third level of generalization (across application classes), some forms of personalization made by a user in, for example, his or her Web browser may also be relevant to his or her e-mail client. Positioning of the toolbars within the window or even removal of toolbars altogether, as well as default font sizes, may be candidates. Another point of generalization at this level may be related to individual differences; feature-shy users may want all of their applications to have feature-reduced interfaces. The general goal would be to reduce the effort involved in repeating similar customizations across applications.

RESEARCH PROJECT 2: THE APHASIA PROJECT

The second project we highlight is related to designing technology for people with aphasia. As outlined in the first part of this chapter, one of the main goals in HCI research is to achieve generalization in both design and evaluation methods. However, in our research that applies these methods to designing technology for people with aphasia, we have met significant challenges in achieving such generalization. We begin this section by describing aphasia. We then describe four subprojects within the Aphasia Project that highlight the challenges we have encountered to generalizing within this domain. Finally, we conclude with a discussion of the approaches we have used to mitigate those challenges.

Aphasia, which is estimated to affect 1 million Americans, is an acquired language disorder impacting an individual's language abilities, including speaking, comprehension of spoken language, reading, and writing (National Aphasia Association, n.d.). It is most often caused by a stroke, and so the majority of people with aphasia are older. However, it can also be caused by other forms of brain damage such as a tumor or injury, and thus it affects individuals of all ages (National Aphasia Association).

One of the main challenges for designing technology for individuals with aphasia is addressing the high degree of variability inherent to the disorder. The manifestation of aphasia can vary considerably among individuals with aphasia: The components of language skill can be affected to varying degrees and in any combination. Furthermore, there can also be variability within individuals. For some people, their communication ability changes day by day; for example, a note written one day can become incomprehensible the next. In addition, using language can become increasingly difficult as an aphasic individual grows weary or tense.

The Aphasia Project (n.d.) is a multidisciplinary research project investigating how technology can be designed to support individuals with aphasia in their daily life. Although there is technology for individuals who have communication impairments, the majority is in the form of augmentative and alternative communication devices, which focus on enabling individuals to express basic needs and wants. Moreover, these devices always require someone other than the end user (such as a caregiver or therapist) to import and organize the contents of the system, such as icons, images, sound, and text (see, for example, van de Sandt-Koenderman, Wiegers, & Hardy, 2005). The Aphasia Project seeks to design applications that can be used independently and that go beyond supporting basic needs. Example subprojects we have undertaken to date include the ESI Planner (Figure 13.2), the FileFacility, the Visually Enhanced Recipe Application (VERA), and PhotoTalk (the latter three are shown in Figure 13.6). With the exception of VERA, which was designed for the Tablet PC, all the other applications have been designed for a personal digital assistant, or PDA, which is a small mobile handheld computer. The next section provides an overview of each of these subprojects, providing the context necessary for our subsequent discussion of the challenges to generalization we have faced in this work.

Four Aphasia Project Subprojects

The ESI Planner   Some individuals with aphasia maintain jobs, but unlike others in today's technology-supported workplace, people with aphasia cannot make use of standard electronic daily planners, which are all text based (e.g., Palm Pilot). We designed the ESI Planner, a multimodal application that combines triplets of images, sound, and text to represent appointment data, to address this problem (Moffatt, McGrenere, Purves, & Klawe, 2004). We hypothesized that these triplets would make it easier for people with aphasia to comprehend the information presented within a daily planner because people with aphasia generally retain their ability to recognize images (Thorburn, Newhoff, & Rubin, 1995). A participatory design process was used: We worked with four people with aphasia to envision and iteratively design the planner application. A laboratory experiment followed to compare two high-fidelity prototypes: the ESI Planner and a text-only equivalent. The experiment, which included eight individuals with aphasia, showed that the participants completed significantly more tasks correctly with the ESI Planner than the text-only equivalent, and that the ESI Planner was generally preferred, especially for individuals with large impairments.

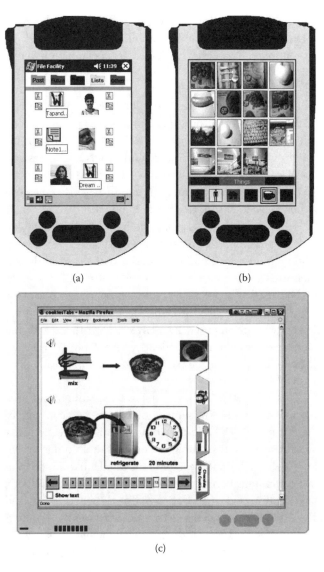

Figure 13.6   Images of (a) the FileFacility, (b) PhotoTalk, and (c) VERA.

The FileFacility   In this subproject, an ethnographic study that involved 70 hours of data collection over several months was conducted with one relatively high-functioning and computer-literate participant with aphasia (Davies, Marcella, McGrenere, & Purves, 2004). The goals were both to learn about communication strategies used by people with aphasia, and to observe how a PDA is incorporated into those strategies. The most significant PDA usability issues found were file access and organization: File access was too demanding, in both time and attention, within the context of interactions, and file organization was not adequately supported, particularly of multimodal data. A participatory design phase followed with the same participant, resulting in a paper prototype of a file management system for the PDA that addressed the key usability issues identified. The participatory approach continued during the implementation of a high-fidelity prototype.

VERA   Although cooking is a daily activity for many people, traditional text recipes are often prohibitively difficult to follow for people with aphasia. VERA is a multimodal application that provides a presentation format that can be more easily followed than a traditional text recipe (Tee et al., 2005). In this subproject, we first designed a visual language for communicating cooking instructions, which allows instructions to be systematically mapped from text to a primarily visual representation. We developed this mapping from a survey of a range of recipe types from several cookbooks to ensure that it would be intuitive and would not require user training. We then developed a prototype based on this visual language, with input from 11 nonaphasic participants, people without experience in aphasia but whom we could recruit easily. Finally, we performed a case study with four aphasic participants: VERA was compared to an aphasia-friendly text-only version of a recipe in the context of fully preparing real recipes. The results of our evaluation were not straightforward, but suggested that the combination of visual instructions and navigational structure imposed by VERA helped those with relatively large language deficits to cook more independently: Fewer interventions were required from the researcher in order for the participants to complete a recipe.

PhotoTalk   This application allows people with aphasia to capture and manage digital photographs to be used in support of face-to-face communication (Allen, McGrenere, & Purves, 2007). For example, a user might take pictures of friends he or she ran into during the day or things he or she saw, in order to share his or her daily activities with his or her spouse later in the day. Unlike any other augmentative and alternative communication device for people with aphasia, PhotoTalk focuses solely on image capture and organization and is designed to be used completely independently. The PhotoTalk subproject used a streamlined process with three phases: (a) a rapid participatory design and development phase with two speech–language pathologists acting as representative users; (b) an informal usability study with five aphasic participants, which uncovered usability problems and provided preliminary feedback on the usefulness of PhotoTalk; and (c) a one-month field evaluation with two aphasic participants. The field study showed that both participants used it regularly (at least 2 out of every 3 days) and fairly independently (the researcher had to intervene on only a few occasions for each participant), but that it was not always used for its intended communicative purpose. In particular, one of the participants decided to use PhotoTalk primarily as a language rehabilitation tool: He took images of objects (such as household items), entered captions for each, and practiced reading and saying the names of those items. Our field study demonstrated PhotoTalk's promise in terms of its usability and usefulness in real-life situations.

Generalization in Research With Cognitively Impaired Individuals

With respect to generalizability of design and evaluation, the core challenge in the Aphasia Project has been in identifying representative users. Within the non–cognitively impaired user population, the variation in user abilities and needs is already large; this variation is compounded substantially by the language variability in the population of people with aphasia. Classically, the size of a representative sample is related to the variability in the population from which the sample is drawn. Given the large variation in the aphasic population, this would argue for drawing a large sample in order to achieve representation. Unfortunately, finding and recruiting participants comprise a significant challenge as one of the main side effects of aphasia is withdrawal and isolation from society. It is for this reason that we have relatively few aphasic participants in either the design or evaluation stages of our research. The comparison of sample size is quite striking, for example, between the evaluations done within the Aphasia Project and those done in our personalization research.

In terms of the design stage, as is evident in the subproject overviews, we often include an upfront participatory design phase. We have been successful in including a small number of target users in some of our subprojects (e.g., the ESI Planner); however, this has not always been feasible or practical.[4] One alternative approach we have investigated is to design with domain experts acting as representative users, a role that some have called "proxies" (Boyd-Graber et al., 2006). For example, in the PhotoTalk project, two speech–language pathologists took part in the participatory design. This is a departure from classical participatory design and comes with drawbacks, namely, that only a true user can fully speak on behalf of his or her needs and wants. On the positive side, one domain expert, through his or her experience with many impaired individuals, may be able to represent a broader, more generalizable view of needs and wants within the target population than any single target user. A potential danger of involving too few individuals in participatory design is that the resulting application may become overly specialized to the individual(s) involved in its design. Getting the right balance has been a challenge in our work, which is reflected in the differing strategies used in each of the projects.

An approach we have found useful in terms of generalizing in the evaluation stage is to perform detailed functional assessments of each participant's abilities. We often include the Western Aphasia Battery (WAB; Kertesz, 1982), a standardized test administered by a speech–language pathologist, as part of our evaluation methodology. The WAB is administered by a speech–language pathologist. It tests the four main components of language: speech, auditory comprehension, reading, and writing. Each of these main components includes several subcomponents: For example, the reading component measures comprehension of sentences, ability to read aloud, and ability to perform written commands. This test has proven to be highly effective at helping us to interpret data that otherwise would have been too variable to understand.

The value of the WAB was particularly striking in the VERA subproject, where the case study results were very mixed. At first glance, we expected that the differences in performance between VERA and the text-only recipe might be explained by the assessment of participants' reading abilities, but their overall reading scores were in fact relatively even. It was only by delving deeper into the assessments that we were able to discover that performance varied with participants' abilities to follow written instructions, which unsurprisingly is related to skill at following a written recipe. Thus, the value of the WAB was that it provided a detailed assessment that broke down various aspects of language ability. These assessments provided more than mere confirmation of our informal intuition regarding participants' language skills. At the subcomponent level, informal assessments are difficult to accurately formulate, especially for nonclinicians. Moreover, many aphasic individuals develop compensatory skills (such as the use of gestures and drawings) to aid them in communication. These skills can mask the full extent of their communication deficits.

To conclude this section on the Aphasia Project, the extent to which we will be able to achieve even modestly generalizable solutions for people with aphasia remains an open question. We have been stretching traditional HCI design and evaluation methods to provide a better fit for our particular population, but it is not clear how far we can push this approach. Just as in our first project, where personalization is needed to counteract feature complexity, a strong theme has been emerging in the Aphasia Project, namely, to have designs that support personalization. Although there have been requests for both more and less features, across all these subprojects, there have also been specific requests for modifications to interaction styles and interface elements. For example, in the PhotoTalk field evaluation, the application had to be personalized upfront for one of the participants by increasing the size of the images to account for the individual's large hands and slight tremor. Understanding the extent to which personalization support is needed remains an area for future work.

FINAL THOUGHTS

Generalization in human–computer interaction is achieved largely through the design and evaluation stages of interactive systems. Developing systems that can be used by a broad user population allows for the most effective use of development resources and provides the best economic incentive for software makers. In this chapter, we have identified two challenges for generalization in HCI: (a) Generalization of system requirements may lead to an overgeneralized interface, where an individual user may use only a small subset of features in the interface; and (b) when systems are aimed at highly variable user populations, it may be more difficult to provide a generalized solution.

The two projects highlighted in this chapter strongly reflect these challenges. The personalization project focuses on relatively mature interactive applications, such as word processors and presentation software, which have been subject to feature bloat. By contrast, the Aphasia Project focuses on the creation of new applications for a highly variable user population. The latter project illustrates that generalization of findings is negatively impacted by the inability to identify and recruit a sufficient sample of representative users. As a result, there is considerable research yet to be done to achieve any degree of generalized application solutions for aphasic users. Interestingly, despite the relative immaturity of the Aphasia Project applications, we are already seeing a strong need for personalization, with respect to both numbers of features and interaction styles and elements.

This chapter has highlighted a tension between generalization and the need for personalization. They need not be seen entirely as dichotomous, but rather the generalization of traditional user-centered design methods and strong support for personalization within the resulting applications can be seen as complementary—generalization is required for an application to be *useful* to a broad population, but for the application to be *usable* by the individuals in that population requires personalization support. This is evident for many classes of application and user populations, and is especially the case for highly variable user populations.

ACKNOWLEDGMENTS

The research projects described in this chapter reflect the work of many students, all of whom have been supervised or co-supervised by Dr. Joanna McGrenere. The multiple-interfaces design is Joanna McGrenere's own doctoral research. The mixed-initiative project is Andrea Bunt's PhD research, co-supervised by Dr. Cristina Conati. The research on findability and awareness within multilayered interfaces is Leah Findlater's PhD research. The ESI Planner is Karyn Moffatt's MSc research, co-supervised by Dr. Maria Klawe. FileFacility and Phototalk are Rhian Davies' and Meghan Allen's MSc research projects, respectively. VERA is a joint research project with undergraduate students Kim Tee and Eve McGregor, as well as Karyn Moffatt, Leah Findlater, and Dr. Sid Fels. Dr. Barbara Purves has had strong involvement in all the Aphasia Project subprojects described here. We would also like to acknowledge the rest of the Aphasia Project team for their input into those projects.

NOTES

1. Other factors have also contributed to feature-rich software, including "innovative" developers, customer demand, evolving technology environments, and apathy to drop little-used commands.
2. *Commands*, *features*, and *functions* are all words used to describe software options available to the user. They have subtle differences in meaning but are largely used synonymously in this chapter.
3. Smart menus are designed such that when you open a menu, only the most recent and frequent menu items used by the given user are shown, but the user can easily access the full menu contents.
4. What is practical in terms of time to recruit and work with subjects is related to the length of study for graduate degrees. The subprojects described in this part of the chapter are all the thesis work of MSc students, who typically have one year to complete the research component of their degree.

REFERENCES

Allen, M., McGrenere, J., & Purves, B. (2007). *The design and field evaluation of PhotoTalk: A digital image communication application for people with aphasia.* Retrieved November 17, 2009, from http://people.cs.ubc.ca/~meghana/assets019-allen.pdf

The Aphasia Project. (N.d.). *Aphasia Project: Overview.* Retrieved November 15, 2009, from http://www.cs.princeton.edu/aphasia/

Boyd-Graber, J., Nikolova, S. S., Moffatt, K. A., Kin, K. C., Lee, J. Y., Mackey, L. W., et al. (2006). Participatory design with proxies: Developing a desktop-PDA system to support people with aphasia. In *CHI '06: Proceedings of the SIGCHI conference on Human Factors in Computing Systems (2006)* (pp. 151–160). Retrieved November 17, 2009, from http://www.eecs.berkeley.edu/~lmackey/papers/esiplannerii-chi06.pdf

Bunt, A., Conati, C., & McGrenere, J. (2007). Supporting interface customization using a mixed-initiative approach. In *Proceedings of ACM Intelligent User Interfaces* (pp. 92–101). New York: Association for Computing Machinery.

Carroll, J. (2000). Introduction to the special issue on "scenario-based systems development." *Interacting with Computers, 13,* 41–42.

Cooper, A. (1999). *The inmates are running the asylum.* Indianapolis, IN: Macmillan.

Davies, R., Marcella, S., McGrenere, J., & Purves, B. (2004). The ethnographically informed participatory design of a PDA application to support communication. In *Proceedings of ACM Assets 2004* (pp. 153–160). New York: Association for Computing Machinery.

Findlater, L., & McGrenere, J. (2007). Evaluating reduced-functionality interfaces according to feature findability and awareness. In *Proceedings of Interact 2007* (pp. 592–605). Berlin: Springer.

Greenberg, S. (1993). *The computer user as toolsmith: The use, reuse, and organization of computer-based tools.* Cambridge: Cambridge University Press.

Hewett, T., Baecker, R. M., Card, S., Carey, T., Gasen, J., Mantei, M., et al. (1996). *ACM SIGCHI curricula for human-computer interaction.* Retrieved June 13, 2007, from http://sigchi.org/cdg/cdg2.html

Kaufman, L., & Weed, B. (1998). Too much of a good thing? Identifying and resolving bloat in the user interface: A CHI 98 workshop. *SIGCHI Bulletin, 30*(4), 46–47.

Kertesz, A. (1982). *Western Aphasia Battery.* New York: Grune and Stratton.

Mackay, W. E. (1990). Patterns of sharing customizable software. In *Proceedings of ACM CSCW'90* (pp. 209–221). New York: Association for Computing Machinery.

Mackay, W. E. (1991). Triggers and barriers to customizing software. In *Proceedings of ACM CHI'91* (pp. 153–160). New York: Association for Computing Machinery.

McGrath, J. (1995). Methodology matters: Doing research in the behavioral and social sciences. In R. M. Baecker, J. Grudin, W. S. Buxton, & S. Greenberg (Eds.), *Readings in human-computer interaction: Toward the year 2000* (pp. 152–169). San Francisco, CA: Morgan Kaufman.

McGrenere, J., Baecker, R. M., & Booth, K. S. (2007). A field evaluation of an adaptable two-interface design for feature-rich software. *Transactions on Computer-Human Interaction, 14*(1), 3.

McGrenere, J., & Moore, G. (2000). Are we all in the same "bloat"? In *Proceedings of Graphics Interface 2000* (pp. 187–196). Retrieved November 17, 2009, from http://www.graphicsinterface.org/proceedings/2000/144/PDFpaper144.pdf

Moffatt, K., McGrenere, J., Purves, B., & Klawe, M. (2004). The participatory design of a sound and image enhanced daily planner for people with aphasia. In *Proceedings of ACM CHI 2004* (pp. 407–414). New York: Association for Computing Machinery.

National Aphasia Association. (N.d.). *Aphasia: The facts*. Retrieved May 14, 2007, from http://www.aphasia.org/naa_materials/aphasia_facts.html

Royce, W. W. (1970). Managing the development of large software systems: Concepts and techniques. In *Proceedings of WESCON*. Los Alamitos, CA: IEEE Computer Society Press.

Shneiderman, B. (1997). *Designing the user interface: Strategies for effective human-computer interaction* (3rd ed.). Reading, MA: Addison-Wesley.

Shneiderman, B. (2003). Promoting universal usability with multi-layer interface design. In *Proceedings of Conference on Universal Usability* (pp. 1–8). New York: Association for Computing Machinery.

Shneiderman, B., & Maes, P. (1997). Direct manipulation vs. interface agents: Excerpts from debates at IUI 97 and CHI 97. *Interactions, 4*(6), 42–61.

Tee, K., Moffatt, K., Findlater, L., Macgregor, E., McGrenere, J., Purves, B., et al. (2005). A visual recipe book for persons with language impairments. In *Proceedings of ACM CHI 2005* (pp. 501–510). New York: Association for Computing Machinery.

Thorburn, L., Newhoff, M., & Rubin, S. S. (1995). Ability of subjects with aphasia to visually analyze written language, pantomime, and iconographic symbols. *American Journal of Speech-Language Pathology, 4*, 174–179.

van de Sandt-Koenderman, M., Wiegers, J., & Hardy, P. (2005). A computerized communication aid for people with aphasia. *Disability and Rehabilitation, 27*, 529–533.

14

Supporting Student Learning With Adaptive Technology
Personalized Conceptual Assessment and Remediation

KIRSTEN R. BUTCHER and SEBASTIAN DE LA CHICA

INTRODUCTION

When people talk about creating technological tools to support learning, they usually want to support educational experiences that will result in knowledge that is both meaningful and robust. Meaningful learning requires not only that students can remember the to-be-learned information but also that they are able to use this knowledge to solve new problems, to apply to new situations, and to build upon during future learning opportunities. Designing effective educational technology that supports deep, generalizable learning requires attention to at least three interrelated goals for student cognition. First, technology should target deep understanding of key conceptual ideas in the domain of study. That is, it should promote successful learning of critical conceptual information that supports the organization and interpretation of new knowledge. Second, technology should encourage the development of metacognitive skills that allow students to monitor the level of their understanding and to choose useful learning strategies. Third, technology should support the use of cognitive processes involved in sensemaking and integration, so that relevant information is processed in a manner that results in deep understanding.

CLICK: Automatic Support for Conceptual Learning

We have been developing a customized, learner-centered technology that uses personalized conceptual knowledge assessment to target the intersection of these goals. This technology, the Customized Learning Service for Conceptual Knowledge (hereafter referred to as CLICK) is a Web-based service that supports the development of personalized instructional interventions in two ways. First, CLICK uses techniques in computer science and natural language processing to achieve the automatic assessment of individuals' existing conceptual domain knowledge. This automatic assessment of a learner's conceptual knowledge produces a detailed knowledge profile that is used to inform the second CLICK instructional intervention: automatically generated recommendations of learning resources. CLICK uses its assessment of student knowledge to create automatically generated recommendations of learning resources in digital libraries or other managed collections that focus on the particular information that the student needs to learn.

CLICK's automatic knowledge assessment and automatic resource recommendations represent next-generation personalization capabilities that can be used in a variety of educational technologies. To date, we have explored the use of CLICK to support student essay writing, using this task as the guiding learning scenario to inform the design and development of CLICK's personalization capabilities. However, CLICK's personalizations target knowledge integration processes and comprehension monitoring strategies that can be used to support deep and meaningful learning in a variety of learning situations. The wide applicability and generalizability of CLICK-targeted cognitive processes and strategies have led us to design CLICK using an open technology architecture; this is a service-oriented approach that promotes integration and reuse of CLICK's personalization capabilities by third parties in novel learning situations. Developers of educational technology can use CLICK's assessments of students' existing conceptual knowledge and its recommendations of relevant learning materials to support a variety of personalized learning technologies that focus on conceptual knowledge development, such as other essay-writing applications, Web-based research tools, or intelligent tutoring applications.

Automatic Customization: Next-Generation Conceptual Intervention

As described later in this chapter, we have used the CLICK service to develop and analyze a lightweight, prototype essay-writing application in order to assess the promise of CLICK's personalized conceptual support. In this essay-writing application, CLICK's conceptually informed, personalized feedback and remediation support generalization of learning by helping students assess the state of their knowledge and by supporting deeper processing of important domain information. Unlike existing technologies that require intense preprogramming to achieve individualized knowledge assessment and conceptual remediation, CLICK represents a paradigm shift in supporting generalizable knowledge by using automatic methods to provide customized, conceptually detailed feedback during interaction with instructional technology. CLICK leverages existing digital resources and extends current computational and natural language processing techniques to create scalable methods for conceptually based, personalized knowledge assessment and remediation that can be embedded in a variety of learning technologies.

In this chapter, we describe the development of CLICK as a learner-centered educational service that produces instructional artifacts to support conceptually customized technology for science learning. We have organized this chapter into four sections. In the first section, we address relevant cognitive science learning research that provides the theoretical rationale for our focus on conceptual knowledge development and effective learning processes. In the second section, we outline the ways in which CLICK's technological scaffolds target the metacognitive skills and learning processes that are critical in effective, conceptually customized learning technology. In the third section, we discuss preliminary results from a learning study in which we used CLICK in a lightweight prototype system that supports customized student interactions for a common instructional task: essay writing. In the fourth section, we discuss the advantages of CLICK's generalizable computational techniques for supporting scalable and customized tools in a variety of contexts. We conclude by outlining future directions, and discussing remaining challenges for personalized learning technologies.

USING CUSTOMIZATION TO SUPPORT GENERALIZATION OF LEARNING

We define *generalization of learning* as the process by which learned information and skills are transferred and applied to new problems or situations in a variety of contexts. From a cognitive science perspective, the development of robust, generalizable learning requires flexible forms of knowledge that can be used to organize and interpret new information, as well as effective cognitive processes that promote sensemaking in multiple domains (e.g., Barnett & Ceci, 2002; Halpern, 1998). For learner-driven activities, where the learner decides when and how to engage with the task, effective support also should extend to metacognitive skills that support deeper engagement and more effective approaches to learning. Successful educational technologies, then, should assist students in assessing their existing knowledge and acquiring missing information using effective learning processes and strategies.

Knowledge Representations for Deep Understanding

Cognitive science research has long recognized the distinction between shallow, rote knowledge and deeper understanding (e.g., Hilgard, Irvine, & Whipple, 1953; Olander, 1941). Whereas shallow knowledge typically is measured by tests of recall, deep understanding has been measured by inference verification (Royer, Carlo, Dufresne, & Mestre, 1996; Wiley & Voss, 1999), card-sorting tasks that reveal underlying knowledge structures (McNamara, Kintsch, Songer, & Kintsch, 1996; Wolfe et al., 1998), transfer tasks in which students reason about new situations (Goldstone & Son, 2005; Mayer, Bove, Bryman, Mars, & Tapangco, 1996), prediction of system behaviors (Hegarty, 1992), and other measures that target overall conceptual understanding such as mental model drawings (Butcher, 2006). From a comprehension perspective, these measures target learning at a situation model level (Kintsch, 1988, 1998; van Dijk & Kintsch, 1983). The situation model is formed when the learner makes inferences that go beyond the presented information and integrates new information with existing, relevant knowledge. The situation model can be distinguished from a *text base representation*, which refers to a shallower level of knowledge consisting only of the propositions in a to-be-learned text. The text base representation reflects memory for—but not understanding of—information (for a discussion, see Kintsch, 1998). Deep understanding is achieved by integrating current information with prior knowledge, resulting in the development of a situation model representation. The situation model is a long-lasting, flexible representation that can be applied to new contexts and situations.

Integration of new information with existing knowledge can be achieved by active processes that attempt to build a coherent model of the situation described by a text (Graesser, Singer, & Trabasso, 1994) or attempts to self-explain information during study (Chi, Bassok, Lewis, Reimann, & Glaser, 1989; Chi, de Leeuw, Chiu, & LaVancher, 1994). In many complex domains, a situation model level of understanding can be considered a specific instance of a general, domain-level representation of objects and functional relationships between these objects that form a mental model (Hegarty & Just, 1993; Johnson-Laird, 1983). A complete and coherent mental model supports reasoning about the relationships among key concepts for a topic or domain and provides a structure to make relevant inferences (e.g., cause and effect).

Targeting Key Knowledge Deficits
To support deep thinking and effective reasoning successfully, situation models or mental models must include sufficient information to form a coherent representation of the topic or domain in question. Missing information or unspecified connections between ideas can limit the potential for successful knowledge acquisition, application, and transfer. A critical first step in supporting student development of rich understanding, then, is to accurately assess whether a student possesses the necessary conceptual information in a domain. In this chapter, we focus on knowledge acquisition activities that are intended to enrich the student's current understanding (Carey, 1991). Enrichment, in this sense, refers to the addition of missing or incomplete information depending upon the state of a student's prior knowledge (Chi, 2008). Under these conditions, effective remediation must focus on providing information and links between relevant ideas based on individual learner profiles. Knowledge enrichment that is tailored to specific students poses a grand challenge: Diverse groups of learners, with distinct profiles of prior knowledge, create the need for conceptually customized interventions that can target unique combinations of knowledge gaps and misunderstandings in a domain. Educational technologies offer a potential solution to this customization challenge by using automated methods to perform a detailed assessment of each student's knowledge needs and to automatically select individually tailored remediation for individual students. These automated methods,

then, can achieve a detailed level of personalized conceptual instruction that is not practical in a normal classroom environment.

Personalization in Intelligent Tutoring   Intelligent tutoring systems are an example of existing, personalized educational technology. These tutors perform detailed assessment of student knowledge in order to select targeted instructional sequences (Graesser et al., 2004; Graesser, Person, Harter, & the Tutoring Research Group, 2001; Koedinger, Anderson, Hadley, & Mark, 1997; VanLehn et al., 2005). Intelligent tutors typically compare student knowledge to an expert or ideal model in order to assess current student knowledge and to choose appropriate remediation. For example, Cognitive Tutors use the step-by-step problem-solving performance of students to generate a model of student competency for mathematical skills. The Cognitive Tutor then uses this model to select problems that provide additional practice for unlearned skills (Corbett, McLaughlin, & Scarpinatto, 2000). AutoTutor (Graesser et al., 2004) assesses qualitative physics knowledge through tutoring conversations, using student responses to diagnose problems in current understanding and to trigger targeted remediation dialogues. Although these systems have been very successful in supporting student learning in their target domains, identification and representation of expert knowledge models have proven to be significant barriers to broad implementation of these systems in a variety of domains. It has been estimated that one hour of cognitive tutor instruction requires approximately 200 development hours (Koedinger, Aleven, Heffernan, McLaren, & Hockenberry, 2004). Building on the experiences of these successful educational-technology research efforts, CLICK's knowledge modeling and conceptual assessment algorithms have been designed to generalize to a variety of domains (see also Butcher et al., 2009) and to support a variety of instructional interventions.

From a generalization of learning perspective, it is important to note that existing intelligent tutors support student learning using instructional sequences that are controlled by the system rather than the learner. There is little known about how personalized knowledge remediation can be successfully implemented for learner-driven tasks, where students are responsible for diagnosing and revising their own understanding. Our position is that generalization of learning will be best supported by systems that can effectively target the acquisition of key conceptual information in a domain at the same time that they support student development of important metacognitive skills and integration processes.

Metacognitive Monitoring: Supporting Self-Sufficient Learning

In this chapter, we define *metacognitive monitoring* as the process by which students evaluate the state of their own knowledge compared to an ideal or desired understanding. When a student engages in monitoring, she assesses the accuracy of her comprehension as well as the completeness of her understanding (Griffin, Wiley, & Thiede, 2008).

Research in metacomprehension has generally found that students' ability to monitor their comprehension of written texts is quite poor (for a review, see Lin &

Zabrucky, 1998). However, students can improve their monitoring accuracy when prompted to use effective strategies. Accurate learner assessment of understanding has been improved both by passive strategies such as rereading (e.g., Griffin et al., 2008; Rawson, Dunlosky, & Thiede, 2000) or delays in making learning judgments (Thiede & Dunlosky, 1994), and by strategic processes such as self-explanation (Griffin et al., 2008) and keyword generation after a delay (Thiede, Anderson, & Therriault, 2003). These successful, active strategies share a common approach of prompting student analysis and articulation of their current knowledge.

Accurate metacognitive monitoring should support successful learning if the outcome of such monitoring serves to inform students about how to focus their learning activities. Students who spend more of their study time on materials that they perceive as not well learned perform best on subsequent tests of comprehension (Nelson, Dunlosky, Graf, & Narens, 1994; Thiede, 1999). Furthermore, students can use the outcome of metacognitive monitoring activities to inform self-regulated learning processes—choosing what to study and for how long (Thiede et al., 2003).

In light of these findings, the CLICK service provides tools that can be used to enhance student learning with personalized educational technology. CLICK supports customized interventions by providing two types of support for metacognitive monitoring. First, CLICK creates a targeted knowledge assessment that can be used to help students focus their monitoring activities on the portions of their work that are more likely to represent significant gaps in conceptual knowledge. Second, CLICK provides personalized recommendations of learning resources that are specifically targeted to students' knowledge problems, making it more likely that students will be able to recognize deficiencies in their current understanding.

Knowledge Integration: Processes for Deep Understanding

To support generalization of learning using educational technology, we need to prompt students to target the right conceptual information while also promoting effective integration of this information with relevant prior knowledge.

We define *knowledge integration* as the combining or linking of relevant information based on deep, conceptual connections. As such, integration of information during learning requires that students make explicit inferences that help them link domain content in meaningful ways. These active inferences should not be confused with the automatic inferences that occur during normal reading, which serve to integrate developing representations of a text (e.g., McKoon & Ratcliff, 1992). Instead, we are focused on more strategic learning processes in which students actively work to make sense of a domain from multiple information sources. This type of meaningful knowledge integration requires that learners are able to focus on and analyze deep aspects of relevant problems or ideas. However, being able to identify and analyze meaningful information often poses a considerable challenge for learners without ample existing domain knowledge. Expert–novice research has shown that novices often focus on superficial similarities rather than deep, conceptual similarities between problems (e.g., Chi, Feltovich, & Glaser, 1981). Novice learners are often unable to recognize relevant aspects of a multimedia display (Lowe, 1993) or to work successfully with multiple representations of conceptual phenomena (Kozma, 2003). Even when information does not need to be translated across representations, learners can fail to adequately understand the meaning and importance of incoming material. For example, prior presentation of incorrect text information can impede the integration of new, correct text information unless the new information provides a clear, alternative causal explanation (Johnson & Seifert, 1994). Thus, learners often need help in recognizing, understanding, and linking information derived from distinct sources.

Student learning can be enhanced by promoting active-learning strategies appropriate to a learner's level of background knowledge (e.g., McNamara et al., 1996). In addition, learning is supported when students can successfully integrate information across multiple sources or representations. For example, creating arguments from multiple texts (Wiley & Voss, 1999) and multimedia materials (e.g., Mayer, 2001) supports deep understanding of domain ideas. Recent research on learning from text and diagrams (Ainsworth & Loizou, 2003; Butcher, 2006; Hegarty & Just, 1993; Schnotz & Bannert, 2003) has demonstrated positive changes to critical learning processes when diagrams are added to a text. These results from prior research have important implications for students' online learning. To successfully integrate materials, learners must recognize relevant information in each source, make connections across the resources, and integrate the resulting information into prior knowledge.

CLICK leverages these findings in order to support students learning from existing digital sources of information. When working with existing, digital educational materials, recognizing and integrating relevant knowledge may be especially difficult. Existing resources in digital libraries represent diverse collections of materials that have been created by different authors and institutions for different goals using a large variety of formats and representations. Diverse and independently developed digital resources are unable to achieve the consistency and simplicity that are included in recommended design elements for supporting integration in Web documents (Britt & Gabrys, 2002). For example, independently created Web pages necessarily result in multiple pages—rather than a single page—that present related information, and those pages are unlikely to present a consistent look and feel. Despite these challenges, it is important to find ways to support student integration of existing digital materials because they represent an important opportunity to leverage a wealth of educational content that does not require new development time or resources.

DESIGNING SUPPORTS FOR GENERALIZATION OF LEARNING

We are exploring the principled design and implementation of a customized learning service for concept knowledge, called CLICK. Our initial target domain has been earthquakes and plate tectonics at a high school level; this domain has been used for the development of our computational techniques and a learning study. CLICK currently leverages the Digital Library for Earth System Education

(DLESE; n.d.) as its pedagogical content knowledge base, but CLICK's computational algorithms are designed to generalize to different digital libraries and other managed collections of digital resources. DLESE provides the educational content for CLICK to model important concepts about a scientific domain, and also serves as a large repository of learning resources that can be used to construct personalized instructional interventions. From a pedagogical perspective, CLICK focuses on identifying conceptual knowledge deficiencies in student work, such as essays, and on suggesting digital library resources that can remediate specific knowledge gaps and misunderstandings. Because CLICK supports ongoing formative assessment during the completion of a learning task, it enables online learning applications to scaffold the development of highly generalizable metacomprehension strategies and learning processes.

Targeting Knowledge Conditions for Conceptual Understanding

To develop a useful representation of the conceptual knowledge in a domain that can be used to assess student understanding, CLICK uses multidocument summarization techniques to capture important pedagogical concepts about earthquakes and plate tectonics from carefully selected (on-topic and age-appropriate) collections of resources in DLESE. CLICK generates concept inventories that consist of sentences extracted automatically from the digital library resources, encoded as a knowledge map (e.g., O'Donnell, Dansereau, & Hall, 2002) that spatially encodes the relationships between these concepts. This knowledge map constitutes a domain competency model that contains the scientific concepts, ideas, and processes learners should know and understand within the target domain.

Assessing What Students Should Know About a Domain   Because the CLICK domain competency model will be used for instructional purposes, it is important that the model reflect pedagogically sound conceptual knowledge. Initial evaluation results have indicated that the CLICK-generated domain competency model successfully captures the pedagogical concepts about earthquakes and plate tectonics that experts identify as important for high school–aged learners. We have compared the concept inventory sentences that CLICK automatically extracts from digital library resources to those selected by two geology experts and two instructional design experts using the same resources. Using a vector space representation of the sentences extracted by CLICK and those selected by the experts, we have computed cosine distance as a measure of linguistic similarity (Salton & Lesk, 1968) between the concept inventory generated by CLICK and the one created by the experts. Cosine distance is a straightforward approach for measuring the similarity of sentences based on the words contained in those sentences and is widely used in computational linguistics. We have chosen to begin our assessment with this standard measure, but there are a large number of other cosine-based comparisons to explore at a later date. Latent semantic analysis (Landauer & Dumais, 1997) is one example. Latent semantic analysis builds upon a basic cosine comparison approach, but it requires the construction of a specialized semantic space from domain- and age-appropriate collections of documents in order to perform additional mathematical procedures that extract semantic similarity of non-identical words.

Our analysis of CLICK-selected and expert-selected digital library concepts yields a cosine value of 0.83, indicating that the sentences extracted by CLICK are very close to the concepts selected by the experts with regard to term selection and frequency of use (de la Chica, Ahmad, Sumner, Martin, & Butcher, 2008). In addition, de la Chica et al. found that the sentences extracted by CLICK resembled the linguistic surface structure of the concepts in an expert-created domain knowledge map because 60% of the terms extracted by CLICK appear in the same relative order as in the domain knowledge map that was collaboratively constructed by the experts.

Assessing Students' Current Understanding

To assess a student's existing conceptual understanding in a domain, CLICK needs to represent current student knowledge in a format that can be compared to the domain competency model. CLICK processes student essays by using natural language processing techniques to capture the internal lexical cohesion of the essays, which CLICK then uses to generate a knowledge map that approximates the learner's current conceptual understanding. These CLICK-generated learner knowledge maps directly use sentences from the student essays as concepts and leverage the presence of thesaurus relationships (e.g., synonyms) between words in neighboring sentences to establish links between concepts (de la Chica et al., 2008).

To assess the accuracy of the CLICK-generated learner knowledge maps, we have compared the degree of overlap between these maps and knowledge maps created manually by the geology and instructional design experts from student essays. This comparison examines CLICK agreement with the experts in terms of sentences selected for representation in the knowledge maps and connectivity between those sentences. We determine agreement using a kappa measure that accounts for prevalence of yes-no judgments and biases amongst the annotators, called prevalence-adjusted bias-adjusted kappa (PABAK) (Byrt, Bishop, & Carlin, 1993). PABAK values range from −1 to +1, where PABAK is zero with 50% observed agreement. The CLICK-generated learner knowledge maps show very substantial agreement with the experts on the selection of essay sentences to represent student understanding in a knowledge map, as evidenced by a PABAK value of 0.92 (Butcher et al., 2009). In addition, CLICK shows substantial agreement with the experts on the connectivity between the selected sentences (PABAK = 0.66) (Butcher et al., 2009).

Assessing Student Knowledge Problems Through Concept Map Alignment

CLICK's automatically generated domain and learner knowledge maps provide the computational infrastructure for CLICK to support highly personalized learning interactions. CLICK supports these customized learning interactions through its diagnostic and recommendation capabilities.

Figure 14.1 depicts CLICK's overall approach to personalized conceptual diagnosis: CLICK aligns concepts from the learner knowledge model (1) to related

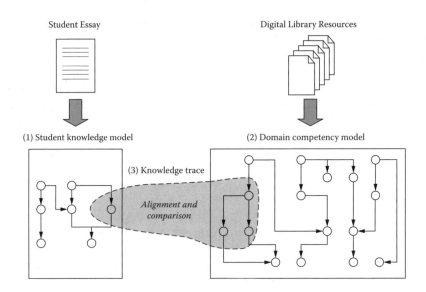

Figure 14.1 CLICK diagnosis of learner conceptual understanding.

concepts in the domain knowledge model (2). This alignment allows CLICK to use both shallow linguistic analysis and graph analysis techniques to form a knowledge trace (3) that diagnoses current learner understanding and allows us to identify conceptual areas requiring improvement. One strength of this computational approach is the significant savings in the time and effort necessary to create educational interventions that are tailored to an individual student's knowledge. Intelligent tutoring systems targeting inadequate student conceptions, such as AutoTutor (Graesser et al., 2004), often leverage detailed inventories of typical student misconceptions obtained through complex and time-consuming learning research efforts in specific content areas, such as gravity for physics students. Motivated by our interest in a more generalizable approach, and by the lack of such misconception inventories for earthquake and plate tectonics, CLICK follows a domain-independent approach to identify areas for conceptual knowledge improvement. CLICK identifies incorrect and missing knowledge by targeting the following three common classes of conceptual deficiencies in students' scientific knowledge:

- *Incorrect statements* correspond to concepts expressed in the student essay that contradict the scientifically accurate concepts in the domain knowledge map.
- *Incomplete understandings* correspond to one of two possible situations:
  - The student provides a correct but only partial description of a science concept or process.
  - The student fails to mention a core concept about the domain.

- *Knowledge integration issues* occur when the student provides correct descriptions of two related science concepts or processes but fails to make an explicit connection between such concepts in his or her essay.

CLICK's diagnosis of current student understanding produces a detailed assessment comprising the specific student statements that it has identified as problematic and a characterization of the type of knowledge problem identified (i.e., incorrect statement, incomplete understanding, or knowledge integration issue). CLICK bases this diagnosis and assessment on comparisons between relevant portions of the automatically generated domain and learner knowledge maps. The rationale for the CLICK diagnostics are represented as internal connections between the student statements identified as erroneous or problematic, the corresponding nodes and links in the learner knowledge map, and the nodes and links from the domain knowledge map that align to the student's knowledge. These three types of data are used to identify information that is necessary to improve the student's current conceptual understanding of the domain, thus forming the conceptual and computational underpinning for CLICK's digital learning resource recommendations. CLICK's recommendations—described later—are the core form of support used to guide students' metacognitive monitoring.

Evaluating CLICK Performance on Knowledge Assessment   Initial evaluation results suggest that CLICK identifies these conceptual knowledge deficiencies nearly as adeptly as geology and instructional design experts (Butcher et al., 2009). CLICK performs very well at identifying essay statements that require conceptual improvement, overall returning 78% of all the essay statements that were selected by our domain and instructional design experts as needing instructional remediation. By comparison, experts on average selected only 69% of the essay statements identified by each other as knowledge deficiencies. On the more rigorous examination of what portion of the essay statements identified as problematic by CLICK coincides with expert judgments, we have observed a modest but encouraging 37% overlap. Our experts showed an average overlap with each other's judgments of 68%. The discrepancy between CLICK–expert agreement and expert–expert agreement in targeting specific portions of student essays is, in large part, due to the fact that experts routinely ignore a number of knowledge problems from student essays that they characterize as low priority. In contrast, CLICK returns *all* problematic statements that it identifies in student essays. To most accurately reflect expert remediation strategies, CLICK likely will need to implement prioritization methods to select the most critical knowledge problems for initial remediation. Overall, initial evaluation results indicate the promise of the CLICK computational approach to identify areas where student knowledge may be incorrect, incomplete, or lacking conceptual coherence.

Supporting Effective Metacognitive Monitoring

CLICK analyzes the contents of student essays and identifies incorrect or problematic statements based on comparisons with the concepts and relationships in the domain knowledge map. CLICK leverages this diagnosis to provide the learner with highly contextualized formative feedback that clearly indicates the sentences that it has targeted for improvement. This approach promotes the development of monitoring strategies because learners receive specific feedback on what aspects of their understanding may be inadequate and prompts them to assess their understanding in the context of specific conceptual ideas.

Customized Feedback on Knowledge Deficiencies

CLICK encourages students' monitoring of their own understanding by singling out specific learner statements that should be assessed and by providing a general prompt for each statement identified as a knowledge deficiency. These prompts are designed to support student knowledge construction, but they are content free in the sense that they do not provide domain-relevant information or remediation (Chi, Siler, Jeong, Yamauchi, & Hausmann, 2001). Chi et al. (2001) demonstrated these content-free prompts to be as effective as explanations and feedback from human tutors in supporting student learning, and we have selected and adapted our prompts from their materials. Because CLICK focuses on supporting student-driven learning interactions, we have selected content-free prompts that include active language and are most likely to elicit a response from learners as they complete a self-driven, interactive learning task. We also modified the prompts to include concept-centric terminology aligned to the three types of knowledge deficiencies captured by CLICK. For example, an incorrect statement may be prompted by "Why don't you explain this sentence again?" A knowledge integration issue between two disconnected statements would be prompted by "Could you connect what you wrote in these sentences?" Our adapted prompts are included in the appendix at the end of this chapter.

Customized Recommendations for Digital Learning Resources

Once CLICK has identified a student's specific knowledge deficiencies and has selected a prompt that is relevant to each type of deficiency, CLICK needs to suggest relevant digital library resources that the student can use to revise his or her current understanding. CLICK personalizes its recommendations based on the student's prior knowledge and learning needs using a novel variation of traditional information indexing and retrieval techniques (van Rijsbergen, 1979). CLICK creates an index of the digital library resources available for recommendation and computes which resources are most relevant, and therefore "closest," to the current level of student understanding and learning needs.

CLICK's information-indexing approach represents an innovative departure from traditional information indexing and retrieval because it uses an internal graph structure to capture the index of important terms representing student knowledge, student learning needs, and digital library resources. CLICK analyzes the sentences contained in its internal domain and learner knowledge maps and extracts the terms necessary to represent student knowledge and learning needs. This analysis considers only domain and learner knowledge map sentences (concepts) closely aligned to the student statement that CLICK has identified as a knowledge deficiency. The end result is a graph representation comprising terms the student knows or should know about a science concept and the corresponding relationships between those terms. CLICK compares this graph of student knowledge terms to the graphs representing those same terms as presented in the available digital library resources and determines the similarity between the graphs. Based on these comparisons, CLICK identifies the most promising selection of digital learning resources and Web pages within those resources for addressing a student's learning needs.

Such deeply personalized recommendations free learners from the difficulty associated with choosing appropriate search engine keywords, processing search engine results, and locating the information that best matches their current state of knowledge. This allows learners to more quickly approximate the search processes of experts, who spend more time scanning and analyzing content for relevant information compared to novices, who spend a disproportionate amount of time formulating and modifying queries for relevant information (Marchionini, 1995). CLICK's highly targeted content recommendations enable learners to effectively employ metacognitive monitoring in order to grasp the true nature and extent of deficiencies in their conceptual knowledge. The development of effective monitoring skills should, in turn, result in more meaningful revisions of knowledge as learners review and revise their conceptual understanding using deeper assessment of the learning materials and connections to prior knowledge.

Supporting Knowledge Integration for Deep Learning

CLICK creates opportunities for learners to integrate their prior knowledge—as expressed in their essays—with the scientific information contained in suggested digital library resources. CLICK learning resource recommendations provide access to materials at two levels: broad and specific. CLICK recommendations link to both an overall digital library resource—which may consist of many individual Web pages—and a single Web page within that resource. CLICK's resource and Web page recommendations aim to maximize the overlap between the student-generated concepts that CLICK has flagged as problematic, the related domain knowledge map concepts, and the scientifically accurate concepts presented in the available digital library resources. As a result, the recommended learning resources are deeply personalized to the current level of learner understanding and contextualized around the corresponding scientifically correct domain concepts. This approach to resource recommendation is both learner centered and knowledge centered, in that it attempts to bridge the conceptual gap between what learners currently know, what they should know, and what digital learning resources can bridge this gap by being integrated into current knowledge.

Besides providing learners with resources that should be more easily integrated into existing knowledge, CLICK also provides learners with multiple recommendations for each identified knowledge deficiency. Given the wide variety of resources contained in digital libraries such as DLESE, learners may receive recommendations from CLICK that include a variety of pedagogical content styles and presentation forms. For instance, a student who writes about plate tectonics may be presented with a Web site containing the textual definition of the three types of faults (convergent, divergent, and transform), along with a resource featuring pedagogically sound animations depicting plate boundary movement at the three types of faults. Providing access to such varied perspectives on a scientific concept or process may help promote deeper comprehension of the underlying content, as learners have the opportunity to integrate textual and multimedia-oriented content to construct more robust conceptual knowledge.

LEARNING STUDY: EVIDENCE FOR EFFECTIVENESS OF CLICK SUPPORT

To evaluate the impact that CLICK's rich set of personalized, pedagogical interactions may have on the learner's cognitive processes, we designed and conducted a controlled, two-part learning study using undergraduate learners studying a science topic. Our goal was to explore the kinds of conceptual knowledge development and metacognitive strategies that learners engaged in while working with the customized learning support offered by CLICK when compared to students offered similar but more general support for remediation.

Subjects

Our participants were 32 undergraduates from the University of Colorado at Boulder. Participants received course credit in an Introductory Psychology class. Participants volunteered for this study using an automated Web site; thus, we did not control for specific demographic variables. In total, 32 undergraduate students (20 females and 12 males) took part in the study, and they were randomly assigned to the experimental ($n = 16$) and control ($n = 16$) conditions.

Materials

We directed an instructional designer with considerable domain expertise in geology to select five educational digital resources from DLESE that provided background information on the theory of plate tectonics and its relationship to earthquakes, volcanoes, and mountain formation. We also collaborated with the same instructional designer to develop a general knowledge assessment consisting of 10 questions with five true-false answer choices for each question. This assessment targets general, factual student knowledge about the following concepts: internal structure of the Earth, plate boundaries, plate movement, subduction, faults, transform faults, earthquakes, seismic waves, and volcanoes.

To isolate the effects of CLICK's personalized prompts and resource recommendations on student learning, we measured students' knowledge development and essay revisions when students used either a CLICK-supported instructional interface (the experimental condition) or a standard digital library interface (the control condition). Students were randomly assigned to an interface, which they used to investigate materials and revise essays. Their first essays were written during an initial research session in which they also had read a set of general domain resources from the Web. We designed a learning environment for the students in the control condition that was equivalent to the CLICK-supported experimental condition in terms of access to resources, essay feedback, and self-regulated learning. Materials for students in the control condition included printed essay feedback based on CLICK's assessment of their essays, as well as a digital library search interface to help students locate relevant digital library resources on earthquakes and plate tectonics. The printed feedback included a copy of the original student essay with the top five knowledge deficiencies identified by CLICK shown in boldface and underlined. Printed feedback for the control condition also presented the following list of five revision prompts to support students in making successful revisions: (a) Explain or restate what you wrote in your original essay, (b) clarify what you wrote in your original essay, (c) be specific when describing concepts, (d) describe concepts using your own words, and (e) explain how concepts may be related to each other. These strategies captured, in general but descriptive text, the revision strategies that were targeted by CLICK's content-free prompts in the experimental condition.

To support resource exploration by students in the control condition, we developed a digital library search interface for DLESE (Figure 14.2). This interface was designed to help students in the control condition search over the same set of resources used by CLICK to generate recommendations for the students in the experimental condition. The digital library search interface allowed control condition students to enter keywords and keyword combinations and to narrow searches using subject and resource type selections similar to those supported on the DLESE Web site (DLESE, n.d.; Weatherley, 2005). Figure 14.2 shows a query

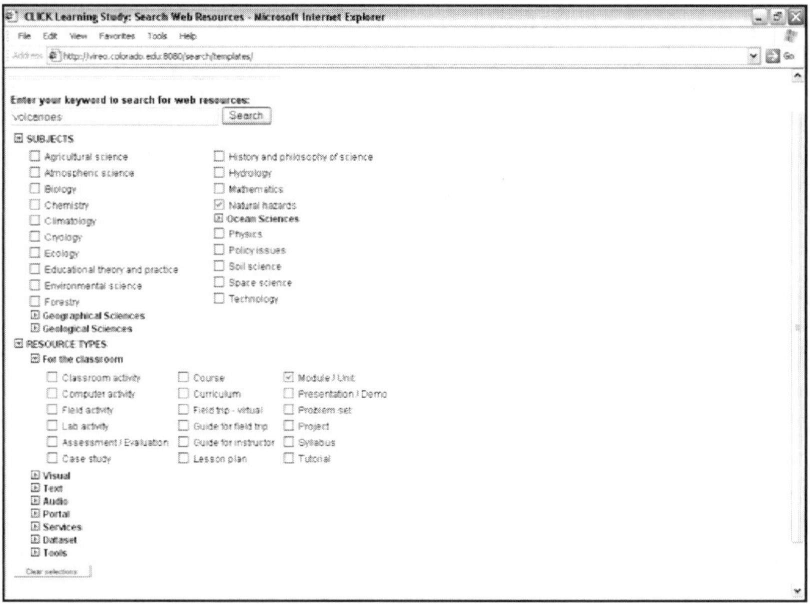

Figure 14.2   Control condition digital library search interface.

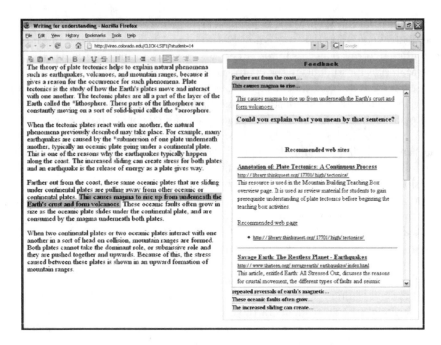

Figure 14.3   Click-based personalized essay-writing application.

being initiated for the keyword *volcanoes*, the subject *natural hazards*, and the resource type *module/unit*.

In contrast to students in the control condition, students in the experimental condition used a simple, Web-based essay-writing application that was developed for this learning study. This Web-based application used CLICK to personalize learning interactions for students doing research online to write essays about earthquakes and plate tectonics (Figure 14.3). As seen in Figure 14.3, the student writes his essay using the text-editing area on the left-hand side of the application, and CLICK provides feedback to the student using the scrollable area on the right-hand side. This feedback area highlights the specific essay sentences that were identified by CLICK as knowledge deficiencies. Each targeted essay sentence corresponds to an entry in the feedback area and is displayed on a clickable bar using the opening words of the sentence in boldface font. When the student clicks on the bar for a specific essay sentence targeted by CLICK, the application highlights the target sentence in the student's essay and displays the personalized feedback related to that sentence. This personalized feedback includes the text of the sentence in question, a relevant content-free prompt, and a list of recommended resources and Web site pages generated by CLICK.

The content-free prompt that follows each targeted essay sentence aligns to the type of knowledge deficiency identified by CLICK. In Figure 14.3, CLICK has identified the student's statement as an incorrect statement; therefore, the interface selects and displays one of the content-free prompts aligned to this type of problematic statement. The content-free prompt (i.e., "Could you explain what you mean by that sentence?") is intended to support the student in reflecting upon his or her current level of understanding and in processing the information contained in the list of recommended Web sites that follows the prompt.

The list of recommendations includes three resources from DLESE identified by CLICK as best fits to help the student improve on his or her current state of knowledge. Each recommendation includes the title of the digital library resource, the resource Web site URL, a short description of the resource, and a recommended Web page within the site. In the example shown in Figure 14.3, the recommended learning resources contain a mixture of text-based and multimedia-centric content that provides the student with the opportunity to integrate conceptual definitions with descriptions of the dynamic geological processes associated with volcano formation in the context of the theory of plate tectonics.

The major difference between the feedback provided in the CLICK condition and that provided in the control condition is that the CLICK condition receives personalized, conceptually relevant resource suggestions for each targeted sentence. However, it should also be noted that there are differences in the presentation of revision prompts for the CLICK and control conditions. Whereas students in the control condition are provided with a list of revision prompts on paper, students in the CLICK condition see only a single prompt—which CLICK thinks is relevant for the identified knowledge problem—for each targeted sentence. Although the overall strategies provided by the prompts in both conditions are comparable, it is possible that revision prompts are more effective when they are selected for and embedded with a particular knowledge problem. Thus, the current study cannot pinpoint the source of potential personalization benefits, but rather seeks to determine whether an overall approach to conceptual personalization will promote effective learning processes and deep knowledge revisions.

Procedure

The learning study consisted of two sessions. All students completed the same set of tasks during the first session. In session 1, prior factual knowledge about the domain was assessed by the true-false test of general knowledge that we had developed with our domain expert. Students were given 20 minutes to complete this test. Students then read about the topic for 15 minutes using the collection of five hand-picked Web sites on the theory of plate tectonics, earthquakes, volcanoes, and mountain formation. At this point, students were given 5 minutes to complete a learning styles assessment as a distraction task. Finally, all students were given 30 minutes to write an essay about earthquakes and plate tectonics of at least 250 words using a word processor. To guide the essay-writing activity, all students were given the following essay-writing prompt:

> Prior to the development of the theory of plate tectonics, geologists had difficulty understanding the origins of earthquakes and mountains. How does the theory of plate tectonics help us explain natural phenomena such as earthquakes, volcanoes, and mountain ranges? Please be as specific as you can in your explanation.

Students were randomly assigned into the experimental and control conditions; analyses show no differences in initial true-false test scores across conditions. On the 50-point true-false test, students demonstrated low prior domain knowledge in both the experimental ($M = 28.5$, $SD = 4.2$) and the control ($M = 28.4$, $SD = 5.9$) conditions. Following session 1, student essays were processed by CLICK to generate learner knowledge maps and to identify erroneous and problematic statements. This CLICK diagnosis was fed into the Wizard of Oz component (Kelley, 1983) of this study, in which two research team members used rich textual descriptions of algorithms under development to manually select five issues identified by CLICK for remediation to present to each student and to select the recommended digital library resources and Web pages.

Students returned to participate in the second session at least one week after their first session. Students in the control condition received a 5-minute tutorial on how to use the digital library search interface for DLESE (shown in Figure 14.2) prior to beginning the essay revision task. These students had access to printed feedback for their essays, including the top five knowledge issues identified by CLICK and the essay revision strategies described earlier. Students revised their original essays using a word processor, and used the digital library search interface to search for and locate informational resources to help them improve their essays. Students were allowed up to 35 minutes to review and revise their original essays.

Students in the experimental condition received their essay feedback integrated within the CLICK essay-writing application shown in Figure 14.3. This feedback included the top five knowledge deficiencies identified by CLICK, a content-free prompt contextualized to the type of deficiency identified, and three resources recommended by CLICK. Students received a 5-minute tutorial using a sample essay on how to operate the CLICK essay-writing interface. Students in the experimental condition were limited to the recommended resources; they did not have access to any additional search engine capabilities. Like students in the control condition, students in the CLICK condition were given up to 35 minutes to review and revise their original essays.

During the essay revision task, we captured all interactions between the user and the available software using off-the-shelf screen capture tools for students in both conditions. After completing the essay revision task, students in both conditions were given 20 minutes to complete a revision questionnaire. This questionnaire prompted students to describe the strategies and operations they had used to address the knowledge deficiencies targeted by CLICK. After completing the revision questionnaire, students in both conditions were given 20 minutes to finish the true-false general knowledge assessment. This assessment contained the same items as in session 1, but item order was randomized to minimize incidental learning.

Results: Metacognition and Strategies for Knowledge Development

Student responses on the revision questionnaire were assessed for metacognitive monitoring, revision strategies, and learning strategies. The revision questionnaire asked students to comment on four sentences that had been selected for review by the CLICK system. For each of these sentences, students were asked to respond to three prompts:

- Why do you think the system identified this statement for revision?
- Describe how your revised statement is different from your original one. Please be as specific as you can.
- Explain what you did to revise your original statement and why. Please be as specific as you can.

We did not constrain student responses by length or structure—students were free to respond to these queries in any manner that they chose.

We conducted an in-depth analysis of student responses on the revision questionnaire, breaking student responses into idea-units that were coded for their category (e.g., diagnosis or revision strategy) and depth of processing (e.g., shallow vs. deep). Diagnosis categories were coded when students provided a reason or rationale for why a specific sentence had been targeted for revision. Deep diagnosis categories reflected metacognitive analysis of essays that focused on the correctness or completeness of domain information (e.g., missing content or incorrect statements). Shallow diagnosis categories reflected metacognitive analysis that focused on superficial aspects of writing style that did not relate to domain content (e.g., wordiness or grammatical mistakes). Revision strategies were coded when students indicated how they had attempted to fix targeted sentences. Deep revision strategies were those that concerned changes to domain content (e.g., adding new content, or revising or refining described relationships among concepts). Shallow revision strategies were those that reflected superficial, stylistic changes that did not refine domain content (e.g., fixing grammar or spelling). Overall responses to each revision inquiry were also coded for overall research process (e.g., did the student use digital library resources?) and stated goal of the revision (e.g., express the same idea vs. revise or change the idea).

Because such detailed analysis of text responses is resource intensive, we selected the first one third of the data sample for coding. We coded revision questionnaires for six students in each condition (12 total students), for each of the four sentences targeted for revision, on responses to each of the three prompts we provided. This results in a maximum of 72 revision responses in each condition (6 Students × 4 Sentences × 3 Prompts). In three cases (two students in the CLICK condition and one student in the control condition), CLICK identified only three sentences that needed improvement. Thus, the total number of coded revision responses was 66 in the CLICK condition and 69 in the control condition.

Essay Diagnosis   As seen in Table 14.1, students who received CLICK's customized, conceptual-based recommendations for digital library resources more often reported that they engaged in deep diagnosis of the CLICK-identified conceptual issues in their essays (interaction between depth of processing and condition: $F_{(1,10)} = 4.2$, $p < .07$, $\eta_p^2 = .30$). Although all students were provided with essay feedback generated by the same CLICK algorithms, personalized recommendations for remediation provided a mechanism for deeper analysis of the essay

TABLE 14.1   Percentage of Total Statements in a
Category Reflecting Shallow Versus Deep Processing

Students' Self-Reported Strategies	Control	CLICK
Essay diagnosis: Metacognitive processing		
Shallow (grammar, wordiness, spelling, writing style)	36%	17%
Deep (incorrect, missing content, too vague or broad)	64%	83%
Essay revision: Knowledge development		
Shallow (reword, fix grammar/spelling, delete)	67%	37%
Deep (revise or add content, describe relationships)	33%	63%

content. Rather than positing superficial reasoning for CLICK-targeted sentences (e.g., that the sentence was too wordy or poorly written), students using the CLICK interface were more likely to analyze potential problems with their essay's scientific content (e.g., the sentence did not include information on the three kinds of faults). CLICK's customized recommendations supported metacognition in the sense that students monitored the state of their knowledge with regard to scientific content when diagnosing why CLICK had targeted particular sentences.

Essay Revision   CLICK's potential to support knowledge integration was evident in the revision strategies that students reported using. Students who received CLICK resource recommendations frequently reported that they attempted to change or revise the science content that they described in their essays (e.g., described the relationship between plate tectonics and earthquakes) rather than shallow features of their essay (e.g., reworded the sentence to make it sound better). Thus, students who received personalized, conceptually targeted resource recommendations were more likely to engage in deep knowledge revision and development during learning ($F_{(1,10)} = 6.6$, $p = .03$, $\eta_p^2 = .40$). It should be noted that highly successful essays can benefit from both deep knowledge development and attention to stylistic and grammatical changes. However, stylistic changes are problematic and result in poorer quality essays when used in lieu of content knowledge development.

The revision questionnaires also include information about students' overall learning strategies, as evidenced by their self-reported behaviors during revision. When receiving CLICK's personalized, conceptually informed suggestions for Web resources, students were more than three times as likely to report that they used digital library resources to investigate and evaluate the knowledge they needed for revision (see Table 14.2) compared to students in the control condition. This difference is statistically significant ($F_{(1,10)} = 5.4$, $p < .05$, $d = 1.35$), and has

TABLE 14.2   Revision Strategies of Experimental
Conditions, as Percentage of Total Revisions

Self-Reported Process and Goals	Control	CLICK
Digital resources consulted to inform revision	13%	46%
Revision preserves same idea	75%	29%

positive implications for improving the accuracy of metacognitive monitoring and providing increased opportunities for knowledge integration. Knowledge change is unlikely if students fail to engage with learning resources. Indeed, students in the control condition reported trying to reexpress the same conceptual idea as in their original, CLICK-targeted sentence 75% of the time, compared to only 29% of the time for students who received CLICK resource recommendations ($F_{(1,10)}$ = 4.2, $p < .07$, d = 1.18).

It is important to note that the students in the control condition were not operating under an impoverished learning environment in this study. For both the control and experimental conditions, CLICK's conceptual analysis was used to identify problematic sentences from student essays for revision. Control students were provided with the results of this personalized knowledge assessment and had access to a full range of digital library resources—including the resources that were recommended by CLICK in the experimental condition. Moreover, the 50-point, true-false general knowledge assessment demonstrated that students overall demonstrated a gain in performance ($F_{(1,30)}$ = 4.6, $p < .04$, $d = .45$) from pre- ($M = 28.4$, $SD = 4.621$) to posttest ($M = 30.69$, $SD = 5.048$), but condition did not affect development of factual knowledge. This result argues against the possibility that students in the CLICK condition were exposed to more information or learned more facts about the domain. However, the true-false assessment is not intended to be a measure of deep comprehension. To assess deep comprehension, an analysis of the quality and content of students' actual essays is ongoing.

Because we controlled both the amount and type of feedback and instruction that we offered students in this study, the key difference between the control condition and the CLICK condition lies in the personalized recommendation of learning resources that are aligned with identified conceptual issues. Our current results show that personalized recommendation of learning resources increased students' self-reported metacognitive knowledge monitoring and promoted focus on scientific content. But is there evidence that students' essays reflected deep knowledge development that would be consistent with what we would expect if these differences in monitoring and learning strategies supported deep comprehension? To address this question, we conducted a detailed, qualitative analysis of two students' essay revisions for a similar, CLICK-identified knowledge deficiency.

Qualitative Analysis Example

We selected the students in this analysis—one in the control condition and one in the experimental condition—because each wrote a problematic statement about volcano formation and independently received essay revision feedback that targeted this statement. We examined the sentence transformations made by each student for two essay sentences: (a) the sentence targeted by CLICK as an incorrect statement of a scientific concept, and (b) a nontargeted but contiguous sentence that is closely related to the knowledge deficiency expressed by the student.

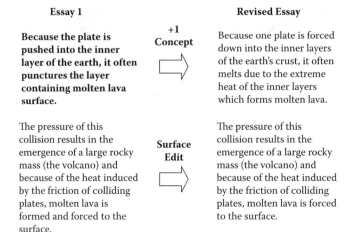

Figure 14.4 Control student essay transformations.

The scientifically accurate description that accounts for the formation of volcanoes is that volcanoes are more likely to occur at convergent plate boundaries, where one plate is being pushed down under another in a process known as *subduction* (see Svitil, n.d.). During this subduction process, molten rock, or magma, is produced through the heating of the crust that is being pushed down beneath the surface into the Earth's mantle. The resulting magma collects in weak patches of crust, called *magma chambers*. If the pressure in the magma chamber builds high enough, the magma will rise to the surface and possibly erupt, and a volcano will be formed.

Figure 14.4 depicts the sentence transformations related to the volcano formation knowledge deficiency identified by CLICK for a student in the control condition. The revisions in Figure 14.4 fit the typical pattern seen for students in the control condition: These students tended to focus on surface-editing activities of limited scope; new content was rarely generated, and, if it was, it often appeared only within the exact sentence containing the original problematic conceptual knowledge.

The problematic statement in the first essay, flagged by CLICK as an incorrect statement, is shown in boldface type ("Because the plate is pushed ..."). In this sentence, the student correctly describes the process of subduction (although the term is never mentioned), but then goes on to erroneously describe the process of lava creation as being caused by "puncturing" of layers. We also examine the following, related sentence from the first essay ("The pressure of this collision ...") and note the existence of a scientifically inaccurate description of volcano formation as a result of "[t]he pressure of this [plate] collision" and as the "emergence of a large rocky mass." This sentence also erroneously describes the process of magma formation as the result of "the friction of colliding plates."

In the second essay, the student modified the sentence originally flagged by CLICK as problematic by adding the correct concept that lava forms due "to the

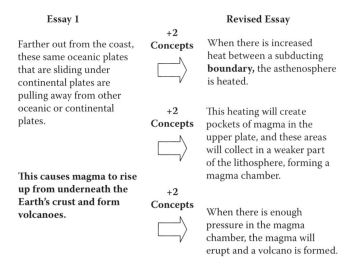

Figure 14.5   Experimental condition essay transformations.

extreme heat of the inner layers [of the Earth]," but the overall student understanding of the geological process is still incorrect. The student made no significant changes to the contents of the following sentence, other than removing the
concept of lava formation. As a result of this shallow content editing, the sentence
still contains problematic statements about volcano formation and about friction
causing "lava [to be] forced to the surface." On the revision questionnaire, the
student describes the reason for this revision to be the inaccuracy of the original
statement and notes that she or he did further research on the topic to make the
sentence "more accurate." It should be noted that these strategies are counted as
potentially useful approaches to learning in our quantitative analysis, but that the
student fails to note how the essay's scientific content was changed or augmented
during revision. Given this student's minor addition of scientific content and failure
to address the remaining problems, it is clear that even useful strategies can fail to
be implemented in meaningful ways.

Figure 14.5 depicts the sentence transformations related to the volcano formation knowledge deficiency identified by CLICK for a student in the experimental
condition. The revisions in Figure 14.5 fit the overall pattern of revisions seen for
students in the experimental condition: Students using the CLICK-based interface
typically focused on knowledge generation activities of wider scope, characterized
by the introduction of new scientific concepts, more domain-appropriate terminology, and new sentence generation.

In the first essay, the student provided an incorrect description of volcano formation ("This causes magma to rise ...") shown in boldface in Figure 14.5. This
sentence and its implicit reference to the preceding one represent not only an incorrect account of the process of volcano formation (resulting from rising magma), but
also an erroneous inference that connects volcano formation with oceanic plate
divergence.

In the second essay, the student replaces the original two sentences with three newly generated ones containing an expanded and scientifically improved account of the process of volcano formation. In the first new sentence, the student correctly introduces the concept of subduction using the appropriate terminology, "a subducting boundary." It should be noted that, in addition to the correct concept introduced in the first sentence, the student also has introduced a concept that is not entirely accurate when she or he refers to "increased heat … [in] the asthenosphere." Although the concept of subduction and increased heat at plate boundaries is indeed related to the asthenosphere, the asthenosphere of the Earth is already hot. Our consulting domain expert characterizes this as a minor knowledge problem, but it is important to recognize that knowledge development does not always proceed without error. We believe that it is important to address potential knowledge development errors by implementing iterative feedback cycles using CLICK, unlike the single feedback cycle used in this experimental setting. In this case, the student goes on to add additional, correct conceptual information to the essay. The second new sentence introduces two scientifically correct concepts related to how "the heating will create pockets of magma," and how this magma collects in "weaker part[s] of the lithosphere" using the correct terminology, "magma chambers," to name these structures. Finally, the third new sentence also introduces two scientifically correct concepts related to "pressure in the magma chamber" and how this pressure can cause "the magma [to] erupt and a volcano [to be] formed."

Given the degree of scientific accuracy introduced in this essay revision, we analyzed the screen capture data collected during essay revision to address the potential concern of low-level copy-and-paste activities and potential plagiarism. That is, we wanted to know whether the quality of the revisions was attributable to direct lifting of content from the consulted resources. The video evidence shows the student first deleting the original two sentences, and then alternating between reading a CLICK-recommended resource from the Public Broadcasting Service (Svitil, n.d.) and writing the new sentences from scratch. The video of student activities while making these revisions does not show a single occurrence of copy-and-paste operations from the resource. We also identified the sentences from this resource that most closely related to the student's essay edits and compared them to the sentences generated by the student. Comparison of the sentences on volcano creation from the PBS resource and the student's revised essay shows that the three sentences generated by the student are not taken directly from the resource. Rather, the student works with the resource to paraphrase and summarize parts of the original resource content. Nevertheless, a fully implemented essay-writing tutor using CLICK would be well advised to implement some or all of the cheat prevention techniques used by other writing tutors (e.g., Wade-Stein & Kintsch, 2004).

On the revision questionnaire, the student hypothesized that this sentence was targeted by CLICK because it was too vague. The student goes on to explain that she or he used digital resources to find more detail about "how the magma is created and what causes the volcano to form." Thus, the student spontaneously went beyond a broad characterization of learning strategies and offered a content-focused explanation of his or her knowledge revision activities. Further, the strength of the student's revisions makes it likely that the student has deeply engaged with relevant content in the recommended resources. When the student is guided to appropriate, conceptually related resources, learning strategies may be more likely to result in deep and coherent knowledge development.

In summary, analysis of the sentence-editing operations for the student in the control condition indicates that the student made limited improvements with the introduction of only one correct concept: Heat causes lava formation. However, the student failed to make connections between this new concept and his or her prior understanding as evidenced by persistent misunderstandings in the essay related to the process of volcano formation. The presence of only minor essay changes may indicate that this student had difficulty identifying the flaws in his or her understanding of the process of volcano formation, pointing to a lack of support for metacognitive monitoring.

Conversely, the student in the experimental condition engaged in more complex sentence transformations that reflect a significant change in the student's conceptual knowledge about the process of volcano formation. In this case, the student advances from an incomplete and flawed model that included erroneous connections between plate divergence and volcano formation to a more complete and coherent description of the underlying geological processes. To accomplish this transformation, the student discarded the two original sentences and replaced them with three new sentences that provided a scientifically accurate description of the geological processes of volcano formation. Our analyses of student behaviors using screen capture show that these sentences were not directly copied from the digital resources that were consulted. The student summarized new knowledge and integrated new information with previous ideas. The strength of these revisions likely indicates deeper processing of the digital library resources, and suggests that the student was engaged in effective metacognitive monitoring while using CLICK support. The student also introduces correct scientific terminology (i.e., subduction and magma chambers) to revise and enrich the original description of what causes magma to rise to the surface. This new description of volcano formation provides very specific details about the relevant geological processes that significantly extend and enrich the student's initial, simplistic understanding that magma rising up in the Earth forms volcanoes.

It should be noted that these students were selected for analysis based only on the similarity of sentence content in a CLICK-targeted knowledge problem. These two students provide a convenient—and easily comparable—case study of student learning activities that also fit the observed pattern of behaviors of students in each condition. However, we are currently conducting a larger scale analysis to assess the quality of essay revisions in each experimental condition when considering a larger sample of students. Together, the quantitative and qualitative findings presented here provide an initial—and promising—assessment of the effects of personalized, conceptually relevant learning recommendations on student knowledge development.

GENERALIZABLE LEARNING TECHNOLOGY INFRASTRUCTURE

CLICK's service-oriented architecture provides important advantages over typical intelligent tutoring applications. Typical intelligent tutoring systems (e.g., AutoTutor; see Graesser et al., 2004) may best be characterized as architecturally closed systems that target a specific application interaction, thus limiting the generalizability and transferability of their approach. Even though several of these tutoring systems, such as Practical Algebra Tutor (Koedinger et al., 1997), Cognitive Tutor (Ritter, Anderson, Koedinger, & Corbett, 2007), and AutoTutor (Graesser et al., 2004; see also Graesser, Lin, & D'Mello, this volume, chap. 10), have shown impressive learning results in large classroom deployments, these systems may face significant challenges integrating their capabilities into third-party applications due to their application-centric architectures. In contrast, service-oriented architectures encapsulate useful functionality as external computational components that may be integrated into a variety of end-user applications. Educational Web services, such as CLICK, accordingly provide a rich set of capabilities useful for the development of a wide range of online educational-technology applications. CLICK's personalization capabilities are deployed within a service-oriented paradigm that supports seamless integration into various (even unforeseen) Web-based pedagogical applications. For example, CLICK can support an interactive concept-mapping tool, a presentation builder, or a collaborative science research report tool. Application developers can leverage the representational and computational capabilities of CLICK to seamlessly introduce personalization capabilities into their learning environments, while maintaining control over how learners ultimately interact with the learning task of interest.

Embedding CLICK Capabilities in New Learning Technologies

Figure 14.6 depicts an example of an online collaborative science research and writing environment that has been developed to support students in researching and writing reports on the science that underpins news on natural disasters, called SciNews Online (de la Chica, 2007).

SciNews Online uses CLICK's ability to generate a domain knowledge map from Web resources to produce a conceptual knowledge map, shown in the Explore tab of the application. The map represents the connections between important concepts found in Web sites that the learners have selected as references for their report. These reference resources are shown under the "My References" heading in Figure 14.6. Learners can further explore important science concepts depicted in the knowledge map, view the contents of their references using the Read tab, write their explanations using the Write tab, and initiate feedback requests on the content of their reports using the Check tab. The Check function of SciNews Online leverages the diagnostic and personalization capabilities of CLICK to identify problematic statements in the student reports and to provide a customized list

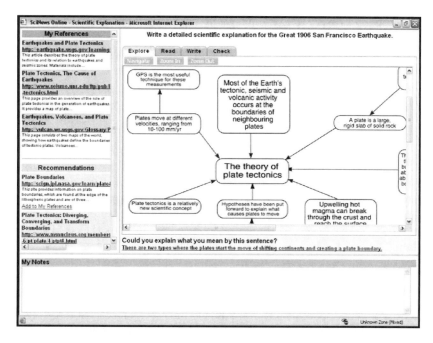

Figure 14.6   SciNews Online, a Click-based application for collaborative Web reports on the science behind the news on natural disasters.

of recommended digital learning resources related to the Great 1906 San Francisco Earthquake.

Extending CLICK to Multimedia Representations

CLICK has the potential to leverage multiple representations during remediation, with the use of the domain knowledge map providing a clear way to use visual representations of conceptual knowledge to support remediation. CLICK could select fragments of the domain knowledge map to present to the learner that align with erroneous or problematic statements. Such feedback would enable pedagogical interactions that encourage learners to perform visual comparisons between their conceptions and the scientifically correct domain knowledge. Such comparisons constitute a form of monitoring understanding about the topic, and represent a potentially useful way to support student engagement with science content. Previous research has shown that knowledge map representations can serve as a meaningful context for computer-supported collaborative learning (e.g., Suthers, Vatrapu, Medina, Joseph, & Dwyer, 2007) as well as individual searches for learning resources (Butcher, Bhushan, & Sumner, 2006). Butcher et al. (2006) found that a knowledge-map search interface prompted students to engage more deeply with science content as they searched for relevant learning resources in a digital library.

As described earlier, CLICK internally represents both domain and learner knowledge as knowledge maps that are directly readable and can also be used to extract compact visual knowledge representations. Selected pieces of CLICK knowledge representations could be used to support a variety of pedagogical interactions. For example, problematic portions of the students' knowledge map could be made directly editable. Students could represent their changing ideas by adding content nodes or changing the connections between nodes. This graphical knowledge map editing could be used to support reasoning about the domain knowledge map. Learners who directly compare their own knowledge map with that of an ideal understanding may develop a deeper understanding of knowledge organization in a domain. Moreover, the ability to support student learning activities using multiple representations (e.g., text and knowledge maps) may better match the expectations of students, who expect technology to be used in meaningful ways and to present opportunities for interactive learning experiences (Hanson & Carlson, 2005).

CONCLUSIONS AND FUTURE DIRECTIONS

CLICK is designed for scalability, minimizing the potential costs of targeting new domain knowledge and facilitating large deployments for highly diverse learner populations. CLICK obviates the need for expensive human-directed knowledge-engineering efforts typically associated with personalized educational-technology research efforts (Ritter, Anderson, Cytrynowicz, & Medvedeva, 1998; Susarla, Adcock, Van Eck, Moreno, & Graesser, 2003), although it should be noted that CLICK targets conceptual knowledge development rather than the problem-solving skills that are often trained by intelligent tutoring systems. To this end, CLICK automatically generates both domain and learner knowledge maps and uses linguistic and graph analysis techniques to identify areas for improvement in learner essays. Furthermore, CLICK does not target specific erroneous or incomplete scientific conceptions, rather focusing on three broad groups of conceptual deficiencies, namely, incorrect statements, incomplete understanding, and knowledge integration issues. As a result, CLICK does not require ongoing updates either to keep up with evolving science or to maintain comprehensive lists of issues to target for specific learner populations during the diagnosis of learner understanding. These automatic domain knowledge model generation and generic student knowledge diagnostic algorithms make CLICK a highly scalable technology infrastructure in design and purpose with a high potential for generalizing to a variety of domains and learning contexts.

Our initial results demonstrate that CLICK's personalized, conceptual support promotes students' diagnosis of their current understanding, and encourages learning processes and strategies associated with increased metacognitive monitoring and knowledge integration. Detailed, qualitative analysis of student essays suggests potential for CLICK to support deep integration of science content with prior domain ideas, without disrupting the acquisition of general, factual knowledge.

Effective support of generalization of learning will require that CLICK becomes increasingly adept at prioritizing conceptual knowledge deficiencies for remediation. To efficiently support conceptual knowledge development, CLICK will need to identify effective processes to distinguish between critical and supporting concepts in a domain. Pedagogical interactions targeting those critical, core concepts may need to be ordered—when a student's knowledge problems include multiple, overlapping concepts, remediation may need to begin with the concepts upon which the other ideas build. As we saw in the example from Figure 14.5, students also can develop new errors during knowledge development. Iterative cycles of feedback may catch errors that can be introduced as students deepen and enrich their domain understanding. Developing mechanisms to deal with these knowledge dependencies represents a significant pedagogical, and computational, challenge.

CLICK also may support generalization of learning by developing techniques to strategically vary the format of the resources that it suggests for knowledge remediation. When sufficiently diverse educational resources are available, it may be useful to select resources that target the same conceptual knowledge using a variety of formats and activities. For example, CLICK may select a textual resource, a multimedia presentation, and an interactive simulation that target a particular knowledge deficit. Selection of diverse resources may provide additional opportunities to generalize knowledge across learning contexts, and also may offer additional advantages in terms of increased learner engagement and time on task.

Overall, educational technologies that leverage personalized, conceptual assessment and remediation have significant potential to change the nature of instructional interventions. Although significant challenges remain, CLICK demonstrates the potential of these systems to promote deep understanding and effective student approaches to learning.

APPENDIX

This appendix contains the list of adapted content-free prompts adapted from Chi et al. (2001) and used in the design and implementation of CLICK. Text in **bold** is revised compared to Chi et al. (2001).

Incorrect Statements

Could you explain the concept **you discussed in this sentence**?
Could you explain what you mean by **that sentence**?
Could you restate what you **wrote in that sentence**?
Why don't you explain this sentence again?
What makes you say that/think so?

Incomplete Understanding

Partial Description of Concept or Process	Missing Core Domain Concept
Anything else you can tell me about **this concept**?	Could you explain the concept **discussed in this sentence**?
Could you explain what you mean by **that sentence**?	Please explain what this **concept** says.
Could you elaborate on what you **said in that sentence**?	What does this **concept** tell us?
Could you be a little bit more specific **about this concept**?	Could you explain/put this **concept** in your own words?
Could you clarify what you **wrote in this sentence**?	What's the main point of this **concept**?

Knowledge Integration

Is there something else you want to tell me **about these concepts**?

Could you connect what you **wrote in these sentences**?

How are these two concepts related?

ACKNOWLEDGMENTS

This work was funded in part by National Science Foundation through NSF Award No. IIS/ALT 0537194. The opinions, findings and conclusions, and recommendations expressed in this material are those of the author(s) and do not necessarily reflect the views of the National Science Foundation.

The authors thank Holly Devaul for her advice on issues of domain accuracy and her assistance in developing domain-relevant assessments. We thank Faisal Ahmad and Qianyi Gu for important contributions to the development of the CLICK service and the research interface. We also thank Marguerite Roy, Robert Hausmann, and Donna Caccamise for helpful comments on earlier versions of this manuscript.

REFERENCES

Ainsworth, S., & Loizou, A. T. (2003). The effects of self-explaining when learning with text or diagrams. *Cognitive Science, 27,* 669–681.

Barnett, S. M., & Ceci, S. J. (2002). When and where do we apply what we learn? A taxonomy for far transfer. *Psychological Bulletin, 128,* 612–637.

Britt, M. A., & Gabrys, G. (2002). Implications of document-level literacy skills for Web site design. *Behavior Research Methods, Instruments, & Computers, 34,* 170–176.

Butcher, K., Bhushan, S., & Sumner, T. (2006). Multimedia displays for conceptual search processes: Information seeking with strand maps. *ACM Multimedia Systems Journal, 11,* 236–248.

Butcher, K., de la Chica, S., Ahmad, F., Gu, Q., Sumner, T., & Martin, J. H. (2009). Conceptual customization for learning with multimedia: Developing individual instructional experiences to support science understanding. In R. Zheng (Ed.), *Cognitive effects of multimedia learning* (pp. 260–287). Hershey, PA: IGI Global.

Butcher, K. R. (2006). Learning from text with diagrams: Promoting mental model development and inference generation. *Journal of Educational Psychology, 98*, 182–197.

Byrt, T., Bishop, J., & Carlin, J. B. (1993). Bias, prevalence, and kappa. *Journal of Clinical Epidemiology, 46*, 423–429.

Carey, S. (1991). Knowledge acquisition: Enrichment or conceptual change? In S. Carey & R. Gelman (Eds.), *The epigenesis of mind: Essays on biology and cognition*. Hillsdale, NJ: Lawrence Erlbaum.

Chi, M. T., Bassok, M., Lewis, M. W., Reimann, P., & Glaser, R. (1989). Self-explanations: How students study and use examples in learning to solve problems. *Cognitive Science, 13*, 145–182.

Chi, M. T., de Leeuw, N., Chiu, M.-H., & LaVancher, C. (1994). Eliciting self-explanations improves understanding. *Cognitive Science, 18*, 439–477.

Chi, M. T., Feltovich, P. J., & Glaser, R. (1981). Categorization and representation of physics problems by experts and novices. *Cognitive Science, 5*, 121–152.

Chi, M. T. H. (2008). Three types of conceptual change: Belief revision, mental model transformation, and categorical shift. In S. Vosniadou (Ed.), *International handbook of research on conceptual change* (pp. 61–82). Hillsdale, NJ: Lawrence Erlbaum.

Chi, M. T. H., Siler, S. A., Jeong, H., Yamauchi, T., & Hausmann, R. G. (2001). Learning from human tutoring. *Cognitive Science, 25*, 471–533.

Corbett, A. T., McLaughlin, M., & Scarpinatto, K. C. (2000). Modeling student knowledge: Cognitive tutors in high school and college. *User Modeling and User-adapted Interaction, 10*, 81–108.

de la Chica, S. (2007). *SciNews Online: Scaffolding the construction of scientific explanations.* Paper presented at the 2007 SIGCHI Conference on Human Factors in Computing Systems, Extended Abstracts—ACM Student Research Competition, San Jose, California.

de la Chica, S., Ahmad, F., Sumner, T., Martin, J. H., & Butcher, K. (2008). Computational foundations for personalizing instruction with digital libraries. *International Journal of Digital Libraries, 9*(1), 3–18. (Special Issue on Digital Libraries and Education)

Digital Library for Earth System Education (DLESE). (N.d.). [Home page]. Retrieved November 17, 2009, from http://www.dlese.org

Goldstone, R. L., & Son, J. Y. (2005). The transfer of scientific principles using concrete and idealized simulations. *Journal of the Learning Sciences, 14*, 69–110.

Graesser, A. C., Lu, S., Jackson, G. T., Mitchell, H. H., Ventura, M., Olney, A., et al. (2004). AutoTutor: A tutor with dialogue in natural language. *Behavior Research Methods, Instruments, & Computers, 36*, 180–192.

Graesser, A. C., Person, N. K., Harter, D., & the Tutoring Research Group. (2001). Teaching tactics and dialogue in AutoTutor. *International Journal of Artificial Intelligence and Education, 12*, 257–279.

Graesser, A. C., Singer, M., & Trabasso, T. (1994). Constructing inferences during narrative text comprehension. *Psychological Review, 101*, 371–395.

Griffin, T. D., Wiley, J., & Thiede, K. W. (2008). Individual differences, rereading, and self-explanation: Concurrent processing and cue validity as constraints on metacomprehension accuracy. *Memory & Cognition, 36*, 93–103.

Halpern, D. F. (1998). Teaching critical thinking for transfer across domains. *American Psychologist, 53*, 449–455.

Hanson, K., & Carlson, B. (2005). *Effective access: Teachers' use of digital resources in STEM teaching*. Retrieved November 15, 2007, from http://www2.edc.org/gdi/publications_SR/EffectiveAccessReport.pdf

Hegarty, M. (1992). Mental animation: Inferring motion from static displays of mechanical systems. *Journal of Experimental Psychology: Learning, Memory, and Cognition, 18*, 1084–1102.

Hegarty, M., & Just, M. A. (1993). Constructing mental models of machines from text and diagrams. *Journal of Memory and Language, 32*, 717–742.

Hilgard, E. R., Irvine, R. P., & Whipple, J. E. (1953). Rote memorization, understanding, and transfer: An extension of Katona's card-trick experiments. *Journal of Experimental Psychology, 46*, 288–292.

Johnson, H. M., & Seifert, C. M. (1994). Sources of the continued influence effect: When misinformation in memory affects later inferences. *Journal of Experimental Psychology: Learning, Memory, and Cognition, 20*, 1420–1436.

Johnson-Laird, P. N. (1983). *Mental models*. Cambridge, MA: Harvard University Press.

Kelley, J. F. (1983, December 12–15). *An empirical methodology for writing user-friendly natural language computer applications*. Paper presented at the 1983 SIGCHI Conference on Human Factors in Computing Systems, Boston, MA.

Kintsch, W. (1988). The role of knowledge in discourse comprehension: A construction-integration model. *Psychological Review, 95*, 163–182.

Kintsch, W. (1998). *Comprehension: A paradigm for cognition*. Cambridge: Cambridge University Press.

Koedinger, K. R., Aleven, V., Heffernan, N., McLaren, B. M., & Hockenberry, M. (2004). Opening the door to non-programmers: Authoring intelligent tutor behavior by demonstration. In J. C. Lester, R. M. Vicari & F. Paraguaçu (Eds.), *Proceedings of the 7th annual Intelligent Tutoring Systems Conference* (pp. 162–174). Berlin: Springer-Verlag.

Koedinger, K. R., Anderson, J. R., Hadley, W. H., & Mark, M. A. (1997). Intelligent tutoring goes to school in the big city. *International Journal of Artificial Intelligence in Education, 8*, 30–43.

Kozma, R. (2003). The material features of multiple representations and their cognitive and social affordances for science understanding. *Learning and Instruction, 13*, 205–226.

Landauer, T. K., & Dumais, S. T. (1997). A solution to Plato's problem: The latent semantic analysis theory of acquisition, induction and representation of knowledge. *Psychological Review, 104*, 211–240.

Lin, L.-M., & Zabrucky, K. M. (1998). Calibration of comprehension: Research and implications for education and instruction. *Contemporary Educational Psychology, 23*, 345–391.

Lowe, R. K. (1993). Constructing a mental representation from an abstract technical diagram. *Learning & Instruction, 3*, 157–179.

Marchionini, G. (1995). *Information seeking in electronic environments*. Cambridge: Cambridge University Press.

Mayer, R. E. (2001). *Multimedia Learning*. New York: Cambridge University Press.

Mayer, R. E., Bove, W., Bryman, A., Mars, R., & Tapangco, L. (1996). When less is more: Meaningful learning from visual and verbal summaries of science textbook lessons. *Journal of Educational Psychology, 88*, 64–73.

McKoon, G., & Ratcliff, R. (1992). Inference during reading. *Psychological Review, 99*, 440–466.

McNamara, D. S., Kintsch, E., Songer, N. B., & Kintsch, W. (1996). Are good texts always better? Interactions of text coherence, background knowledge, and levels of understanding in learning from text. *Cognition & Instruction, 14*, 1–43.

Nelson, T. O., Dunlosky, J., Graf, A., & Narens, L. (1994). Utilization of metacognitive judgments in the allocation of study during multitrial learning. *Psychological Science, 5*, 207–213.

O'Donnell, A. M., Dansereau, D. F., & Hall, R. H. (2002). Knowledge maps as scaffolds for cognitive processing. *Educational Psychology Review, 14*, 71–86.

Olander, H. (1941). Children's knowledge of the flag salute. *Journal of Educational Research, 35*, 300–305.

Rawson, K. A., Dunlosky, J., & Thiede, K. W. (2000). The rereading effect: Metacomprehension accuracy improves across reading trials. *Memory & Cognition, 28*, 1004–1010.

Ritter, S., Anderson, J., Cytrynowicz, M., & Medvedeva, O. (1998). Authoring content in the PAT Algebra Tutor. *Journal of Interactive Media in Education, 98*, Article 9. Retrieved May 31, 2008, from http://www-jime.open.ac.uk/98/9/

Ritter, S., Anderson, J. R., Koedinger, K. R., & Corbett, A. T. (2007). Cognitive tutor: Applied research in mathematics education. *Psychonomic Bulletin & Review, 14*, 249–255.

Royer, J. M., Carlo, M. S., Dufresne, R., & Mestre, J. (1996). The assessment of levels of domain expertise while reading. *Cognition and Instruction, 14*, 373–408.

Salton, G., & Lesk, M. E. (1968). Computer evaluation of indexing and text processing. *Journal of the ACM, 15*, 8–36.

Schnotz, W., & Bannert, M. (2003). Construction and interference in learning from multiple representation. *Learning & Instruction, 13*, 141–156.

Susarla, S. C., Adcock, A., Van Eck, R., Moreno, K., & Graesser, A. (2003, July 20–24). *Development and evaluation of a lesson authoring tool for AutoTutor.* Paper presented at the 11th International Conference on Artificial Intelligence in Education, Sydney, Australia.

Suthers, D. D., Vatrapu, R., Medina, R., Joseph, S., & Dwyer, N. (2007). Conceptual representations enhance knowledge construction in asynchronous collaboration. In C. Chinn, G. Erkens, & S. Puntambekar (Eds.), *The Computer Supported Collaborative Learning (CSCL) Conference 2007* (pp. 704–713). New Brunswick, NJ: International Society of the Learning Sciences.

Svitil, K. (N.d.). *Mountains of fire.* PBS Online. Retrieved November 18, 2009, from http://www.thirteen.org/savageearth/volcanoes

Thiede, K. W. (1999). The importance of monitoring and self-regulation during multitrial learning. *Psychonomic Bulletin & Review, 6*, 662–667.

Thiede, K. W., Anderson, M. C., & Therriault, D. (2003). Accuracy of metacognitive monitoring affects learning of texts. *Journal of Educational Psychology, 95*, 66–73.

Thiede, K. W., & Dunlosky, J. (1994). Delaying students' metacognitive monitoring improves their accuracy in predicting their recognition performance. *Journal of Educational Psychology, 86*, 290–302.

van Dijk, T. A., & Kintsch, W. (1983). *Strategies of discourse comprehension.* New York: Academic Press.

VanLehn, K., Lynch, C., Schulze, K., Shapiro, J. A., Shelby, R., Taylor, L., et al. (2005). The Andes physics tutoring system: Lessons learned. *International Journal of Artificial Intelligence and Education, 15*, 147–204.

van Rijsbergen, C. J. (1979). *Information retrieval* (2nd ed.). Glasgow: Department of Computer Science, University of Glasgow.

Wade-Stein, D., & Kintsch, E. (2004). Summary Street: Interactive computer support for writing. *Cognition and Instruction, 22*, 333–362.

Weatherley, J. (2005, June 7–11). A Web service framework for embedding discovery services in distributed library interfaces. Paper presented at the 5th ACM/IEEE-CS Joint Conference on Digital Libraries, Denver, CO.

Wiley, J., & Voss, J. F. (1999). Constructing arguments from multiple sources: Tasks that promote understanding and not just memory for text. *Journal of Educational Psychology, 91,* 1–11.

Wolfe, M. B. W., Schreiner, M. E., Rehder, B., Laham, D., Foltz, P. W., Kintsch, W., et al. (1998). Learning from text: Matching readers and texts by latent semantic analysis. *Discourse Processes, 25,* 309–336.

15

Beyond Human–Computer Interaction
Metadesign in Support of Human Problem–Domain Interaction

STEFAN PARRY CARMIEN and GERHARD FISCHER

INTRODUCTION

The history of interactions between computational machinery and humans has been one of increasing specificity, from the complete generality of machine languages to specialized domain-oriented design environments. However, as designers, we need to balance the ease of use of specific tools with the flexibility and scope of general ones. Our research over the last 2 decades has been focused on creating sociotechnical environments to empower human beings as designers and users of computational artifacts. This chapter explores the issues involved with creating environments that broadly support domain activities yet are open enough to accommodate changing user and task needs.

The development of computational environments has been driven by the fundamental design trade-off between generality and specificity. In this context, *generality* and *specificity* refer to an axis of plasticity in the composition of computationally based tools intended for end users (in contrast to tools intended for professional programmers). On one end of the continuum, there is assembly and machine language, the basic instruction set for instructing a computer with which everything is possible but the expertise needed to use them is reserved for systems programmers, high-tech scribes. At the other end are computer devices and systems that are specifically designed to do one thing; ATM machines are good examples, as are modern elevator controls. These systems are easy to use and efficient in supporting the user's desires (e.g., getting 100 euros from an ATM, or going to the 13th floor) by supporting the demands of specific tasks. Generality seems to be a highly desirable goal because the same tool could be used in many different contexts; however, being broadly applicable for all kinds of users and all kinds of tasks comes with a substantial cost that can be characterized by the Turing tar pit (Perlis, 1982): "Beware of the Turing Tar Pit, in which everything is possible, but nothing of interest is easy."

These environments are based on a level of representation that is too far removed from the conceptual world of the knowledge workers in specific domains. They emphasize *objective computability* (i.e., what can be computed in principle), but they pay little attention to *subjective computability* (i.e., what people can do with a reasonable amount of effort and with limited detailed knowledge about the computational environment).

The other end of the design spectrum can be characterized by the *inverse of the Turing tar pit*: "Beware of the overspecialized systems, where operations are easy, but little of interest is possible." These systems can be so fitted to the tasks they are designed for that doing anything besides the exact task in the specific way it is tailored for is difficult or impossible. Modifying these systems to do things differently than the way provided leads to frustration or abandonment.

In our research over the last 2 decades, we have explored different approaches to create more usable, useful, effective, and enjoyable human-centered computational environments (Norman, 1993) with the following research activities and developments:

- Creating a deeper understanding of design and its support with *domain-oriented design environments* (Fischer, 1994).
- Advancing human–computer interaction (HCI) to *human–problem domain interaction* (Fischer & Lemke, 1988).
- Supporting not only reflective practitioners (Schön, 1983) but also *reflective communities* (Fischer, 2005); reflective practitioners engage in reflection-in-action, meaning reflection that is triggered by breakdowns that occur in the action mode of design. *Domain-oriented design environments* support reflection-in-action with critics (to interrupt action and notify the designer of a possible breakdown) and argumentation (to support reflection). Supporting reflective practitioners is important, but it is not enough. Complex design problems need *reflective communities* because they require more knowledge than any single person possesses and the knowledge relevant to a problem is usually distributed among stakeholders.
- Exploring *metadesign* as "design for designers" (Carmien & Fischer, 2008).

In this chapter we analyze these developments from the perspective of the design trade-offs between *domain specific* and *domain general*. This differentiation can be applied to the computational environments constructed and to the knowledge background of the people using these environments. We will be discussing two specific applications: (a) a sociotechnical environment supporting and empowering people with cognitive disabilities, and (b) an educational framework illustrating that the principles applied to the design of computational systems can be successfully applied to the design of social systems. A social system can be considered as a web of interrelated communications that support the unity, the existence, and the evolution of the system (Luhmann, 1996). We will conclude by presenting several possible lessons learned and challenges ahead that our research and projects have illuminated.

FROM HUMAN–COMPUTER INTERACTION TO HUMAN PROBLEM–DOMAIN INTERACTION

When computer systems first emerged, users were required to express themselves in the machine language of that system. These languages were completely general: Their semantics were not tied to any specific problem domain. The conceptual distance for a human (working in a certain domain) who wanted to model a problem was very large, as indicated in Figure 15.1.

The first fundamental development was the creation of assembly languages and high-level programming languages, as indicated in Figure 15.2. These developments still retained the generality, but they facilitated and supported specific domain-oriented operations (high-level computer languages such as APL, LISP, and Smalltalk were designed to make certain abstractions easier to implement and manipulate; APL was focused on matrices, LISP on dynamic data structures and recursion, and Smalltalk on object-oriented programming). At the same time, these developments led to a division of labor (Levy & Murnane, 2004): Compiler developers emerged as a new class of computer professionals that developed compilers, thereby allowing most of the professional programmers to program in higher level languages.

The initial developments (moving from the architecture in Figure 15.1 to Figure 15.2) represented the beginning of creating computational environments to support users engaged in specific domains. In the history of computers and computer languages, the concept of *domain* has always been an important dimension, albeit most often an implicit one. In this chapter, *domain* indicates a grouped set of human actions in the world that are together aimed at a common goal: The domain of kitchen design consists of all the design activities that lead to the plan (and implementation) of a kitchen; and, similarly, the domain of supporting activities of daily living (ADLs) by persons with cognitive disabilities consists of persons with cognitive disabilities, caregivers, and the artifacts that aid them in this process. Domains have specific (and bounded) areas of interest and expertise. The names of early high-level programming languages such as COBOL and FORTRAN reveal their focus on specific domains: (a) COBOL is an acronym for Common Business-Oriented Language, defining its primary domain in business, finance,

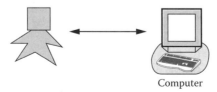

Computer

Figure 15.1   Programming—in the very early days.

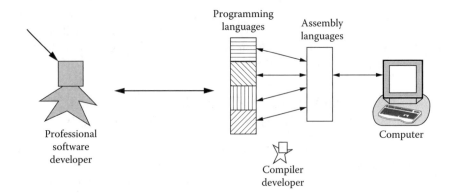

Figure 15.2 Support for human-computer interaction with high-level programming languages.

and administrative systems for companies and governments; and (b) FORTRAN, derived from the phrase "The IBM Mathematical *For*mula *Trans*lating System," was designed with features especially suited to numeric computation and scientific computing.

Our research objectives to support not just human–computer interaction but also *human–problem domain interaction* (Fischer & Lemke, 1988) extended the architectures of Figure 15.2 further by introducing *domain-oriented design environments* (see Figure 15.3). Domain-oriented design environments are both human centered and domain oriented; their domain orientation is a result of embedding accumulated metaknowledge about the task into the design environment. An example of this in a kitchen design system might be the rule that windows should not be located over kitchen ranges, or that the spatial relationship between the work centers should stay within certain ranges to facilitate smooth workflow in the kitchen. These developments were driven by the objective that if the most important role for computation is to provide people with a powerful

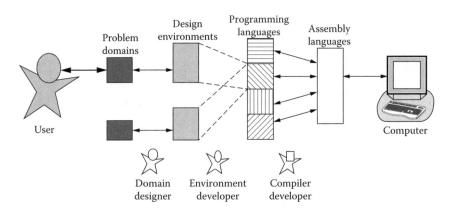

Figure 15.3 Layered architecture in support of human problem–domain interaction.

medium for expression, then the medium should support them in working on the task, rather than require them to focus their intellectual resources on the medium itself. When users suffer from a *tool mastery burden*, their tasks fade to the background because most of their efforts are put toward mastering the tool. To bring tasks to the forefront, computers must become "invisible" (Norman, 1998) and disappear into the background.

The shift from human–computer interaction to human–problem domain interaction is a movement toward putting users, the owners of problems, in charge. As long as users must interact with the computer rather than the problem domain, they are not in charge of their problems, and must instead rely on computer specialists. In analogy to writing and its historical development, a major goal of HCI should be "to take the control of computational media out of the hands of high-tech scribes."

Domain orientation requires the existence of specialized features in the design environment that support the specifics of the particular domain for which it was created. Examples of specific domains that we have explored in our research are as follows:

- Kitchen design supporting professional kitchen designers (see Figure 15.4) and empowering them to create new design (in the "Work Area") by engaging in (a) design by composition (using domain-oriented parts from the "Appliance Palette"—see the upper-left section of Figure 15.4), and (b) design by modification (modifying existing designs contained in the "Catalog"—see the lower-left section of Figure 15.4) (Fischer, 1994).

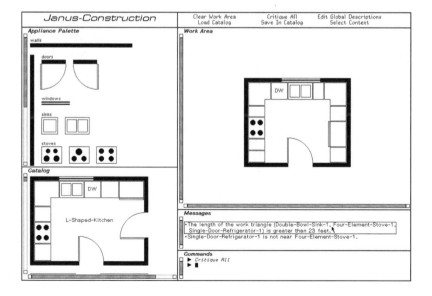

Figure 15.4   A domain-oriented design environment for kitchen design.

- Construction and use of multimedia scripts to support task accomplishment by persons with cognitive disabilities. The Memory Aiding Prompting System (MAPS) system (Carmien, 2007) helped caregivers provide appropriately configured instructions to young adults with cognitive disabilities.

These domain-oriented design environments provided extensive support for certain problem contexts but created the fundamental problem of how their users (being knowledge workers in the domain rather than computer programmers) could extend the systems to fit unanticipated new requirements and tasks. End-user development and end-user modification were required to find effective mixes between domain-specific support and generality (Eisenberg & Fischer, 1994; Myers, Ko, & Burnett, 2006).

The next section will describe a research project in the area of *design for all*, an approach to design that emphasizes usability for as many differently abled people as possible, in contrast to requiring add-on adaptations, often described as *universal design*; in this case, it is to create environments to support and empower people with cognitive disabilities. The discussion will explore how new mixes between specificity and generality can be supported.

SOCIOTECHNICAL ENVIRONMENTS FOR PEOPLE WITH COGNITIVE DISABILITIES: FACING THE CHALLENGE OF A *"UNIVERSE OF ONE"*

In evaluating the impact and utility of a computationally supported tool in use, it is necessary to look at the artifact, the user(s), and the interaction between them, particular the changes caused and required in work practice by the adoption of such systems. One way of doing this is to study the system from the perspective of sociotechnical systems (Mumford, 1987). Sociotechnical systems have both technical and human-social aspects that are tightly bound and interconnected. Sociotechnical design is an approach to complex organizational work design that recognizes the interaction between people and technology in workplaces.

People with cognitive disabilities represent a "universe of one" problem (Carmien & Fischer, 2008). Persons with cognitive disabilities often will have several different disabilities, and each specific combination of cognitive, motoric, sensory and psychological impairments together defines a need for deeply customized assistive technology such that a solution for one person will rarely work for another. The "universe of one" conceptualization includes the empirical finding that (a) *unexpected islands of abilities* exist: Clients can have unexpected skills and abilities that can be leveraged to ensure a better possibility of task accomplishment; and (b) *unexpected deficits of abilities* exist (Cole, 2006). Unexpected missing abilities often occur in otherwise high-functioning individuals. Accessing and addressing these unexpected variations in skills and needs, particularly with respect to creating task support, require an intimate knowledge of the client that *only caregivers* can provide. Compounding this problem is the fact that currently a substantial portion of all assistive technology is abandoned after initial purchase and use—as high as 70% in some cases (Martin & McCormack, 1999; Reimer-Reiss, 2000). This fact results in the consequence that the very population that could most benefit from technology is paying for expensive devices that end up in the back of closets after a short time.

The fundamental challenge derived from supporting the "universe of one" requirement is that it requires highly specific systems—so how can we achieve generalization? Our answer to this challenge is a design methodology based on metadesign.

Metadesign

Metadesign, or "design for designers" (Fischer & Giaccardi, 2006), is grounded in the basic assumption that future uses and problems cannot be completely anticipated at design time, when a system is developed (Suchman, 1987). It is an emerging conceptual framework aimed at defining and creating social and technical infrastructures in which new forms of collaborative design can take place.

The rationale to apply metadesign to address the universe of one was identified by analyzing the Visions System (Baesman & Baesman, 2003), which assisted people with cognitive disabilities by supporting task completion using a PC and touch screens located in the residence of a client with cognitive disabilities. Although the Visions System was effective in supporting tasks that were anticipated by the designers, it was often abandoned because caregivers were not provided with the tool appropriate to their limited computer-programming ability to personalize the environment to the needs of their clients. The Memory Aiding Prompting System (Carmien, 2006), which will be described in this chapter, eliminated these shortcomings of the Visions System by creating a sociotechnical environment based on a metadesign framework by providing the caregivers the design power to modify and evolve the technical systems according to the needs of individual clients.

Metadesign extends the traditional notion of system design beyond the original development of a system to include the coadaptive processes in which the users become codevelopers or codesigners. It is a design method that can address the need of situatedness to account for changing tasks, defining when and what computer artifacts to embed in daily life and practices. This extension is supported by a metadesign distinction between metadesign tool design time and design time; there are two design processes here. First is the creation of a tool that supports metadesign activity; second, in what would more commonly be called *use time*, is the use of the metadesign tool to create a sociotechnical environment that is more fitting to the domain of use. Codevelopment has the end user involved in the ordinary design process; metadesign supports the end user in a continuous refinement process of designing a tool. Another way to differentiate between the two is to note that one way of talking about metadesign is *design over time* (Carmien, 2007): The design of a codeveloped application ends at some point, and use time of that application ensues, whereas the design time of a metadesigned tool never ends.

Metadesign is the antidote to strong-specific (i.e., deeply focused to a niche in a particular domain) tools becoming unusable due to change. It tries to break new ground between generality and specificity by identifying different objectives for *design time* and *use time* of an environment. In all design processes, these two basic stages can be differentiated. At design time, system developers (with different levels of user involvement) develop environments and tools creating complete systems for a *world-as-imagined*. This world-as-imagined is a result of the systems designers understanding their system in use in specific contexts and doing specific tasks. At use time, users use the system, but because their needs, objectives, and situational contexts could be only broadly anticipated at design time, systems require modification to fit the real needs of users. To accommodate unexpected issues at use time, systems need to be underdesigned (Brand, 1995) by providing a context and a background against which situated cases can be interpreted, thereby allowing the "owners of problems" to create the solutions themselves at use time. By *underdesigned*, we mean that a functional system or building is delivered, but that room is internally provided for the user to tailor it to her precise needs. A common example of underdesigned is the German approach to rented flats. Most often a rented apartment is not provided with a finished kitchen; the designing, purchasing, and installing of it are left to the tenant. Although many might find this an overly onerous burden to moving in (and sometimes the old tenant sells the kitchen to the new tenant in a separate transaction not involving the landlord), it does mean that the boundary between *my* home and a *rental* home becomes blurred.

Memory Aiding Prompting System (MAPS)

The Memory Aiding Prompting System (Carmien, 2006) provides an environment in which caregivers can create scripts that can be used by people with cognitive disabilities ("clients") to support them in carrying out tasks that they would not be able to achieve by themselves. The challenge that MAPS addressed was the need for deep customizing of scripts. Prompting is an established technique used for both learning and performing a task by adults and older children with cognitive disabilities (Snell, 1987). Independent living transition professionals teach ADL performance by prompting the person with cognitive disabilities through a task by verbally instructing him through each step, either with or without instructional cards, until it has been internalized by the promptee, such that he could successfully perform the task unaided. Prompting has been historically part of instructional ADL techniques for persons with cognitive disabilities: being prompted through tasks in a rehearsal mode, and then using the memorized instructions at use time (Aist, 1973; Reed, 1989). Prompting consists of breaking down a task into constituent parts and creating prompts, consisting of pairs of images and verbal instructions, for each step. A prompting script is a sequential set of prompts that when followed perform a task. Special education and rehabilitation studies focus on comparing techniques and creating a principled understanding of prompting techniques with a perspective of maximizing internal recall and the *unaided* performance of the steps to complete a task by persons with cognitive disabilities (Reed, 1989). With the arrival of tools like MAPS, the memorization and decision-making elements of the task could be offloaded to the device and the system that supported it. Prompting studies provide a background for the study and design of computationally based prompting (Lancioni, Van den Hof, Furniss, O'Reilly, & Cunha, 1999; Lynch, 1995).

Key to the production of efficacious task scripts is the appropriate segmentation of the chosen task into subtasks of suitable granularity (Saskatchewan Learning—Special Education Unit, 2003; Snell, 1987). The prompts must be scaled to the cognitive level of the user. For some users, that may be as complex as "Go to the post office and get stamps," whereas for others "Get out two slices from the open bag of bread" may be an optimal segment size. The size of the triggered segment is dependent on the set of existing internal scripts that the prompt can trigger. The smaller the size of the internal scripts, the larger the external prompting script must be. Figure 15.5 illustrates the relations between internal scripts and external scripts in MAPS.

To account for the great diversity among clients, MAPS was developed as a metadesign environment, empowering caregivers to develop personalized prompting systems for the specific needs of individual clients. It is based on a codesign of social and technical systems, and it uses models and concepts that not only focus on the artifact but also exploit the social context in which the systems will be used. For instance, in the field study of MAPS adoption, one of the end users, a teenage girl, used a script made by her mother to allow her to shop at the local supermarket by herself for the first time. In this script the steps and stages of the shopping process, including an explicit photo and voice prompt shopping list, were made by the mother, which she then put on her daughter's PDA using MAPS. Near the end of the script there was a checkout section that included a photo of the checkout clerk that the mother and daughter had been going to for many years. That specific photo anchored both the physical context (i.e., "Go to that checkout line, and get ready for the steps in the checkout/payment process") and social environment (e.g., "Here is the nice lady you have known all these years who will help you, just like with Mom"). Both of these social context triggers and reinforcements made a difference in the actual use of the device, reducing anxiety and directing her to the one checkout person most likely to be sensitive to the special needs of the end user.

The two end users of MAPS were tightly connected. Every young adult with cognitive disabilities had a caregiver, be she family or institutional. MAPS was designed from the beginning to present a script designer interface to the caregiver (who was assumed to be not more than basically skilled with PCs) and a person with cognitive disabilities who would use the system to "play" the scripts

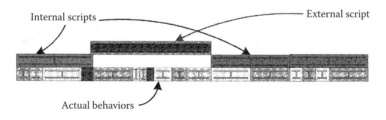

Figure 15.5   Behaviors, internal and external scripts.

in pursuing ADLs. From the perspective of the metadesign tool designer, the end user was one person in two roles, sometimes in the role of a script designer (the caregiver) and sometimes in the role of a script user (the client).

MAPS consists of two major subsystems that share the same fundamental structure but present different *affordances* for the two sets of users (an affordance is an aspect of an object that makes it obvious how the object is to be used, for example buttons or scroll bars in a computer application). One of the attributes of good design is that the affordances presented to the user are intuitively usable. MAPS-DE for caregivers (see Figure 15.6) employs Web-based script and template repositories that allow content to be created and shared by caregivers of different abilities and experiences.

MAPS-PR (see Figure 15.7) for clients provides external scripts that reduce the cognitive demands for the clients by changing the task from learning and remembering what to buy and how to maneuver through the supermarket, picking items, to following the instructions provided by the prompting systems.

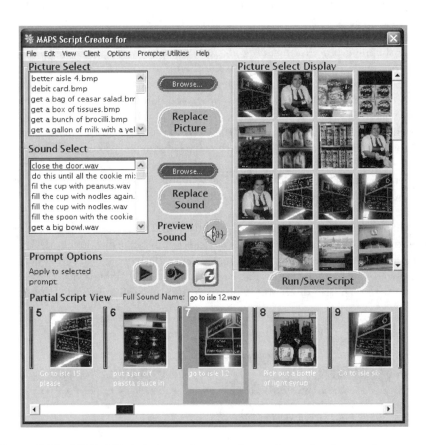

Figure 15.6   MAPS-DE: A design environment for creating scripts by caregivers.

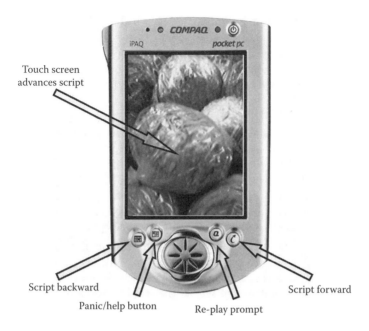

Touch screen
advances script

Script backward   Script forward

Panic/help button   Re-play prompt

Figure 15.7   MAPS-PR: A personal assistant for clients.

The Importance of Representation

Because of the needs and abilities of the end users with cognitive disabilities, abstract representations of the components of goals such as icons are often not effective. Used as indicators to identify specific objects in the world, icons, simplified abstract visual symbols of objects, are not as accurately or as quickly identified with their referent by persons with cognitive disabilities, even those icons that are specifically designed for this purpose. In a test with typical young adults and with young adults with cognitive disabilities, use of actual photos enabled quicker and more accurate identification of the target for those subjects with significant cognitive impairments (Carmien & Wohldmann, 2008). So in designing the MAPS system, the specifications called for support from photos to act as one part of the prompt and specific verbiage recorded by specific voices as the other part. MAPS evaluation collected several illuminating examples of this. In one instance, a prompt for a teenage girl was not recorded by her mom, because of typical teenage power issues. In another, a young adult woman used the prompter system to support employment in a used-clothing store as part of the process of transitioning from high school to employment; to support this transition, the state provided her with a certain amount of assisted employment. Assisted employment meant that she would have a job coach with her for the first several months of employment, guiding her through internalizing the scripts of the tasks that constituted her prospective job. At the end of her job training with the coach, she expressed anxiety on "graduating" to unsupported employment; she was told by her coach that if she needed a hand to hold, her (the job coach's) voice would be with her in the form of the recordings of the prompts. As a result, when supporting caregivers act as multimedia programmers, they had to take into account, on one hand, the need for arbitrary images and sounds to be used and, on the other hand, the need to produce scripts in a particular format.

The need for adaptation of the scripts over time for the young person with cognitive disabilities using the MAPS-PR prompter came from the situated use of the scripts. In some cases, internalized subtasks or the discovery that, for *this* person, certain subtasks needed more support provided a functional requirement that could be satisfied by a metadesign approach. From the perspective of the metadesign tool designer, the end user was a dyad, both generating and consuming scripts. Mediating between these two roles is feedback (or system backtalk) in the form of information about how the script was used in the specific task. This backtalk came in the form of observations by the caregiver and also a log of script use that the MAPS-PR prompter provided at the end of each session. By supplying a tool to the caregivers that supported both script modification (expanding or contracting task support scaffolding) and support script reuse among these user dyads composed of a caregiver and a person with cognitive disabilities, a correct balance between the two tar pits could be navigated. The underlying architecture of MAPS provided local and networked databases of scripts that could be modified to suit current needs and saved so that the original script was still available for use as a template of successful scripts by other dyads (after appropriate anonymization) or to regress to earlier versions of the same script if needed.

A unique challenge of metadesign in the domain of cognitive disabilities is that the clients themselves cannot act as designers, but the caregivers must accept this role. Figure 15.8 illustrates the entire process, from metadesign tool design to its use in the world, with the caregiver creating scripts, the scripts being used by the person with cognitive disabilities, and then the revision and updating of the scripts on the basis of the script's match to the person, task, or environment in use.

Potential Pitfalls and Shortcomings of Domain Orientation

Opponents and critics of domain-oriented approaches have argued that the following problems exist with domain-oriented design approaches:

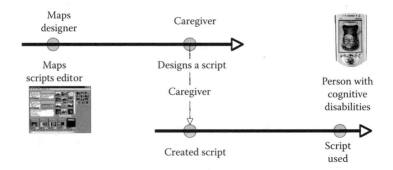

Figure 15.8   Empowering caregivers to act as designers.

1. The lack of a profound theory of what domains are will restrict the development of domain-oriented design environments on ad hoc intuitions about what constitutes a domain.

We argue that domains are not fixed, given entities that should be regarded as well defined and unchanging (Rittel & Webber, 1984). It is one of the foundations of our approach to understand domains as being "constructed" by a design community as opposed to existing in some objective, supergeneral form. This has set our work apart from other approaches such as domain analysis and modeling (Sutcliffe, 2004) and has provided the foundation for a process model (called the *seeding, evolutionary growth, reseeding* [SER] *model*; Fischer & Ostwald, 2002) of how domains and the *domain-oriented design environments* supporting them should evolve over time.

2. Domain specificity poses a major limitation for design productivity; every domain will have to have its own purpose-built environment.

As indicated above, we are aware of the tension and the design trade-off between *the Turing tar pit* and the inverse of it. Referring back to human organizations and domain expertise, our society educates its members in domains, and switching from one domain to another is a nontrivial undertaking. So why should we expect that we will get a new domain-oriented design environment in a different domain for free?

Making a tool domain specific does not necessarily mean shackling its flexibility in that domain. To a large extent the designer can mitigate the error of forcing the user to solve every problem in the domain in the same way, as Tufte (2003) pointed out about PowerPoint users becoming limited in their expressivity. One way to avoid this is to carefully choose the metaphor that the tool is based upon; in the kitchen design environment that metaphor was an architect's desk and stencil templates, and in the case of MAPS it was a sequential filmstrip. In the MAPS case, this was the result of a summer spent making various lo-fi mockups of possible design metaphors and "playing" scenarios with them, a sort of supported cognitive walkthrough (Lewis & Rieman, 1993). Although the filmstrip metaphor was successful, for one of the dyads a further elaboration was needed. For the dyad of the job coach and young woman in assisted employment referred to in the "The Importance of Representation" section, the job coach–student employee pair needed the ability to fork and loop over sets of scripts in order to accommodate the need for "bridging" tasks to give the client support for soft skills. *Soft skills* are the auxiliary, human politeness behaviors that young adults with cognitive disabilities often lack; it is soft skills that more often cause job termination than simple poor job performance. The job coach needed to provide the opportunity for the client to select one of three tasks at use time. The MAPS-PR system was modified to successfully support this (see Figure 15.9); however, it was clear that the lack of time spent in designing the underlying metaphor led to a design that was more constrained (to just this set of tasks) than the more general original MAPS design.

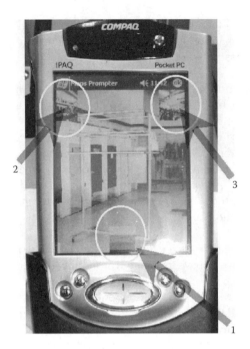

Figure 15.9   MAPS-PR with the optional three-script screen interface.

No one with any concerns for productivity would limit her or his learning efforts and work products to a specific domain if they could be applied more generically. To address this issue, in addition to metadesign we have developed a general-purpose software architecture that can be instantiated for different application domains. This architecture, called the *multifaceted architecture* (Fischer, 1994), provides support to avoid rebuilding domain-oriented design environments from scratch for a new domain, while maintaining the domain-specific orientation and support. Without paying the price of working in a domain, computational environments will be severely limited in the amount of support they can provide, specifically to capture the interest of end users and provide them with control over their tools.

Human-centered design is focused on making the human the focus in the design of technology. Although technology has grown exponentially, internal human capabilities (without taking advantage of external supporting sociotechnical environments) have not fundamentally changed over time (our neurons do not fire faster, and our memory has not increased in capacity). The fundamental challenge to improve human learning, working, and collaboration requires external environments that complement more effective human abilities and knowledge in specific tasks. There are interesting trade-offs between generic systems (providing breadth and generality in the form of superappliances such as Swiss Army knives) and very specific domain-oriented tools (such as the elaborate tool sets used by mechanics) (Buxton, 2002).

The next section will discuss this design trade-off between generality (breadth) and strong-specific (depth) systems in the context of creating innovative educational environments in which the minds of tomorrow are educated.

EDUCATIONAL IMPLICATIONS: HOW DO WE EDUCATE THE "RENAISSANCE SCHOLAR" OF THE 21ST CENTURY?

The smartest people in the world do not generally look very intelligent when you give them a problem that is outside the domain of their vast experience.

—Herbert Simon (1996)

The design principles that we have explored in the preceding sections about computational environments are equally relevant for social design as applied to education and collaboration in groups and communities. There is an ongoing debate in education about how to cope with the design trade-off between *discipline specialization* (depth) versus *general knowledge* (breadth) in a world in which there are too many things to learn and to know. For example, given the constraints on human ability, how can we expect an individual in the context of developing a sociotechnical environment such as MAPS to maintain the requisite specialist knowledge in his or her technological discipline, while at the same time have the needed competence and understanding about people with cognitive disabilities?

The "Renaissance scholar" is not a reasonable model for the 21st century because

> nobody knows who the last Renaissance man really was, but sometime after Leonardo da Vinci it became impossible to learn enough about all the arts and the sciences to be an expert in more than a small fraction of them. (Csikszentmihalyi, 1996)

Simon (1996) argued that when a domain reaches a point at which the knowledge for skillful professional practice cannot be acquired in a decade, specialization increases (Kaufman & Baer, 2004), collaboration becomes a necessity, and practitioners make increasing use of media supporting distributed intelligence (Hollan, Hutchins, & Kirsh, 2001; Salomon, 1993). One of the potential answers to these challenges is (as argued before) to educate people to become members of reflective communities (Fischer, 2005) rather than acting only as reflective practitioners (Schön, 1983).

The *fish scale model* (Figure 15.10) (Campbell, 1969) is a qualitative model illustrating an interesting structure of reflective communities: It tries to achieve "collective comprehensiveness through overlapping patterns of unique narrowness." The model depicts a competence that cannot be embodied in a single mind. The inevitably incomplete competence of an individual (sometimes referred to as *symmetry of ignorance*; Fischer, 2000; Rittel, 1984) requires reflective communities in which there is the right mixture between sufficient overlap and complementary competence. The fish scale model provides a viable path toward a new design

Figure 15.10   The fish scale model.

competence, based on the integration of individual and social creativity (Fischer, Giaccardi, Eden, Sugimoto, & Ye, 2005).

This abstract model can be contextualized to the application of creating computational environments for people with cognitive disabilities, and in this way we can create a team in which depth and breadth are achieved simultaneously (Center for LifeLong Learning & Design, 2004). In this model, teams consist of software professionals and domain experts who are engaged in an interdisciplinary collaboration (see Figure 15.11, left pane). In the Center for LifeLong Learning & Design's case, the team included (a) special education teachers working with people with cognitive disabilities, and (b) software professionals developing environments such as MAPS. To make this collaboration productive and effective, the specialists acquired some knowledge in the other disciplines that created a common language and a shared understanding (Figure 15.11, right pane).

CONCLUSIONS

As cultures evolve, specialized knowledge will be favored over generalized knowledge (Csikszentmihalyi, 1996; Simon, 1996), and specialized artifacts and technologies will come to the forefront of common usage (Basalla, 1988; Buxton, 2001). Will this cultural fragmentation lead to a new "Tower of Babel," and how can new

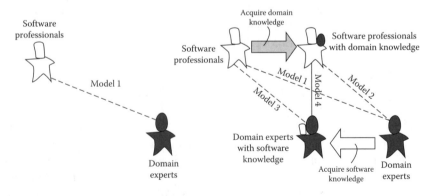

Figure 15.11   Interdisciplinary collaboration and reflective communities.

frameworks and approaches be developed that overcome some of these limitations? The conceptual frameworks presented in this chapter (domain-oriented design environments, metadesign, and reflective communities) explore new synergistic efforts to support the development of specialized and generalized knowledge. In doing so, we worked under the basic assumption that there are no decontextualized "sweet spots" but only *design trade-offs* (a) between specific environments well suited to a task and general environments applicable to a large set of tasks, and (b) between breadth-first and depth-first education.

REFERENCES

Aist, E. H. (1973). *The effect of two patterns of visual prompting on learner achievement in industrial arts*, Unpublished doctoral dissertation, Arizona State University.

Baesman, B., & Baesman, N. (2003). The Visions System. Retrieved November 15, 2009, from http://www.thevisionssystem.com

Basalla, G. (1988). *The evolution of technology*. New York: Cambridge University Press.

Brand, S. (1995). *How buildings learn: What happens after they're built*. New York: Penguin

Buxton, W. (2001). Less is more (more or less). In P. J. Denning (Ed.), *The invisible future: The seamless integration of technology in everyday life* (pp. 145–179). New York, McGraw-Hill.

Campbell, D. T. (1969). Ethnocentrism of disciplines and the fish-scale model of omniscience. In M. Sherif and C. W. Sherif (Eds.), *Interdisciplinary relationships in the social sciences* (pp. 328–348). Chicago: Aldine.

Carmien, S. (2006). *Socio-technical environments supporting distributed cognition for persons with cognitive disabilities*. Department of Computer Science, University of Colorado at Boulder. Retrieved November 13, 2009, from http://l3d.cs.colorado.edu/~carmien/

Carmien, S. (2007). *Leveraging skills into independent living: Distributed cognition and cognitive disability*. Saarbrücken: VDM Verlag.

Carmien, S., & Fischer, G. (2008). Design, adoption, and assessment of a socio-technical environment supporting independence for persons with cognitive disabilities. *Proceedings of CHI 2008: ACM Conference on Human Factors in Computing Systems*. New York: ACM Press.

Carmien, S., & Wohldmann, E. (2008). Mapping images to objects by young adults with cognitive disabilities. *Research in Developmental Disabilities, 29*, 149–157.

Center for LifeLong Learning & Design. (2004). CLever: Cognitive levers—helping people help themselves. Center for LifeLong Learning & Design, University of Colorado at Boulder. Retrieved November 15, 2009, from http://l3d.cs.colorado.edu/clever/assets/20001018-l3d-meeting/gf-l3d-presentation.pdf

Cole, E. (2006, April). Patient-centered design as a research strategy for cognitive prosthetics: Lessons learned from working with patients and clinicians for 2 decades. Keynote address to the SIGCHI 2006 Workshop on Designing Technology for People with Cognitive Impairments, Montreal, Canada.

Csikszentmihalyi, M. (1996). *Creativity: Flow and the psychology of discovery and invention*. New York: HarperCollins.

Eisenberg, M., & Fischer, G. (1994). Programmable design environments: Integrating end-user programming with domain-oriented assistance. In *Human Factors in Computing Systems, CHI'94 (Boston, MA)* (pp. 431–437). New York: ACM.

Fischer, G. (1994). Domain-oriented design environments. *Automated Software Engineering, 1*(2), 177–203.

Fischer, G. (2000). Social creativity, symmetry of ignorance and meta-design. *Knowledge-Based Systems Journal*, *13*(7–8): 527–537. (Special Issue on Creativity & Cognition)

Fischer, G. (2005, July). From reflective practitioners to reflective communities. In *Proceedings of the HCI International Conference (HCII), Las Vegas* [CD-ROM].

Fischer, G., & Giaccardi, E. (2006). Meta-design: A framework for the future of end user development. In H. Lieberman, F. Paternò, & V. Wulf (Eds.), *End user development: Empowering people to flexibly employ advanced information and communication technology* (pp. 427–457). Dordrecht, the Netherlands: Kluwer Academic.

Fischer, G., Giaccardi, E., Eden, H., Sugimoto, M., & Ye, Y. (2005). Beyond binary choices: Integrating individual and social creativity. *International Journal of Human-Computer Studies*, *63*(4–5), 482–512 . (Special issue on creativity)

Fischer, G., & Lemke, A. C. (1988). Construction kits and design environments: Steps toward human problem-domain communication. *Human-Computer Interaction*, *3*(3), 179–222.

Fischer, G., & Ostwald, J. (2002). Seeding, evolutionary growth, and reseeding: Enriching participatory design with informed participation. In *Proceedings of the Participatory Design Conference (PDC'02), Malmö University, Sweden, CPSR*.

Hollan, J., Hutchins, E., & Kirsh, D. (2001). Distributed cognition: Toward a new foundation for human-computer interaction research. In J. M. Carroll (Ed.), *Human-computer interaction in the new millennium* (pp. 75–94). New York: ACM Press.

Kaufman, J. C., & Baer, J (2004). Hawking's haiku, Madonna's math: Why it is hard to be creative in every room of the house. In R. J. Sternberg, E. L. Grigorenko, & J. L. Singer (Eds.), *Creativity: From potential to realization* (pp. 3–19). Washington, DC: American Psychological Association.

Lancioni, G., Van den Hof, E., Furniss, F., O'Reilly, M., & Cunha, B. (1999). Evaluation of a computer-aided system providing pictorial task instructions and prompts to people with severe intellectual disability. *Journal of Intellectual Disability Research*, *43*(1), 61–66.

Levy, F., & Murnane, R. J. (2004). *The new division of labor: How computers are creating the next job market*. Princeton, NJ: Princeton University Press.

Lewis, C., & Rieman, J. (1993). *Task-centered user interface design: A practical introduction*. University of Colorado at Boulder. Retrieved November 15, 2009, from http://hcibib.org/tcuid/

Luhmann, N. (1996). *Social systems* (Trans. J. Bednarz & D. Baecker). Stanford, CA: Stanford University Press.

Lynch, W. (1995). You must remember this: Assistive devices for memory impairment. *Journal of Head Trauma Rehabilitation*, *10*(1), 94–97.

Martin, B., & McCormack, L. (1999). Issues surrounding assistive technology use and abandonment in an emerging technological culture. In *Proceedings of Association for the Advancement of Assistive Technology in Europe (AAATE) Conference*.

Mumford, E. (1987). Sociotechnical systems design: Evolving theory and practice. In G. Bjerknes, P. Ehn, & M. Kyng (Eds.), *Computers and democracy* (pp. 59–76). Aldershot, UK: Avebury.

Myers, B. A., Ko, A. J., & Burnett, M. M. (2006, April). Invited research overview: End-user programming. Paper presented at the Human Factors in Computing Systems, CHI2006 conference, Montreal, Canada.

Norman, D. A. (1993). *Things that make us smart*. Reading, MA: Addison-Wesley.

Norman, D. A. (1998). *The invisible computer*. Cambridge, MA: MIT Press.

Perlis, A. J. (1982). Epigrams on programming. *SIGPLAN Notices*, 7–13.

Reed, R. W. (1989). An investigation of two prompting/fading procedures to teach independent fire evacuation behaviors to individuals with severe/profound mental retardation. Doctoral Dissertation, University of New Orleans.

Reimer-Reiss, M. (2000). Assistive technology discontinuance. Paper presented at the Technology and Persons with Disabilities Conference.

Rittel, H. (1984). Second-generation design methods. In N. Cross (Ed.), *Developments in design methodology* (pp. 317–327). New York: John Wiley.

Rittel, H., & Webber, M. M. (1984). Planning problems are wicked problems. In N. Cross (Ed.), *Developments in design methodology* (pp. 135–144). New York: John Wiley.

Salomon, G. (Ed.). (1993). *Distributed cognitions: Psychological and educational considerations*. Cambridge: Cambridge University Press.

Saskatchewan Learning—Special Education Unit. (2003). Task analysis. Regina, SK: Author.

Schön, D. A. (1983). *The reflective practitioner: How professionals think in action*. New York: Basic Books.

Simon, H. A. (1996). *The sciences of the artificial*. Cambridge, MA: MIT Press.

Snell, M. E. (1987). *Systematic instruction of persons with severe handicaps*. Columbus, OH: Merrill.

Suchman, L. A. (1987). *Plans and situated actions*. Cambridge: Cambridge University Press.

Sutcliffe, A. G. (2004). *The domain theory: patterns for knowledge and software reuse*. Hillsdale, NJ: Lawrence Erlbaum.

Tufte, E. (2003). *The cognitive style of PowerPoint* (2nd ed.). (Available from the author at http://www.edwardtufte.com/tufte/books_pp)

In Summary

MARIE T. BANICH and DONNA J. CACCAMISE

S o what insights can we glean regarding generalization through the diversity of approaches outlined in this volume? We believe that a number of broad-brushstroke themes emerge. One important theme that comes through clearly across many of the chapters is the idea that generalization is an overarching concept that can be thought to occur at various levels: across items, across domains, and across people. For example, at the level of items, Williams and Tanaka discuss generalization of perceptual expertise, as exhibited by individuals who become experts at recognizing birds or cars. In such cases, an individual is exposed to a variety of exemplars and learns to generalize what constitutes membership to a given category. In Chapter 1, Huff and LaBar discuss how emotions, in particular fear, get generalized. In both these cases, the ability to generalize is examined by providing the individual with a novel set of specific items and seeing the degree to which generalization has occurred. At the level of domains, generalization is examined by determining whether information learned in one arena can be generalized to another arena. For example, at this level Hall, Wieckert, and Wright show how a cluster analysis method used in evolutionary biology is applied by a group of entomologists to identify groups or taxa of termites related by their capacity for secreting particular hydrocarbons.

As discussed by Poldrack, Carr, and Foerde, these two forms of generalization appear to be supported by distinct neural systems. One system that involves generalizing across basic perceptual and motor aspects of a given task requires a very similar context in which a skill or item was learned to be reinstantiated. It was thought to involve sensory and motor regions of the brain, and the basal ganglia (see also Chapter 2 by Williams and Tanaka). The other system relies on the hippocampus, which allows for flexible associations across contexts and situations. The neural architecture of each of these systems has characteristics that support these two distinct types of generalization.

At the next level, we can ask how generalizations are transmitted culturally across individuals (again, see Hall et al.) or through things created by humans, such as computer programs, which can be considered cultural artifacts (see Grasser, Lin, and D'Mello, Chapter 10). Consideration of these distinct levels of generalization is important not only for our understanding of what generalization is, but also in considering the design of systems that aid generalization. For example, in Chapter 13, McGenere's work on computer systems that support generalization makes it clear that an individual needs to be able to take operations and generalize them across specific instances (e.g., the cut-and-paste functions being used for a specific research grant and also for a specific manuscript to be submitted for publication); across domains, such as would occur if a user was to employ both Word and WordPerfect; and across individuals, such as the conventions that occur across a community of software designers for cut-and-paste functions.

Another theme that arises across these chapters is that generalization is an associative mechanism. This idea is formalized into mathematical terms by Griffiths in Chapter 7, in which he discusses a Bayesian approach to generalization. In this conceptualization, generalization is bootstrapped through being aware of the probability, based on past events or experiences, that a particular event, characteristic, or situation will occur given a particular context. This formulation makes clear that there are two important factors: the experience and the context.

The chapters on development discuss empirical evidence that demonstrates how experiences and their context serve as a powerful learning mechanism during development. Fischer demonstrates how perceived perceptual similarity across objects, with regard to characteristics in both the auditory and visual domains, allows for generalization so that certain classes of objects are given similar verbal labels. In their chapter, Gerken and Balcomb show the strength of such mechanisms in that children can learn to generalize from a relatively small number of types of input, given they receive multiple versions of each type. What is notable is that such mechanisms serve as a means of induction, allowing for hypothesis testing regarding what serves as a valid generalization. These hypotheses in turn guide additional learning and generalization. In Chapter 6, Lany and Gómez show how these mechanisms can work as a scaffold, such that prior information and experience can enable learning of new and novel structures. The richness of the data set for aiding in generalization is also demonstrated in Chapter 12 by Thompson, in which she discusses findings examining language retraining in persons with agrammatic aphasia as a result of brain damage. She finds that the best performance and generalization occur when they are given more complex sentence structures that then generalize to simpler forms, rather than vice versa.

Another idea that emerges from these chapters is that the extent or degree to which one is willing to generalize (in Bayesian terms, the size of the search space) has important implications. Put another way, the question is "How far afield will an individual go to consider a new item or situation as relating to old ones?" Often in infant and machine learning, it appears better to learn in incremental steps, so you do not get stuck in a rule or generalization that is good for the particular set of items to which you have been exposed but not for a larger set. An example is provided by the findings of Levering and Kuntz with regard to category formation; They suggest a differential reliance on feature similarity versus relational similarities, given prior knowledge. Another situation in which the willingness to venture far afield may be limited is in the case of expert learners, and here some costs become apparent. Over time, experts have built up an elaborated model or hypothesis of how certain items are related, which serves them well within a particular domain. Yet, the more elaborated the hypothesis, the harder it may be to change. This may explain why experts, although showing superior behavior in a particular domain, may actually show costs in performance in other domains.

In fact, for connections to be made across more disparate instances or domains, one needs a much less conservative mechanism. Such mechanisms may support the "Aha" moment, where information from another domain or approach is applied in a novel or creative manner to a new situation. Yet linkage of information too far afield has it costs. For example, it leads to overgeneralization as observed during language development in children and in the realm of emotion, which can lead to overgeneralization that is detrimental. As discussed by Huff and LaBar, overgeneralization of fear is what characterizes anxiety disorders. Although not discussed in this volume, another situation in which generalization can have detrimental effects, here at the societal level, is when overgeneralization of conceptions of certain social or ethnic groups leads to prejudice. These considerations highlight that generalization has both costs and benefits, which make clear the need to create a model that can explain how a learner finds the "sweet spot" between generalization that is too restricted and narrow versus generalization that is too broad.

Another theme that arises within the volume is how context has a large influence on generalization. One can think of the set of items or experiences to which one has been exposed as the context in which generalization can occur. This holds whether one is talking about specific instances or about the social systems, the set of people, systems, and cultural artifacts within which a person who is attempting to generalize finds him or herself. In educational and real-world settings, context is a complex construct, and one aspect of this is the notion of formal versus informal learning settings—a continuum beset with yawning gaps when encountered in real-world settings. Graesser, Lin, and D'Mello describe the use of computerized tutors that create a virtual world that they believe will play a significant role in filling these contextual gaps. During the symposium, it was noted that current educational practices (e.g., case-based instruction) favor students arriving at answers, while ignoring or forgetting the history that leads to those answers. Educational research suggests that this format is not conducive to generalization across problem domains, and it was argued that perhaps virtual learning environments, with their tireless instructional capacities, can be designed to fill this void—a promise from technology-driven educational applications that has yet to be fully realized.

Yet another theme is the idea that some aspects of generalization are supported implicitly, whereas others are supported explicitly. This maps in a rough way to the distinction between declarative and procedural learning systems discussed in Chapter 3 by Poldrack et al. In some cases, no explicit knowledge of the generalization is required for it to occur, as with the perceptual expertise discussed by Tanaka and Williams or the emotional generalization discussed by Huff and LaBar. Yet to design systems that support generalization, the implicit must become explicit. In Chapter 8, Huenerfauth's chapter on representation, explicit supports are necessary to develop a computer-based sign language interpreter and signer, which hinges on how the designer represents meaning in this system to maximize generalization. In fact, as we move from the biological and developmental perspectives of generalization in learning to applications in educational and other assistive technology, the explicit support for generalization takes center stage and how one conceptualizes artifact design is critical to its success. Even the technological medium itself becomes a new context for understanding generalization. Whereas others tend to look at generalization in terms of the ability of an individual to generalize or transfer learning, software designers are concerned with how to make interactive software generalize to a large user population. The fact that the goal is about being able to do more with less requires that the designers attempt to create that perfect solution that allows for maximum human generalization of the program features so as to do all that they hoped to do with the technology, gaining maximum benefit. Carmien and Fischer frame the issue as a Turing machine, noting that one can create a product that is so general that the user has a huge, and often insurmountable, learning curve to customize the general features to his or her unique needs. In contrast, software that is designed too narrowly may be usable for a specific task, but its lack of generalizability makes it uninteresting and relatively useless. The just-right solution involves design software architecture that is generalizable in a way that users can create an individualized interface design that fits their unique needs from the same software building blocks that build other projects.

Another innovative example of explicit supports to generalization designed for a "just-right" solution leverages existing communities of practice and databases of knowledge to provide individualized tutoring in a scalable format. Butcher and de la Chica examine technology-based educational tutors and define a service-based infrastructure that appears to expand context and flexibility over current "hard-wired" computer-based tutors where the scope and sequence are controlled more by the system and less by the learner. Butcher and de la Chica do this by taking advantage of media-based distributed cognition. In this student-driven scheme, learners must actively develop and employ metacognitive skills and integration processes, the stuff of leading cognitive theory of comprehension, with tantalizing but as yet undetermined outcomes to the generalization of learning. The goal is for the computational techniques used in this service approach to generalize to any topic domain, so that large repositories of information available in Internet libraries are instantly available in a personalized tutoring environment.

As this volume demonstrates, although a multidisciplinary perspective on generalization can help to extract some basic principles, much remains to be understood. Yet understanding generalization is critical and indeed essential for optimal learning. Whether knowledge is acquired through formal schooling, training, or extended or momentary real-world experiences, its usefulness generally depends on how well it can be applied to new problems and also to new situations or contexts. Aside from fixed tasks where rote behaviors suffice, new circumstances routinely challenge the learner: new sentences to comprehend for the language learner, new flight patterns to coordinate for the air traffic controller, new Web pages to navigate for the educational database user. For formal education to be effective, learning must generalize at a number of different levels. Hence, it remains for future research to continue to elucidate how generalization can be understood and harnessed to support optimal learning.

Index